Fodor's EXPLORING

# LONDON

FODOR'S TRAVEL PUBLICATIONS, INC.
NEW YORK • TORONTO • LONDON • SYDNEY • AUCKLAND

WWW.FODORS.COM

**Important Note**
Time inevitably brings changes, so always confirm prices, travel facts, and other perishable information when it matters. Although Fodor's cannot accept responsibility for errors, you can use this guide in the confidence that we have taken every care to ensure its accuracy.



Published in the United States by Fodor's Travel Publications, Inc.
Published in the United Kingdom by AA Publishing.

Fodor's is a registered trademark of Random House, Inc.

ISBN 0–679–00478–5
Fourth Edition

**Fodor's Exploring London**

Author: **Christopher Catling**
Revisions: **Louise Nicholson**
Accommodations and Restaurants: **Elizabeth Carter**
Series Adviser: **Ingrid Morgan**
Joint Series Editor: **Susi Bailey**
Copy Editor: **Nia Williams**
Revisions Editor: **Grapevine Publishing Services Ltd**
Cartography: **The Automobile Association**
Cover Design: **Tigist Getachew, Fabrizio La Rocca**
Front Cover Silhouette: **Dallas & John Heaton/Westlight**

**Special Sales**
Fodor's Travel Publications are available at special discounts for bulk purchases (100 copies or more) for sales promotions or premiums. Special editions, including personalized covers, excerpts of existing guides, and corporate imprints, can be created in large quantities for special needs. For more information contact your local bookseller or write to Special Marketing, Fodor's Travel Publications, 201 East 50th Street, New York NY 10022. Inquiries from Canada should be directed to your local Canadian bookseller or sent to Random House of Canada, Ltd., Marketing Department, 2775 Matheson Blvd. East, Mississauga, Ontario L4W 4P7.

Printed and bound in Italy by Printer Trento srl.
10 9 8 7 6 5 4 3 2 1

# How to use this book

## ORGANIZATION

### London Is, London Was

Discusses aspects of life and culture in contemporary London and explores significant periods in its history.

### A–Z

Breaks down the city into regional chapters, and covers places to visit, including walks and drives. Within this section fall the Focus On articles, which consider a variety of subjects in greater detail.

### Travel Facts

Contains the strictly practical information vital for a successful trip.

### Accommodations & Restaurants

Lists recommended establishments throughout London, giving a brief summary of their attractions.

## ABOUT THE RATINGS

Most places described in this book have been given a separate rating. These are as follows:

- ▶▶▶ **Do not miss**
- ▶▶ **Highly recommended**
- ▶ **Worth seeing**

## MAP REFERENCES

To make each particular location easier to find, every main entry in this book has a map reference to the right of its name. This comprises a number, followed by a letter, followed by another number, such as 176B3. The first number (176) refers to the page on which the map can be found, the letter (B) and the second number (3) pinpoint the square in which the main entry is located. The maps on the inside front cover and inside back cover are referred to as IFC and IBC respectively.

# Contents

*De Hems, a Dutch-style pub in Macclesfield Street*

**Christopher Catling is the author of numerous books and articles on travel, including *The Economist Business Traveller's Guide to China*, the *Shell Guide to East Anglia* and the *Insight Guide to Oxford*.**

# My London

One of my earliest childhood memories is of listening to a radio report which said that London was no longer the world's biggest city, having been overtaken in population by Tokyo. This stuck in my memory because it puzzled and upset me: how could London not be the world's capital? Surely it was part of the natural order of things that this city, the fount of democracy, should always be preeminent in the world.

That was my first lesson in the relativity of all cultural assumptions—since then I have got used to the idea that London is not the world's largest city. But it remains one of the world's greatest cities, comparable for complexity, diversity, history, and vitality with Rome, Paris, New York, Cairo and New Delhi. Its social, political, and economic life is simultaneously a product of its past, but is yet dynamically contemporary and truly international.

London's 1980s renaissance has made it a city for people, a place characterized by sheer vitality. In 1974, when I was working as an archeologist on London's waterfront, I could look across the Thames to crumbling Victorian warehouses, intersected by dark alleys and fronted by rotting timber wharfs. Now, this same part of London forms part of a vibrant and developing Bankside community. The city's resurgence is just as vibrant today, partly because people have decided they want to live in the center of London again. Developers have refurbished warehouses into apartments instead of offices. Where people settle, restaurants, stores, and entertainment centers soon thrive.

Ambitious Millennium projects have created fresh focuses for London. Most obvious is the Millennium Dome at Greenwich. Bankside Power Station houses a new branch of the Tate Gallery; and a new pedestrian bridge across the Thames will link this branch of the Tate to St. Paul's. The British Museum Great Court has been opened up again, restoring the museum to its original layout, while the ousted British Library has a fine new home at St. Pancras. Among theaters, the rebuilt Sadler's Wells and remodeled Royal Opera House are major new achievements. London, in other words, is entering another place in its evolution: it never stays still, and repays frequent revisiting.

**Christopher Catling**

# London Is

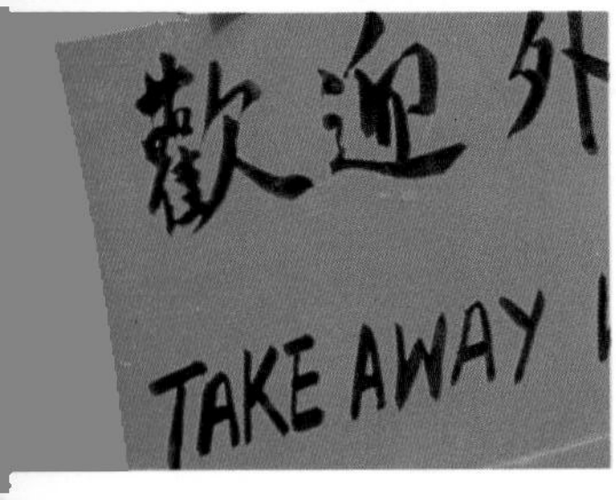


*London is truly cosmopolitan, embracing people of every race and religion. Throughout history, it has served as a magnet to foreign traders, offered a place of refuge to those fleeing persecution, and, as the capital of an empire that once spanned the globe, absorbed great numbers of immigrants. The result is a multiethnic, integrated community where a variety of cultures thrive side by side.*



As early as the 7th century, the Venerable Bede called London "a mart of many peoples," and social historians say that the rapid growth in London's population during the Middle Ages can only be explained by large-scale immigration. Among the later migrants were Jews expelled from Portugal and Spain, who arrived via the Netherlands after 1656, when Oliver Cromwell extended an official welcome. Other newcomers were the Huguenots from France, who arrived and settled in the Soho and Spitalfields areas when Louis XIV denied their right to religious freedom by revoking the Edict of Nantes in 1685.

*In London's Chinatown*

It was during this period that London became the most populous city in Western Europe, overtaking Paris, Venice, Naples, and Milan as its total number of inhabitants, increased from around 200,000 in 1600 to 600,000 by 1700.

From the late 18th century onward mass migration, reflecting the miseries of war, tyranny, and political upheaval, swelled the population of London even further: refugees from the French Revolution and its aftermath began to arrive from 1794 on, followed by Scottish and Irish settlers during the famine years of the 1840s.

Anti-Semitic pogroms in Russia and Eastern Europe brought Jewish refugees in the 1880s, and another wave arrived in the 1930s fleeing Fascist persecution. Londoners might have reacted antagonistically to all these newcomers but most did not. When Sir Oswald Mosley, leader of the Fascist Blackshirts, tried to march through the streets of the East End in 1936, 500,000 Londoners turned out to stop him.

**POSTWAR MIGRATION** In the postwar years, many Londoners made homeless by the Blitz were rehoused in new towns (such as Bracknell, Harlow, and Hemel Hempstead); others left the country altogether, seeking a new life in Australia, Canada, or New Zealand. To compensate for the labor shortage, Commonwealth citizens were encouraged to settle in London to work in the transportation system, the National Health Service or on construction projects such as Heathrow and Gatwick airports.

Greek and Turkish Cypriots, Vietnamese, Chinese, Bangladeshi, and Ugandan Asian refugees, fleeing from warfare or dictatorship, came to live in London, although not all of them managed to find work; unemployment in London is highest among ethnic minorities.

**INTEGRATION** Despite, or perhaps because of, this long history of migration, London is generally free of racial tension. A wide range of ethnic traditions has been absorbed into London life. It has the biggest Caribbean carnival in Europe—the Notting Hill Carnival that takes place during the last weekend in August; the splendid Central Mosque has added to the city's rich architectural heritage; and there is a huge range of good, cheap restaurants serving worldwide cuisines, most notably Chinese and Indian. Thanks to hard-working Asian entrepreneurs, every neighborhood has corner shops that are open all hours; and the Brick Lane area has been transformed into a hub for Bangladeshi Asians, full of street stalls, stores selling exotic fabrics, and restaurants.

❑ London's population reached a peak of around 8½ million in 1939. Since then it has fallen to about 7 million in 1995, but it is still the highest of any city in Europe and about 12 percent of the total UK population. After a period when people were more inclined to move out to greener suburbs and commute into the city to work, there is now a return to London living and a significant population rise will show in the 2001 census. Nevertheless, around 1¼ million commute daily from places as far afield as Oxford, Brighton, or Peterborough. London also receives 29 million visitors a year. Not surprisingly, therefore, the capital's bus and subway network carries 5 million passengers a day. ❑

*A city of ethnic diversity*

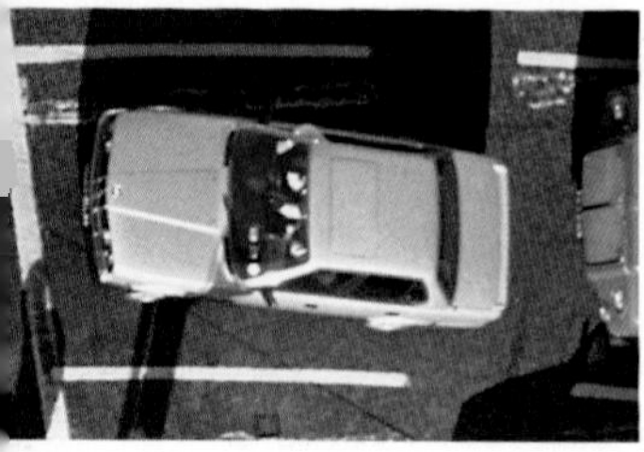

*London is full of symbolic monuments and buildings, none more potent than the Houses of Parliament, known as "the mother of Parliaments." To many Londoners, however, politics is not just something that goes on within the House of Commons: it is part of daily life, affecting everything from litter to the state of the city's roads and transportation.*



Since 1986, London has been the only major city in the world that has not had a single elected body responsible for its infrastructure. Instead, this work has devolved to the 30 or so independent London boroughs. This came about when, after many years of conflict with central government, the controversial Labour-controlled G.L.C. (Greater London Council) was abolished by Margaret Thatcher's Conservative régime.

In 1997, however, the Conservative party was soundly defeated by Labour, in both national and London polls. Labour immediately announced plans to reintroduce a unified body that would be responsible for those issues that cross borough boundaries, and which therefore have an effect on all of London (e.g. transportation and pollution, see page 13). A referendum, which will ask Londoners their views on the issue, is planned. If successful, the newly created job of London mayor elected by all Londoners (a position superior to the local mayors of the City and Westminster) will have its first incumbent in 2000.

❑ Visitors sometimes expect to see the city as Dickens described it, its dark medieval alleys made darker still by fog as thick as pea soup. Smog (a mixture of smoke and fog) killed plants and trees, turned honey-colored buildings black, left encrustations on the varnish covering historic paintings, bleached clothes and ancient fabrics and caused great damage to human health. In the worst winter smogs of the 19th century, theatergoers could hardly see the actors on stage for smoke, and pedestrians could only just see their feet. One of the last smogs to hit the city, the "killer smog" of December 1952, caused an estimated 4,000 deaths among bronchial sufferers, and the resulting outcry led to London being declared a smokeless zone under the Clean Air Act of 1956. ❑

*Sleeping on the streets*

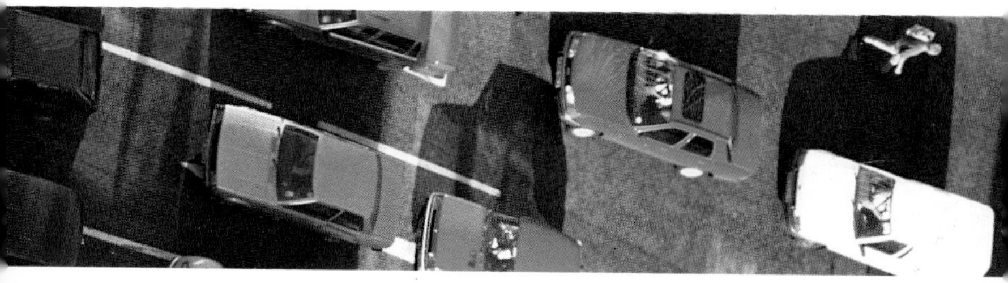

## LITTER AND HOMELESSNESS

Political conflict did not end with the G.L.C.'s abolition; it simply moved onto a broader stage. The national government has a powerful grip on the budgets of local authorities and often intervenes, through a process known as "capping," if any borough threatens to overspend. Some boroughs have responded by cutting expenditure on street cleaning and other services, arguing that limited funds must be spent on essentials, such as housing and education. Litter has thus been turned into another pawn in the political game and is an all too familiar sight in certain parts of the city.

More distressing is the huge number of homeless people on London's streets, huddling for shelter in doorways because they have nowhere else to go. The sight provokes puzzlement and anger in Londoners, most of whom are unsure of the causes or the solution. The situation is slowly improving, however. At one time in the early 1990s about 2,000 people slept outdoors; now many of them go to charitable hostels, while others have managed to find more permanent lodgings.

## TRANSPORTATION AND POLLUTION

Another pressing problem is the sheer quantity of traffic and the resulting pollution. London made great strides to solve its pollution problems following the Clean Air acts of 1956 and 1968. Smog, a noxious mixture of smoke, chemical fumes and fog that had characterized London for several hundred years, became a thing of the past when coal burning was banned, and industry and homeowners were encouraged to switch to oil, gas, and electricity for heating and power. Many buildings were cleaned of the sooty encrustations blackening their stonework—the Houses of Parliament, Westminster Abbey and most other landmarks were restored to pristine condition.

A new menace, however, is not so visible but nevertheless equally damaging: photochemical smog (the action of sunlight on vehicle exhaust emissions), which causes a condition similar to hay fever. Several measures to discourage car use have been proposed, including a much improved and subsidized public transportation system. The River Thames could also play an important role in the future.

*Combating vehicle pollution*

*Many of the 29 million visitors to London come for the same reason as the cat in the nursery rhyme: to look at the Queen, or at least to look at the palaces, jewels, and ceremonies associated with royalty. Fascination with things royal tends to be strongest among visitors from republican countries, while the fashion among the Queen's own subjects is to be increasingly skeptical about the role of the monarchy.*



The fire that damaged the State Apartments at Windsor Castle in 1992 did not provoke sympathy for the Queen. In fact, there was a public outcry that taxpayers should fund the palace's restoration while the Queen, the richest woman in the world, contributed nothing. In responser, the Queen funded it herself by opening Buckingham Palace to paying visitors.

The controversy came at the end of a year which the Queen described as an *annus horribilis* (a dreadful year). It had seen the breakup of two royal marriages (one was Prince Charles's to Lady Diana), and calls for the Queen to pay tax on her vast annual income. This last demand was one to which the Queen did concede, marking an important stage in a long-running saga: the definition of an appropriate role for monarchy in the modern age. The death of Diana, and the way the royal family were perceived to have reacted to it, reopened this debate.

One poll suggested that half Britain's population would like to see an end to the monarchy, and some say that Britain would long ago have become a republic but for the thought of who might be elected President instead.

**THE SUCCESSION** If Britons were allowed to elect a monarch from the present royal family, Prince Charles, the heir to the throne, might have competition from his sister, the Princess Royal (Princess Anne). She represents the modern face of monarchy better than any of her siblings and is widely admired for her work for the Save the Children Fund. However, Charles wins sympathy for his involvement with a host of issues, including his youth programs, and green views.

*Trooping the Colour*

**THE ROYAL YEAR** The Queen's official life follows an established pattern. The New Year is usually spent at Sandringham, in Norfolk, which was bought in 1861 for the Prince of Wales (later Edward VII). February and March often involve overseas tours but she returns to London, dividing her time between Buckingham Palace and Windsor Castle, for the spring and early summer. On the second Saturday in June she travels down the Mall in a horse-drawn carriage for the Trooping the Colour ceremony in Horse Guards, in celebration of her official birthday (her real one is on April 21). June is also the month when the Queen goes to the races, often to see her own horses compete, for the Derby and for Ascot Week (when women wear flamboyant hats). In July the Queen hosts garden parties at Buckingham Palace for the great and worthy, before heading north to Scotland, to visit Holyrood House (Edinburgh), and then Balmoral Castle for the grouse-shooting season. Foreign tours may take place in September, but the Queen is back for the State Opening of Parliament (late October or early November), which takes place in the House of Lords; no monarch has been admitted to the Commons since 1642, when Charles I burst in demanding the arrest of five Members of Parliament. On Remembrance Sunday, the Sunday nearest November 11, the Queen lays a wreath to commemorate the war dead at the Cenotaph in Whitehall.

❑ The stormy marriage of Prince Charles and Diana, Princess of Wales, was charted daily by the world's press, as was Charles's brother Prince Andrew's to Sarah Ferguson. Both ended in divorce, and both women continued to live in the public eye, apparently by choice. But after Diana's death in 1997, the press began to exercise some self-control toward Prince Charles's sons, princes William and Harry; and softened their attitude toward Prince Charles's longterm affection for Camilla Parker Bowles. The marriage of the Queen's youngest son, Prince Edward, at Windsor in 1999, enjoyed more privacy. Meanwhile, the Queen herself is more actively in touch with her people, giving the monarchy a new humanity. ❑

*The Queen in bejeweled splendor*

*London is a style capital, giving birth to new ideas that become international fashions. London's position was established during the 1960s style revolution, epitomized by the Beatles and Mary Quant, and confirmed during the emergence of punk in the 1970s, when designers from Tokyo to New York embraced black clothes with studs, zips, and safety-pin decoration. Today, London continues to lead in fashion, music, and art of all kinds.*



London stars in the 1950s were singers such as Tommy Steele and Joe Brown, with their Cockney accents—quite acceptable to most parents. Youngsters dressed like their parents, except for the Teddy Boys, who were generally thought of as a rough crowd.

**SWINGING SIXTIES** By the mid-1960s, youth had begun to create its own fashions. The King's Road and Carnaby Street became the center of all that was hip and new in the London of the Swinging Sixties. Boutiques like Mary Quant's Bazaar became the trendsetters for those "dedicated followers of fashion" so pilloried by the well-known Kinks song. London also dominated the music scene, especially after the Beatles made this city their home. They, the Who, and the Rolling Stones dominated the pop charts on both sides of the Atlantic.

*Patriotic punk*

Thirty years later, the innocent, fun London pictured with its "Bobbies on their bicycles, two by two" in songs such as "England Swings Like a Pendulum Do" is just a memory, but anyone nostalgic for the past can join a Beatles Tour (tel: 020-8898 3606), which takes in places such as Abbey Road, where the eponymous album cover was shot, the clubs where they performed, and the rooftop building in Savile Row where they made their last public appearance together in February 1969.

**PUNK** By contrast, punk's lasting influence is the dynamic and daring experimental street fashion confidently worn by many young people, as if they are moving, living art works. Museum-piece punks hang around the King's Road on summer weekends, but these are semiprofessionals: usually art students who supplement their grants by dyeing their hair lurid colors and posing for photographs (they expect a tip, of course). They have little in common with the raw, vicious, anti-establishment music, clothing, and attitudes that were born in London during the long, hot summers of 1976 and 1977. However, punk ideas have been absorbed into the amorphous style that characterizes many of today's young Londoners.

**YUPPIES AND THE ME GENERATION** In the 1980s London took its tune from America, in a new materialism and ostentatious spending. Teenage Porsche owners did global deals over their cellular phones and put down options on penthouse apartments (yet to be built) in the Docklands. Something of this still hangs around among young businessmen who flaunt their designer clothes in fashionable restaurants—but they make less of an impression today.

*Mary Quant, 1960s fashion queen*

**DYNAMIC VARIETY** Changes in the 1990s have prepared the city for the 21st century. London is alive with creative talent working in all styles, leaving Londoners free to enjoy their individuality and particular tastes. London Fashion Week is an important event, when young British designers set the tone for world fashion. Art and crafts are so lively that east London now supports the largest community of artists in Europe, an estimated 10,000 people. Music is vibrant in all its forms—jazz, pop, rock, reggae, trance, salsa, hip hop, garage, house, jungle and many others, reflecting the cosmopolitan culture of the capital, and the consequent club scene is large, fast and ever-changing. Theater follows a similar pattern, with landmark, innovative productions staged from the top Royal National Theatre down to the small fringe theaters such as the Almeida and Young Vic, with productions regularly moving on to New York. Restaurants, which burgeoned in the 1990s while undergoing a welcome revolution to find more authentic ingredients and recipes, now offer quality dishes from almost all the world's food traditions. Meanwhile, health and the environment have a central position: diet, exercise, pollution, and waste are daily considerations in the lives of many Londoners.

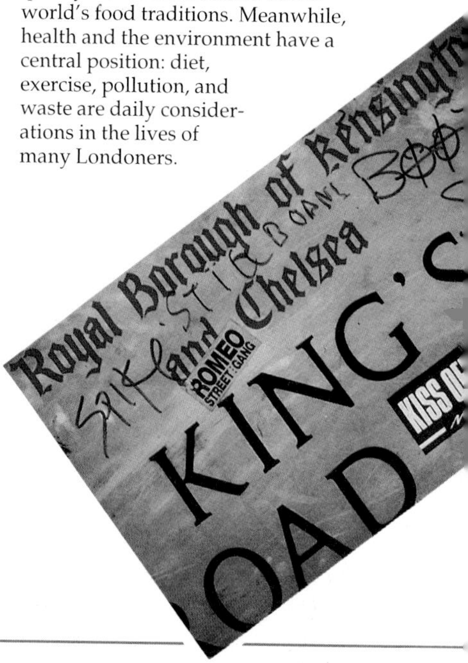

*From double-decker buses to soldiers dressed in red tunics and bearskin helmets guarding Buckingham Palace, London is a city steeped in tradition and pageantry. No matter what time of year you visit, there is bound to be some colorful event going on.*



The most famous of London's regular events is the Changing of the Guard. It is worth remembering that this takes place in several different locations. In summer the crowds at Buckingham Palace often block the view, and you may prefer the alternative ceremonies at Whitehall or St. James's Palace, while the hour-long event at Windsor Castle, with its marching bands and music, is perhaps the best of all.

January's big event is the Lord Mayor of Westminster's New Year's Day Parade. This only started in 1986 but has become a popular attraction, with floats, bands, and American-style cheerleaders, who march from Piccadilly to Hyde Park starting at 12:30 PM. On the anniversary of Charles I's execution (January 30) members of the Royal Stuart Society, in appropriate costume, retrace the monarch's route to the scaffold from St. James's Palace and lay a wreath on his statue at the head of Whitehall.

Shrove Tuesday, which usually falls in February, is celebrated with pancake races in Carnaby Street; seven weeks later, on Easter Sunday, there is a carnival in Battersea Park, while on Easter Monday there is a parade of working horses (still used to draw brewers' carts) in Regent's Park at noon.

*Bearskins and bayonets*

❑ The Trooping the Colour ceremony takes place in June, but there is a public lottery for the tickets (50,000 people apply for 4,000 seats). To try, write requesting tickets (a maximum of two) with a stamped, addressed envelope to The Brigade Major, Trooping the Colour, Household Division, Horse Guards, Whitehall, between January 1 and March 1. You can also apply for tickets to the dress rehearsals on the two preceding Saturdays, with a better chance of success. ❑

In May and June another piece of pageantry takes place in Horse Guards Parade, called Beating the Retreat, when military bands mark the setting of the sun and perform by floodlight (advance reservations from the Trooping Office essential: for details, tel: 020-7930 4466).

Chelsea Pensioners parade in honor of their founder, Charles II, on Oak Apple Day, May 29 (see pages 92–93), and most Wednesday evenings in May and June you can watch traditional Morris dancers performing their routines outside Westminster Abbey.

There are festivals galore in July (one of the best is the City of London Festival, tel: 020-7377 0540 for details) but for something more unusual you can watch the start of the Swan Upping ceremony at Temple Stairs on the Embankment. From here, the

Queen's Swan Keeper travels upriver to Henley-on-Thames to mark the beaks of the newly born cygnets, which are all owned by (and therefore enjoy the protection of) the Queen and the Dyers and Vintners livery companies.

The annual Costermonger's Harvest Festival, held in early October at St. Martin-in-the-Fields, Trafalgar Square, brings together the hardy characters who sell fruit and vegetables from stalls all over London. It is here that you are most likely to see London's famous Pearly Kings and Queens, so called because of their coats covered with buttons made of mother of pearl. They were originally elected by costermongers to act as unofficial community leaders, sorting out disputes between street traders, who were reluctant to involve the police in their affairs. Today most Pearly Kings and Queens devote their spare time to raising money for charity.

On the first Sunday in November you can watch the start of the London to Brighton Veteran Car Run; only cars made before 1905 can take part, and their owners dress in period costumes. The rally commemorates the abolition in 1896 of the law requiring all cars to be preceded by someone walking with a red warning flag. The second Saturday in November sees the colorful Lord Mayor's Show (see page 163). The State Opening of Parliament, usually held in late October or early November, marks the new parliamentary year with the Queen's grand procession from Buckingham Palace to the Houses of Parliament—this and the indoor ceremonies are televised. Numerous events lead up to Christmas, including carol-singing around the tree in Trafalgar Square (every day at 4 PM from mid-December onward).

*The Lord Mayor's Show*

*London is in an almost constant state of flux, as buildings are knocked down and new ones are put up in their place, or historic buildings are restored to their former pristine splendor. Here is a summary of the main changes that have taken place within the last 10 years and of the major developments that are still on the drawing board.*

**FLEET STREET** Although Fleet Street still looks the same, the newspaper printworks and the journalists have gone, scattered to various parts of the city, including Marsh Wall (the *Daily Telegraph*) and Wapping (*The Times*, *Sunday Times*, *Sun*, and *News of the World*). Strikes and violence accompanied the breakup of Fleet Street (and the breakup of the once powerful print unions), as newspaper proprietors, led by Rupert Murdoch, embraced new technology and moved into new premises. Some of these are important architectural landmarks. Rick Mather designed *The Saturday Times*'s La Lumière building at Wapping; Bernard George created the striking art deco façade in Kensington where Associated Newspapers has its headquarters; Nicholas Grimshaw designed the Financial Times Print Works built at East India Dock.

*Lloyd's (by Richard Rogers)*

**THE THAMES EMBANKMENTS** The 1990s revitalization of London is especially striking along the Thames. At Vauxhall Bridge a conspicuous green and white building, completed in 1992, houses the headquarters of the secretive MI6, the government organization responsible for foreign intelligence (or, in plain terms, spying). Farther east, one of the leading proponents of the postmodernist style, Terry Farrell, designed the eight-story office building above Charing Cross Station, which seems to hover like a giant glowering beetle above the water. On the opposite bank, Nicholas Grimshaw's great glazed and curving arch is Waterloo International Terminal, opened in 1994 to serve trains and passengers using the Channel Tunnel to move directly between the city centers of London, Paris, Lille and Brussels. Indeed, the whole south bank of the Thames from County Hall to London Bridge is now revitalized. Stops along the riverside walkway include the London Aquarium, the IMAX Cinema, the Tate Gallery of Modern Art and Shakespeare's Globe Theatre.

**DOCKLANDS** London Docks was once the world's busiest port. At its peak in 1964, it employed 100,000 people and handled 61.6 million tons of cargo in giant enclosed docks. Then, with the arrival of container ships, the port moved downriver to modern, mechanized Tilbury. Between 1968 and 1981 all the docks closed, leaving an area of waterscape 11 miles long containing 450 square

*The International Finance Centre*

acres and 55 miles of water's edge silent and empty. In 1981, the London Docklands Development Corporation was formed, intended as a catalyst to reshape and revive the area, backed by government incentives and tax relief. Its brief was to regenerate the land and buildings, encourage industry and commerce, create an attractive environment and promote housing. Two decades and much controversy later, its success can begin to be assessed. More than 80 national and international awards have been won for buildings, landscaping and conservation, including Canary Wharf, St. Anne's Church and the Royal Docks landscaping, but it is perhaps Canary Wharf tower and squares that impress the first-time visitor the most.

**THE FUTURE NOW** Docklands regeneration launched the revival of east London and, in the following years, the whole of London's riverside. With it came a new way of living: derelict warehouses were converted into spacious loft apartments with river views. The focus of the capital's new developments is increasingly returning to the Thames. In the city center they include the Tate Modern, housed in Giles Gilbert Scott's brick power station at Bankside, the revitalization of Sir William Chamber's palatial 1770s Somerset House, and the new Millennium Bridge over the Thames. In the east, the Museum in Docklands fills a waterside Georgian warehouse, and the vast Millennium Dome is dominant. Away from the river, developments include major overhauls at the Royal Opera House, the British Museum, Victoria and Albert Museum and Science Museum.

*Battersea Power Station*

**THE CRADLE OF THE NATION** London is a city so steeped in history that it sometimes seems as if every building has its own story to tell, from the humblest pub with its low, beamed ceilings to the grandest palaces and cathedrals.

London has played an extraordinarily dominant role in the history of both Britain and the world. Within living memory London was the biggest city on the earth, the capital of a powerful empire spanning the

continents, upon which it was said that the sun never set. Since the end of World War II, with the rapid break-up of the empire, Britain and London have diminished greatly in importance and influence. That process seems set to continue, as closer integration with Europe will inevitably mean that less power is wielded by London-based politicians and a great deal more by institutions based in Brussels or Strasbourg. Even so, London retains many reminders of its past history, in its buildings, its museums, its stately palaces, its statues and works of art. Visiting them reminds us of all the many great events that the city has witnessed in its long history, such as the first performances of Shakespeare's plays or the creation of the first democratic parliament.

*Little did the Romans suspect that the city they founded on the north bank of the Thames in AD 43 would eclipse Rome itself and grow to be the biggest city in the world. Surprisingly enough, substantial remains of that first Roman city can still be seen today, despite 2,000 years of rebuilding and development.*



London owes its existence to chance and the building of a bridge. The Emperor Claudius had intended that Colchester, in Essex, should be the capital of Roman Britain, and that is where the Roman invasion force headed in AD 43 after landing near the site of today's Richborough, in Kent. To reach Colchester, the seat of King Cunobelin (Shakespeare's Cymbeline), who ruled all of south-east England, the Romans had to cross the Thames at some point. A few years after their triumph, the Romans constructed a wooden bridge near the site of today's London Bridge—in fact, though rebuilt many times since, it has remained close to the spot the Romans originally chose. London's bridge became the focus of the road network that the Romans built to enable troops to be moved quickly around the newly conquered province of Britannia. Market forces began to operate, for where there is a major road junction, with troops stationed and ships calling, merchants will inevitably set up stores. Before very long, Londinium was a thriving settlement and port.

*Mithras, the Roman army's cult god*

**THE BOUDICCAN REVOLT** Londinium was strategically important to the Romans and, as a new settlement, was a symbol of Rome's colonial ambitions. As such it was a target for those disaffected Iron Age peoples who had not welcomed the invasion. They formed an alliance under the leadership of Boudicca (Boadicea), leader of the Iceni tribe, whose territory covered much of modern Norfolk. Boudicca chose her time well, waiting until Suetonius Paulinus, the Roman governor, was putting down a revolt in Anglesey, before destroying Colchester and then marching on Londinium in AD 60. The city was burned to the ground and its inhabitants massacred. What happened after that is not entirely known. Flushed with victory, Boudicca's troops pursued the Roman cavalry to a battle site somewhere in the Midlands, where, according to Tacitus, the Romans achieved an easy victory through superior discipline, killing 80,000 British, while only 400 Romans died. Boudicca is said by Tacitus to have poisoned herself, but other contemporary writers suggest that she died of an illness. It is said that the Britons gave her a rich burial, and legend has it that she is buried, complete with chariot and retainers, beneath the round barrow, or burial mound, that sits on Parliament Hill, on Hampstead Heath. Boudicca has

*Boudicca, the Celtic warrior queen*



become a popular folk figure, a symbol of resistance against tyranny. Ironically, the magnificent bronze statue of her that stands on the Thames at Victoria Embankment was made in the 1850s, at exactly the time when Britain was itself pursuing a policy of imperial expansion.

**ROMAN LONDON** London was rapidly rebuilt and, because its location was clearly more convenient than Colchester, it became the official administrative capital of Britannia sometime around AD 100. As such, London had its full complement of civic buildings, palaces, and temples; the Museum of London (see page 166) has excellent reconstructions showing the appearance and development of the Roman city from this time. Of visible remains, there is the Temple of Mithras (see page 167) and substantial parts of the city wall built around AD 200; one well-preserved stretch can be seen just north of Tower Hill, by the Underground station, and there is another good stretch still serving as the churchyard boundary wall next to the church of All Hallows on the Wall, near the corner of London Wall and Broad Street. You can follow the route of the wall (1¾ miles) with the aid of the *London Wall Walk* leaflet published by the Museum of London.

*Major developments took place in the medieval period that have had lasting effects on the shape of London—most notably, the founding of Westminster Abbey and its adjacent royal palace, which was to become the focus of law-making and administration, while the City developed as an important commercial and industrial center.*



**SAXONS AND VIKINGS** The period that followed the withdrawal of Roman troops from Britain in AD 410 is one of the most intriguing in history, precisely because so little is known about it. We do know that the first churches were built in London in the 7th century, if not before, and archeological finds suggest that the port of London continued to thrive, exporting wool and cloth.

London appears in the historical record again in the 9th century, when chroniclers noted "great slaughter" resulting from Viking raids. In 994 the city was again attacked by Sweyn Forkbeard, son of the Danish King, who was eventually bought off—London was a major contributor to the *danegeld* tax that the Danes demanded in return for peace. In the end, Sweyn's son, Canute, was accepted as "King of all England" in 1017 and crowned in London.

*Glass in the medieval Guildhall*

❑ **Monarchs and their reigns**

**Normans**
William I 1066–1087
William II 1087–1100
Henry I 1100–1135
Stephen 1135–1154

**Plantagenets**
Henry II 1154–1189
Richard I 1189–1199
John 1199–1216
Henry III 1216–1272
Edward I 1272–1307
Edward II 1307–1327
Edward III 1327–1377
Richard II 1377–1399

**Lancastrians**
Henry IV 1399–1413
Henry V 1413–1422
Henry VI 1422–1461 (deposed); 1470–1471 (restored)

**Yorkists**
Edward IV 1461–1470; 1471–1483
Edward V 1483
Richard III 1483–1485 ❑

**EDWARD THE CONFESSOR** London as we know it today began to develop during the reign of Edward the Confessor, who came to the throne in 1042. He devoted his income to a magnificent new abbey church at Westminster, building a royal palace alongside it. This marked a decisive shift away from the old Roman city, and from that time onward London consisted of two distinct parts: the royal center around Westminster and the commercial center in the City.

**THE NORMANS** The importance of Westminster was confirmed when William I, the Norman Conqueror, was crowned King of England in the abbey. A huge number of immigrant merchants began to settle in London in the wake of the Conquest, including Jewish bankers, who occupied the area still known as Old Jewry. This street runs down to Cheapside, which was one huge open-air marketplace. Other streets leading off Cheapside were devoted to particular crafts or products, as names such as Bread Street, Poultry Lane, Goldsmiths Row, and Friday Street (the site of the Friday fish market) still recall.

**LAW AND LITERACY** As a system of law and concepts such as trial by jury were established, London developed new institutions, such as the Inns of Court, built midway between the City and Westminster during the 13th century for the training and housing of law students. While the universities of the period trained students to become clergymen, the Inns of Court were more like business schools, turning out advisers to the king, ambassadors and administrators. One such was Geoffrey Chaucer, whose career included spells as Controller of Customs, ambassador to France, and Clerk of the King's Works. In between he found time to write (but never complete) *The Canterbury Tales* (begun around 1387), a book that helped to establish English as a respectable, poetic language, well able to compete with Latin and French. The widespread availability of Chaucer's work resulted from the activities of William Caxton, who studied printing in Cologne. Edward IV encouraged him to set up a press at Westminster in 1476, and between then and his death in 1491 he published a total of 80 books. Caxton's apprentice, Wynkyn de Worde, took over the business and moved the press to Fleet Street in 1500, thus beginning that street's long association with the printed word.

*Geoffrey Chaucer, poet and clerk*

❑ One of London's most impressive medieval buildings is the Guildhall, which dates to around 1411 but existed as early as the 12th century. The size and splendor of this hall reflects the strength of London merchants, who were organized into guilds to protect their interests: they regulated prices and, through apprenticeship schemes, effectively controlled who could and who could not enter their lucrative professions. Under the medieval system of government each ward or district of the City appointed an alderman, usually from the elite of the guilds, and together the aldermen ran all the City's affairs, guided by their leader, the mayor. The aldermen and mayor still exist, but their powers are now more limited. ❑

*The Tudor era brought far-reaching changes to London, sparked off by Henry VIII's decisive break with the Church of Rome and the dismantling of monastic power. The effect was to usher in the more confident and secular age of Elizabeth I.*



**HENRY VII** The Tudor era began with a great act of piety: the building of a beautiful fan-roofed chapel in Westminster Abbey by Henry VII, a shrewd financier and politician who was determined to strengthen the role of the monarchy. The chapel was still unfinished in 1509, when Henry VII died, and it was completed by his son, Henry VIII.

**HENRY VIII AND THE DISSOLUTION** Soon Henry VIII was busy with demolition, rather than building. He produced the final answer to a debate that had been raging since early medieval times (and that had resulted in countless wars and the martyrdom of Saint Thomas à Becket); he declared himself, rather than the Pope, to be the absolute head of the church in England. Conveniently this meant that he could appropriate the vast wealth of the church; the church tithe (a tax of one-tenth of all crops and revenues) was diverted to the Crown in 1534, and in 1536 Henry dissolved the monasteries, gaining a vast stockpile of property with which to reward his supporters. Religious houses in and around London were converted to mansions by favored courtiers; Blackfriars, for example, became the estate of the Master of Revels, Thomas Cawarden. A huge amount of property in the City that had previously been owned by the church was sold or given away, so that rents plummeted and houses stood empty.

*The Tower of London in 1509*

❑ **Monarchs and their reigns**
**Tudors**
Henry VII 1485–1509
Henry VIII 1509–1547
Edward VI 1547–1553
Mary I 1553–1558
Elizabeth I 1558–1603 ❑

**POPULATION GROWTH AND PLANNING LAWS** This situation did not last long, however, for the reign of Elizabeth I was marked by a fourfold growth in London's population, resulting in serious overcrowding and the passing of the first ever planning law. This was issued as a royal proclamation in 1580 (and made law in 1592). It prohibited any new building within a 3-mile radius of the city, and any subdivision of existing buildings. This and similar laws issued in the early 17th century were totally ignored, with the effect that the many monastic gardens and

*Gross genius: Henry VIII*

❑ London Bridge was one of the wonders of Tudor London. Since its completion in 1209 it had acquired some unusual features: One was the sheer number of stores and houses packed onto the bridge, resulting in great congestion. Another was the ornate Nonsuch House, built toward the Southwark end of the bridge in 1577; this folly was so called because there was "none such" like it. The heads of traitors executed in the nearby Tower of London were displayed on poles above the gatehouse of the bridge, having been boiled and dipped in tar to preserve them. This practice ended in 1661, and the bridge itself, having stood for 600 years, was replaced in 1831 by a new bridge designed by Sir John Rennie. In 1972 Rennie's bridge was replaced, only to be sold and re-erected in Lake Havasu City, Arizona. ❑



fields that had previously existed within the boundaries of the city rapidly became clogged with shoddy timber buildings. Much of the Elizabethan city was destroyed a century later by the Great Fire, but the spirit of the period lives on in Shakespeare's great plays, and in the comedies of his contemporary, Ben Jonson, whose *Bartholomew Fair* gives a pretty clear idea of the rough life of the early 17th century.

**EXPANDING TRADE** No area was rougher than Southwark, where Shakespeare's Globe Theatre was built in 1598–1599, alongside the brothels, taverns, bear pits, and cockpits to which apprentices would come for entertainment. This area developed rapidly as London burst beyond its Roman and medieval limits, and the south bank became the place where poorer, semiskilled, or manual laborers lived. They were joined by a growing population of sailors and shipbuilders as London's overseas trade contacts expanded. The Royal Exchange was opened in 1570 by Elizabeth I, designed to compete with powerful markets in Antwerp and Amsterdam (though, ironically, the original building was built from Dutch and Flemish materials), and British merchants such as Thomas Gresham made vast fortunes from trade with Russia, the Levant, and the East Indies.

*The 17th century began with the coronation of James I in 1603; since he was already James VI of Scotland, the two kingdoms were united for the first time and conciliation was the theme of the Jacobean age. But soon Britain would be gripped by civil war and a king would lose his head, while London would be decimated by plague and then destroyed by fire.*



**THE GUNPOWDER PLOT** In the early years of James I's reign an event took place that is still commemorated with bonfires and fireworks all over Britain. Catholic conspirators, who looked to Rome and the Pope as head of the church, sought to further their cause by placing explosives in the cellars beneath the House of Lords, with the aim of killing the King and all the assembled peers. The plan, known as the Gunpowder Plot, failed, and Guy Fawkes was caught before lighting the gunpowder fuse, on November 5, 1605.

**THE CIVIL WAR** Parliament was again the scene of an explosive event on January 4, 1642, when Charles I burst into the House of Commons demanding the arrest of five Members. This was the culmination of a bitter power struggle between the King and Parliament, which then erupted into war. London took the side of Parliament in the battles that ensued, and City merchants made a substantial contribution to the cost of the Parliamentary army that finally defeated the Royalists at Naseby. In 1649 the King was beheaded and, after a period of instability, Oliver Cromwell became Lord Protector, imposing a puritanical rule that lasted until his death in 1658. In 1660 the monarchy was restored.

❑ **Monarchs and their reigns**
**Stuarts**
James I 1603–1625
Charles I 1625–1649
The Commonwealth 1649–1653
The Protectorate 1653–1659
Charles II 1660–1685 ❑

*Fires lit to fend off the plague*

*London's burning*

**THE GREAT PLAGUE** Two great disasters were to hit the city in the 1660s. The first signs of the Great Plague were detected at Christmas 1664 and soon all those who could afford it, including most of the city's doctors, had fled. Many theories were propounded about the cause of the plague—dogs and cats were blamed and killed by official exterminators, which only exacerbated the problem, for the rats, the true carriers of plague, simply multiplied. At the height of the plague, 14,000 people were dying every week, their corpses dumped into vast plague pits.

The cold winter of 1665 brought a decline in casualties, and by February 1666 the King and court had returned to London. At least 100,000 people had died, but the city soon returned to its normal bustle.

**THE GREAT FIRE** A mere six months later, on the night of September 2, 1666, a baker's shop caught fire in Pudding Lane. The Lord Mayor was alerted but is reported to have said that the fire was so trivial that "a woman might piss it out." Samuel Pepys, on rising from his bed the next day, was horrified to learn that 300 houses were already burned by "an infinite great fire," and that nobody was attempting to quench the flames. Remarkably, only nine people lost their lives in the Great Fire, which raged for three days, but the damage to property was immense. Nearly every building within the 395 acres of the City had been destroyed: 13,200 houses, 44 guildhalls, and 87 churches. St. Paul's Cathedral was so badly damaged that repair was impossible. Those Londoners who had survived the Great Plague were now camped in the fields around the smoldering ruins of their city, wondering what further disaster might occur.

❑ The Great Plague of 1665 was only one of a series to hit the city. The Black Death of 1348–1349 carried off at least half of the city's population, and the plague recurred, on and off, for the next 300 years. Ordinances were passed banning the slaughter of animals in the city—the waste was thought to be the source of disease. Burning fires in the streets to purify the air and breathing the scent of nosegays made of herbs were tried as preventative measures, and arsenic was prescribed as a cure. Finally the Great Fire put an end to the epidemics, destroying the rat-infested buildings in which the plague had thrived. ❑

*Out of the ashes of the Great Fire a new and prosperous city soon arose. During the next 150 years, a huge amount of building took place that totally transformed London's appearance, resulting in the city that we see today.*



**SIR CHRISTOPHER WREN** The task of rebuilding London after the Great Fire fell to Sir Christopher Wren, Surveyor General to the Crown, but all his initial proposals met with resistance. Wren planned a radical redevelopment of the medieval city, replacing the narrow alleys and jumbled wharfs with a new waterfront and graceful public buildings. His visionary scheme foundered on practicality; comprehensive redevelopment was prevented by the complex pattern of land and property holding in the city, and by the fact that Londoners themselves wanted to rebuild their houses and stores as quickly as possible. The city was reconstructed along the existing street pattern, but using brick, stone, and tile, instead of timber and thatch, as a precaution against fire.

Wren's scheme for St. Paul's was also frustrated. Faced with the challenge of building the world's first Protestant cathedral, he produced a building that broke with the past, as his "Great Model" in the cathedral crypt shows. His clients, however, wanted to cling to their medieval liturgy, which required a processional nave and a chancel, so the design was eventually altered—some would say compromised—in order to meet their wishes.

*Wren, the idealistic architect*

❑ **Monarchs and their reigns**
James II 1685–1688
William and Mary 1689–1702
Anne 1702–1714

**Hanoverians**
George I 1714–1727
George II 1727–1760
George III 1760–1820
George IV 1820–1830
William IV 1830–1837 ❑

**THE GREAT BOOM** Over the next decades, the city developed its own character and became a place where people worked, rather than lived. Looking down from the dome of St. Paul's, a mason employed on its construction in the last years of the 17th century would have seen large private gardens, fields, orchards, and grazing animals only a short distance away. Soon that view was to change, for a huge building boom began that continued at breakneck pace for the next century. The private gardens lining the Strand were developed first, followed by Covent Garden, Holborn, Spitalfields and Soho, St. James's and Mayfair. Many of the residential areas built at this time bear the names of landowners who grew rich on bricks and mortar: the Curzons, Portmans, Cadogans, Camdens, Sloanes, and Grosvenors.

These residential areas, such as St. James's and Mayfair, were built for wealthy aristocrats and courtiers, with elegant houses set around garden squares. The subsequent building boom was, however, fueled by the rise of the professional classes. Doctors, lawyers, underwriters, stockbrokers, and merchants, even actors, artists, and publishers, had the means to move out of the cramped and overcrowded city into West End property. London must have resembled a vast building site for much of the period, especially toward the end of the 18th century and the beginning of the 19th, when major public buildings, such as the Mansion House, the Bank of England, and the British Museum, were erected. Two projects epitomize the buoyancy of this era. The architect John Nash undertook the remodeling of a whole swathe of London, from the Mall northward to Regent's Park, providing the kind of dramatic vistas that London had so far lacked; it also provided the stimulus for London's expansion northward that eventually linked it to hilltop Hampstead. Meanwhile, Trafalgar Square was cleared of its royal stables and transformed into a public space leading toward Whitehall, where new buildings such as the Admiralty symbolized England's colonial might. One medieval building remained in the midst of the new monuments: the Palace of Westminster. It had such a long history that nobody dared suggest rebuilding it, although it was archaic and impractical. Few were sorry, then, when the palace finally went up in flames in November 1834, marking the end of an era.

❑ Before the Great Fire London was built largely of timber; the city lacks any local source of good building stone. Stone for prestigious churches such as St. Paul's had to be brought by sea from Portland in Dorset or along the Thames from the Cotswolds. After the Great Fire, new building laws restricted the use of wood. Bricks became the standard material, made locally by extracting clay from farmland on the fringes of the city. The pits were then filled in with domestic garbage and the land leased to speculative builders. By the 19th century, bricks were being brought in by rail or canal, principally from the clayfields and brick kilns of Bedford, Fletton, and Peterborough. ❑

*Wren's masterpiece, St. Paul's*

*Queen Victoria came to the throne in 1837, aged only 18. During the 63 years of her reign London continued its inexorable growth. It was a city at the heart of a vast empire, the financial capital of the world, a city of magnificent buildings and great institutions; at the same time it had a huge population of extremely poor people living in squalid conditions. The word "slum," which had been introduced by Jewish immigrants, began to be applied to parts of London at this time.*

**THE GREAT EXHIBITION** The most spectacular public event of Queen Victoria's reign was "The Great Exhibition of the Works of Industry of All Nations," staged in Hyde Park in 1851. Six million people poured through the turnstiles between May 1 and October 15 to see the exhibits housed in Joseph Paxton's Crystal Palace. The profits were sufficient for a new museum complex to be set up, including the Victoria and Albert, the Science and the Natural History museums. They were constructed over the former market gardens of South Kensington.

The Great Exhibition, with its emphasis on technology and industry, set many of the themes of the period—even the Crystal Palace itself, basically a greenhouse or conservatory on a massive scale, inspired scores of similar buildings using iron as the core structural material, rather than wood, brick, or stone. Examples range from the Agricultural Hall in Islington to covered markets such as Leadenhall, Smithfield, and Covent Garden. The same technology was used for railway stations such as the beautifully restored Liverpool Street, or Paddington, the terminus of the Great Western Railway (where restoration work is in progress).

*Queen Victoria*

**THE TRANSPORTATION REVOLUTION** Paddington Station was built in its present form in 1854, but the line itself opened in 1838, offering a service to West Drayton. In 1842, Queen Victoria set the royal seal of approval on this new form of transport by taking her first train journey along the same line, traveling from Slough to Paddington, a distance of 17 miles, in 23 minutes—an average of 44 m.p.h.; Prince Albert is reported to have instructed the conductor: "Not so fast

next time." By the end of Victoria's reign, 390,000 commuters were being carried in and out of the city every day, traveling a distance of up to 30 miles, an indication of just how far London had spread by then.

Meanwhile, London's docks were expanding rapidly. Smaller boats, mainly carrying cargoes such as coal and grain from other British ports, still used riverside wharves, but congestion on the Thames was such that purpose-built docks were needed to handle the big oceangoing vessels. Whole new villages and communities grew up to serve the docks, but poverty was endemic because wages were extremely low. London was becoming an increasingly stratified city, with a relatively prosperous West End and a poor East End. Model dwellings to house the poor began to appear—the American philanthropist, George Peabody, left substantial funds for their construction—but never enough to make any serious dent in the growing problem of the slums. The situation gave rise to many philanthropic initiatives, such as the founding in 1878 of William Booth's Salvation Army, which set up soup kitchens and hostels to help the very poor. Ultimately, the extreme poverty in London was to have massive and worldwide repercussions: Karl Marx's observations on its causes and solutions were to become the basis for Communist-inspired revolutions in several parts of the world.

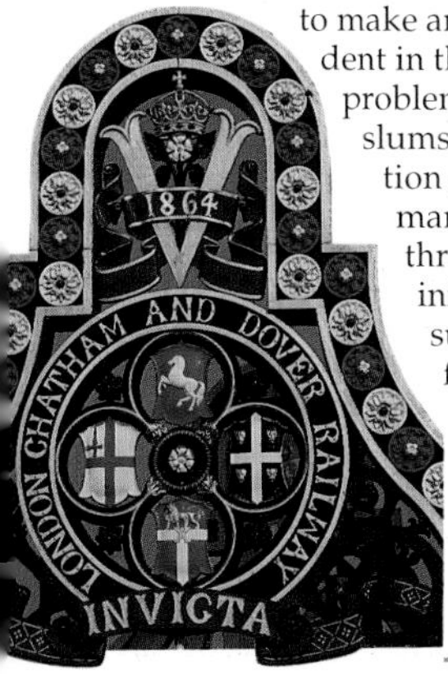


❑ London lacked any kind of system for disposing of waste until the mid-19th century. Garbage and sewage were dumped into its rivers, earning it the names "Venice of drains" and "capital of cholera." The first covered sewers were introduced in 1858, known as "the Year of the Great Stink" because they were completely ineffectual. Nobody went anywhere near the Thames unless they had to and the windows of the newly rebuilt Houses of Parliament were draped with sheets soaked in chloride of lime to keep the smell at bay. The savior of London, whose name is nearly forgotten but who ought to be regarded as a national hero, was Sir Joseph Bazalgette. His system of brick-lined sewers, linked to treatment plants and pumping stations, came into operation in the 1860s. Bazalgette's 1,300-mile system, carrying 70,200 gallons a day, still forms the basis of London's drainage system. ❑

*Not long after the century turned, Victoria died and modern history began. Cultural values and attitudes began to change, and in place of the* laissez-faire *attitude to development, the London County Council began to impose order. All was to be shattered, however, in the Blitz, when German bombers attacked London repeatedly between September 1940 and May 1941, reducing large parts of the capital to rubble.*



The London County Council was officially created in 1888 as a directly elected body with substantial powers. It needed them to tackle the problems of a city that had grown out of control, but it was not until the early 20th century, under Progressive (Liberal) leadership, that it began to show its muscle. Soon the L.C.C. was involved in everything from slum clearance to building houses. It also created many parks and open spaces, including the Green Belt, designed to halt the city's spread. Some of the L.C.C.'s housing plans, such as the Boundary Street development in Bethnal Green, became the models for developments in parts of continental Europe.

**THE INTER-WAR YEARS** The pace of building continued after World War I; in the words of a slogan of the time, Britain needed "homes fit for heroes." Increasingly these were high-rise blocks of flats (apartments) of five stories or more and regarded with suspicion because residents of flats enjoyed none of the benefits of street-based community life.

The middle-class dream was to escape the city, made possible by the creation of a comprehensive and cheap public transit system, the Underground, whose first line had opened in 1863. (Its later, deep-dug tunnels gave the system its nickname, "the tube.")

Rapid expansion in the 1920s and 1930s enabled more people to live in new suburban housing developments, where houses had running water and electricity. Soon, however, the Underground would serve another purpose: providing shelter for Londoners during nightly air raids at the height of the Blitz.

❑ **Monarchs and their reigns**
Victoria 1837–1901
Edward VII 1901–1910
George V 1910–1936
Edward VIII 1936
George VI 1936–1952
Elizabeth II 1952–present ❑

**THE BLITZ** The *Blitzkrieg* ("lightning war") was Hitler's weapon for beating Britain into submission, although its effect was to strengthen resistance. Recognizing that aerial bombing would play a major role in the war, the authorities had already evacuated 690,000 children to temporary rural homes in September 1939. Many poor evacuees from the East End thereby gained their first glimpse of farm animals, and rural people discovered that the children of the East End were not the degenerates, the "people of the abyss," that they were often portrayed.

Meanwhile, German bombs began to rain down, and a nightly pattern was established: a two-minute siren wail would warn Londoners of approaching aircraft, giving them time to take cover in basements, in Anderson shelters (arches of corrugated metal covered with earth) dug into the back of private yards, or in the Underground. Even Churchill, the wartime leader, had an underground bunker, now an

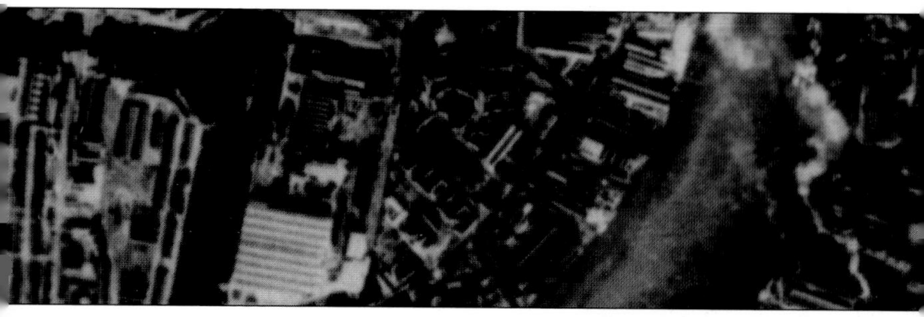

intriguing museum, in the Cabinet War Rooms in Whitehall.

Throughout the Blitz, everyone tried to live life as normal, although bus and train services were constantly disrupted, along with gas, electricity, and water supplies. Even so, nightclubs and theaters remained open. The Café de Paris, which optimistically called itself "the safest nightclub in town" and had mirrored walls copied from the ballroom of the *Titanic*, received a direct hit in March 1941. It was just one event in the raids that left 29,890 dead and 3½ million buildings in London severely damaged or destroyed.

The worst of the Blitz was over by May 1941. Toward the end of the war, however, a new bombing campaign began. In reprisal for British air raids on German cities, Hitler unleashed his new "wonder weapons," the V1 flying bomb and the V2 rocket, from June 1944. These created havoc, caused great loss of life in the last months of the war.



**ST. PAUL'S** Throughout the Blitz, a special effort was made to protect St. Paul's, which survived intact, even when every building around it was flattened. Prompt action enabled potentially dangerous fires to be put out, but luck played a part as well; the cathedral received a direct hit on September 12, 1940, but the bomb failed to explode and was extracted from the foundations three days later. It was then driven to Hackney Marsh and exploded creating a crater more than 115 feet wide.

*Life goes on, despite the war*

*Nikolaus Pevsner, founder of the* Buildings of England *series of books, observed that postwar planners and architects caused greater damage to England's historic cities than the Luftwaffe ever did during the Blitz. More recently the sentiment has been repeated by Prince Charles, an outspoken critic of much modern architecture. The postwar rebuilding of London certainly transformed the city, yet by 2000 Britain's capital had acquired many impressive buildings and developments.*



Immediately following the war, two key pieces of planning legislation were passed to improve the look of London. Under the Town and Country Planning Act of 1947, protection was given to historic buildings, which could no longer be demolished or altered at will. The Civic Amenities Act of 1967 extended this concept to whole areas of London, thus creating the notion of "conservation areas" within which development was severely restricted. The other great step forward was the 1956 Clean Air Act, which successfully eradicated London's smog.

**BUILDINGS OF THE AGE** Set against these triumphs, London acquired a large body of mediocre and alienating buildings, some of which have since been demolished while others face an uncertain future. One example is the South Bank complex, a legacy of the 1951 Festival of Britain. The Royal Festival Hall was put up in a great hurry when this celebration was first conceived as a way of cheering up the nation after the rationing and austerity that followed the war. As a symbol of the bright new world, the Festival Hall is uninspiring; it is, nevertheless, regarded with some affection by Londoners for the simple reason that it is not as ugly as the bunkerlike structures that surround it, such as the Hayward Gallery and the National Theatre. A new facing has been proposed as a way of improving their appearance, but this has not yet been undertaken despite years of complaints.

**LONDON'S FIRST AIRPORT**
Heathrow Airport was transferred from military to civil use in 1946. In 1955 its first major passenger terminal was completed; this, like much of the airport, was built by Sikh laborers from the Punjab (a region of India and Pakistan), encouraged to move to London to fill labor shortages.

Heathrow quickly became one of the world's busiest freight and passenger airports, making a huge impact on west London and its economy. To cope with the massive increase in air traffic, four other airports have been built: Stansted, Gatwick, Luton, and the London City Airport in the Docklands.

*Makeshift antismog masks*

**THE DOCKS** By contrast, east London went into dramatic decline as manufacturing industries began to relocate out of London, and the docks, much rebuilt after devastating war bomb damage, began to close down with astonishing speed. The increased use of container ships led to the relocation of London Port to Tilbury, downriver. By 1981 the 11-mile stretch of docks was entirely closed.

**BRAVE NEW WORLD** In the four decades following World War II, all but 70 of the City's 667 acres have been rebuilt. At first, repairing war damage was a priority. However, after the Big Bang of 1985–1986, a revolution in financial services demanded completely different office space. Meanwhile, the government kick-started the total regeneration of the Docklands area in 1981 and were luring companies eastward. The City fathers recognized a threat to their supremacy and responded quickly. In just eight years, from 1986 to 1993, the equivalent of one half of the entire stock of City office buildings had been rebuilt. Just as the centerpiece of Docklands is Canary Wharf, so the City's is Broadgate—400 million square feet of office and recreation space built on disused railway land surrounding Liverpool Street Station. These massive developments, together with the regeneration of the riverside, especially along the south bank, have shifted the focus of the capital eastward, yet kept its financial heart in the City. As the century drew to a close, a host of ambitious Millennium projects, aided by grants from the Lottery Fund further suggested that London's seemingly infinite expansion westward has paused and turned around.



*Visiting the Festival of Britain*

**BUS TOURS**
Joining a London Transport Official Sightseeing Tour is a good way to get your bearings. English-language tour buses have live commentary. All buses operate a hop on, hop off service at more than 70 stops with a 6-minute frequency in summer (10–15 minutes in winter). Starting points include: Baker Street Station; Victoria Station, Grosvenor Gardens; Piccadilly Circus, Haymarket; Waterloo (Eurostar exit); Charing Cross Station; Marble Arch Station (exit 4).

*Right: outside the Houses of Parliament*

**LONDON BY AREA** London resembles a giant patchwork quilt, made up of many different districts and communities that have grown up around two ancient, once separate cores: the City of London, known as the City, and the City of Westminster. In and around them, there are parks, monumental palaces, museums, and churches. This rich tapestry can seem complex, but today's Central London still retains distinctly discernable districts that reflect the city's amalgamation over the centuries.

**WESTMINSTER** Retains its ancient, original purpose: to be the political, religious and royal hub of the capital, England and Great Britain. The Houses of Parliament, Westminster Abbey, and Trafalgar Square are its historic landmarks, while government offices line Whitehall. Art treasures fill the Tate Gallery of British Art, the National and National Portrait galleries and Banqueting House.

**ST. JAMES'S AND THE MALL** Privileged Londoners process along Mall, wander St. James's Park, and frequent gentlemen's clubs, Christie's art auctioneers, Floris the perfumer, and other long-established stores. With Buckingham Palace central, courtly tradition prevails.

**MAYFAIR AND PICCADILLY** Lying between Oxford Street and Piccadilly, Mayfair was built by the rich for the rich. Today, the grand Georgian streets and squares are temporary homes to the international wealthy. High style is the key-note in the super-deluxe hotels, the Bond Street and Regent Street stores, and the art galleries.

# A-Z London by area

**CHELSEA AND KNIGHTSBRIDGE** Village Chelsea, inner Knightsbridge, and the core of South Kensington retain their gentle, residential pace. Between them, streetwise shoppers check out the latest fashion statements along the King's Road and around Brompton Cross. Here, too, are Harrods and the South Kensington museums.

**KENSINGTON, NOTTING HILL, AND HYDE PARK** Built up around the homely Kensington Palace, stuccoed Kensington family homes set the tone. This informal mood pervades Kensington Gardens and adjoining Hyde Park, where Londoners of all ages come to relax, and extends through leafy Holland Park to fashionable Notting Hill and its Portobello Road antiques market.

**REGENT'S PARK AND MARYLEBONE** The great, elegant swathe of Regent's Park is the back garden for north Londoners, with its roses, zoo, lake, and theater. There is more entertainment nearby at Lord's Cricket Ground, Madame Tussauds, the Planetarium, the BBC Experience and along Regent's Canal at Camden Lock markets.

**BLOOMSBURY AND FITZROVIA** In the streets surrounding leafy Georgian squares, university buildings and museums buzz with the hot debates of London's students and intellectuals. The British Museum is its focus; its satellites include Dickens' House and the British Library.

**SOHO AND COVENT GARDEN** This amorphous mass of lanes lying between the two cities, London and

**WALKING TOURS**
These are a comprehensive, and often very entertaining way to get to know London. The best operators are the Original London Walks (tel: 020-7624 3978), though there are several other companies; see the listings magazine *Time Out* for details.

Westminster, is one big entertainment center. Theaters stage plays and musicals, bars are hives of gossip, and restaurants still serve food to reflect the area's cosmopolitan immigrant past.

**HOLBORN AND THE STRAND** The riverside strip linking the City to Westminster is punctuated by the silent medieval Inns of Court, the Temple, and the Courtauld Gallery.

**THE CITY** London began here. It was mostly rebuilt in the showy 1980s, but today's City traders still walk past Roman temple remains, medieval halls, Wren churches, and Victorian monuments to British imperial power.

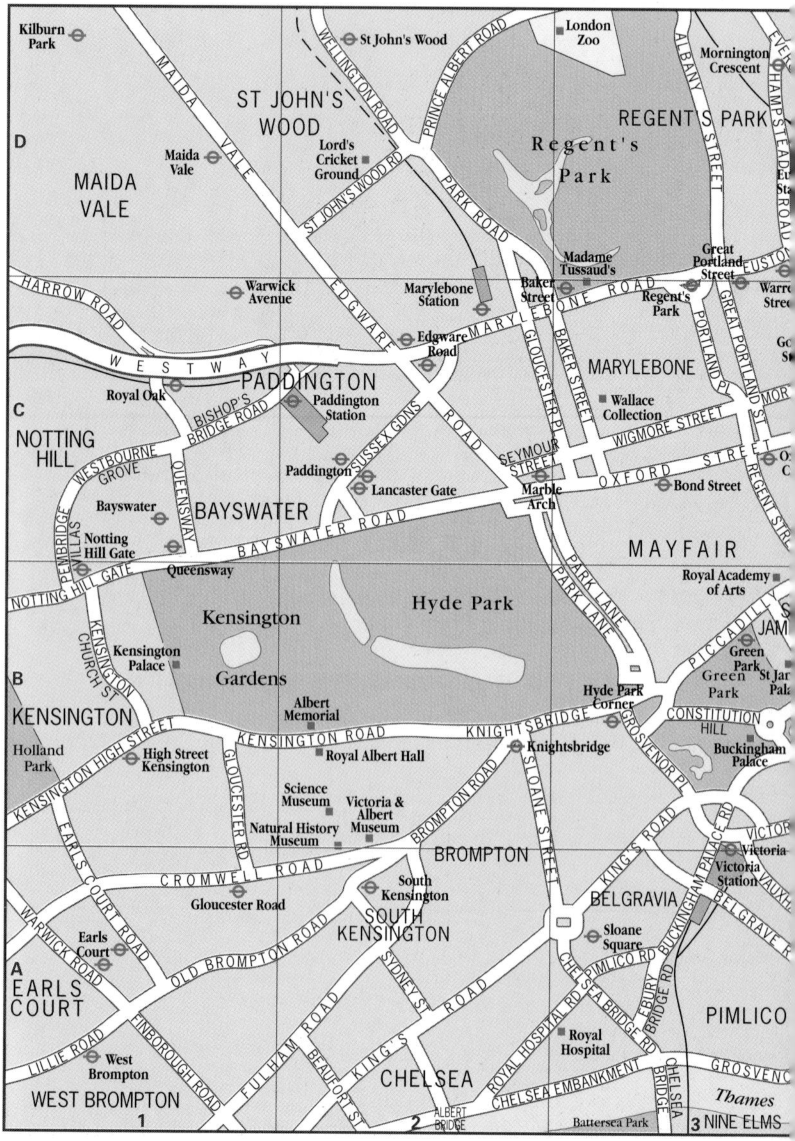

**CLERKENWELL, ISLINGTON, AND THE EAST END** Clerkenwell buzzes with craftspeople, Islington mixes Georgian terraces, avant-garde theaters, and restaurants; the East End retains its grit, wit and immigrant flavor.

**DOCKLANDS** The huge river landscape stretching downstream from the City is a blend of old villages, modern architecture and riverside warehouse apartments, crisscrossed by the high level Docklands Light Railway.

**BANKSIDE** A riverside strip of continuous entertainment from Westminster to London Bridge provides concert halls, theaters, museums, an aquarium, and a cathedral.

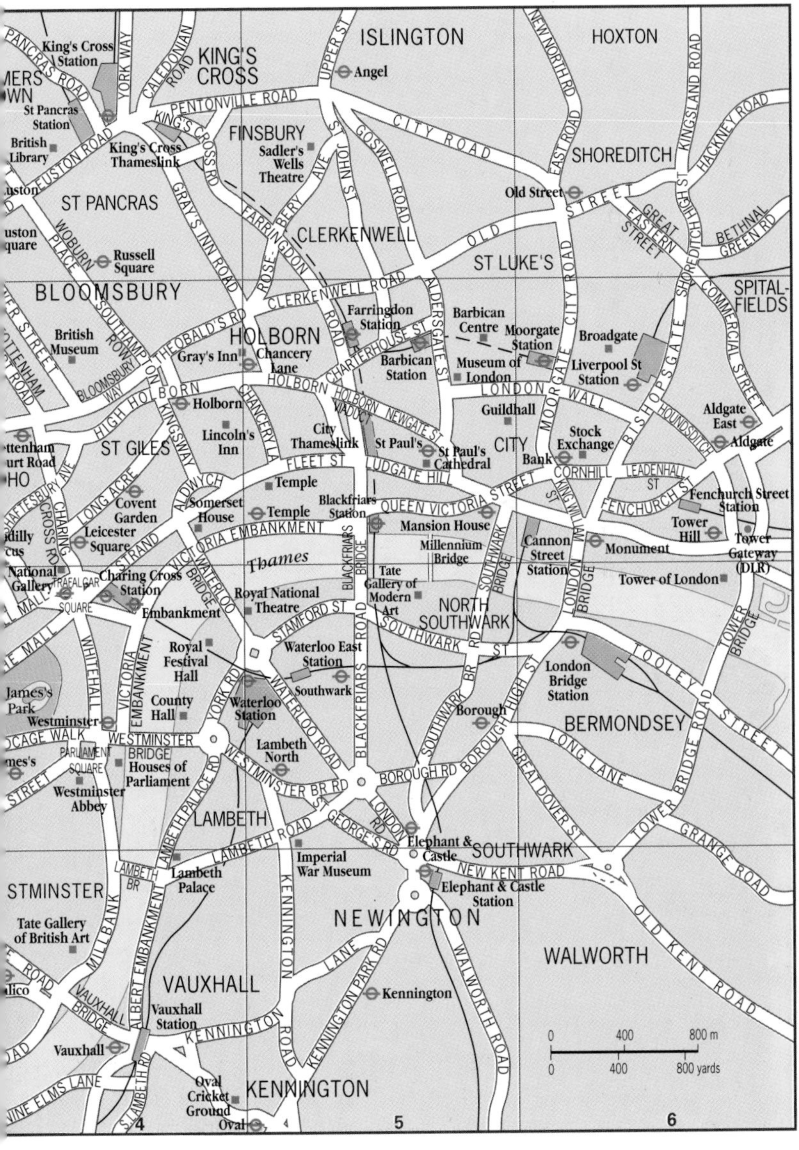

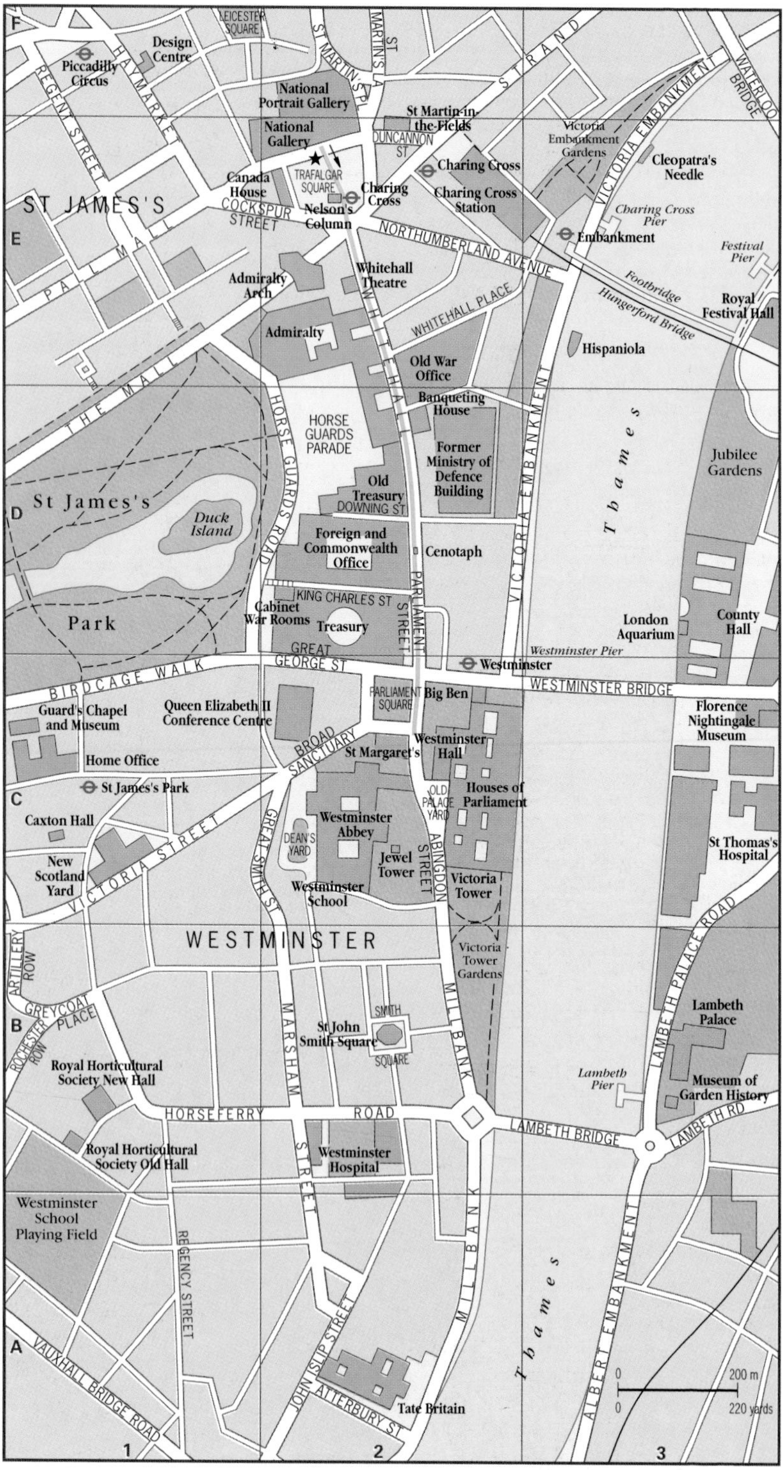
ST JAMES'S
Piccadilly Circus
Design Centre
HAYMARKET
REGENT STREET
LEICESTER SQUARE
ST MARTIN'S PL
ST MARTIN'S LA
STRAND
National Portrait Gallery
National Gallery
St Martin-in-the-Fields
DUNCANNON ST
Canada House
TRAFALGAR SQUARE
Nelson's Column
Charing Cross
Charing Cross Station
COCKSPUR STREET
NORTHUMBERLAND AVENUE
Victoria Embankment Gardens
VICTORIA EMBANKMENT
Cleopatra's Needle
Charing Cross Pier
Embankment
Festival Pier
WATERLOO BRIDGE
Footbridge
Hungerford Bridge
Royal Festival Hall
PALL MALL
Admiralty Arch
Whitehall Theatre
WHITEHALL PLACE
Admiralty
WHITEHALL
Old War Office
Hispaniola
THE MALL
Banqueting House
HORSE GUARDS PARADE
Former Ministry of Defence Building
Thames
Jubilee Gardens
Old Treasury
DOWNING ST
St James's
Duck Island
HORSE GUARDS ROAD
Foreign and Commonwealth Office
Cenotaph
KING CHARLES ST
Cabinet War Rooms
Treasury
PARLIAMENT STREET
Park
London Aquarium
County Hall
Westminster Pier
GREAT GEORGE ST
Westminster
BIRDCAGE WALK
WESTMINSTER BRIDGE
PARLIAMENT SQUARE
Big Ben
Guard's Chapel and Museum
Queen Elizabeth II Conference Centre
Florence Nightingale Museum
Westminster Hall
BROAD SANCTUARY
St Margaret's
Home Office
St James's Park
OLD PALACE YARD
Houses of Parliament
Caxton Hall
Westminster Abbey
DEAN'S YARD
GREAT SMITH ST
New Scotland Yard
VICTORIA STREET
Jewel Tower
ABINGDON STREET
St Thomas's Hospital
Victoria Tower
Westminster School
WESTMINSTER
Victoria Tower Gardens
ARTILLERY ROW
LAMBETH PALACE ROAD
GREYCOAT PLACE
MARSHAM STREET
SMITH SQUARE
St John Smith Square
MILLBANK
Lambeth Palace
ROCHESTER ROW
Royal Horticultural Society New Hall
Lambeth Pier
Museum of Garden History
HORSEFERRY ROAD
LAMBETH BRIDGE
LAMBETH RD
Royal Horticultural Society Old Hall
Westminster Hospital
Westminster School Playing Field
REGENCY STREET
ALBERT EMBANKMENT
JOHN ISLIP STREET
VAUXHALL BRIDGE ROAD
ATTERBURY ST
Tate Britain
0
200 m
0
220 yards
A
B
C
D
E
F
1
2
3

**WESTMINSTER** Gossip and intrigue—political, royal, and religious—have filled the streets and buildings of Westminster since it first developed, two miles southwest of the City of London. It was Edward the Confessor who began the original Westminster Abbey after he moved the royal court out of the City in 1042, triggering London's westward expansion. Since then, Westminster has been synonymous with government. Its major buildings house the Treasury and the Foreign and Commonwealth Office. At its heart stand the Abbey and the Houses of Parliament. Trafalgar and Parliament squares, its focal points, are being pedestrianized during 2000.

**WESTMINSTER WALK** Start in Trafalgar Square, on the steps of the National Gallery.

**Trafalgar Square** is the center of the city—a bronze plaque in the pavement behind Charles I's statue marks the spot. The square was laid out in 1829 in honor of Lord Nelson's naval victory against Napoleon in 1805. Its centerpiece is a statue of Nelson on a Corinthian column, 175 feet tall. Beyond is a fine view down Whitehall and to the left is the church of **St. Martin-in-the-Fields.**

Walk down into the square, where there is plenty to see: fine reliefs of Nelson's greatest triumphs decorating the base of his column, Sir Edward Landseer's four bronze lions added in 1867, Sir Edwin Lutyens's pools with their playful dolphins added in 1939. Now walk toward **Whitehall.** Stranded on an island at the head of the broad avenue is Hubert le Sueur's animated statue of Charles I on horseback (1633) looking toward Banqueting House, the scene of his execution in 1649. The first building on the right, the **Admiralty**, is fronted by Robert Adam's stone screen (1759) adorned with two sea horses. The country's naval affairs were run from this building when the British fleet was considered the most powerful in the world. Next comes **Horse Guards**, where two members of the Household Cavalry mount guard on horseback daily between 10 and 4—a tradition that survives even though all that remains of the former royal palace is the **Banqueting House** opposite. Beyond Horse Guards is **Downing Street**, the official residence of the Prime Minister (No. 10) and the Chancellor of the Exchequer (No. 11), though the present Prime Minister, Tony Blair, and his family live at No. 11, which is bigger than No. 10. Farther down Whitehall, in the middle of the road, is the **Cenotaph**, designed by Sir Edwin Lutyens (1920) to commemorate the dead of World War I. Whitehall comes to an end at Parliament Square, with the **Houses of Parliament** to the left and **Westminster Abbey** to the right.

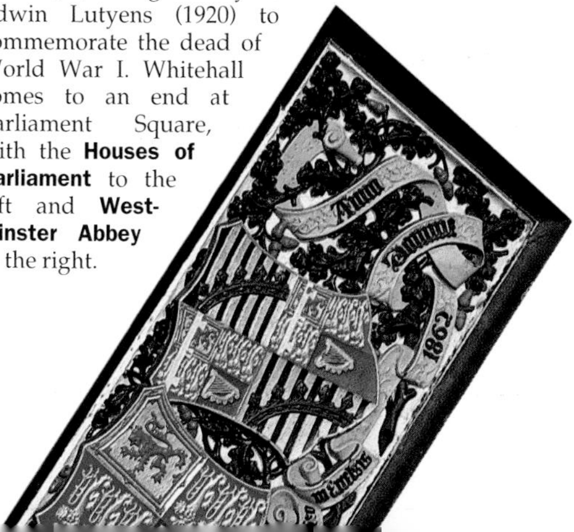

*Previous page: Trafalgar Square*

**THE EXECUTION OF CHARLES I**
Charles I is said to have faced death with exemplary courage, wearing two shirts so that he would not shiver in the January cold and give the impression that he was afraid. Andrew Marvell, the poet who witnessed the execution, wrote of the king that "He nothing common did or mean/Upon that memorable scene." Many went to the scaffold both before and after Charles I, but never an anointed monarch, and many considered his execution an unforgivable act of regicide. To this day, Charles I continues to have his admirers, who place wreaths on his statue, at the head of Whitehall, on January 30, the anniversary of his death.



*Rubens's ceiling paintings in the Banqueting House*

## ▶▶▶ Banqueting House *44D2*

*Whitehall, SW1 (tel: 020-7930 4179)*
*Open: Mon–Sat 10–5. Admission charge includes excellent acoustiguide*
*Underground: Charing Cross, Westminster*

The Banqueting House (closed Sunday) contains one of London's finest rooms. It was built between 1619 and 1622 by Inigo Jones, who had trained in Livorno (Tuscany), and absorbed the influence of the architect Andrea Palladio. He introduced the purity of classical design to London, first with the Queen's House, Greenwich (now part of the National Maritime Museum complex, see page 218), then with this sophisticated and seminal building.

Banqueting House is now hemmed in by other classical buildings. It is difficult to imagine how exotic and different it would once have appeared, crisply faced in white Portland stone, and surrounded by the ramshackle brick and timber buildings of the rambling Whitehall Palace Henry VIII seized from Cardinal Wolsey, enlarged and used for courtly entertainment. When fire destroyed part of the palace, James I employed Inigo Jones to rebuild it on a massive scale (modeled on the Tuileries Palace in Paris), but only the Banqueting House was completed. The exterior is relatively restrained, except for the frieze of garlands running beneath the parapet. James II added the weathervane on the north side of the roof to inform him when William of Orange might be blown across the English Channel.

The real wonder of the building lies inside and upstairs: the magnificent ceiling paintings commissioned by Charles I and designed by Peter Paul Rubens, who was knighted for this work. Painted in Antwerp and installed in 1635, the nine pictures are intended to emphasize the divine authority of the monarch (a contentious political issue at the time): James I (Charles' father) is shown being received into heaven, while other scenes depict the

*Churchill's office and bedroom in the Cabinet War Rooms*

claimed benefits of his rule: peace, prosperity, and the Union of England and Scotland. This forthright pictorial propaganda is designed to be seen from the doorway, the visitor's viewpoint, as explained on the acoustiguide.

Rubens's ceiling paintings are quite ironic in light of subsequent events, for Charles I went to his execution from this room on January 30, 1649, having fought and lost the seven-year Civil War against Oliver Cromwell and the Parliamentarians. A scaffold was erected outside the north annex (since demolished) of the Banqueting House, and it was from here, through a window, that Charles I stepped out onto the scaffold to meet his death. A bust of Charles I over the staircase entrance marks the spot.

## ▶ Cabinet War Rooms 44D2

*Clive Steps, King Charles Street, SW1 (tel: 020-7930 6961)*
*Open: Apr–Sep 9:30–6; Oct–Mar 10–6. Admission charge*
*Underground: Westminster*

This labyrinth of underground rooms provides an intriguing glimpse of the spartan conditions under which Sir Winston Churchill, the War Cabinet, and the Chiefs of Staff operated during World War II. From the cramped confines of this dark basement, they directed the strategies and forces of a global war. Deep below ground, the suite of 21 rooms offered a degree of protection against German aerial bombardment.

The rooms are equipped exactly as they were during this traumatic period. Highlights include the Cabinet Room, arranged as if for a meeting; the Prime Minister's room, which served as a combined office and bedroom for Churchill (here is the desk from which he made some of his most famous and morale-boosting radio broadcasts to the nation and the British Empire); the Map Room containing a map of the world, on which the Allied campaign was charted; and the Telephone Room containing the hotline telephone on which Churchill discussed his plans of strategy with President Franklin D. Roosevelt.

### ▶▶▶ REGION HIGHLIGHTS

**Banqueting House** *page 46*

**Houses of Parliament** *pages 48–49*

**National Gallery** *pages 50–51*

**National Portrait Gallery** *page 52*

**Tate Britain** *pages 56–57*

**Upriver cruises** *page 55*

**Westminster Abbey** *pages 59–61*

### HENRY VIII'S WINE CELLAR

Behind the Banqueting House stands the former Ministry of Defence (M.O.D.) head office. In its basement is a surviving part of the original royal palace of Whitehall; a simple vaulted brick chamber known as Henry VIII's Wine Cellar. This was considered such an important monument that it was moved over 39 feet from its original site when the M.O.D. building was constructed in the 1940s. Sadly, visits are not possible.

*Parliament*

**THE GUNPOWDER PLOT**
One of the most celebrated dates in British history is November 5, 1605, when Guy Fawkes and a number of other Roman Catholic conspirators attempted to blow up Parliament, along with James I and his ministers. Effigies of Guy Fawkes (and other unpopular figures) are burned on bonfires at firework parties all over the country on this date, and the cellars of the House are still checked to this day by the Yeomen of the Guard before the ceremonial State Opening of Parliament. The Queen presides over the State Opening from the House of Lords; no monarch has ever been admitted to the Commons since 1642, when Charles I forced his way in and tried to arrest five Members of Parliament, an event that sparked off the seven-year Civil War between Royalists and Parliamentarians.

### ►►► Houses of Parliament *44C2*

*St. Margaret Street, SW1 (tel: (020-7219 4272/3107)*
*Open: when Parliament in session, Mon–Thu; call for precise timings. Admission free*
*Underground: Westminster*

The public may attend debates when Parliament is in session; stand in line at the St. Stephen's porch entrance, which is clearly marked. At other times, the Houses of Parliament are closed for security reasons, but visits can be arranged.

Although access to this monumental building complex is restricted, the exterior alone is a splendid sight. The best views are from the far side of Westminster Bridge, looking across the Thames to the 270-yard frontage, with its symmetrically placed towers and pinnacles. The Parliament Square façade is much more varied, stretching from the Clock Tower (popularly known as Big Ben) to the Victoria Tower. In between lies the low roof of Westminster Hall, constructed by William the Conqueror's son, William Rufus, in 1099, where Parliament met for over two centuries. Its magnificent hammerbeam roof, completed in 1402, is the largest unsupported span in England and the finest medieval timber roof in northern Europe.

Edward the Confessor built the Palace of Westminster on this site in 1049, and successive monarchs used it as their main London residence until 1529, when Henry VIII decided to move to the nearby Palace of Whitehall (see Banqueting House, page 46). Parliament (from the Old French *parlement*, a discussion or debate) first met in the Chapter House of Westminster Abbey, but transferred its sessions to the vacated Palace of Westminster in 1547, where it has met ever since.

Fire destroyed most of the old Palace of Westminster in 1834, and the design for the new buildings was the subject of a public competition. From 97 entries, Charles Barry's was selected as the winner. A.W. Pugin, the expert on Gothic detailing, assisted him. The result is a palatial construction in the Tudor Perpendicular style, which perfectly suits its role as the building from which the nation is governed.

The interior of "The House," as it is known to those who work in it, is a cramped warren containing 1,100 rooms, 100 staircases, and almost 2 miles of corridor. Portcullis House, a new, precision crafted, wing of offices should ease the space; designed by Sir Michael Hopkins and Partners, it is being built on top of Westminster Underground Station on Bridge Street; some MPs already have offices just beyond this site, in Norman Shaw Building. The public areas are magnificently decorated in neo-Gothic and Arts and Crafts style. The actual debating chambers are so small that seating in the House of Commons can only accommodate 346 of the 659 elected Members of Parliament (the rest have to stand). This intimacy lends the House a clublike atmosphere and encourages the noisy barracking that some regard as undignified, others as an essential feature of parliamentary debate. The layout of the Commons, and of the second chamber, the House of Lords, reflects the fact that parliament formerly met in a chapel: the seating is ranged, like choir stalls, in parallel rows with the Speaker's chair where the altar would have stood.

The House of Lords has been televised since 1985, and the House of Commons introduced the cameras, with trepidation, in 1989.

## ▶ Jewel Tower *44C2*

*Abingdon Street, SW1 (tel: 020-7222 2219)*
*Open: Apr–Sep, daily 10–6; Oct–Mar 10–4. Admission charge*
*Underground: Westminster*

The Jewel Tower, which was built in 1366, stands opposite the Houses of Parliament, and once formed part of the original Palace of Westminster. The name refers to the fact that it was built as a strongroom to store the royal jewels and other valuables during Edward III's reign. It was carefully restored in 1956, after suffering bomb damage, and is now used to display an exhibition tracing the history of English parliaments, including a virtual reality tour of the Houses of Parliament. Look for the hefty 1621 iron door, on the first floor, made when the Jewel Tower was still being used to store all parliamentary records.

**BIG BEN**
Big Ben is the bell that tolls out the hours from the clock tower alongside the Houses of Parliament—a sound that is broadcast live at the beginning of some news programs. The first bell cracked in 1857, after it was cast, and had to be replaced with a new one, made in 1858. Nobody knows how the bell got its name. Some say it was named after "Big Ben" Caunt, a heavyweight boxer of the day, while others suggest it was named after Sir Benjamin Hall, the rotund man who was in charge of building works at Westminster. The tower has four massive clock faces; the minute hands are nearly 16½ feet long and made of hollow copper. Gunmetal was originally used, but proved to be too heavy. Each minute space is 12 inches across. Old pennies are used whenever any slight adjustments are needed to the weight of the clock's pendulum—but only very rarely has the time been out by more than a fraction of a second.

*Left: the king of clocks, high above the Houses of Parliament*

*The entrance terrace of the National Gallery*

**NATIONAL GALLERY TOP TEN**
Ten pictures in the National Gallery to look out for:
1 *The Wilton Diptych*
2 *The Battle of San Romano* by Paolo Uccello
3 *The Baptism of Christ* by Piero della Francesca
4 *The Virgin and Child with Saint Anne and Saint John the Baptist* by Leonardo da Vinci
5 *Bacchus and Ariadne* by Titian
6 *Giovanni Arnolfini and his Wife* by Jan van Eyck
7 *Self Portrait* (1669) by Rembrandt
8 *The Haywain* by John Constable
9 *Rain, Steam and Speed* by J. M. W. Turner
10 *Une Baignade, Asnières* (also called *Bathers at Asnières*) by Georges Seurat

### ►►► National Gallery 44E2

*Trafalgar Square, WC2 (tel: 020-7839 3321)*
*Open: Mon, Tue, Thu–Sat 10–6, Wed 10–9, Sun 10–6.*
*Admission free*
*Underground: Charing Cross*

The National Gallery fills the whole of the north side of Trafalgar Square. Few people notice that the building itself is a rather uninspired piece of classical design because there are so many competing attractions in the square. The view from the entrance terrace is superb, however. Beyond Sir Edwin Lutyens's elegant fountains, Nelson's Column, the pigeons, and the crowds there is a view down Whitehall to the Houses of Parliament; to the right is Canada House (1824), the headquarters of the Canadian High Commission; to the left, the church of St. Martin-in-the-Fields is partnered by Sir Hubert Baker's beautifully crafted South Africa House (1935), the Embassy of the Republic of South Africa. Its facade has lively carvings of South African flora and fauna.

Two bronze statues stand outside the Gallery: Grinling Gibbons's James II (1686), and George Washington, presented by the people of the United States in 1921.

The National Gallery itself was begun in 1824 when the government decided that London needed a national art collection to compete with other European galleries, such as the Uffizi in Florence, and the Louvre in Paris. It just happened that John Julius Angerstein's Pall Mall house was for sale at the time, along with his collection of 38 paintings, including works by Raphael and Rembrandt. These were purchased for £57,000 and Angerstein's house was used as the first gallery, until the present building was completed in 1838. In the meantime, a number of important pictures were added to the collection through gifts and bequests, but many of the best known works were acquired by shrewd gallery directors scouring Europe for masterpieces that could be bought cheaply because the artists were temporarily out of fashion.

Because space in the gallery was limited (originally it was only one room deep), the directors pursued a policy of quality rather than quantity. The result is one of the world's richest art collections, covering most schools and periods of painting up to the 20th century (the national collection of modern art, along with British works of all periods, is now housed in the two Tate Galleries; see pages 56–57 and 204–205). The gallery shop provides a leaflet explaining where to see the 20 most popular masterpieces and you can check on the day's free lectures and guided tours at the information desk and obtain a room-by-room guide.

If you intend to spend all day at the gallery, enter at the new Sainsbury Wing annex, to the left of the main entrance. The Sainsbury family donated the funds for the building, designed by the American architect Robert Venturi. Since the annex houses Renaissance works (in fact its collection begins ca1260), the architect incorporated motifs inspired by 16th-century Italian *palazzi*. Brilliantly colored paintings are dramatically framed by doorway arches carved in gray *pietra serena*, the stone that lends such grace to many of the best Italian Renaissance buildings. Thus the annex makes a fitting and complementary setting for the varied works of Jan van Eyck, Botticelli, Uccello, and for Leonardo da Vinci's entrancing cartoon of the *Virgin and Child*. The Sainsbury Wing also stages an extensive exhibition program in the basement, has a large first floor store, and has a bar and restaurant on the second floor with views over Trafalgar Square.

A bridge leads to the main gallery, where the full riches of European art are displayed. The many works by Rubens include his *Samson and Delilah* and *Le Chapeau de Paile*. Here, too, is Van Dyck's stunning equestrian portrait of Charles I, Poussin's *Triumph of Pan*, Constable's *The Haywain* and Seurat's *Bathers at Asnières*. New acquisitions include Durer's *St. Jerome*, Stubbs's *Whistle Jacket* and an exquisite Virgin and Child by Clarisse Master.

**NATIONAL GALLERY MOSAICS**

Do not miss the floor mosaics of the National Gallery's main staircase and vestibules, designed by the Russian-born artist Boris Anrep between 1928 and 1952. Those in the west vestibule illustrate the *Labours of Life*. Those in the north vestibule include portraits of Winston Churchill and T. S. Eliot, exemplifying Defiance and Leisure respectively, in a series entitled *The Modern Virtues*. Best of all, the *Awakening of the Muses* on the half-landing includes portraits of the most beautiful women of the 1930s: Greta Garbo as Melpemone (Muse of Tragedy), Virginia Woolf as Clio (Muse of History), and Diana Mitford as Polyhymnia (Muse of Song).

Giovanni Arnolfini and his Wife *by Jan van Eyck*

*Gallery of the great and good*

## ►►► National Portrait Gallery 44F2

*2 St. Martin's Place, WC2 (tel: 020-7306 0055)*
*Open: Mon–Sat 10–6; Sun noon–6. Admission free*
*Underground: Charing Cross*

Tucked away at the back of the National Gallery, the National Portrait Gallery is a virtual "Who's Who" of all the famous names in British history, science, and the arts. The collection consists of some 7,000 paintings, drawings, sculptures, and photographs collected because of the eminence of the subject, regardless of the merits of the artist; even so, many important artists are represented, from Hans Holbein to David Hockney, and the collection as a whole provides an intriguing overview of the development of portraiture from the stylized iconograph representation of early monarchs to the psychological expressiveness of later works. In all this, the gallery is probably the best place to get an idea of the range of exceptional people who made up the story of London—and Britain—and continue to do so.

The portraits are displayed chronologically, with the earliest on the top floor. Here, among the medieval portraits, you will find the poet Geoffrey Chaucer and his patron, Richard II, portrayed as a sensitive young man.

Two towering monarchs dominate the Tudor Rooms: Henry VIII, portrayed by Holbein and surrounded by several wives and advisers who fell from grace and lost their handsome heads, and Elizabeth I, partnered by her favorites, the Earls of Leicester and Essex. The portraits of Elizabeth I are a *tour de force* of political propaganda: Marcus Gheeraerts's work shows her triumphantly standing on a map of Britain with storm clouds behind (which were intended to represent the defeated Spanish Armada) and bright skies ahead.

Monarchs, politicians, and soldiers dominate the early part of the collection; later rooms have more of writers, artists, and scientists. There are portraits of Shakespeare, John Donne, Samuel Pepys, Sir Christopher Wren, and Sir Isaac Newton. Among the most popular literary portraits are the romantic depiction of the young Lord Byron, the only known picture of Jane Austen (by her sister Cassandra), and a tender portrait of the Brontë sisters by their brother Branwell.

The late Victorian and 20th-century displays are among the most perceptive and striking. Some pictures are self-portraits (Sir Stanley Spencer, Graham Sutherland, David Hockney, Dame Laura Knight) or depictions of one artist by another (Vanessa Bell by Duncan Grant, Henry Moore by Marino Marini). The first- and second-floor galleries display the museum's contemporary portraits plus major annual competitive shows, while the new wing open in 2000 has a rooftop café, bookstore, and other facilities. This is where you the visitor can judge the gallery's choice. It's worth renting the informative audio CD guide.

**NATIONAL PORTRAIT GALLERY TOP TEN**

1 *Richard II*
2 *Henry VIII* by Hans Holbein
3 *Elizabeth I* by Marcus Gheeraerts
4 *Sir Francis Drake* by Nicholas Hilliard
5 *Oliver Cromwell* by Samuel Cooper
6 *Emma, Lady Hamilton*, Nelson's mistress, by George Romney
7 *Lord Byron* by Thomas Phillips
8 *Jane Austen* by her sister Cassandra
9 *The Brontë Sisters* by their brother Branwell
10 *Virginia Woolf* by Duncan Grant

### ▶ St. John Smith Square 44B2

*Smith Square, SW1 (tel: 020-7222 1061)*
*Open: to concert-goers only*
*Underground: Westminster*

This church is hidden away in the residential streets south of the Houses of Parliament, where several Members of Parliament have flats; the area is known as the "Division Bell" district because many of its pubs and restaurants are wired up to the division bell that rings to summon M.P.s to vote on issues under debate in the House of Commons. M.P.s then have exactly eight minutes in which to rush back to the chamber.

The church itself is sometimes called "Queen Anne's footstool" after the story that Queen Anne, when asked how she would like the church to look, tipped over her footstool! Built in 1728, this is in fact a bold example of English baroque architecture. It was bombed during World War II, but has been carefully restored. It is now a busy concert hall, with almost nightly recitals. A licensed restaurant, "The Footstool," is located in the basement and makes a good spot for a pre-concert meal.

### ▶ St. Margaret Westminster 44C2

*Parliament Square, SW1 (tel: 020-7222 5152)*
*Open: daily 9:30–4:30. Donation*
*Underground: Westminster*

This fine 16th-century church is often overlooked because it stands in the shadow of Westminster Abbey but the stained-glass windows alone make it worth a visit. The

**THE MONUMENTS OF ST. MARGARET CHURCH**

St. Margaret Westminster contains memorials to many eminent people. A tablet near the altar marks the spot where Sir Walter Raleigh, the explorer and writer, who was beheaded for treason outside the Palace of Westminster in 1618, is said to be buried. Another tablet commemorates William Caxton, the printing pioneer, who was buried here in 1491. James Rumsey, laid to rest in 1792, has a memorial recalling his role as a pioneer of American steam navigation. There is also a remarkable number of Elizabethan and Jacobean monuments, of which the best is the alabaster effigy of Mary, Lady Dudley (died 1660) in the south aisle.

*The handsome church of St Martin-in-the-Fields*

**FAMOUS PARISHIONERS**
Many famous people are associated with the church of St. Martin-in-the-Fields. George I was the first churchwarden here, and his coat of arms appears on the pediment and above the chancel arch. Charles II was christened in an earlier church on this site in 1630 and his mistress, Nell Gwyn, was buried in the churchyard, as was Chippendale. The original burial ground is gone, however, cleared away in 1829 to make room for Duncannon Street, which runs to the south.



east Crucifixion window was commissioned by Ferdinand and Isabella of Spain and made in the Netherlands around AD 1500 for the marriage of their daughter, Catherine of Aragon, to Prince Arthur. Arthur died in 1502 and Catherine became the wife of his brother, Henry VIII. After nearly 20 years of marriage had failed to produce a male heir, Henry sued for divorce (and broke away from the Catholic church in the process), on the grounds that it was not legal to marry your brother's widow. The south aisle windows contain abstract glass by John Piper (1966), while the north aisle window commemorates John Milton, who was married in this church in 1656, as were Samuel Pepys in 1655 and Winston Churchill in 1908.

### ► St. Martin-in-the-Fields 44E2

*Trafalgar Square, WC2 (tel: 020-7930 1862)*
*Open: daily 8–6:30. Donation*
*Underground: Charing Cross*

For many people this lovely church is by far the best building in Trafalgar Square. It was designed by James Gibbs and built between 1721 and 1726. Its large portico and soaring spire that rises to 185 feet, a fraction taller than Nelson's Column, give it a memorable silhouette. If the arrangement of portico and steeple seems familiar, it is because this architectural masterpiece has inspired the plan of many churches worldwide, especially in early colonial America. Inside, on either side of the chancel, are boxes for members of the royal family (on the left) and the staff of the Admiralty, whose office is nearby in Whitehall. This was the original home of the Academy of St. Martin-in-the-Fields, and their tradition of free lunchtime concerts continues: the quality musicians make this one of the best places to find lunchtime peace in the busy city. The church also houses a bookstore, brass rubbing center, art gallery, and café (in the crypt), while a daily craft market is located at the rear. St. Martin-in-the-Fields is often referred to as the "church of the homeless." This is because Dick Sheppard, vicar from 1914 to 1927, opened a shelter in the crypt just after World War I to help unemployed and destitute ex-soldiers. Today the work continues with soup kitchens and general assistance for the homeless available in the parish rooms' basement.

*Choristers from the famous Westminster School, founded ca1200*

*Westminster Pier, which extends alongside Westminster Bridge on Victoria Embankment, is the central departure point for trips up and down the River Thames. The number of riverboats is increasing as the river regains popularity, and there are several pier stops between Westminster and the Greenwich Peninsula. Most boats have a bar or café and the tours are narrated. You can buy a ticket on the spot, but it is best to reserve your place in advance through a travel agent.*

**Upriver cruises** These run from March to the end of October and go to Kew (for the botanical gardens) and then continue all the way to Hampton Court Palace—you need to set aside a whole day for this trip, and perhaps return by train. They pass through some of the most beautiful rural scenery that London has to offer. Numerous parks (such as Kew, Syon, and Richmond) extend to the water's edge. In between are graceful Victorian suspension bridges (notably Chelsea, Albert, and Battersea bridges) and fine views of the riverside houses and pubs of Chelsea, Chiswick, and Richmond (tel: 020-7930 4721 for further information).

**Downriver cruises** By contrast, these run all year and offer fine views of the City skyline, the Tower of London, the rejuvenated Docklands district, and Greenwich, home of the National Maritime Museum, and, beyond, the Millennium Dome. Longer cruises continue past the Millennium Dome to the Thames Flood Barrier at Woolwich, a remarkable piece of engineering designed to prevent London from being flooded. The barrier consists of ten movable gates, straddling the river, which can be raised to hold the water back or lowered to let ships through. (For further details about downriver cruises, tel: 020-7930 4097. The Millennium Express service from Central London to the Dome continues after 2000; for information from City Cruises, tel: 020-7237 5134; an "affinity pass" halves ticket prices.)

**THE THAMES FLOOD BARRIER**

Each of the Thames Flood Barrier's gates weighs 3,000 tons and is 50 feet high. Together they constitute the world's biggest movable flood barrier. A visitor center on Unity Way explains the barrier's workings, and you can tour around the structure by boat.

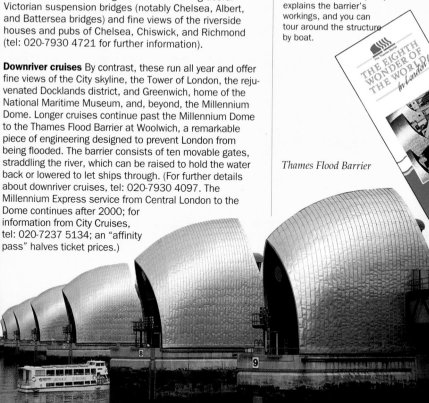

*Thames Flood Barrier*

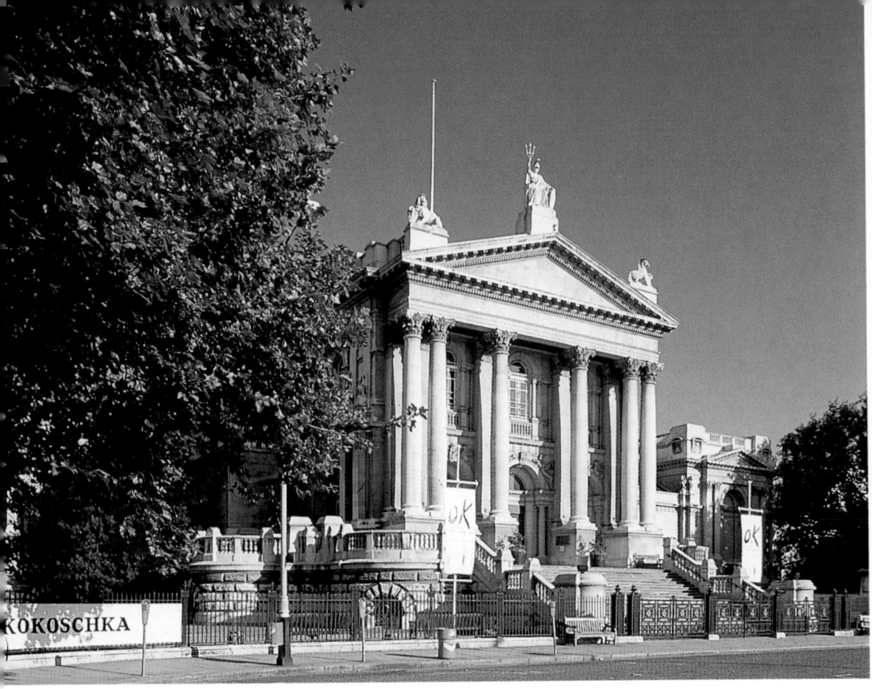


*Tate Britain on Millbank*

**LONDON ARTISTS TODAY**

London is the center of contemporary art in Europe. Thousands of artists live here, and the commercial galleries reflect the diversity of their work—most stock current copies of the free, thick *Galleries* magazine, which lists them by area, together with useful maps. The annual Turner Prize is the most prestigious (and controversial) art award. Previous winners include Damien Hurst, whose name has become synonymous with pickled or clipped sheep, sharks, and cows, Rachel Whiteread, known for her representations of inside spaces, Gillian Wearing and Chris Ofili. Jenny Saville paints slowly but achieves the most sumptuous flesh since Rubens. Amongst the senior generation, look out for works by Howard Hodgkin, Lucian Freud, Alan Jones, Richard Hamilton, Maggie Hambling, and Francis Bacon.

## ▶▶▶ Tate Britain 44A2

*Millbank, SW1 (tel: 020-7887 8000)*
*Open: daily 10–5:50. Admission free; there may be a charge for some loan exhibitions*
*Underground: Pimlico*

Until 1999, the national collections of British and modern international art were crammed together here. Then, under the dynamic directorship of Nicholas Serota, the collection split in two so that both can have sufficient space. By 2002, the Tate Gallery's redevelopment as the new home for the national collection of British art will be complete. Meanwhile, the national collection of modern international art has already left Pimlico and gone to Bankside (see pages 204–205).

The story of the Tate begins with Henry Tate, the sugar millionaire who was determined that London should have a showcase for British art. He offered his own collection of Victorian paintings to get it going, together with funds for a gallery. Finally, the government took up his idea and Sidney Smith's building was constructed on Millbank in 1812–1821. Piecemeal additions and donations followed, including the central cupola and sculpture galleries gifted by the notorious art dealer Joseph Duveen and his son in 1937, and the Whistler Restaurant with its landscape murals by Rex Whistler in 1983.

The Clore Gallery, designed by Stirling and Wilford, opened in 1985 to house the extensive Turner Bequest. It resembles a garden pavilion, and the top-lit galleries bring natural light to J.M.W. Turner's fragile watercolors without damaging them. Turner charted new territory in his depiction of pure light, away from realism and toward abstraction, and is seen as the father of modern British—if not European—painting. He left his personal collection to the nation at his death in 1851, stipulating that the finished works should be displayed together. It took 136 years for that wish to be fulfilled. Now, with the international collection gone, the British collection can spread out. It is not small, however: 3,500 paintings plus the prints and sculptures—and always growing. The redevelopment will increase gallery space by a third, but not everything will change: the popular annual Tate Gallery rehangs begun by Serota in 1990 will continue, when specific aspects of this vast collection are emphasized by rehanging old favorites and exhibiting others unseen for some time.

In all, Henry Tate's vision of an impressive showcase for the range of British art, from the 16th century to the present day, will be realized. The restaurants and stores, already known for their quality, will encourage visitors to spend a whole day at the Tate appreciating art in a leisurely environment.

The atmosphere of the Tate has always been relaxed. It is a place that stimulates discussion and delight, disapproval and sometimes disgust. There is the naïve formality of Tudor and Stuart portraits, most strongly visible in *The Cholmonley Sisters* (1600–1610). There is the passion and realism of the 18th-century paintings of the Enlightenment—William Hogarth's portraits, Stubbs's studies of horses, the aristocratic portraits of Reynolds, and liquid brushstrokes of Gainsborough.

These paintings, seemingly calm now, challenged convention in their day; but William Blake's visionary illustrations for Dante's *The Divine Comedy* seem as daring today as when they were created in the 19th century—at the same time as Constable and Turner were painting. The Tate's collection of Pre-Raphaelite paintings is particularly rich, and includes Millais' *Ophelia* (1851–1852). The different paths taken by British art in the 20th century can be seen in the Tate's Bankside building.

**TATE GALLERY TOP TEN**

Ten works of art to look out for in the Tate Gallery:

1 *The Cholmonley Sisters*
2 *Sir Benjamin Truman* by Thomas Gainsborough
3 *Flatford Mill* by John Constable
4 *Snowstorm: Hannibal Crossing the Alps* by J. M. W. Turner
5 *Haymakers* by George Stubbs
6 *The Annunciation* by Dante Gabriel Rossetti
7 *Paradise Lost* illustrations by William Blake
8 *Miss Cicely Alexander* by Rex Whistler
9 *The Awakening Conscience* by Holman Hunt
10 *Ophelia* by Sir John Everett Millais

Norham Castle, Sunrise
*by J.M.W. Turner*

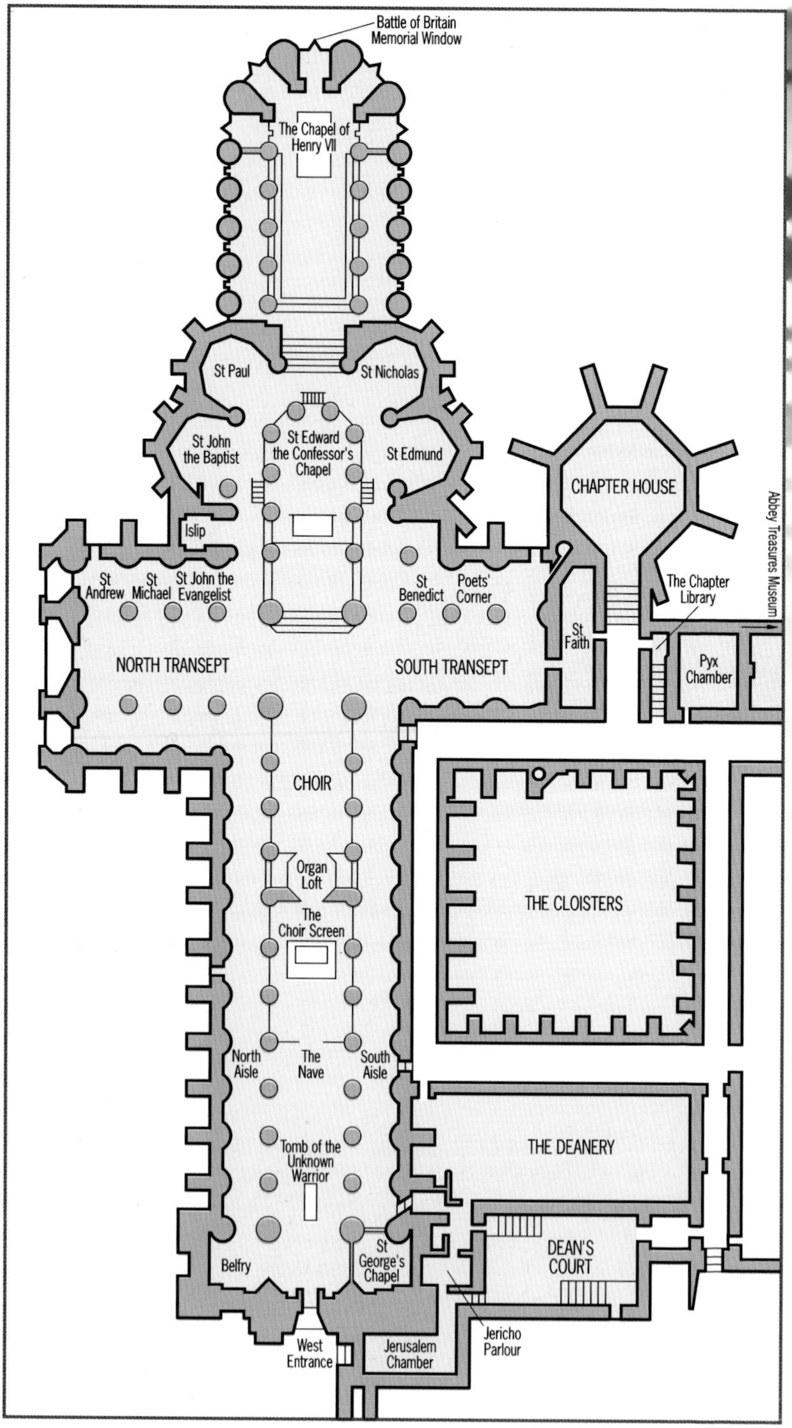




*Floor plan of Westminster Abbey*

## ▶▶▶ Westminster Abbey 44C2

*Broad Sanctuary, SW1 (tel: 020-7222 5152/7110)*
*Open: Nave and Royal chapels Mon–Fri 9:30–3:45; Sat 9:30–1:45; Wed eve 6–7. Chapter House, Pyx Chamber, Abbey Museum and College Garden: daily, call for times. Admission charge. Open for services*
*Underground: Westminster*

Westminster Abbey is a huge monument, crowded at all times. To experience the full serenity of the building, attend a service and hear the choirboys of Westminster School, accompanied by the abbey organ on which Henry Purcell once played.

**History** The church that gave its name to Westminster stood here by the 8th century, but the present building was begun by Edward the Confessor around 1050. He died a week after its consecration, on January 6, 1066 and was the first monarch to be buried here. Almost a year later, on December 25, 1066, William the Conqueror was crowned here, confirming the royal status of the church, which has seen the coronation of every subsequent English monarch.

Edward the Confessor was later canonized, and Henry III embarked on large-scale rebuilding in 1245 to make a shrine fit for the veneration of the sainted king. Today's church, greatly influenced by the French Gothic cathedrals of Amiens and Reims, was the result. In 1503, the Lady Chapel at the east end was replaced by the Henry

*The fan-vaulted Henry VII Chapel*

**THE TOMB OF THE UNKNOWN WARRIOR**
Of the many monuments in Westminster Abbey, the Tomb of the Unknown Warrior, located just in front of the west door, is perhaps the most moving. The simple grave, covered with a black marble slab, contains one anonymous soldier, symbolizing more than a million on the British side alone who gave their lives in World War I. He was buried here on November 11, 1920, in soil brought from the battlefields of France and Belgium. In front is another simple memorial, to Winston Churchill, who died in 1965 and lies buried at Bladon in Oxfordshire, near his birthplace.

**MORE MONUMENTS**
The north transept contains monuments to many eminent statesmen, including Peel, Gladstone, Palmerston, and Pitt the Elder, while the north choir aisle near the organ is dedicated to musicians, including Purcell, Elgar, Vaughan Williams, and Britten. One of the best monuments here is to the relatively unknown Lady Elizabeth Nightingale. She died in 1731 (the monument erroneously says 1734) of a miscarriage, having been frightened by lightning. A dramatic monument by the French sculptor Roubiliac (in the St. Michael Chapel) depicts her lying in her husband's arms as Death aims a spear at her heart.



VII Chapel, the architectural high point of the church. The west front was not completed until 1745, when the two towers were built to Nicholas Hawksmoor's design.

**The Nave** Entering the west door, look upwards to the majestic nave roof. An astonishing feature of the church is its great height (105 feet) in relation to its width. The complex patterning of the vault carries the eye eastward; only by looking up can you appreciate the enormous length of the building, since at ground level the view is stopped by the 19th-century screen that separates the nave from the choir and crossing. Before moving on, note the Tomb of the Unknown Warrior straight ahead and St. George's Chapel to the right, now dedicated to the dead of two world wars. Just outside the chapel, on a pillar to the left, is a portrait of Richard II (1377–1399), the oldest known true portrait of an English monarch.

**The Choir and Sanctuary** To pass beyond the choir screen and enter the ceremonial heart of the church where services—and royal coronations—take place, you have to pay an admission fee. There are good views to the left and right of the huge and intricate rose windows of the transept. The sanctuary itself is railed off. The floor has a very rare cosmati-work pavement, a form of mosaic made of glass and precious stones, dated 1268, but this is usually covered by a carpet.

*Hawksmoor's towers*

**Henry VII Chapel** Continuing round the north side of the sanctuary, you are led first into the north aisle of the Henry VII Chapel to view the white-marble effigy of Elizabeth I (died 1603), who shares a tomb with her half sister, Mary I (died 1558). From the aisle you enter the main part of the Henry VII Chapel. This is the most exciting part of the abbey, with its exquisite fan-vaulted ceiling, and makes an impressive setting for the royal tombs that are arranged around the altar and aisles. Among the finest of these is the tomb of Henry VII, in front of the altar, and of his mother, Lady Margaret Beaufort, near the south aisle altar. Mother and son both died in the same year (1509), and both tombs are the work of the Florentine sculptor, Pietro Torrigiani (who, as a boy, was often involved in fights with Michelangelo). The tombs were the first examples of Renaissance carving to be seen in Britain.

The chapel is used for installing Knights of the Bath, an order founded by Henry IV in 1399, and their banners hang above the flamboyant canopies of the wooden stalls. More down to earth are the stall misericords, which are carved with depictions of mermaids, monsters, and a wife beating her husband.

**The Confessor's Chapel** A bridge leads from the Henry VII Chapel to the Confessor's Chapel, where the king who founded the abbey is buried, along with Henry III, who rebuilt it. Their tombs are plain by comparison with that of Queen Eleanor (died 1290), portrayed in an effigy of bronze. Here, too, is the wooden Coronation Chair made in 1300, on which all British monarchs are crowned. Until recently it incorporated the ancient Scottish throne stone, the Stone of Scone, which dates back to at least the 9th century and was captured by Edward I in 1297. Finally in 1996, after years of pressure from Scottish nationalists, the stone was returned north of the border.

**Poets' Corner** The south side of the sanctuary leads back to the south transept, which, since the 16th century, has been where great poets, authors, artists, and actors are honored with memorials (though not all are buried here).

**The Cloister, Chapter House, Pyx Chamber and Undercroft Museum** A door in the south choir aisle leads to the cloister, with its fine, flowing tracery and superb views of the flying buttresses that support the nave. The Chapter House is an octagonal building of 1253, whose floor is covered in its original tiles. It was here that parliament met between 1257 and 1547, before moving to the Palace of Westminster. For children, the Abbey's highlight is the Norman undercroft, one of the few remaining parts of Edward the Confessor's original church. Here macabre wax effigies of Queen Elizabeth I, Charles II, and Lord Nelson are displayed, made using death masks and the real clothes of the people: Nelson's hat and eyepatch are those he wore in life. Some effigies were used to substitute the body for lyings-in-state; others were made in the 18th century to attract visitors to the Abbey. The Pyx Chamber is a survivor of the original abbey and contains the building's oldest altar, dated ca1240. It is now home to original pyxes (money chests) and the Abbey's church plate.

**POETS' CORNER**
Among the best monuments in Poets' Corner are the busts of Dryden, Jonson, Milton, and Blake—the last sculpted in bronze by Sir Jacob Epstein in 1957. There is also a fine statue of Shakespeare, paid for by public subscription and made in 1740. Two non-poets, however, have the finest monuments of all, both carved by Roubiliac: the composer Handel, on the west wall, holding pages from his oratorio *Messiah*, and the soldier-statesman John, Duke of Argyll and Greenwich, to the left of Handel, surrounded by figures symbolizing Liberty, Eloquence, and Wisdom.

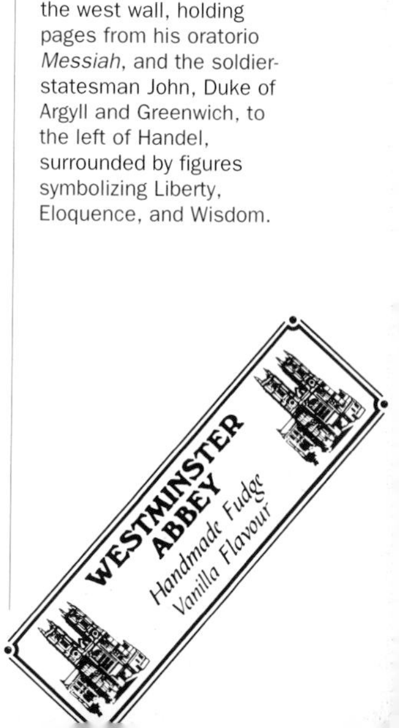

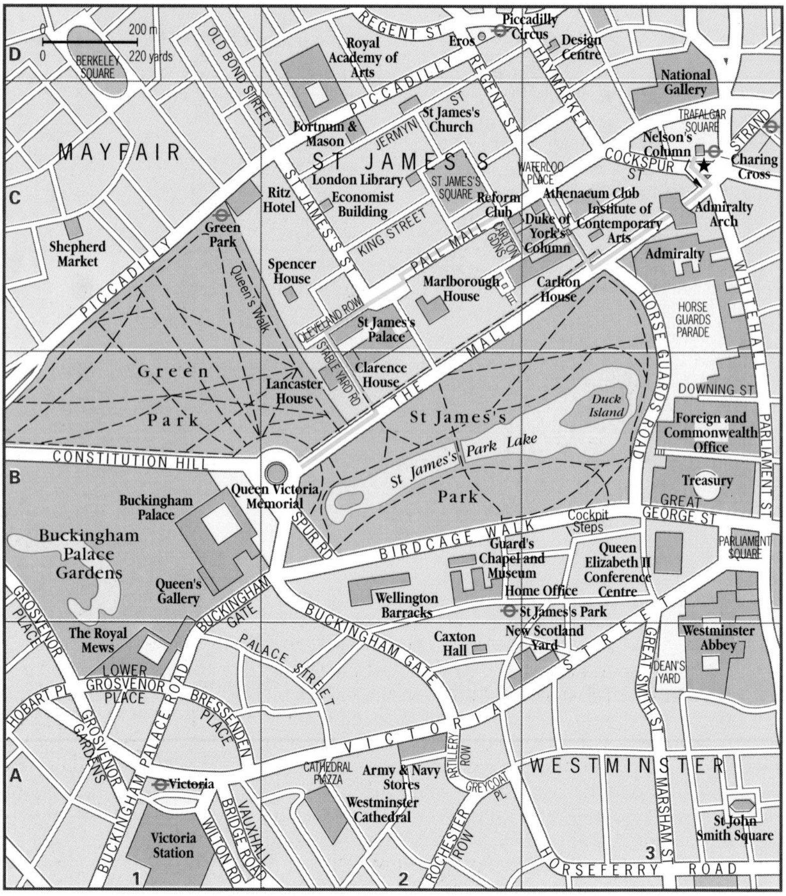




**THE GAME OF PELL MELL**
The Mall and Pall Mall, which runs parallel to the north, are both named after the game of *paille maille* (French for "ball mallet"), or "pell mell" in English. This was a sort of cross between golf and croquet, very popular in the time of Charles II, when London had several such alleys laid out for the game. The aim was to hit the wooden ball through an iron hoop suspended above the alley. No doubt its popularity was partly due to the money that changed hands in the bets that tended to accompany the game.

**ST. JAMES'S AND THE MALL** If Westminster is the center of government, then its neighbor, St. James's, is the elegant, formal seat of royalty. Buckingham Palace, the Queen's official London residence, sits at one end of the Mall, a wide avenue laid out in 1660 that forms the ceremonial route taken by the royal family on great state occasions, such as Trooping the Colour and the State Opening of Parliament.

Not far away is the much older St. James's Palace, surrounded by buildings of aristocratic elegance that house such institutions as the Royal Society, the Royal Fine Art Commission and the Institute of Directors. Gentlemen's clubs, such as the Athenaeum and the Reform, dominate Pall Mall and St. James's Street, and the exclusive tone of the whole district is confirmed by Jermyn Street's long-established specialist stores.

**ST. JAMES'S AND THE MALL WALK** If you begin this walk around 10 AM you should reach Buckingham Palace in time for the Changing of the Guard ceremony (Mar–Aug daily 11:30 AM; alternate days for the rest of the year and no ceremony in very wet weather; tel: 0839 123411 for recorded information).

# St. James's and the Mall

Starting from Trafalgar Square, walk through Admiralty Arch, built in 1910 as a memorial to Queen Victoria. Ahead lies Buckingham Palace. On the right is the front of **Carlton House Terrace**, built in 1832 to the designs of John Nash; the **Institute of Contemporary Arts** is at the No. 12, an unlikely-looking site presenting innovative art, drama, film, and video. The Duke of York Steps are beside it, at the top of which is the **Duke of York's column**, erected in 1833 to commemorate the son of George III, who commanded the British army during the Napoleonic Wars. Beyond lies **Waterloo Place**, with more memorials, notably an equestrian statue of Edward VII; another, to the right, of Captain Scott, the Antarctic explorer; and, ahead, the Guards' Crimean Memorial, with a statue of Florence Nightingale, the "lady with the lamp."

Turn left onto Carlton House Terrace, and take the first right onto Carlton Gardens to reach Pall Mall. On the right corner, the Reform Club's home is Charles Barry's masterpiece, an Italian palazzo adapted for London weather, built 1837–1841. Turn left onto Pall Mall, and keep straight on to Cleveland Row to get to **St. James's Palace**, a surprisingly homey brick mansion built during the reign of Henry VIII. It was the chief royal residence until Queen Victoria moved to Buckingham Palace in 1837, and it is now the London residence of Prince Charles and his sons. **Clarence House**, to the west of the palace, is the home of the Queen Mother; there is no public access, but you can see the sentries on duty outside the gatehouse.

Walk past the gatehouse and turn left onto Stable Yard Road, passing **Lancaster House**, on the right. This was the venue for the Lancaster House Conference of 1978, when Lord David Owen, then Foreign Secretary, presided over talks that led to the end of white rule in Rhodesia (now Zimbabwe). The building is currently used by the government to entertain important foreign visitors.

Once you are back in the Mall, turn right and walk up toward Buckingham Palace.

*Above: Lock & Co. Below: outside Buckingham Palace*

*Above: Buckingham Palace and the Queen Victoria Memorial*



**▶▶▶ REGION HIGHLIGHTS**



**THE COURT AND THE SEASON**

When the Queen is in residence at Buckingham Palace, the Royal Standard (the flag bearing the arms of the British sovereign) is raised. The Queen holds court in London, during "the Season," April to mid-August. Formerly, young ladies making their first official appearances in public ("debutantes" or "debs") were "presented" at court. Other events of the Season, such as Royal Ascot and the Queen's Garden Parties, are still eagerly awaited. Come mid-August, the Queen moves between her other residences at Windsor, Sandringham, and Balmoral.

## ▶▶▶ Buckingham Palace 62B1

*Buckingham Gate, SW1 (tel: 020-7930 4832/7799 2331/7321 2233)*

*Open: Buckingham Palace State Rooms: most of Aug and Sep, daily 9:30–4:30. Ticket office opens 9 and closes when last ticket sold; tickets can be reserved in advance. Queens Gallery: daily during exhibitions 9:30–4:30. The Royal Mews: Oct–Dec, Mon, Wed noon–4; Apr–Oct, Mon–Thu noon–3:30. Admission charges*

*Underground: Victoria, St. James's Park*

The royal court has moved several times in the last 900 years: first from the City to the Palace of Westminster under Edward the Confessor, then to Whitehall Palace under Henry VIII, then to St. James's Palace under Charles II. St. James's remained the official residence of the sovereign throughout the 17th and 18th centuries, and it was here that the big state functions took place. (Foreign ambassadors are still officially accredited to "the Court of St. James's.") Nevertheless, sovereigns often left the cramped Tudor buildings to sleep at Kensington Palace —William and Mary had forsaken Whitehall Palace for this healthier, more rural home (see pages 112–113).

It was at Kensington that Queen Victoria lived from her birth in 1819 until her accession to the throne in 1837. She chose to make Buckingham Palace the official London residence of the sovereign, as it remains today.

The palace is named after Buckingham House, built for the Duke of Buckingham in 1705. It was purchased by George III in 1761, lavishly remodeled by George IV (1820–1830), and given Sir Aston Webb's 363-foot facade in 1913. Against this classical backdrop one of London's most popular events takes place Mar–Aug daily at 11:30 AM (alternate days for the rest of the year), when sentries of the Guards Division in full dress uniform perform the Changing of the Guard. Spectators watch from the palace railings with their five wrought-iron and bronze gates, decorated with cherubs and erected in 1906. An alternative vantage point is the Queen Victoria Memorial, which stands in the traffic island in front of the palace (although climbing it is discouraged). This marble column, erected in 1911, is topped by the gilded figure of Victory, while Queen Victoria sits facing down the Mall.

**The Queen's Gallery** Although Buckingham Palace is only open in August and September, you can visit the Queen's Gallery at the rear of the building all year. Opened in 1962, it was originally built as a garden conservatory, then converted to the palace chapel in 1893 and finally turned into an art gallery in 1962. Here you can see exhibitions of paintings, drawings, and furniture drawn from the vast Royal Collection, including works by Rubens, Rembrandt, and Canaletto, as well as watercolors painted by Queen Victoria. The works on display are changed every six months or so. New developments will be completed in time for the Queen's Golden Jubilee in 2003, so the public can see more of her stupendous collection.

**The Royal Mews** Located farther along Buckingham Palace Road from the Queen's Gallery, these were built in 1824–1825 to house the royal household's horses and coaches. The splendid state carriages used on major state occasions are displayed here. They include the richly carved and gilded Gold Carriage, made for George III in 1762 and used for coronations; the Irish State Coach, bought by Queen Victoria in 1852 and used for the State Opening of Parliament; the so-called Glass State Coach, bought in 1910 and used to carry visiting dignitaries and overseas ambassadors; and the open-top landau used for the weddings of the Prince and Princess of Wales in 1981 and the Duke and Duchess of York in 1986.

**VISITING THE PALACE**
Buckingham Palace has been open to the public since 1993, for six weeks a year, from mid-Aug through Sep (when the Royal Family are away in Scotland). The State Rooms on view are furnished with some of the most important pictures and works of art from the Royal Collection (one of the finest art collections in the world). There is no need to wait in line, as tickets may be bought in advance by credit card or, during the opening season, from the ticket office in Green Park. Funds raised contribute to the restoration of Windsor Castle (see pages 236–237).



*Mounted officers leaving Buckingham Palace*

*These two streets are packed with stores that are worth seeing whether you intend to buy anything or not. Some stores have been trading here since the 1760s and several retain their 18th-century frontages and fittings. In keeping with the tone of the whole area, these stores cater largely to traditional, upscale tastes of wealthy men, although there are stores here that have among their merchandise women's clothes, food, antiques, and jewelry as well.*

**BY ROYAL APPOINTMENT**
Several stores in the Jermyn Street area display a royal coat of arms, indicating that they have been granted a coveted Royal Warrant of Appointment. Royal Warrants can be granted by the Queen, the Queen Mother, the Prince of Wales, and the Duke of Edinburgh. To qualify, the store must have had the royal patron's custom for at least three years. A handful (including Harrods of Knightsbridge, Piccadilly booksellers Hatchards, and the General Trading Company of Sloane Street) hold all four warrants.



*Clothes for the fastidious at Turnbull & Asser*

A good place to start is the **Design Centre**, 28 Haymarket. This is run by the government-sponsored Design Council and exhibits the best examples of British design, ranging from furniture to industrial tools. There are also gifts and books and magazines on design, art, and architecture on sale.

**Jermyn Street** From Regent Street westward, this makes a perfect window-shopping stroll, just as it did for courtiers from St. James's Palace when it was laid out in the 1660s. On the right, **Herbie Frogg** (No. 18) sells men's clothes of modern cut. Next door is **Geo F. Trumper**, hairdresser to some of the most eminent heads in London, followed by **Bates the Hatter**, selling deerstalkers and Panama hats. The masculine tone continues on the opposite side of the road with **Astley's** (No. 109A), selling briar pipes. Next comes **Russell & Bromley's** shoe store (No. 95) and **Robin Symes** (No. 94), an antiques dealer specializing in Greek and Roman sculpture. Next door is the cheesemonger, **Paxton & Whitfield** (No. 93). The shop front is mid-Victorian and the company, founded in 1740, stocks a huge array of cheeses, game pies, hams, pâtés, and wines. The Queen Mother buys her provisions here, while both the Queen and the Prince of Wales patronize **Floris**, the

perfumier (No. 89), founded in 1730 by a Spaniard from Minorca, Juan Fameias Floris, and still a family firm today. These stores all stand opposite the back entrance to St. James's Church (see page 79). Farther down on the right is the short Princes Arcade, built in the 1880s, while farther up is the Piccadilly Arcade with its gleaming bow windows, built in Georgian style in 1910.

Passing several more clothing and antiques stores you will come to **Wiltons** restaurant (No. 55), known for its oysters and traditional English cooking (game is a specialty). **Turnbull & Asser** (No. 71), nearly opposite, is a custom tailor specializing in silk and cotton shirts, famous for attention to clients' often idiosyncratic tastes. For made-to-measure shirts you must allow time for fittings and order a minimum of six; ready-made shirts are also available for the less fastidious. At the end of Jermyn Street, turn left into St. James's Street.

**St. James's Street** This wide street lined with gentlemen's clubs, long-established stores and new gourmet restaurants, sweeps down to St. James's Palace. Walking down the hill, you will pass the **Economist Building** (No. 25), an example of modern architecture (1964) that fits in well with the surrounding 18th-century premises of leading clubs (see pages 68–69). The second left, King Street, leads to **Christie's**, the auctioneers established in 1766 (No. 8), where new heights were scaled in 1997 when Gustav Klimt's *Schloss Kammer an Altersee No. 2* sold for almost £24 million ($40 million). **Spink & Son** (No. 7) is perhaps best known as a dealer in coins, medals, and paper money, but the gallery also displays English and Oriental art.

Back on St. James's Street, you will find **John Lobb** (No. 9) the shoemaker, where the staff makes models of patrons' feet in wood for shoes that are a uniquely perfect fit. **Lock & Co** (No. 6) does the same thing for heads (established in 1700, it made Lord Nelson's famous cocked hats). Two doors down is an alley leading to Pickering Place, a paved courtyard typical of many that once existed in 18th-century London. **Berry Bros & Rudd** (No. 3) is early Georgian and hardly changed; customers scrutinize the wine list, and staff fetch bottles of rare wines and liquors from the cellars below. There is a huge 17th-century scale to the left of the entrance, which was once used to weigh customers, since public scales were not introduced into England until 1799.

*The pick of pipes*

**THE ECONOMIST BUILDING**

The Economist Building in St. James's Street is one of a very small number of modern buildings that has been listed Grade II, meaning that it is considered such an important example of architecture that it may not be altered or demolished without government approval. The complex, designed by Alison and Peter Smithson and built between 1962 and 1964, is grouped around a quiet plaza containing Henry Moore's *Reclining Figure* (1969) and other modern sculptures. The buildings house the offices of *The Economist* magazine, a bank, and apartments. They are faced in Portland stone and seem to have a sculptured quality all of their own. The careful siting of the different offices within the complex allows framed glimpses of the Georgian and Victorian buildings that surround it. The building also contains a stunning minimalist bar, called Che.

*St. James's contains many of London's most exclusive gentlemen's clubs. Most were founded in the 18th century, when many aristocrats lived nearby, and flourished in an age when men and women led separate social lives, the woman's domain being confined to the home. Some clubs also served as gambling dens, where many an aristocratic fortune was thrown away over an evening's game of cards.*



**PUBS AND RESTAURANTS**
Though you are not allowed inside London's exclusive clubs, you can at least try one of the nearby restaurants that have a clublike atmosphere. One of the best is Greens (35–36 Duke Street, tel: 020-7930 4566), where they serve the sort of traditional food that club members enjoy: steak and kidney pie, followed by jam roly-poly pudding, for example. Wiltons (55 Jermyn Street, tel: 020-7629 9955) is renowned for game, seafood, oysters, and fine port wines. Less expensive is the Red Lion (2 Duke of York Street, tel: 020-7930 2030), a well-preserved Victorian pub full of mahogany paneling and cut glass.

As men began to spend more time at home with their families, the appeal of clubs began to decline, and by the 1930s they were known as the last bastion of crusty, reclusive, and conservative bachelordom. In recent years, though, clubs have undergone something of a revival, partly because some provide excellent sports facilities and an overnight place to stay. Even so, the main attraction remains the same as ever: the snob appeal of belonging to an exclusive circle (mostly of men, since few clubs admit women as members even today).

Walk westward down Pall Mall from Trafalgar Square, and you will encounter the **Institute of Directors**, a club for business leaders, and the **Athenaeum,** standing on opposite sides of Waterloo Place. If the buildings seem to echo each other, it is because both are the work of Decimus Burton. The Athenaeum is named after Athena, Goddess of Wisdom; her statue stands on the porch, and a frieze, based on the sculptures of the Parthenon, runs beneath the cornice. Founded in 1824 as a club for writers and artists, the Athenaeum's members today include bishops, scientists, and civil servants.

The Athenaeum's neighbors are the **Travellers' Club** and the **Reform**. When the former was founded in 1819, members had to prove that they had traveled more than 500 miles from London—not so easy in the pre-railway age. The Reform, as its name suggests, was formed by supporters of the 1832 Reform Act, which paved the way for an electoral system based on one person, one vote. Today, its members include men and women. James Barry was the architect for both buildings; despite their measured Renaissance-style exteriors, the interiors are particularly sumptuous.

The same is true of **The Royal Automobile Club** (No. 89), where members enjoy the use of a marble-lined swimming pool. The R.A.C. stands opposite St. James's Square, first laid out in 1663. The houses around the perimeter were intended for members of the nobility who wanted to live close to St. James's Palace, where Charles II used to live.

**No. 5** was the Libyan People's Bureau; the flowers in the gardens opposite mark a memorial to Yvonne Fletcher, the policewoman who was killed by a Libyan gunman during the siege of April 1984. **No. 10** (Chatham House) is the former residence of three Prime Ministers, William Pitt, the Earl of Derby, and William Gladstone. The

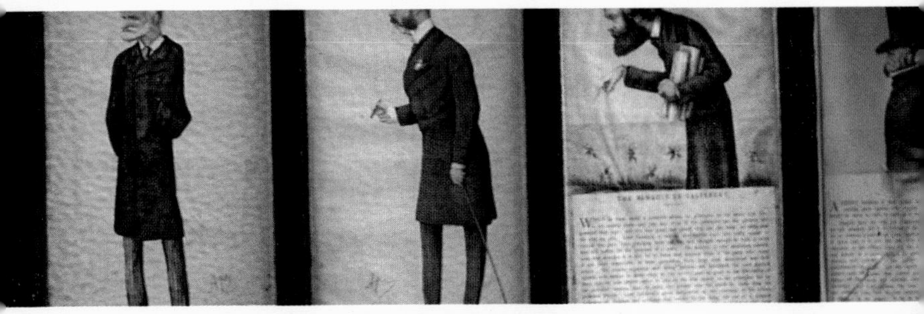

London Library at **No. 14** is not a club, though you do have to be elected to membership and pay a fee. It was founded in 1841 by the historian and polemicist, Thomas Carlyle, and the book collections include many rare and out-of-print volumes. It is much used today by academics, journalists, and writers.

Continuing up Pall Mall, you will pass the **Oxford and Cambridge Club** before turning right onto St. James's Street. This street has several of London's oldest clubs, as well as numerous buildings that were built as clubs but have since been turned to other uses. Many are built in Palladian style with fine Venetian windows, columns, and balustrades. The prestigious **Carlton Club** is at Nos. 69–70, whose members include many Conservative Party M.P.s.

The Carlton Club is a relative newcomer on the scene, having been founded in 1832. By contrast, **Brooks's Club** (No. 61), started up in 1764; **Boodles** (No. 28), started in 1762; and **White's** (No. 37), the oldest institution of them all, evolved from White's Chocolate and Gaming House in 1693.

**THE ARTS AND SCIENCES**

Besides its clubs, St. James's houses the premises of several prestigious bodies. The Royal Society, at No. 6 Carlton House Terrace, was founded by Charles II in 1660 as a scientific society with Samuel Pepys, Christopher Wren, and Isaac Newton among its early presidents. Today it lists many Nobel Prize winners among its members. Nearby, at No. 17 Carlton House Terrace, you will find the Mall Galleries (*Open* daily, 10–5 during exhibitions), which display landscapes, portraits, and watercolor paintings by members of the Federation of British Artists; most are for sale. This work tends to be traditional, in contrast with experimental works exhibited at the Institute of Contemporary Arts (Nash House, The Mall. *Open* daily noon–7:30 or later).



*The Athenaeum, on Pall Mall, was founded in 1824*

*Scott's Government Offices above the trees of St. James's Park*

**SPENCER HOUSE**

Built in 1756–1766 for the first Earl Spencer (an ancestor of Diana, Princess of Wales), Spencer House (27 St. James's Place, tel: 020-7499 8620, Sun 10:30–5:30. Admission charge) is London's finest surviving 18th-century town house, now fully restored and lavishly furnished under the patronage of Lord Rothschild. Access to its eight opulent rooms is by a one-hour guided tour, of which the highlights are the Palladian gilded Palm Room by John Vardy, and the elegant mural decorations and gilded furniture of the Painted Room by Vardy's successor, James "Athenian" Stuart, who designed the first-floor rooms. The house also contains a fine collection of 18th-century paintings and furniture.

## ▶▶▶ St. James's Park 62B2

*Underground: St. James's Park.*

St. James's Park is the most attractive of all London's green spaces. From the footbridge that crosses the lake at the heart of the park there are uninterrupted views westward to the classical facade of Buckingham Palace, while to the east you see the rear of Sir George Gilbert Scott's classical Government Offices, and the turrets and onion domes of the National Liberal Club, framed by the weeping willows whose branches cascade down to the fringes of the lake. Several varieties of wildfowl make the lake their home; many of the birds are quite tame. You can either take a stroll all the way around the perimeter of the lake, or concentrate on the views from the bridge and then head south to Birdcage Walk, the road that forms the southern park boundary (there were aviaries here in the time of James II).

On the opposite side of the road, Cockpit Steps (a reminder that the birds were also used for sport) lead up to Queen Anne's Gate, a charming enclave of early 18th-century houses, several of them with very ornate wooden canopies over their front doors. There is a statue of Queen Anne in front of No. 15 and blue plaques abound, recording the famous people who were born here or who lived here. No. 36 is the home of the National Trust, England's foremost historic preservation body, which owns and manages many of the country's finest houses and gardens.

At the southern junction of Queen Anne's Gate with Broadway you will find the London Transport Headquarters. It stands above St. James's Park Underground station and has fine facade sculptures: Jacob Epstein's bold figures of *Day and Night* flank the entrance, while reliefs symbolizing the winds were carved by five artists, including Eric Gill and Henry Moore.

### ▶ Wellington Barracks 62B2

*Birdcage Walk, SW1 (tel: 020-7930 4466)*
*Open: Chapel, Mon–Fri 9–4. Sun services. Admission free. Guards Museum: daily 10–4. Admission charge*
*Underground: St. James's Park*

This building serves as the headquarters of the Guards Division: the soldiers, resplendent in scarlet dress uniforms and bearskin hats, who perform the Changing of the Guard ceremony at Buckingham Palace. The Guards' Chapel has a moving war memorial cloister. The chapel itself was hit by a bomb in 1944, killing 121 people who were attending a service. It was rebuilt in 1963, incorporating the remains of the 19th-century apse.

The Guards' Museum is for those interested in military history. It explains the background of the regiments that make up the Household Division and the duties they perform as the official bodyguard to the Queen.

### ▶ Westminster Cathedral 62A2

*Ashley Place, Victoria Street, SW1 (tel: 020-7798 9055)*
*Open: Mon–Sat 8–7, and services. Donation. Campanile: Apr–Oct, daily 9–5; Nov–Mar, Thu–Sun 9–5. Admission charge*
*Underground: Victoria*

This exuberant Byzantine-style building, with its echoes of the great Basilica of St. Mark in Venice, is the principal Roman Catholic church in England, the seat of the Archbishop of Westminster. It was begun in 1895 but remains unfinished. It was intended that the whole interior be lined with marble and mosaics but the funds were sufficient only to complete the facing of the lower area, leaving the upper surfaces impressively bare. The fourteen Stations of the Cross, crisply carved by the young Eric Gill in his distinctive style, are on the name piers. For most visitors, the other main attraction is the superb campanile, built, like the rest of the church, of brick alternating with bands of Portland stone, very similar to Siena Cathedral's bell tower. It is 273 feet in height and there are outstanding views from the summit of all the main buildings of central London and far beyond to the surrounding countryside. What's more, you don't have to be in good physical shape to enjoy the view, since there is an elevator to take you to the top.

*Westminster Cathedral, Britain's premier Catholic church, comprises some 12½ million handmade bricks, without any steel reinforcement*

**THE STONES OF WESTMINSTER CATHEDRAL**

The variegated marble that covers the walls of Westminster Cathedral came from some of the most ancient and renowned quarries in Europe. Two columns at the west end are of red Norwegian granite, symbolizing the blood of Christ. The green columns came from Thessaly, the same source as the marble used to build Haghia Sophia in Istanbul, to which this church bears a strong resemblance. The white capitals are of Carrara marble, the stone favored by Renaissance sculptors such as Michelangelo. The high altar is a massive block of Cornish granite and the canopy, or baldachino, is supported on columns of yellow Verona marble.

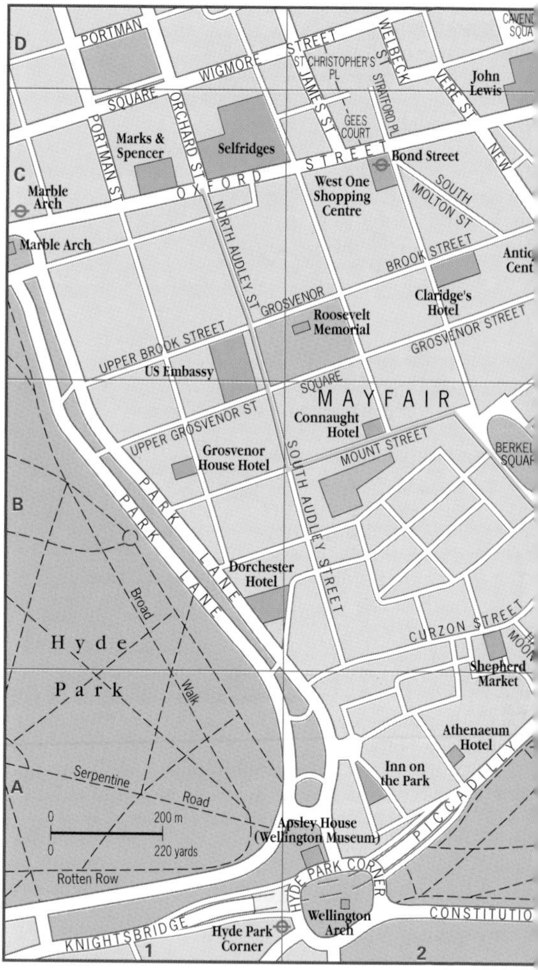


**MAYFAIR AND PICCADILLY** Mayfair contains some of London's most elegant houses, set around leafy squares, but with the exception of several embassies, their original aristocratic tone has mostly been lost as buildings became offices or upscale apartments. The fine Adam-style architecture of Berkeley Square survives, as do the exclusive stores of Bond Street, Piccadilly, and Burlington Arcade. Bordering the north and south sides are Oxford Street and Regent Street, lined with well-known retailers and department stores.

**MAYFAIR AND PICCADILLY WALK** Starting at Green Park Underground station, walk east along Piccadilly to reach **Burlington Arcade**, the fifth turn on the left. Burlington Arcade is a covered promenade, built in 1819—one of England's first shopping malls. The arcade is Regency in style and atmosphere. Exclusive stores selling antiques and clothing line either side. Rules of propriety are enforced by Beadles, in top hats and great coats, who are retired members of the 10th Hussars regiment.

# Mayfair and Piccadilly

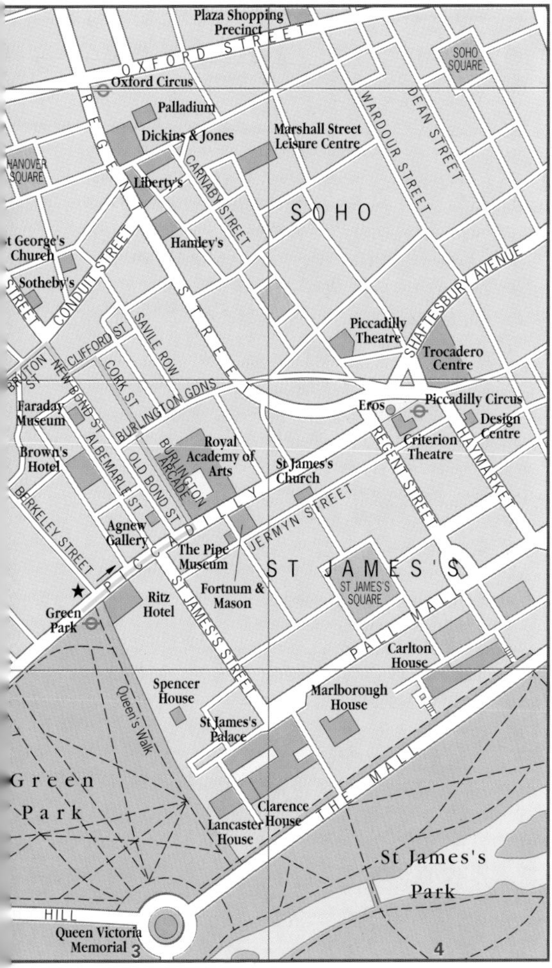


At the opposite end of the arcade, cross Burlington Gardens and walk up Cork Street before turning left onto Clifford Street, past art dealers displaying everything from contemporary art to Old Masters.

Turning right on Bond Street brings you to Bruton Street, on the left; on the corner is the Time-Life Building (1952), with panels carved by Henry Moore set in the terrace parapet. Turn left down Bruton Street to **Berkeley Square**. The west side is lined with Georgian houses; you may glimpse, through the windows, lavishly plastered interiors and grand staircases.

The top left-hand exit out of Berkeley Square leads left onto **Mount Street**. The **Connaught Hotel**, on the right, is probably London's most discreet super-deluxe hotel.

Turn right at The Audley pub on South Audley Street to reach **Grosvenor Square**, the scene of anti-Vietnam war rallies in the 1960s, focused on the forbidding American Embassy on the left.

North Audley Street leads from the top left-hand corner of Grosvenor Square to Oxford Street.

**▶▶▶ REGION HIGHLIGHTS**

**Bond Street**
*pages 74–75*

**Liberty's** *page 81*

**Piccadilly** *pages 78–79*

**Royal Academy of Arts**
*page 82*

**St. James's Church**
*page 79*

**Wellington Museum (Apsley House)** *page 83*

*Old and New Bond streets together form a continuous thoroughfare cutting through the heart of Mayfair and lined with fashionable stores. Starting at the Piccadilly end, there is a succession of picture dealers selling quality works. On the left are Thomas Agnew and Marlborough Fine Art. On the right are the Leger Gallery (No. 13), specializing in 18th- and 19th-century British art, and Colnaghi (No. 14), which deals in European paintings and sculpture. Opposite, Versace's elegant store, with marble floors and stucco ceilings, sells the best of Italian couture.*



**SAVILE ROW**
Parallel with New Bond Street, three blocks east, is Savile Row, a byword for gentlemen's tailoring. Gieves and Hawkes (No. 1), founded in 1785, was the first establishment; the late Tommy Nutter (No. 19) designed Elton John's way-out clothes; at No. 3 the Beatles made their last public appearance, on the roof of the Apple Building in 1969.

*Bond Street stores*

**Bond Street** prices are high, but window shoppers can have a field day. Beyond Stafford Street, on the left, is **Gucci**, followed by the cheerful orange-and-white facade of the **Royal Arcade**, where **Charbonnel et Walker** (No. 1) sell their exquisite chocolates, and other stores specialize in silver, paintings, and antiques. The Arcade leads to **Albemarle Street** with more art galleries, such as Thomas Agnew at No. 3 and Marlborough Fine Art at No. 6, plus **Brown's Hotel** (No. 23), where Eleanor and Franklin Roosevelt spent their honeymoon, and the **Royal Institution** (Nos. 20–21) with its templelike facade. This was founded in 1799 for the promotion of scientific knowledge. A small museum in the basement is devoted to the pioneering electromagnetic experiments of Michael Faraday (*Open* Mon–Fri 10–4:30).

Back on Old Bond Street, the **Ferragamo** boutique stands on the right, and if you turn down **Burlington Gardens**, then left onto **Cork Street**, you will find several galleries specializing in the works of modern artists.

**Asprey & Garrard** (Nos. 165–169 New Bond Street) stands at the junction of Old Bond Street (laid out in 1686) and New Bond Street (extended in 1721). Its big windows of plate glass and iron, considered revolutionary when they were installed around 1848, make it ideal for window shopping. A favorite with royalty worldwide, this is where Prince Charles bought the engagement ring for his fiancée, Lady Diana Spencer.

Farther up, on the corner of New Bond Street and Bruton Street, is **Hermès**, known for its silk scarves. Beyond Bruton Street, on the left, the thoroughly unstuffy **Fine Art Society** store (No. 148), dating from 1876, sells works by 19th- and 20th-century British artists, and is always worth visiting.

**Sotheby's** (No. 35), on the right, has a modest entrance for such a well-known auctioneers' house. There are viewings and sales here most days: details at the information desk (or tel: 020-7493 8080). Antiques can also be found at the **Bond Street Antiques Centre** (No. 124) and the **Bond Street Silver Galleries** (Nos. 111–112).

Designer-label clothing and shoe stores predominate in the upper stretch of New Bond Street, where **Fenwicks**, the stylish department store, is to be found on your right at the Brook Street intersection.

Turning right down Brook Street you will enter **Hanover Square**, laid out in 1717 and named for the Elector of Hanover who took the throne as King George I in 1714. Handel, who lived at No. 25 Brook Street, had his *Messiah* performed annually at The Hanover Square Rooms (since demolished). Turn round, back along **Brook Street** and continue toward **Claridge's Hotel**, where frock-coated doormen admit the tidily dressed to its opulent interior. Before you reach Claridge's, take a detour right down the pedestrian area of **South Molton Street**. Here, chic boutiques belie the street's old nickname, Poverty Lane, and in summer there is a festive atmosphere as shoppers enjoy the sunshine from its pavement cafés.

**ST. GEORGE'S CHURCH**

At the southern end of Hanover Square, in St. George Street, is the church of St. George, built in 1724 by John James and fronted by massive Corinthian columns. The baroque interior retains its 18th-century layout with galleries in the aisles. The Venetian east window is filled with 16th-century stained glass, moved here from a church in Antwerp, showing a Tree of Jesse. St. George's was, and remains, a fashionable place for weddings. Among those married here were Benjamin Disraeli, Mary Anne Evans (better known as the novelist George Eliot), Theodore Roosevelt, and the poet Percy Shelley.

*From Marble Arch in the west to High Holborn in the east, Oxford Street stretches for 1½ miles to form Europe's longest row of department stores and retail outlets. In the weeks leading up to Christmas, when festive lights and decorations are strung across the street, it is the most crowded place in town, with police called in to control not the traffic, which is largely excluded, but the sheer volume of shoppers.*



**THE ROAD TO TYBURN**
Oxford Street used to be known as Tyburn Way because it led to the gallows at Tyburn (at the intersection of Edgware Road and Marble Arch), where public executions took place until 1783. Public hanging was intended to act as a deterrent to the watching crowds, a warning against crime, but it turned into popular entertainment, and high prices were paid for ringside seats.

*Selfridges' department store, right; its clock, below*

**Oxford Street** was so named because it led to Oxford, a name consolidated when the Earl of Oxford bought the open land to the north of it in 1793. Once lined with entertainment halls, it is now Europe's longest retail street, a shopper's delight, even if many stores are chain outlets. One is **Marks & Spencer**, whose flagship store is at Marble Arch (No. 458). The largest and best known store is **Selfridges** (No. 400). The impressive Edwardian building, designed by R.F. Atkinson and Daniel Burnham and built in 1907–1928, introduced American retail ideas to London. Harry Gordon Selfridge, from Chicago, commissioned the steel frame building with its opulent Ionic columns, founding London's only rival to Harrods. The giant Art Deco clock over the main entrance (by Gilbert Bayes) has the regal figure of *The Queen of Time*, standing on a prow that represents the ship of commerce. On a completely different scale **Gees Court**

and **St. Christopher's Place** form a narrow pedestrian alley that is easily missed (entered through a tiny archway between James Street and Stratford Place on the north side of Oxford Street). The lane is lined with small stores and sidewalk cafés, a different and more intimate world than the big modern **West One Shopping Centre** above Bond Street underground station opposite.

**Stratford Place**, the next left, is another surprising interruption to Oxford Street's almost continuous line of store fronts. Set back at the end of this 18th-century cul-de-sac is the elegant and untouched Stratford House of 1723, built in Adam style and housing the Oriental Club, founded in 1824 for colonial civil servants.

Next comes **John Lewis** (Nos. 278–306), another of the street's big stores. Its motto is "We are never knowingly undersold" and the store will refund the difference if you can buy identical goods more cheaply elsewhere.

**Oxford Circus** forms the busy intersection of Regent Street and Oxford Street. Note the northward view to **All Souls Church**, Langham Place (see page 118), with its circular portico and spire, built by John Nash to form the focal point of the view up Regent Street, though today it is rather dwarfed by tall office towers and store signs. Curving facades also give distinction to the buildings of Oxford Circus, but the architecture becomes less impressive as you continue east. In this stretch you will find two well-known music megastores, **H.M.V.** (No. 150) and **Virgin** (Nos. 14–30).

The eastern end of Oxford Street is dominated by the **Centrepoint** building, a rather gloomy structure too tall for its site (400 feet) and set in a windswept plaza. Designed by Richard Seifert, the tower has recently been listed as a building of architectural merit, thus protected from alteration or demolition. The skyscraper marks Oxford Street's junction with Tottenham Court Road, the best place to buy genuine electronic goods at good prices, with reliable after-sales service. From here, New Oxford Street continues east, having sliced through the notorious slums of St. Giles (where the Great Plague of London started in 1665) in 1847 to join up with High Holborn.

The pretty church of **St. Giles-in-the-Fields** still stands to the south. David Garrick, the Shakespearian actor, was married here, the children of the poets Shelley and Byron were christened here, and the satirist and poet Andrew Marvell lies buried in the churchyard.

**MARBLE ARCH**

Marble Arch, designed by Nash in 1827 and inspired by the Arch of Constantine in Rome, was originally intended to form a triumphant gateway to Buckingham Palace. Popular myth says it was moved here in 1851 because it was too narrow for the royal coach to pass through; in fact, it was moved to make way for a new range of buildings. Now it stands in sad isolation at the center of a busy traffic circle, and the central gates remain firmly closed most of the time. To this day only members of the royal family are allowed to drive through.



*St. Christopher's Place, a stylish enclave from which to escape the madding crowd*

*Piccadilly's name has its origins in a mansion built here in 1612 for one Robert Baker. He had made his fortune selling "picadils," a type of stiff collar fashionable with the 17th-century court, and his house (and the area around it) became known as Piccadilly. Today, Piccadilly mixes gaudy neon signs with state-of-the-art entertainment, and splendid old stores.*

**PEPSI TROCADERO**
The Trocadero houses Europe's largest indoor entertainment complex on its seven floors (tel: 0891-881100. *Open* daily, 10 AM–midnight. *Admission free*, but charges for attractions). The biggest attractions are Segaworld, with over 400 cutting-edge arcade-style games to master, the Emaginator Movie Experience, and the huge Pepsi IMAX (it stands for maximum image) 3-D cinema where audience members wear electronic headsets with surround sound to maximize the feeling of virtual reality. Madame Tussaud's Rock Circus is also here (see page 79).



*In Shepherd Market*

**Piccadilly** begins at **Hyde Park Corner**, a spot where cars do battle above while pedestrians get lost in the labyrinthine underpass below. One exit from the underpass leads to the traffic island containing **Constitution** (or Wellington) **Arch**, designed in 1828 by Decimus Burton and intended as a ceremonial gate linking Hyde Park with Buckingham Palace via Constitution Hill. It is topped by animated horses pulling Victory's chariot, a superb bronze sculpture by Adrian Jones (1912). Nearby is a statue of the Duke of Wellington (1888) facing his residence, Apsley House (see page 83). To the north are the luxury hotels of Park Lane; the south side of Piccadilly runs alongside **Green Park**, laid out in the 17th century.

Walking up Piccadilly on the north side, you can detour left up White Horse Street to find the stores, pubs, and restaurants around **Shepherd Market**. These narrow streets and alleys were built in 1735 by Edward Shepherd on the site of the ancient May Fair that gave its name to the district. Here you will find **The Bunch of Grapes** (No. 16 Shepherd Market), a Victorian pub, and **Tiddy Dol's** (No. 55), a restaurant set in an 18th-century house.

Continuing up Piccadilly, **Half Moon Street**, the next on the left, was the home of Bertie Wooster, P.G. Wodehouse's comic creation, as well as of Dr. Johnson's real-life friend and biographer, James Boswell.

Beyond Green Park is the Parisian-style **Ritz Hotel** (1906). Once a haunt of the fashionable set it is still a glamorous place in which to have tea (reservations advised), and its dining room overlooking Green Park is one of London's most beautiful. Farther along on the left are Old Bond Street and Burlington Arcade, opposite Piccadilly Arcade. Although it was built in 1910, it too has bow-fronted shops, specializing in china, rare books, and clothing. Next on the right comes **Fortnum & Mason**, the grocery store founded in 1707, lit by chandeliers and lined with mahogany paneling. Its shelves are piled high with displays of delicious foods. Look for the clock above the entrance: on the hour, music strikes up and Mr. Fortnum and Mr. Mason pop out of their niches and bow to each other. **Hatchards**, next door, with its 18th-century store front, is one of London's best stocked and most congenial bookstores. Opposite is the Royal Academy (see page 82) and farther down on the right, slightly set back, is Sir Christopher Wren's church of **St. James's.**

**Piccadilly Circus** itself is a somewhat confusing sight, which planners have remodeled repeatedly since Nash laid it out in 1819. It marks the junction of five major

streets but lacks the coherence of design to make this clear. These days it is a rather shabby, over-commercialized place, famous for its enormous, illuminated advertising signs and for Alfred Gilbert's tiny figure of a winged archer, popularly known as Eros, the god of Love, but actually designed as the *Angel of Christian Charity*. This was erected in 1893 as a memorial to the philanthropic Earl of Shaftesbury, who did much to improve the lot of factory and mine workers (especially children) in the mid-19th century. Today's children and teenagers, however, are more likely to flock to the all-new pulsating attractions of the **Pepsi Trocadero**, London's indoor high-tech theme park (see panel, page 78), with the latest dare-devil rides. Next door is Madame Tussaud's homage to the world of rock music. **Rock Circus** celebrates Mick Jagger, Jamiroquai and other stars; the visitor can wear special headphones that play the music of the performer they are looking at (*Open* Mar–Aug, Mon, Wed, Thu and Sun 10–8, Tue 11–8, Fri, Sat 10–9; Sep–Feb, Wed–Mon 10–5:30, Tue 11–5:30).

**ST. JAMES'S CHURCH**

St. James's Church (tel: 020-7734 4511; *Open* daily 8:30–7; Oct–Apr 9–6. *Donation*) was the last of some 55 churches that Sir Christopher Wren designed for London and the one that he himself liked best. It was bombed in 1940 but has been superbly restored (you would not guess that the spire of 1968 is made of fiberglass). Its gallery-lined interior contains work by the great carver, Grinling Gibbons, including the angels of the organ case, the Garden of Eden font, and the altarpiece. St. James's today is more than a church: there is a natural foods café (The Wren at St. James's, 35 Jermyn Street) to the rear with works of art for sale on the walls; its courtyard is the venue for a crafts market (Thu, Fri, and Sat). Music lovers should check out the lunchtime recitals (Tue–Sat; full concerts on Thu, Fri, and Sat evenings), and the annual music festival in May and June.

*The* Angel of Christian Charity, *mistakenly known as Eros, watches over Piccadilly Circus*

*Regent Street, named for the Prince Regent, later George IV, was laid out by John Nash between 1813 and 1816 to form a grand boulevard linking Regent's Park with the royal palaces and aristocratic mansions of Carlton House and Pall Mall. Although most of the original buildings have been replaced, Regent Street retains its grandeur, especially at the Piccadilly Circus end. Here, it bends dramatically to the left, obscuring the buildings that lie beyond but promising much. From here up to and beyond Oxford Circus, this grand street is devoted to quality shopping.*



*Above: mural in Carnaby Street*
*Right: Regent Street, facing south*

The eastern side of Regent Street has many of the best buildings. The **Café Royal** (No. 68) opened in 1865 and soon became the haunt of Aubrey Beardsley and Oscar Wilde; the Brasserie retains something of its sumptuous beau monde atmosphere. **Mappin & Webb** (No. 170) and **Asprey & Garrard** (No. 112) sell antique and modern jewelry to the wealthy, including the royal family. Between these two, on both sides of the street, are well-known clothes shops, including **Aquascutum** (No. 100), **Austin Reed** (No. 103), and **Burberrys** (No. 161), makers of distinctive (and expensive) raincoats, hats, and scarves. Farther up, **Hamley's** (Nos. 200–202), established in 1760, is thought to be the largest toy shop in the world; despite its size, expect it to be packed, with lines at the door before Christmas. Two other children's favorites are nearby: the Disney Store at No. 140, and the Warner Bros. Store at No. 172. **Liberty's** comes next with its trademark fabrics (the store front is, in fact, on Great Marlborough Street, not Regent Street itself). The range of tempting stores continues with **Laura Ashley** (No. 256), a prime source for clothes, fabrics, and furnishings. **Dickins & Jones** (No. 224) is a department store selling everything from designer-label clothes to glass and china, and the **Wedgwood Gift Centre**, on Oxford Circus, sells the company's famous Grecian-style pastel ceramics.

**CARNABY STREET**
Running parallel with Regent Street, two blocks to the east, is Carnaby Street, a byword for trendiness in the Swinging Sixties, when Mary Quant was the fashion queen and everyone came here to buy paisley flower-power shirts and bell-bottomed trousers. As fashions changed, so Carnaby Street declined to the point where it became a seedy eyesore. Today it has been revived to cater to young, hip people. Around the corner, at 8 Kingly Street, *Beatles For Sale*, a store entirely devoted to Fab Four memorabilia, is proving a popular attraction for music fans of all ages.

*Liberty's (Nos. 210–220 Regent Street) is a department store unlike any other in London: an Aladdin's Cave housed in a building that is a gem of Arts and Crafts design. A wide and varied range of goods can be bought here, but the distinctive Liberty print fabric is still the main attraction—and carries with it an image of upscale style.*

The store fills two buildings, both designed by E.T. and E.S. Hall and built in 1924. The classical part overlooks Regent Street; above the entrance, a frieze shows Britannia receiving goods from the nations of the world. Inside, the basement is packed with the Japanese ceramics, textiles, and prints that were Arthur Lasenby Liberty's trademark when he opened the store in 1875. The floors above offer a profusion of goods from around the world, from African tribal jewelry to exotic silk fabrics, all arranged to re-create the atmosphere of a bazaar. The first floor stocks Liberty handkerchiefs, scarves and ties.

The top floor, by contrast, resembles an informal museum. On one side you can browse among Arts and Crafts furniture, known for its quality craftsmanship and its straightforward, clean design. On the other, glass cases line the walls, filled with antique silver and pewter pieces specially commissioned from artists such as Archibald Knox; his flowing, Celtic-inspired designs were so popular that "Liberty style" became synonymous with art nouveau. In between is the central stairwell, where you can peer over the banister and look down on oriental carpets and Liberty's own range of fabrics.

Liberty's Tudor-style wing dates from 1924 and is built of timbers salvaged from H.M.S. *Impregnable* and H.M.S. *Hindustan.* A bridge across Kingly Street, linking the store's two parts, has a clock where St. George and the Dragon do battle every hour. Above the Great Marlborough Street entrance is a gilded caravel, the sailing ship that once carried cargoes of silks, porcelain, and spices.

*Liberty's weathervane depicts a caravel, the ship that once sailed the oceans in search of spices and silk. Below, Liberty's stock, laid out like an eastern bazaar*

**THE ROYAL ACADEMY SUMMER EXHIBITION**
The Royal Academy Summer Exhibition is one of the high points of the London Season: tickets to the fashionable and exclusive private preview are much sought after. The exhibition (June–mid-Aug) displays the paintings, sculpture, and architectural drawings of living artists, and much of the work is for sale. Of the 10,000 or so works submitted, the Academicians select just over 1,000 for public display. They have, in the past, been criticized for conservatism and for preferring representational works, while ignoring the abstract. Today, the choice tends to be more adventurous and wide-ranging.

## ▶▶▶ Royal Academy of Arts *73B3*

*Piccadilly, W1 (tel: 020-7300 8000)*
*Open: daily 10–6, plus intermittent late night openings.*
*Underground: Green Park, Piccadilly Circus*

Burlington House, Piccadilly's most imposing building, was built as a Palladian palazzo (mansion) for the Earl of Burlington around 1720. Today it is the home of the Royal Academy of Arts, whose members include many distinguished British artists and architects. Major international exhibitions loaned from collections around the world fill two suites of galleries for most of the year; art in the Summer Exhibition (see side panel) is for sale. Recent exhibitions have included Monet's late works and Picasso's ceramics.

Burlington House is set back from the street, with a courtyard in front that has a statue of Sir Joshua Reynolds. He was elected first President of the Royal Academy when it was founded in 1768, under the patronage of George III, with the twin aims of raising the prestige of the arts and of teaching promising painters (Constable and Turner were among the first students). The two wings on either side house other learned bodies, such as the Society of Antiquaries.

The statues that adorn the Royal Academy's facade represent Raphaël, Titian, Wren, Leonardo da Vinci, and others. The Academy's entrance hall has ceiling paintings by former Academicians—notably Benjamin West's *The Graces* and *The Four Elements*.

The main exhibition rooms are on the second floor; many of them have splendid door frames, ceiling decorations, and fireplaces. The top floor of the building (the Sackler Wing, reached by glass elevator or steps) has been remodeled by Sir Norman Foster, himself an Academician, and is used for smaller exhibitions, including shows by living artists. Here, and not to be missed, is Michelangelo's *Madonna and Child with the infant St John*, a circular relief carved in marble in 1504–1505 and generally considered to be one of his most beautiful works.

The Royal Academy store stocks a wide range of art books, and sells greetings cards, posters and postcards, artists' materials, and gift items ranging from jigsaws to jewelry, often designed by Royal Academicians.

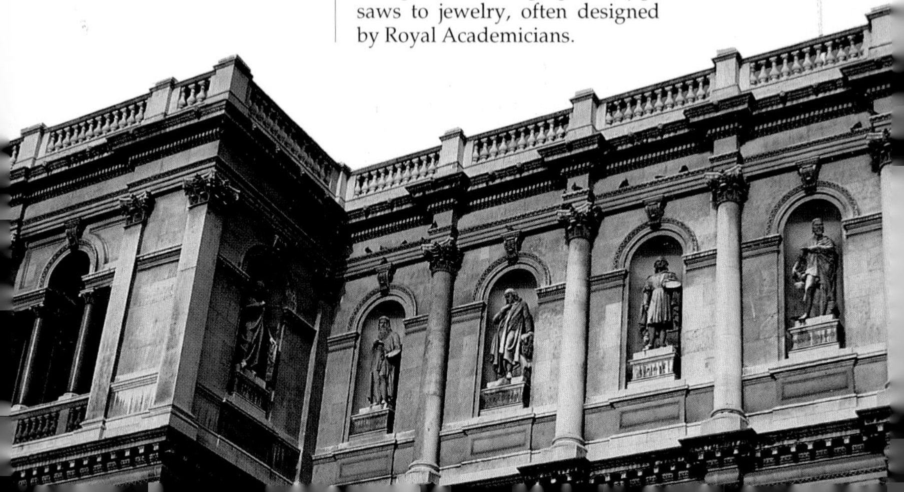

*The Iron Duke, a national hero after his defeat of Napoleon Bonaparte*

## ►►► Wellington Museum (Apsley House) *72A2*

*Hyde Park Corner, W1 (tel: 020-7499 5676)*
*Open: Tue–Sun 11–5. Admission charge*
*Underground: Hyde Park Corner*

When the Duke of Wellington (1769–1852) finally defeated Napoleon at the Battle of Waterloo in 1815, he became the nation's hero. Parliament, in gratitude, voted to give Wellington £200,000 (then a very substantial sum), which he lavished on alterations to his home, Apsley House. The original house was built of brick by Robert Adam in 1778. Wellington's architects (Benjamin Dean Wyatt) wrapped it in Bath stone, added the giant Corinthian portico and pediment, and designed the vast Waterloo Gallery—where the Duke gave an annual banquet to celebrate his triumph at Waterloo.

Apsley House, known as "No. 1, London" in Wellington's day, is today a museum that combines two pleasures: the opportunity (surprisingly rare in London) to see inside an aristocratic 18th-century home; and the chance to admire the Duke's art collection (some of it looted as the spoils of war, some of it bought legitimately, some of it given to Wellington by grateful allies freed from Napoleon's yoke). Yet, in the midst of all this splendor and opulence, it is Napoleon who manages to steal the show: Canova's heroic almost 11-foot marble statue of the French emperor, nude except for a fig leaf, stands at the base of the staircase. Napoleon himself commissioned the work but did not like it because the figure of Victory, in the statue's right hand, appears to be flying away. The statue remained in storage in the Louvre until the British government bought it in 1816 and presented it to Wellington.

Equally intriguing is Goya's *Equestrian Portrait of Wellington*, hung in the Waterloo Gallery. X-rays have shown that this originally depicted Joseph Bonaparte, Napoleon's brother; he was made king of Spain in 1808 but defeated by Wellington at the Battle of Vittoria in 1813, and Goya hastily painted Wellington's head over the original.

**THE IRON DUKE**

The Duke of Wellington is popularly known as the "Iron Duke" but not, as is often supposed, because of his military achievements. Instead the name dates to the later period in his life when, having served as Prime Minister from 1828 to 1830, he resigned in opposition to parliamentary reform and the extension of democracy. This refusal to support the Reform Bill made him so unpopular that rioters broke the windows of Apsley House. Iron shutters were then put up to prevent a reoccurrence — hence the somewhat sarcastic nickname.

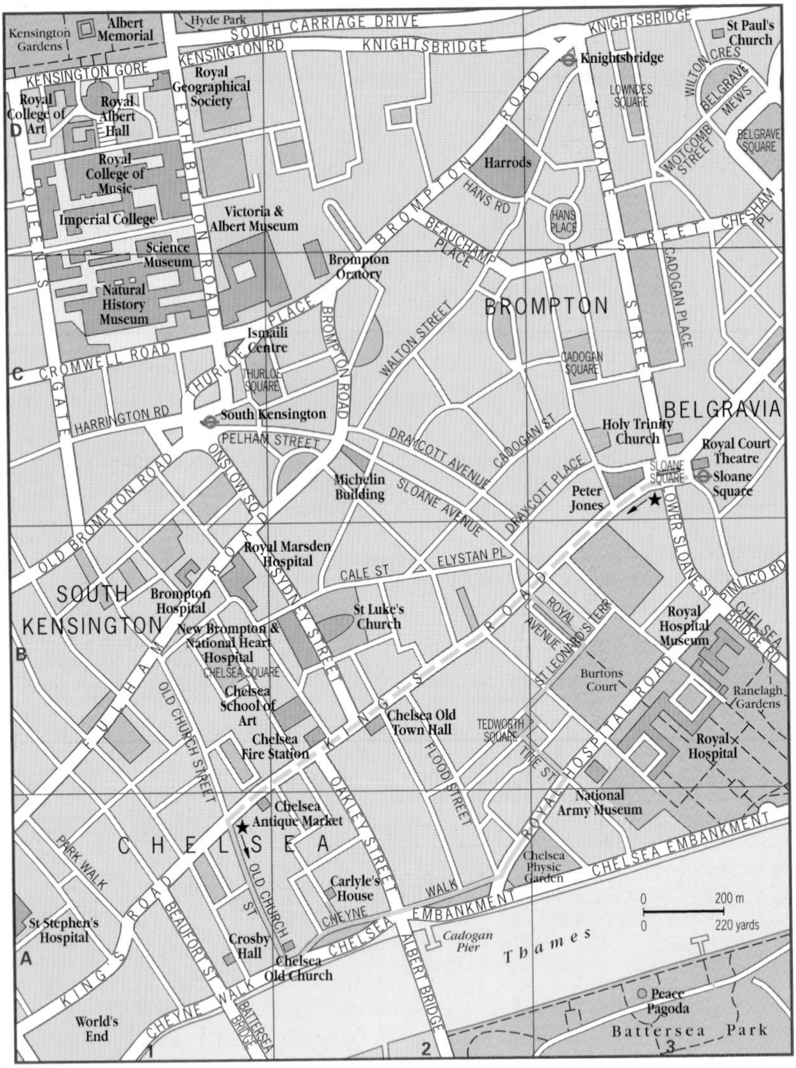

**CHELSEA AND KNIGHTSBRIDGE** These upscale residential areas are kept immaculate for Londoners and temporary residents from abroad. But Chelsea's King's Road, by a twist of irony, continues to stand for youthful, very British rebellion. Its boutiques were the first to sell mini skirts and hippie gear in the 1960s, and punk was born here a decade later. By contrast, the South Kensington museums complex on Cromwell Road presents a wealth of objects, events and images that stimulate curiosity, while London's best-known department store, Harrods, is just a short step away, in Knightsbridge.

**CHELSEA AND KNIGHTSBRIDGE WALK** This walk starts and ends at the King's Road, taking in a range of buildings spanning nearly 500 years of Chelsea's past.

# Chelsea and Knightsbridge

Take Bus No. 22 from Sloane Square Underground station down the King's Road, getting off near the cinema, on the corner of Old Church Street. Walking south down Old Church Street, you will pass two important examples of Modern Movement architecture set among pretty Georgian brick houses: **No. 64** (by Mendelssohn and Chermayeff) and **No. 66** (by Gropius and Fry) were both built in 1936.

Turn left at the end of the street to reach **Chelsea Old Church**, which has a memorial to Sir Thomas More, Henry VIII's Chancellor, who lived near here from 1524 until he was executed in 1535. It is said that Henry VIII secretly married his third wife, Jane Seymour, in this church in 1536. There are many other important monuments at Chelsea Old Church, including an unusual shrouded effigy of Sara Colville (1631).

Turn left from the church onto Cheyne Walk; to the right there is a good view of the Albert Bridge (built 1873).

**Cheyne** (pronounced "Chainy") **Walk** is lined by early Georgian houses, many with elegant railings and balconies. The second street on the left (Cheyne Row) has more modest houses but of the same early 18th-century

*Left: elegant Albert Bridge*

date, including **Carlyle's House** (see page 90). Cheyne Walk continues on the other side of Oakley Street. The most splendid of the houses (**No. 16**) was once the home of Dante Gabriel Rossetti.

Nearby, on Chelsea Embankment, **Swan House** (No. 17), built in 1875, and its neighbor, **Cheyne House** (1876), are pioneering examples of Norman Shaw's Queen Anne style, with oriel windows.

Continue up Royal Hospital Road and take the third left into **Tite Street**, whose playful houses and studios were popular with a number of artists in the late 19th and early 20th century. Oscar Wilde wrote several of his best-known plays at **No. 34**, Whistler lived at **No. 46**, John Singer Sargent at **No. 31**, and Augustus John at **No. 33**.

Turn right onto Tedworth Square (Mark Twain lived at No. 23) and right onto St. Leonards Terrace, with its fine 18th-century houses (Nos. 14–32). Turn left onto Royal Avenue to return to the King's Road.

**▶▶▶ REGION HIGHLIGHTS**


**Carlyle's House**
*page 90*

**Chelsea Royal Hospital**
*pages 92–93*

**Harrods** *page 87*

**Natural History Museum**
*pages 94, 98–99*

**Science Museum**
*pages 100–101*

**Victoria and Albert Museum**
*pages 104–105*

*Some of the world's best-known designers have their boutiques among Brompton Road's chic stores and restaurants. Once lined with rural market gardens, it is now a window shopper's dream—Harrods' window dressing is exceptionally sumptuous. At the same time, some of the buildings themselves warrant a closer look.*

**BROMPTON ORATORY**
Brompton Oratory (tel: 020-7589 4811. *Open* daily 6:30 AM–8 PM. *Admission* free) is the work of Herbert Gribble, a young and almost unknown architect who designed this large and flamboyant baroque building in 1876. The huge Carrara marble statues of the Twelve Apostles in the nave, carved in the 1680s by Giuseppe Mazzuoli, originally stood in Siena Cathedral. On a more intimate scale is the Chapel of St. Wilfrid, with its triptych by Rex Whistler of the *Martyrdom of St. Thomas More and St. John Fisher* (1938).



If you start at South Kensington tube station, it is a short walk down Pelham Street to Fulham Road and the **Michelin Building** (No. 81), a striking art deco building of 1911, decorated with ceramic-tile panels of racing cars. It was built for the French tire company and rescued from the threat of demolition in 1985; now it houses the **Conran Shop**, specializing in imaginative furnishings, and **Bibendum**, an upscale restaurant.

To the south, down Fulham Road, there are other interior furnishings shops. To the north, Brompton Road leads toward Harrods, passing a number of stylish boutiques including **Joseph** (No. 317), **Jasper Conran** (No. 303), **Issey Miyake** (No. 270), and **Emporio Armani** (No. 191).

The huge Italianate baroque church of St. Philip Neri—better known as the Brompton Oratory—stands at the busy intersection of Thurloe Place and Brompton Road. This is a fashionable church for London's Roman Catholic community. Choral mass is held here every Sunday at 11 AM, and the sermons are often highly theatrical, and very entertaining and interesting.

The fourth right turn beyond this church leads to another enclave of chicdom: Beauchamp Place. **Caroline Charles** is at No. 56–57; opposite, **Janet Reger** (No. 2) sells fine lingerie, and **Kanga** (No. 8) carries exotic evening wear.

Back on the right-hand side, Indian cottons in bold colors and patterns based on traditional Mogul designs are the specialty of **Monsoon** (No. 52), while **Annabel Jones**, next door, sells chunky jewelry. If your tastes in fashion are more conservative, try **Michelle Holden** (No. 42) for classic couture (for men, women, and children). On the left, **Bruce Oldfield** (No. 27), one of the established stars of modern British fashion, will create something original—at a price.

*Bibendum in Michelin House: from French tire headquarters to shrine of modern cooking*

*Harrods, at 87–135 Brompton Road, is more than just a store: it is a miniature kingdom, over which the princes of high finance have fought bitter battles. Its vast, terra-cotta building (illuminated at night) has grown to occupy 15 acres—a far cry from its origins as a small grocer's store founded by Charles Henry Harrod in 1849.*

Harrods has 330-plus departments, more than 4,000 staff, and has been known to take in $24 million in a single day (in 1997), although normal turnover is a more modest $2.4 million a day. Harrods' Latin motto (*Omnia, omnibus, ubique*—everything, for everyone, everywhere) sums up the philosophy of a store that attracts visitors from around the world and sells almost everything the world produces.

Pick up the *Store Guide* from information desks at the entrance, and ask about the day's exhibitions, author signings, and product demonstrations.

*Harrods' sumptuous food halls are both a tourist attraction and the local store for Knightsbridge residents*

For many the first-floor food halls are the highlight, partly for the unbelievable range of foods on display, but also for W.J. Neatley's tiled ceilings above the fish, meat, and poultry halls, illustrating *The Hunt* and dating from 1902.

Equally lavish art-deco ceramics decorate both the men's hairdressing rooms and the women's rest room. The store's Egyptian owners have added the highly elaborate central escalator, inspired by the art of Ancient Egypt. Children should not miss the pet shop or the Toy Kingdom on the upper floors.

There is a price to pay for so much free entertainment—the crowds can be unbearable, and the store is best visited early in the day. If you want to take tea in Harrods' 400-seater Georgian Restaurant, it is best to book; otherwise, try any of the 19 other cafés and bars.

Harrods is not open on Sundays.

**HARRODS SALES**

At the legendary January sale, reductions are huge, but so are the crowds, and some people are so eager to secure a bargain that they will camp outside the entrance over Christmas. Once inside the store, even dignified and aristocratic ladies lose all sense of decorum—elbows and fists fly in this test of consumer tenacity that can sometimes resemble a game of rugby.

*London is now one of the world's culinary capitals. This has come about through three profound changes: innovative chefs have reinterpreted traditional British recipes; customers know more about world cuisines, and demand quality and authenticity; and restaurants compete in service, interiors, and food.*

**SOHO**
Soho has a cosmopolitan range of restaurants, but there are some constants that can be relied upon. Alastair Little, 49 Frith Street (tel: 020-7734 5183), modern British, in minimalist setting; Lindsay House, 21 Romilly Street, W1 (tel: 020-7439 0450), modern British, in a sumptuous town-house; The Sugar Club, 21 Warwick Street, W1 (tel: 020-7437 7776), innovative, bold modern dishes in a stylish setting; Yo! Sushi, 52-53 Poland Street, W1 (tel: 020-7287 0443), amusing hi-tech Japanese; and Wagamama, 10a Lexington Street, W1 (tel: 020-7292 0990), a no-frills noodle refectory. In Wardour Street, try Mezzanine at No. 100 (tel: 020-7314 4000), the first-floor canteen section of Conran's mega-restaurant, and Spiga at Nos. 84–86 (tel: 020-7734 3444). In Dean Street, find Pizza Express at No. 10 (tel: 020-7437 9595) for jazz and pizza, and Quo Vadis at Nos. 26–29 (tel: 020-7437 4809), Marco Pierre White's French brasserie.



Here are just a handful of the many good restaurants in town at the moment. The top chefs work in impressive locations; reservations are essential and prices are high. The dress code is smart, and men should wear jackets and ties; if in doubt, check when reserving your table.

**TOP CHEFS AND HAUTE CUISINE** In this category the chef is key; if he has moved on, reconsider your choice. Michel and Albert Roux's Le Gavroche restaurant, 43 Upper Brook Street, W1 (tel: 020-7408 0881) was the training ground for many top chefs. Michel Roux Jnr now runs it, serving classic French food in a formal, flawless setting. Pierre Koffmann has taken La Tante Claire to the Berkeley Hotel, Wilton Place, SW1 (tel: 020-7493 5699), and continues to create perfect French dishes. Gordon Ramsay has moved into Koffmann's old premises, now called the Gordon Ramsay Restaurant, 68 Royal Hospital Road, SW3 (tel: 020-7352 4441). Nico Landenis thrives at his flagship, Chez Nico at Ninety, in the Grovesnor

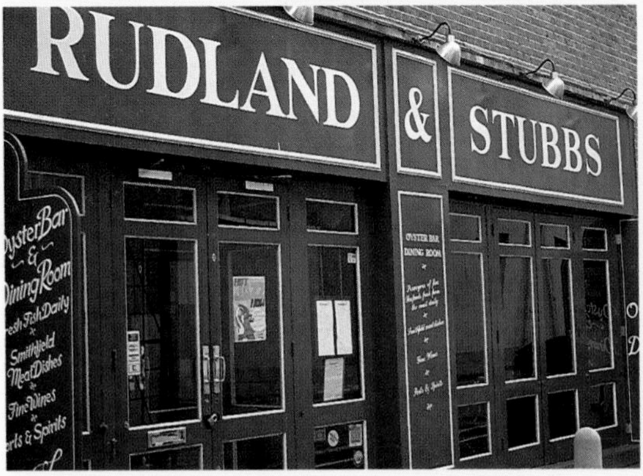


*Oysters and fresh fish are the specialty of Rudland & Stubbs*

House Hotel, 90 Park Lane, W1 (tel: 020-7409 1290), while Marco Pierre White cooks at The Oak Room in Le Meridien, Piccadilly, W1 (tel: 020-7437 0202).

**BRITISH** British food has undergone a revolution. Here is a variety of places to find good dishes. The Ivy (1 West Street, WC1, tel: 020-7836 4751), Le Caprice (Arlington House, Arlington Street, SW1, tel: 020-7629 2239) and Sheeky's at 28–32 St. Martin's Court, WC2 (tel: 020-7240 2565) and 11 Queen Victoria Street, EC4 (tel: 020-7489 8067) are four flawless, professional restaurants run by Jeremy King and Chris Corbin. Other

*The Quality Chop House: the best of British cooking*

restaurants worth investigating include City Rhodes, 1 New Street Square, EC4 (tel: 020-7583 1313), for Gary Rhodes's sophisticated modern dishes; Quality Chop House, 94 Farringdon Road, EC1 (tel: 020-7837 5093), for brasserie food at shared tables; Rule, 35 Maiden Lane, WC2 (tel: 020-7836 5314), for full roasts in Edwardian rooms; St. John, 26 St. John Street, EC1 (tel: 020-7251 0848), for offal, marrow and other British favorites in a minimalist setting, and R.K. Stanley's, 6 Little Portland Street, W1 (tel: 020-7462 0099) for platefuls of sausages in a retro setting, good for families.

**WORLD CUISINES** This is a token selection of the rich choice on offer. For French food, try Maison Novelli, 29 Clerkenwell Green, EC1 (tel: 020-7251 6606), or Marco Pierre White's glamorous Mirabelle, 56 Curzon Street, W1 (tel: 020-7499 4636). For Indian, the choice is very wide but Chor Bizarre, 16 Albemarle Street, W1 (tel: 020-7629 9802), La Porte des Indes, 32 Bryanston Street, W1 (tel: 020-7224 0055), Tamarind, 20 Queen Street, W1 (tel: 020-7629 3561), and Veeraswamy's, 99 Regent Street, W1 (tel: 020-7734 1404) are some of the upscale best. For Japanese, Nobu, The Metropolitan Hotel, 19 Old Park Lane, W1 (tel: 020-7447 4747) is unbeatable; for Italian, try Zaffarano, 15 Lowndes Street, SW1 (tel: 020-7235 5800) or Stefano Cavallini's food at the Halkin Hotel, 5 Halkin Street, SW1 (tel: 020-7333 1234).

**HOTEL RESTAURANTS** Dine in sumptuous surroundings at The Ritz (tel: 020-7493 8181), The Dorchester (tel: 020-7317 6336), Claridges (tel: 020-7629 8860), Savoy (tel: 020-7836 4343/7420 2699), Waldorf Meridien (tel: 020-7836 2400) and One Aldwych (tel: 020-7300 1000). Reservations will be necessary for all of these.

**BREAKFAST AND AFTERNOON TEA**
The British no longer eat huge cooked breakfasts and multi-course afternoon teas with scones and home-baked cakes. However, they are still well prepared in a few restaurants, in particular in the deluxe hotels, which all take breakfast and tea seriously. Away from the hotels, try full breakfast at Mash, 19–21 Great Portland Street, W1 (tel: 020-7637 5555), Sotheby's Café, 34 New Bond Street, W1 (tel: 020-7408 5077), or the little Italian-run cafés tucked into corners. For delicious cakes, go to Patisserie Valerie, 44 Old Compton Street (tel: 020-7437 3466) or to the good cafés in museums, such as at the V&A, Whitechapel Art Gallery, and Kensington Palace's Orangery.

*Chelsea salon; here the Carlyles entertained Dickens*

**"THE FRENCH REVOLUTION"**
Carlyle's most famous work, entitled *The French Revolution* (1837), is a massive tome and a towering achievement, especially since a major part of the book had to be written twice. Carlyle left the manuscript at the house of his friend, the philosopher John Stuart Mill, who lived at No. 17 Kensington Square. To his horror, Mill discovered that his housemaid, thinking that the pile of paper was discarded, was using it to light fires. As a result, Carlyle had no alternative but to sit down and write the whole first volume over again.

### ▶▶▶ Carlyle's House *84A2*

*24 Cheyne Row, SW3 (tel: 020-7352 7087)*
*Open: Easter–late Oct, Wed–Sun 11–5*
*Underground: Sloane Square. Bus: 11, 19, 22*

Few people today read Thomas Carlyle's thunderously oratorical works, such as his history of the French Revolution, but in his day he was regarded with almost religious reverence. Admirers would come from afar to visit the great man, who was renowned for the high moral tone of his work. His wife, the witty Jane Carlyle, poet and letter writer, attracted an equally eminent bevy of admirers, Dickens, Tennyson, Browning, and Thackeray among them. This stream of visitors met for conversation in the upstairs drawing room of Carlyle's house, where he lived from 1834 until his death in 1881.

Visiting the house today, you gain a very real sense of that mid-Victorian era. The house (built in 1703) was described by Carlyle himself as "old-fashioned, eminent, antique," and some of the rooms, to this day, have no electricity. Heavy furnishings and rose-colored wallpapers add to the dark but dignified atmosphere. The walls are hung with portraits of the Carlyle family (including a fine early picture by the pioneer of British photography, Julia Margaret Cameron) and of the men about whom Carlyle wrote in his epic books, most notably Frederick the Great of Prussia.

The top-floor attic was specially built for Carlyle in 1853 and was intended to be a soundproof study, though in fact it had the effect of amplifying the sounds of street and river traffic. A touching reminder of domestic life is Carlyle's hat, hung by the back garden door: Thomas was fond of his pipe but had to go into the garden for a smoke, since Jane could not stand the smell.

## ▶▶ Chelsea Physic Garden *84A3*

*66 Royal Hospital Road (entrance on Swan Walk), SW3 (tel: 020-7352 5646)*
*Open: early Apr–late Oct, Wed 12–5 and Sun usually 2–6; daily during Chelsea Flower Show (last week in May), noon–5*
*Underground: Sloane Square. Bus: 19, 22, 349*

Founded in 1673, the Chelsea Physic Garden is a haven of privacy and tranquillity in the heart of busy London. As the name suggests, it began as a place of scientific research, planted with species valued for their medicinal properties, under the auspices of the Worshipful Company of Apothecaries. That work continues to this day. The beneficial effects of feverfew in the relief of migraine is just one of the many research projects that are currently underway.

Within its high sheltering brick walls, the simple rectilinear beds are planted by genus, according to the method of plant classification established by Linnaeus in the 18th century. (Pick up the useful map by the entrance.) Any suggestion of dull formality is banished, however, by the wild and willful way in which these plants, many of them highly fragrant, thrust their colorful blooms outward and upward, spilling out over the paths so that progress around this crowded garden is necessarily slow.

Many rare trees grow here, some of considerable age, such as the striking golden rain tree (*Kolreuteria paniculata*), with its twisted branches. The woodland areas come into their own at the end of the winter, when the ground beneath is carpeted in snowdrops, cyclamen, and hellebores. The garden also has the first-ever rock garden constructed in England—more a curiosity than a pleasure to the eye. It dates from 1772 and is made from basaltic lava blocks brought from Iceland and old masonry from the Tower of London.

*Informal beds at the Chelsea Physic Garden*

**SIR HANS SLOANE**
A statue of Sir Hans Sloane in wig and gown stands at the center of the Chelsea Physic Garden (there are others in Sloane Square and the British Museum). London owes much to this extraordinary man, who was physician to Queen Anne and George II, President of the Royal College of Physicians, and immensely wealthy. The British Museum was founded from the collection he bequeathed at his death in 1753. In 1712 he purchased the manor of Chelsea, which included the Physic Garden. Sloane ensured the garden's survival by paying for its restoration (at a time when it was in serious decline), and he made financial arrangements to ensure that the site would never be built upon but would always remain a garden.

**OAK APPLE DAY**
Oak Apple Day (May 29) at Chelsea Royal Hospital is one of London's more colorful pageants. The resident veterans parade in their three-cornered hats to honor the birthday of Charles II, their founder. The parade takes place around Grinling Gibbons' statue of Charles II in the Figure Court. The statue is ritually decorated with oak leaves, to commemorate the king's escape from the Battle of Worcester (1651) after defeat at the hands of the Parliamentarians. After hiding in a hollow oak tree, the king was able to escape to France, from where he eventually returned, after the death of Cromwell, to be restored to the English throne in 1660.



*The splendid Great Hall, with Charles II looking on from a distance*

## ▶▶▶ Chelsea Royal Hospital *84B3*

*Royal Hospital Road, SW3 (tel: 020-7730 5282)*
*Open: Mon–Sat 10–noon and 2–4, Sun 2–4 in summer only, plus Sun services. Donation*
*Underground: Sloane Square*

There is a story that Charles II's mistress, the actress Eleanor Gwyn (also known as Nell Gwyn), persuaded the king to found this hospital because she was moved to tears by the sight of a wounded soldier begging for alms. A more realistic version may be that, with the bitter experiences of the Civil War behind him, Charles II realized the importance of maintaining a standing army that would stay loyal to the Crown. His method of winning the army's loyalty was to provide for aged and injured soldiers, rather than simply throwing them onto the streets without so much as a pension.

The Chelsea Royal Hospital was set up in 1682, an institution modeled on Louis XIV's Hôtel des Invalides in Paris (founded in 1670) to provide food, lodging, and medical care for infirm veterans. The architect was Sir Christopher Wren, who, up to now, had concentrated almost exclusively on designing churches for the reconstruction of the City of London after the Great Fire. This was his first full-scale secular work, and he produced a building of almost barracklike simplicity but of great dignity, which was subsequently extended (between 1809 and 1817) by Sir John Soane—see especially Soane's Stables to the right of the entrance.

The central courtyard is known as the Figure Court because of the figure of Charles II standing at the center; this bronze statue, made by Grinling Gibbons in 1676, was brought here in 1692 and depicts the king as a Roman soldier. The central block of the hospital building has an

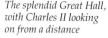

*Chelsea Pensioners in resplendent uniform*

imposing octagonal lobby, with the Great Hall and chapel either side. The paneled Great Hall, where the residents take their meals, is decorated with a huge painting of Charles II on horseback by Antonio Verrio, while the opulent chapel is a typical Wren design with a black and white stone floor, fine plasterwork, choir stalls by Grinling Gibbons and a huge altar-painting—the *Resurrection*—in the vault by Sebastiano Ricci.

Governor's House stands at the river end of the eastern range, its Council Chamber decorated with sumptuous carving and hung with portraits of Charles I and his family (by Van Dyck), Charles II (by Lely), and William III (by Kneller). Lawns sweep down to the Thames and the terrace displays a cannon captured at Waterloo. To the east, the tree-filled Ranelagh Gardens used to be a vast pleasure garden where, in the words of the 18th-century writer Oliver Goldsmith, the public would flock for "fêtes, frolics, fireworks and fashionable frivolity." To the west, the more formal gardens serve as the site for the famous Chelsea Flower Show and provide good views across the river to Battersea Park.

Today, Chelsea Royal Hospital is home to about 500 pensioners (veterans), who wear a distinctive uniform—a dark blue overcoat in winter and a scarlet frock coat in summer—dating back to the time of the Duke of Marlborough (1650–1722). Pensioners must be ex-soldiers of "good character" and are usually at least 65 years old. The pensioners' duties include attending church and occasional parades, in return for which they receive food, lodging, clothing, and a daily ration of beer and tobacco. Chelsea Pensioners sometimes volunteer to show visitors around the Hospital or to pose for photographs, in which case it is customary to give them a tip.

**CHELSEA FLOWER SHOW**

The Chelsea Flower Show is one of the great events of the summer season. Established in 1913, it is held in late May and provides a showcase for all that is novel in the gardening world, from the newest rose varieties to the latest in lawnmower technology. Every devoted gardener attends, from the Queen downward. The horticulturalists who display their stock here spend all year preparing and, by playing tricks with nature, succeed in presenting all the riches of the four seasons in a single week: snowdrops and sweet-smelling narcissi bloom alongside summer-flowering delphiniums and autumnal chrysanthemums. Often, however, the simplest ideas steal the show—window-box displays or meadow gardens of British native wildflowers. Garden snobs claim the Chelsea Flower Show is now too popular, and too dominated by the big commercial growers. They prefer to attend the other shows organized by the Royal Horticultural Society at their exhibition hall in Vincent Square. For details of these, contact the Royal Horticultural Society, 80 Vincent Square, London SW1P 2PE (tel: 020-7834 4333; Chelsea Flower Show hotline tel: 020-7344 4343).

*Chelsea Flower Show*

**THE CRYSTAL PALACE**
The Crystal Palace, which housed the Great Exhibition of 1851, stood on the south side of Hyde Park, near the Royal Albert Hall. It was a stupendous building, three times longer than St. Paul's Cathedral (1858 ft.) and tall enough (at 109 ft.) to contain three elm trees that were already growing on the site. Designed by the great landscape gardener, Joseph Paxton, it was a prefabricated greenhouse on a gigantic scale. Skeptics predicted it would crash to the ground in the first strong gale. In fact, six million visitors passed through before the exhibition closed. The Crystal Palace was then dismantled and moved to Sydenham where, unfortunately, it burned down in 1936. Little now remains (see page 215), though the great greenhouses at Kew Gardens (see pages 226–227) convey an idea of what this splendid Victorian building once looked like.



## ►► National Army Museum 84B3

*Royal Hospital Road, SW3 (tel: 020-7730 0717)*
*Open: daily 10–5:30. Admission free*
*Underground: Sloane Square*

This museum covers the history of the British Army from 1485 (when the Yeomen of the Guard, the first professional army, was formed) to the present day. Audiovisual presentations and dioramas bring the subject to life, and rather than glorifying war, the museum brings home a sense of the hardships experienced by ordinary and very vulnerable soldiers.

Start in the basement, which deals with the period from Agincourt to the American Revolutionary War, and features the best display of British swords in the country. You can also try on an English Civil War helmet, feel the weight of a cannonball, and listen to some contemporary soldiers' songs. Upstairs is the skeleton of Napoleon's favorite charger, Marengo, alongside personal relics of Wellington and some gory battlefield remnants. The exhibits on the next floor move on to the defense of the British Empire and the role of the British soldier in the 20th century. It includes a reconstructed trench, and explores such diverse theaters of war as the deserts of Africa and the jungles of Borneo.

## ►►► Natural History Museum 84C1

*Cromwell Road, SW7 (tel: 020-7938 9123)*
*Open: Mon–Sat 10–5:50, Sun 11–5:50. Admission charge; children free*
*Underground: South Kensington*

The Natural History Museum was created to celebrate the rich variety of life on earth and is housed in a suitably splendid building of cathedral-like proportions. The idea of creating a museum devoted to natural science was first discussed at a controversial time; plans were drawn up in 1862, only three years after Darwin had published *The Origin of the Species*, sparking off a fierce debate between scientists who supported evolutionary theory, and those who insisted on the biblical version of the Creation. The debate even influenced the style of the building. Purists maintained that the neo-Gothic style, then in vogue, should be reserved for places of worship and not employed for secular buildings. The architect, Alfred Waterhouse, sidestepped the problem by looking to French Romanesque architecture for his inspiration.
*Continued on page 98.*

*The Road to Waterloo exhibition includes a huge model depicting the Battle of Waterloo with 70,000 model soldiers*

*The Royal Albert Hall and the buildings that surround it commemorate the vision of Prince Albert, Queen Victoria's husband. The Hall is one of the most prominent among the many grandiose buildings added to the cityscape during Victoria's reign, and has become a familiar landmark.*

*The Royal Albert Hall, home of the Proms and a rock concert venue*



The substantial profits generated by the Great Exhibition of 1851 were used to purchase land to create educational museums, colleges and halls. Presiding over this grand scheme was a Royal Commission, headed by Prince Albert. When Albert died in 1861, the public was asked to donate funds to finance the building of the Albert Memorial (see page 111) and the Royal Albert Hall. The costs of building the Memorial escalated, and plans for the Hall were shelved until 1863, when Henry Cole, in charge of raising funds, hit on the idea of selling 1,300 seats at £100 ($160) each, entitling the owners to attend every event staged over the next 999 years! (This arrangement still stands, although the descendants of the original owners often waive their right to attend.)

Finally completed in 1871, the immense domed building, 274 feet in diameter and 155 feet high, is capable of seating 8,000. All kinds of cultural and sporting events are held here, but to many the Hall is inextricably linked with the Henry Wood Promenade Concerts, better known simply as the Proms, which take place here every evening between mid-July and mid-September, culminating in the emotion and patriotism of the Last Night of the Proms. Essential to the whole concept of the Proms is the availability of cheap tickets, sold on a first-come, first-served basis; the first few hundred people at the head of the line can stand in the arena, right behind the conductor. By the end of 2003 a refurbishing plan will give the Hall new life.

**IN THE VICINITY**
There are several fine buildings near the Albert Hall. Behind it is the Royal College of Music, where a collection of musical instruments is on public display during the school term (Wed 2–4:30); look, too, for the exciting range of concerts given by students. To the west of the Hall, the former home of the Royal College of Organists has a facade decorated with a frieze of musicians—but no organist! On Kensington Gore, the Royal Geographical Society (1875), and Albert Hall Mansions (1886) together form a good example of Norman Shaw's Queen Anne style of architecture.

*The King's Road, as its name indicates, was once a private royal road, linking St. James's Palace and Hampton Court; it was used only by the monarch and courtiers. Humbler folk had to take a boat along the Thames if they wanted to travel west and visit what was then the small fishing village of Chelsea.*

**WORLD'S END**
The main concentration of stores on the King's Road comes to an end at a kink in the road known as World's End, named after the pub of the same name (No. 459). The origin of the name is obscure but, no doubt, the residents of Chelsea feel that the world does end here, on the borders with the less chic Fulham district. Another fine pub here is the Man in the Moon (No. 392), distinguished not only by its engraved glass fixtures but also as a theater pub, mounting productions (usually modern drama) most evenings (tel: 020-7351 2876).



In 1830 the King's Road was opened to the public, and from that time onward Chelsea began to expand, becoming something of an artist's colony, whose residents ranged from the eminently respectable to the downright eccentric.

This mixture survives to the present day and gives the King's Road much of its character: stores selling fine antiques or antiquarian books stand cheek by jowl with avant-garde boutiques; punks with weird clothes and outrageous hairstyles parade alongside immaculately tailored grandes dames taking their coiffeured poodles for a stroll.

The first stretch of the King's Road, leading westward from Sloane Square, is lined with the display windows of **Peter Jones** department store (see page 102). Opposite are the early 19th-century barrack buildings of the **Duke of York's Headquarters**. The second street on the right, Blacklands Terrace, leads to **John Sandoe Books** (No. 10), which is one of the best of the many small bookstores in London.

Farther down on the left, there are glimpses toward Chelsea Royal Hospital down Royal Avenue, a leafy boulevard laid out in 1689, and intended as a route connecting Wren's Royal Hospital with Kensington Palace. This short stretch is all that was built of the route, and it was here that, in Ian Fleming's novels, James Bond had his home.

*A pottery shop in the King's Road*

*Keeping the* Easy Rider *era alive*



At this end of the street, look for the **Designers Sale Studio** (No. 24), where leading fashion designers dispose of their end-of-season items at discount prices.

Beyond the entrance to Markham Square lies the **Pheasantry** (No. 152), an odd building with Grecian-style caryatids. Built for the breeding of pheasants in the late 19th century, it is now a late-night bar, club, and restaurant. Beginning in 1916, for several years the Pheasantry housed a ballet school run by the Princess Serafine Astafieva, where future stars such as Margot Fonteyn and Alicia Markova took their first steps.

Beyond the Pheasantry are some of the King's Road's most interesting stores: **Antiquarius** (Nos. 135–141) is an antiques market where some 70 stallholders sell everything from postcards to Georgian silver. More upscale items, with an emphasis on art nouveau and art deco, are sold at **Chenil Galleries** (Nos. 181–183), and at **Chelsea Antique Market** (Nos. 245–253) you will find books, maps, and prints. Opposite, there is a taste of the country at the **Chelsea Farmers' Market**, with its small food stalls, and the **Chelsea Garden Centre,** a tiny spot crammed with (very expensive) plants, flowers and pots, on the corner of Sydney Street. Farther up Sydney Street is **St. Luke's Church**, all neo-Gothic frills, where Charles Dickens was married to Catherine Hogarth in 1836. Nowadays fashionable weddings are more likely to take place at the Register Office alongside **Chelsea Old Town Hall**, on the opposite side of the street from the Sidney Street turn off.

Continuing up the King's Road, **Green and Stone** (No. 259), the artists' supplies store, is handy for students at the nearby Chelsea College of Art, founded in 1891. Beyond are two interior design premises with contrasting styles: chic, state-of-the-art fabrics at the **Designers' Guild** (No. 271) and classic wallpapers and fabrics at **Osborne & Little**.

The main part of King's Road ends with two innovative stores: **Rococo** (No. 321) sells way-out confectionery, and **World's End** (No. 430) is Vivienne Westwood's original store for her humorous and unconventional fashions.

**THE CADOGAN ESTATE**

If architecture interests you more than shopping, you should explore the maze of streets that lies to the north of the King's Road, especially the Cadogan Estate, which has some of London's most interesting Queen Anne-style buildings. The style developed in the 1870s in rejection of the flat-brick or stucco-fronted facades of the Georgian and Regency era. Suddenly, Dutch gables, projecting windows, balconies, and all sorts of ornament came into fashion. For typical examples, see the west side of Cadogan Square, particularly the buildings designed by Norman Shaw (Nos. 62, 68, and 72).

*The Natural History Museum*

*The beast from Wyoming:* Diplodocus carnegii *has become almost a symbol of the Natural History Museum*

**NATURAL HISTORY MUSEUM HIGHLIGHTS**
The Natural History Museum has more than 67 million items in its collection, an indication of the sheer diversity of the natural world. Among the most intriguing exhibits, look for the skeleton and reconstruction of the extinct dodo in the Bird Gallery, the weird and spiny coelacanth in the Central Hall, and in the section devoted to dinosaurs the giant flesh-eating monster, *Tyrannosaurus rex.* Biggest of all, however, is the Blue Whale model in the Mammal Hall, which measures almost 93 feet in length. The largest land animal—the African elephant—is dwarfed beside it.

*Continued from page 94.*

Waterhouse chose a style that was less familiar to the British and less loaded with religious connotations. The building is clad in a bravura display of colored terra-cotta, with relief panels depicting animals, fossils, plants, and insects running the whole length of the 680-foot facade; living species are depicted to the left of the entrance, extinct ones to the right.

Today, the collections include 28 million insects, 27 million animals, 9 million fossils, 500,000 rocks and minerals, and 3,200 meteorites.

Stepping through the main entrance, with its twin towers, the sense of entering a cathedral is reinforced by the navelike form of the Central Hall, although the voices of hundreds of excited children exploring the dinosaurs on display is a far cry from the hushed tranquility of a church. Soaring staircases provide a viewpoint for admiring the profusion of decoration (note especially the monkeys scampering up and down the arches) and for looking down on the plaster-cast skeleton of *Diplodocus carnegii* (who comes from Wyoming), 150 million years old, 86 feet long, and one of the largest land animals ever to have roamed the earth.

Plans displayed in the Central Hall will help you decide what to see, and there is plenty of choice. Many of the most recent displays were designed specifically with children in mind. The favorite is the Dinosaurs exhibition (turn left to Gallery 21) where a high-level walkway brings you eye to eyesocket with some of these ancient monsters. The lighting is low and atmospheric, and for children weaned on *Jurassic Park*, there is an animatronic re-creation of flesh eaters in action. Moving on to more peaceful matters, the Mammal Hall has the giant life-size

### THE GIANT SEQUOIA TREE

Not all the items in the Natural History Museum are animals. One of the most intriguing exhibits is a section through a Giant Sequoia tree (*Sequoia-dendron giganteum*) displayed on the stairs to the second floor. This was cut down in 1892, by which time it was 277 ft. tall and measured 49½ ft. around the girth. A tree ring count indicates that it was 1,335 years old when felled, having started its life in California in AD 557.



blue whale model—another highlight of the museum. Also in this area is the "Human Biology" exhibition, (through a darkened room that simulates the interior of a womb); this is followed by blinding lights in an attempt to re-create a newborn baby's first view of the world. The rest of this hall explains human reproduction, development, and perception using imaginative models, push-button displays, and sound effects.

There are more ancient creatures to seek out in the Central Hall, while "Creepy Crawlies" takes an entertaining look at insects, and the Ecology Gallery, opposite, demonstrates the interdependence of all living things on earth. The Museum has a good restaurant, and the stores stock some excellent souvenirs and gift ideas.

The former Geological Museum is now the Earth Galleries section of the museum with a series of state-of-the-art displays. These include Visions of Earth, a dramatic, if somewhat ethereal space, which depicts the Earth within the solar system. A central escalator leads up straight through a huge globe to the first floor where displays tell the story of the Earth's formation. Many beautiful mineral and gemstone specimens are also on display. The most popular exhibits, however, are on the top floor; The Power Within focuses on volcanoes and earthquakes and features a simulation of the Kobe earthquake in Japan in 1995, including film footage captured live at the time which shows a supermarket being shaken. The Restless Surface section includes several hands-on stations that demonstrate the forces of wind, water and heat on the landscape. Other galleries focus on the story of Britain from the beginning, and the earth's natural geological treasury of gemstones, and they discuss ways of protecting our world for the future.

**SCIENTIFIC ART**
Some of the Science Museum's exhibits bridge the gulf between art and technology. One of them is a work of art, the dramatically lit painting of *Coalbrookdale by Night* by P. J. de Loutherbourg (1801) in the Iron and Steel Gallery. Another is the intricate Orrery of 1716, a working model of the solar system, demonstrating the movement of the planets, made and named for the Earl of Orrery. Nature's artistry is also demonstrated by the model of the D.N.A. spiral to be found on the second floor, while displays on the same floor show the futuristic possibilities of computer-generated graphics.

## ▶▶▶ Science Museum 84D1

*Exhibition Road, SW7 (tel: 020-7938 8000/8008/8123)*
*Open: daily 10–6. Admission charge*
*Underground: South Kensington*

Even the most technophobic visitors to London will find something to interest them in this fascinating museum, since many of the displays are as entertaining as they are educational. For that reason, the museum is very popular with children and can sometimes resemble a vast, noisy playground. The original museum celebrated the commercial applications of science and technology that gave rise to the Industrial Revolution. This period is best covered on the first floor, where there are engines of all kinds, driven by steam, wind and even atmospheric pressure.

Here you can also see some of the world's earliest motorcars, such as an 1888 Benz three-wheeler and an 1895 Panhard et Levassor. The pioneering days of railroads are represented by *Puffing Billy* (1813), the oldest locomotive in the world, and George Stephenson's record-breaking *Rocket*.

Space exploration is another one of the themes of this floor, and on display are the Apollo 10 capsule that took astronauts around the moon for the first time in May 1969, and a re-creation of a futuristic moon base.

On the second floor is the Launch Pad gallery, where a series of interactive experiments is designed to exercise inquiring minds and fidgety hands. Children are also well catered to in the basement galleries where "The Garden" (actually an indoor area) is popular with three-to six-year-olds and "Things" (as in "How do Things Work?") is designed for seven-to-eleven-year-olds.

The gadget-mad visitor, meanwhile, will enjoy "The Secret Life of the Home", dedicated to domestic labor-saving devices. Adjacent to "Launch Pad" is the "Challenge of Materials" gallery, which makes the world of materials, industry, and engineering both fun and accessible.

*From the Wright Brothers to Stealth bombers, the Flight Gallery is a museum highlight*

As you move around, you will often find clear answers to recurrent long-term questions as to who, what and how—for instance, who invented the plastic bag; what exactly is gravity and how do we overcome it and fly; how precisely does a telephone, fax or e-mail work? The longer you stay, the more your curiosity grows.

The Science Museum can be a daunting prospect in itself. It covers such a wide range with such depth that

*Exploration of the final frontier; from gunpowder rockets to the Apollo missions*

**SCIENCE AND HISTORY**
Among its displays of the cutting edge of technology, the Science Museum also has some ancient exhibits. The oldest of these is the clock mechanism from Wells Cathedral, displayed in the Time Measurement Gallery and still working some 600 years after its construction. An important piece of industrial history is represented by Arkwright's original spinning machine of 1769, one of the pioneering inventions that sparked off the whole Industrial Revolution, with its far-reaching implications for the way we live today.



rigorous selection is essential. It is best to choose just one or two subjects, or perhaps one floor, and stick to that. If, however, you do want to get a taste of every area, buy a copy of the excellent museum guide and follow the "look out for" exhibits. Using this approach, on Floor 2 you will find Edison's early lamps, the ill-fated Ford Edsel of the late 1950s, and the amazing prototype computer "Babbage's Difference Engine." The contrast between this and today's silicon-chip technology, exhibited alongside, is astounding. Here, too, is a beautiful collection of model ships. Flight is the most glamorous topic on Floor 3. Exhibits from the National Aeronautic Collection include early aircraft, such as Alcock and Brown's Vickers-Vimy (1919), the first to cross the Atlantic. Remaining floors house the Wellcome Museum of the History of Medicine, with early medical implements resembling instruments of torture, Napoleon's toothbrush, and Florence Nightingale's moccasins.

The commercial application of science and technology continues to be the museum's driving force. In 2000, a whole new Wellcome Wing opens, devoted to contemporary science, medicine and technology, and including an IMAX movie theater.

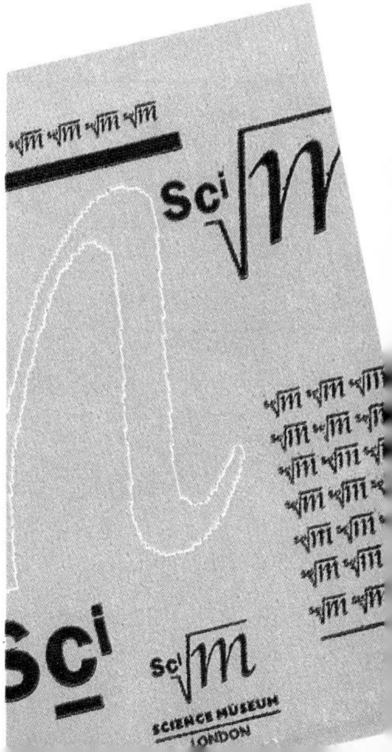

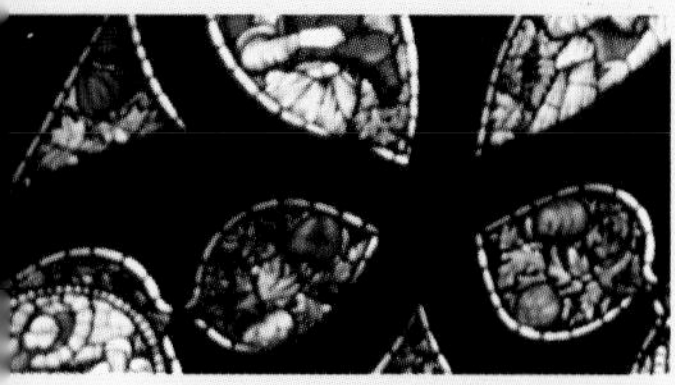

*Sloane Street offers good stores and interesting architecture. Once the haunt of caricatured Sloane Rangers in the 1980s—upper-crust girls (and guys) of good breeding—the top half is now lined with haute couture stores that include the classics Chanel and Valentino.*

*Pont Street*



**THE MEWS PUBS OF BELGRAVIA**

Some of London's most interesting pubs are located in the mews of Belgravia, where they were built to serve the coachmen, grooms, and butlers employed by the big houses, and soldiers from the nearby Wellington Barracks. One such is the Grenadier (18 Wilton Row), full of military mementoes and said to be haunted by the ghost of an officer flogged to death for cheating at cards. Another is the Star Tavern (6 Belgrave Mews), the very model of a perfect traditional tavern, with open fires in winter and antique furnishings.

At **Peter Jones** department store, on the west side of Sloane Square, you can buy everything necessary for decorating and furnishing your home in a conventional or modern British style. The **Royal Court Theatre** stands on the opposite side of the square, famous for radical drama that often satirizes bourgeois values (John Osborne's play *Look Back in Anger* received its first performance here in 1956). In between, at the heart of the square, trees shelter a fountain, which features the figure of Venus (1953, by Gilbert Ledward).

As you head up Sloane Street, one of the first stores you encounter is the **General Trading Company** (No. 144), well stocked with gifts, toys, china, kitchen accessories, furnishings, and a very good glass department. The fact that the store is one of a tiny handful in London to hold all four royal warrants indicates how upscale it is, but it neverthess also sells modestly priced crafts from the Far East and Africa.

**Holy Trinity Church** stands across the street from the General Trading Company, a masterpiece of English Arts and Crafts design, completed in 1890. The huge east window contains 48 panels depicting saints and was designed by Edward Burne-Jones (check the notice board for lunchtime concerts here). Farther up on the right are the gardens of **Cadogan Place**: access is limited to residents of nearby apartments, but you can see over the railings. The view is particularly cheerful when the winter-flowering shrubs and bulbs are in bloom.

From Cadogan Place northward, both sides of Sloane Street are lined with stores bearing famous names. **Valentino**, **Kenzo**, **Joseph**, and **Katharine Hamnett** are among them, as well as more modestly priced fashions at a branch of **Esprit**.

It is tempting to dip into the side streets for their characterful buildings. To the west you can walk through Pont Street, Hans Place, and Hans Road to Harrods. **Pont Street** has plenty of fine Queen Anne-style houses with Dutch gables and terra-cotta decorations. St. Columban's Church, built in 1955, with a striking helm roof, stands at the far end of the street.

**Hans Place** contains houses surviving from the time when Henry Holland first laid out his "Hans Town" development in 1777, building in an area that then consisted of open fields. **Hans Road** boasts some pioneering examples of Arts and Crafts architecture by Mackmurdo (No. 12) and Voysey (Nos. 14 and 16). Jane Austen lived briefly at No. 23 in the year 1815 when she was entertained by the Prince Regent, to whom she dedicated her finest novel, *Emma*.

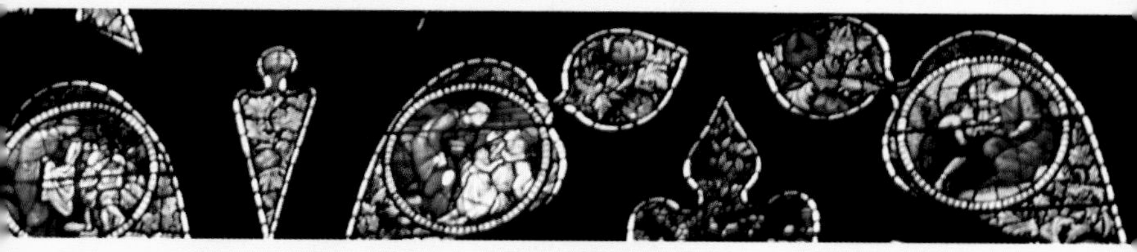

In the opposite direction, the hotel on the corner of Sloane Street and the north end of Cadogan Place is where Oscar Wilde was arrested for homosexual practises in 1895. Beyond lies **Belgrave Square**, at the heart of exclusive Belgravia; many of the huge Regency houses now serve as embassies or ambassadorial residences. The area was developed between 1825 and 1835 by Thomas Cubitt and is characterized by monumental stucco-fronted mansions, backed by cobblestone mews where horses were once stabled and servants lived (today even a simple mews cottage or converted stable is likely to be inhabited by a millionaire). To see the best of this district, visit **Motcomb Street**, with its antiques stores; **Kinnerton Street**, with its pretty courtyards leading off to the left; curving **Wilton Crescent**, and **St. Paul's Church**, in Wilton Place. This last is a Victorian neo-Gothic church, popular for high-society weddings, with a fine timber roof and rich decorations.

**BELGRAVE SQUARE**
Belgrave Square's sunken garden is surrounded by houses designed by George Basevi. For all their monumental proportions, the blank fronts and huge porches have provoked dismissive comments from architectural critics, although the three grand villas at the square's corners (by Kemp, Smirke, and Hardwick) do provide some variety.

*A stage for satire*

*The V&A entrance, modeled on Victoria's crown*

**THE GREAT BED OF WARE**

The Great Bed of Ware is one of the V&A's most celebrated exhibits, partly because of its prodigious size (10 ft. wide and nearly 13 ft. long) but also because of its great age (made around 1590) and its extravagant carved, painted, and inlaid decoration. Another celebrated curiosity is the large model tiger in the Nehru Gallery, which is shown in the act of eating a British army officer. Made in 1790, for Tipu Sultan of Mysore, the model incorporates a small organ that imitates the groans of the tiger's victim.

### ▶▶▶ Victoria and Albert Museum 84C1

*Cromwell Road, SW7 (tel: 020-7938 8500)*
*Open: daily 10–5:45; seasonal late openings on Wed; call for details*
*Underground: South Kensington*

The V&A, as it is affectionately known, is a storehouse of treasures so diverse in their nature as to defy general description. Where else under one roof would you find superb examples of textiles from around the world, architectural fragments from French châteaux, Indian chess sets, medieval reliquaries, and a bed so famous that it featured in the plays of Shakespeare and Ben Jonson? In broad terms, the collection covers applied art from every age and nation, but this description does not do any justice to the immense diversity, eclecticism, and idiosyncracy of its material.

The origin of the museum goes back to the Great Exhibition of 1851, a celebration of the arts, crafts, and industrial products of the British Empire. Prince Albert,

*Renaissance masterpieces in replica in the V&A's Italian Cast Court*

the driving force behind the exhibition, wanted the museum to be a permanent collection displaying the best examples of commercial art and design, which would be a source of inspiration to future generations.

The first museum on the site was a utilitarian structure of iron and glass, nicknamed the Brompton Boilers. As the collection grew, the building expanded to its present size (it covers 13 acres and has over 6 miles of gallery space). Queen Victoria laid the foundation stone for the Cromwell Road facade in 1899 (her last public engagement in London), and the building was completed in 1909. The lantern on top of the entrance is shaped like the Queen's imperial crown.

Wandering at whim through the galleries will probably leave you tired and confused—it is best to pick up a plan at the entrance, make a rigorous selection and then set off. Alternatively take an introductory tour.

From the main hall, the central corridor houses medieval art, one of the best collections of its kind in the world, ranging from 5th-century ivories to Saxon goldwork and Carolingian gospel bindings. This leads to the Pirelli Garden, a good place to rest weary feet. The garden is overlooked by the Renaissance galleries, while straight ahead you will find the Morris, Gamble, and Poynter rooms. These were, originally, the museum tearooms and restaurant, and they retain their Minton tile work, William Morris furnishings, and Edward Burne-Jones stained glass. Running to the right of the entrance hall are the newly designed galleries displaying Art and Design in Europe and America from 1800 to 1890. Twentieth-Century Galleries, on the second floor, bring the story of design right up to date (and have changing exhibits of recent material).

Do not miss the Toshiba Gallery of Japanese art, the Nehru Gallery of Indian Art, or the T.T. Tsui Gallery of Chinese Art, the Cast Court, and the Raphael Cartoons (all on the first floor), or the British galleries upstairs when they re-open in 2002 after three years of refurbishment by top designers. The Cast Court is a magnificent collection of around 500 (mostly) life-size copies of some of the world's most famous sculptures, including Michelangelo's David, and Trajan's Column from the Forum of Imperial Rome AD 113. The most awesome cast is that of the huge 12th-century entrance arch from the famous Spanish cathedral of Santiago de Compostela. The Raphael Cartoons are Raphael's full-scale designs on paper from which weavers worked, in this case to fashion seven huge designs for tapestries intended to hang in the Sistine Chapel. They represent the single most important example of large-scale Renaissance art in England and have inspired generations of English artists and craftsmen ever since they were brought to England in 1623 by King Charles I.

Plans for a major extension have been approved, including The Spiral, Daniel Libeskind and Cecil Balmond's bold new gateway that looks like a precariously balanced pile of giant geometric shapes.

When hunger sets in, head for the restaurant, one of the best of any London museum. Save some time for the excellent store, which sells jewelry, ceramics, and crafts by some of the most innovative designers working in Britain today.

**THE YALTA MEMORIAL**
To the south of the Victoria and Albert Museum, a garden in Thurloe Square contains a moving memorial (1982, by Angela Conner) to the Yalta Victims, the many thousands of people who were forcibly repatriated to the Soviet Union and Eastern Europe between 1944 and 1947, only to face imprisonment and death.

*Morris wallpaper*

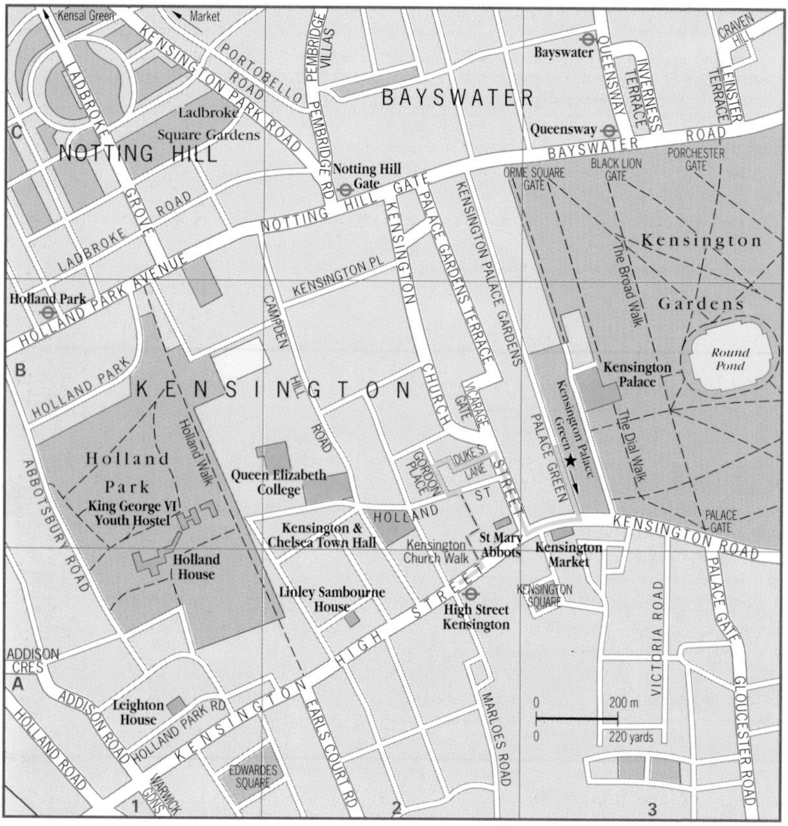




**KENSINGTON SQUARE**
Kensington Square was one of the first developments in the former village after William III moved to Kensington Palace. Nos. 11 and 12, originally one house, are the best preserved and date from 1693. Among the square's early residents was Richard Steele, founder of *The Spectator*. Hubert Parry, composer of *Jerusalem*, lived at No. 17. Edward Burne-Jones, the artist, lived at No. 41 and John Stuart Mill, the political philosopher, lived at No. 18: it was here that Thomas Carlyle's first manuscript of *The French Revolution* was burned by accident (see page 90).

*Singing in the park*

**KENSINGTON, NOTTING HILL, AND HYDE PARK** The great tract of Hyde Park separates the West End from Kensington, which maintains an air of being apart from the rest of central London. Immaculate stucco houses set in leafy avenues make it easy to imagine how 17th-century Kensington really was just a small rural village. Its transformation began in 1689 when William III came to live at Kensington Palace. Today, many of the fine houses have been converted to apartments. The High Street, once a country lane, is now a wide thoroughfare lined with fashionable stores, and the antiques stores of Kensington Church Street stretch unchecked to Portobello Road.

# Kensington, Notting Hill and Hyde Park

**KENSINGTON WALK** This route leads from Kensington Palace Gardens, which provide a glimpse of some of the most aristocratic dwellings surviving in the royal borough, to the present-day focus of Kensington life: the High Street stores.

Start in **Kensington Palace Gardens**, a leafy avenue laid out in 1843 on the site of the kitchen gardens of Kensington Palace. It is closed by entrance lodges at either end to reinforce the sense of privacy and exclusivity. In the 19th century its opulent houses earned it the nickname "Millionaires' Row." Several houses have now been converted into embassies.

Head south toward Kensington High Street. At the southern end of Kensington Palace Gardens (Palace Green) look for **No. 1**, which was designed by Philip Webb in 1863 as an experiment in Arts and Crafts style; and **No. 2**, built for the novelist William Makepeace Thackeray in 1860.

Turn right on to Kensington High Street; then take the next major turning on the right into Kensington Church Street. On Kensington High Street, **St. Mary Abbots Church** stands on the site of Kensington's original village church. It was rebuilt by George Gilbert Scott in the 1870s in a style intended to reflect the area's wealth and has a fine spire.

Take the second left, Duke's Lane, which still has some cottage-style houses reminiscent of the old Kensington. Turn left again onto picturesque Gordon Place, which has houses originally built for coachmen serving Kensington Palace. Gordon Place quickly leads you to Holland Street, where you turn right. Holland Street retains some unspoiled 18th-century houses (**Nos. 10, 12, 13, and 18–26**) and, at its far end, a left turn down the delightful Kensington Church Walk leads back to the bustle of Kensington High Street. Here, above the tube station, is **Barker's** department store, with its splendid art-deco facade (built 1937–1938) and domed atrium. The store, once as famous as Harrods, is now a galleria, occupied by a variety of retailers. Nearby are two fashionable clothing markets: Hype DF, at 48–52 and the Kensington Market, at Nos. 49–53.

*Above: Kensington Church Street*

▶▶▶ REGION HIGHLIGHTS

*A peacock, one of the many birds roaming free in Holland Park*



**HOLLAND HOUSE**
Until it was blitzed in World War II, Holland House was one of the finest Jacobean mansions in London and the glittering center of political and literary society. During the Commonwealth, when Cromwell ruled the land, plays were performed here privately in defiance of the Puritan ban on all forms of theatrical activity. In the early 18th century it was home to Joseph Addison, one of the founders of *The Spectator*, who composed his articles for the magazine while strolling up and down the 116-ft. Long Gallery, taking a sip of wine for inspiration from the glasses he kept at each end. During the first decades of the 19th century it was famous for the salons hosted by Lady Holland and attended by the leading intellectuals of the day, including Byron, Talleyrand, Prince Metternich, and Macaulay. Lady Holland was a passionate supporter of Napoleon. During his brief exile on Elba, she sent him jars of plum jam, books, and a refrigerator, as tokens of her belief in his cause.

### ▶▶ Commonwealth Experience 106A1

*230 Kensington High Street, W8 (tel: 020-7603 4535)*
*Underground: High Street Kensington*
*Currently closed for total redevelopment as an educational resource and exhibition centre, to re-open 2002.*

### ▶▶▶ Holland Park 106B1

*Holland Walk (off Kensington High Street) (tel: 020-7471 9813)*
*Underground: High Street Kensington*
*Entrances on Holland Park, Abbotsbury Road, Holland Walk, and Kensington High Street*
Flower-filled formal gardens and wilder woodland areas can both be enjoyed in this varied 55-acre park hidden behind the grand houses of Kensington and Holland Park. It used to be the private garden of Holland House, built in 1606–1607 (see panel). All that remains of the house today is the first floor and the orangery, which contains a restaurant. The terrace in front of the house, known as the Holland Park Theatre, is used in the summer months for outdoor plays, ballets, operas, and concerts. Surrounding the house are a rose garden, a Dutch garden—laid out in 1812 with flower beds bordered by box hedges, and an iris garden. Peacocks and other ornamental birds wander freely about the park, adding their color to the scene. The woodland areas to the north are best in May, when the rhododendrons and azaleas are in full bloom, complemented by the pink and creamy spires of horse-chestnut blossom. This park, one of London's most romantic and secretive, rewards the curious walker. There is the Japanese Kyoto Garden created in 1991, near the formal Caro's garden sculpture, and the statue of Henry James Fox in the woods.

### ▶▶ Leighton House Museum 106A1

*12 Holland Park Road, W14 (tel: 020-7602 3316)*
*Open: Mon–Sat 10–5:30. Donation*
*Underground: High Street Kensington*
Leighton House is the most remarkable of a cluster of artists' houses in the leafy district of Holland Park. George Aitchison designed it in 1864–1866 for his friend, the artist Frederick Lord Leighton, as the ultimate up-to-date bachelor's indulgence—with only one bedroom; he did not want to be bothered with guests. The result was

London's first full architectural expression of the English Aesthetic Movement. Leighton was 34 years old when he built the house. Born in Scarborough, northern England, he roamed Europe as a young man, returned to England and, aged 25, achieved success by having his Early Renaissance-inspired painting *Cimabue's Madonna* exhibited at the Royal Academy Summer Exhibition. Better still, Queen Victoria bought it. His future sealed, he became a fashionable painter, was appointed President of the Royal Academy (1878–1896) and was created Baron Leighton of Stretton a month before he died in 1896.

During the 1860s Leighton had traveled widely in the Near East. His fondness for things Oriental is immediately apparent. Behind the plain brick exterior, lies one of London's most idiosyncratic rooms, the wonderful Arab Hall, designed by George Aitchison and based on the Moorish buildings of Spain. The hall is lined with tiles, dating from the 13th to the 17th centuries, which Leighton collected on his travels in Damascus, Cairo, and Rhodes; these are supplemented with equally exotic tiles designed by William de Morgan. The domed hall has a fountain at its center, a Romanesque mosaic frieze by Walter Crane, and marble columns with capitals carved by Edgar Boehm. Other rooms, less exotic, but nevertheless finished with red walls and ebonized wood, are hung with paintings by Leighton and other leading Pre-Raphaelites.

The huge studio upstairs where Leighton worked is used for concerts and exhibitions. Leighton's sculpture, *Athlete struggling with a python* (1877), stands in the walled garden, where visitors may picnic, with permission.

**ARTISTIC KENSINGTON**

Kensington—Melbury Road, in particular—was once a hotbed of artiness. George Frederick Watts lived at No. 6, where he made the equestrian figure, *Physical Energy*, now in Kensington Gardens (see page 111). No. 9 (now No. 29) was built by William Burges for himself in 1875–80 and reveals his preoccupation with Gothic detailing. William Holman Hunt, whose painting *The Light of the World* hangs in St. Paul's Cathedral, lived at No. 18. Nearby, No. 8 Addison Road was built in 1906–1907 for Sir Ernest Debenham, founder of the department store, and covered in colorful William de Morgan tiles, earning it the nickname Peacock House.



*Leighton House—the Arab Hall*

*Hyde Park and Kensington Gardens together form an expanse of trees, flowers, and greenery covering 615 acres. The dividing line between them is the road that runs from Alexandra Gate in the south, over the Serpentine Bridge, built in 1826, and up to the Victoria Gate in the north. To the west of this line is Kensington Gardens; to the east is Hyde Park.*

**SPEAKERS' CORNER**
Speakers' Corner is at the northeastern edge of Hyde Park, near Marble Arch. Here, on Sundays, soapbox orators harangue the crowds on issues ranging from politics and religion to vegetarianism or the evils of smoking. The tradition of free speech and assembly dates from the mid-19th century. There have been huge gatherings here in the past, including demonstrations against nuclear armaments. According to law, anyone can speak on any topic, as long as they do not blaspheme, use obscene language, incite racial hatred, or breach the peace.



Kensington Gardens is a relatively quiet area, with surprisingly rich wildlife. Herons and grebes can be seen on the willow-fringed Long Water, to the north of the Serpentine Bridge. Hyde Park is more a place of recreation and entertainment, with boats for rent on the Serpentine in summer; bandstand music at lunchtime in June, July, and August; and occasionally fairs, concerts, or fireworks parties.

The parks escaped being built upon during the great expansion of London in the 18th century because the land belonged to the Crown. Henry VIII had seized it from the monks of Westminster Abbey at the Dissolution of the Monasteries and had turned it into a huge royal hunting ground. Charles I made it London's first public park, open to "respectably dressed people" and it became a favorite resort of Samuel Pepys, among others.

A good place to begin a stroll around Hyde Park is Hyde Park Corner. Here, behind Apsley House (see page 83), you can enter through Decimus Burton's 1828 triple-arched screen or the gates created in honor of the Queen Mother. The road inside is Rotten Row—a corruption of *route du roi* (King's Road)—built to link rural Kensington Palace to Piccadilly and St. James's Palace. It is now

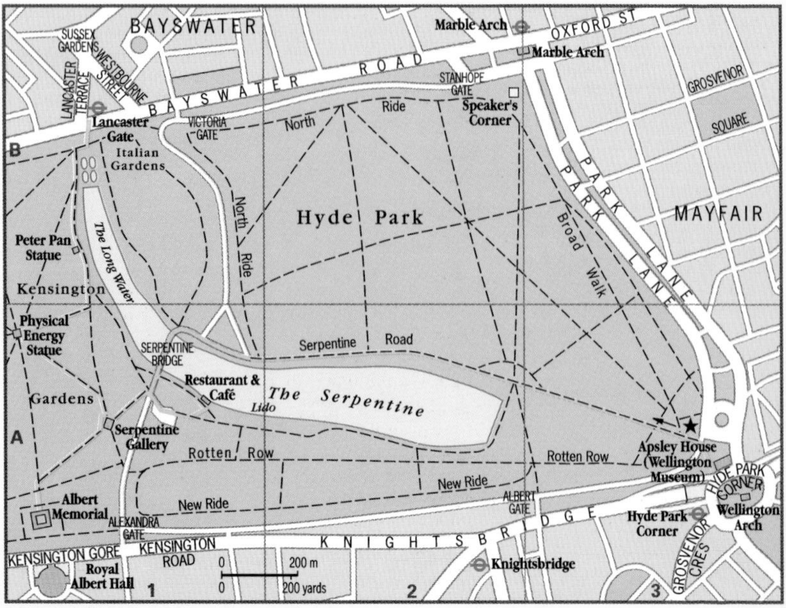

*Audience participation at Speakers' Corner, Hyde Park*



used by the Household Cavalry Brigade for exercising their horses; at around 10:30 AM (9:30 AM on Sunday) and noon, members of the Brigade ride to and from the Changing of the Guard ceremonies, which take place at Buckingham Palace and Horseguards.

Serpentine Road leads straight ahead to the northern shore of the Serpentine. This lake was created by damming the River Westbourne. A beautiful bridge, built in 1826 by George Rennie, spans the water. Swimming in the Serpentine is allowed at the Lido, on the opposite bank, from 10 AM to 8 PM in summer. Hardy members of the Serpentine Swimming Club come here for a daily dip between 6 and 9 AM, even in the depths of winter, and a few always take a dip on Christmas Day.

Nearby is the Serpentine Gallery, which hosts exhibitions of contemporary art (tel: 020-7402 6075/7298 1515. *Open* daily 10–6 during exhibitions. *Admission free*). Walk north to see two sculptures: *Physical Energy* (1904) by George Frederick Watts is a powerful equestrian figure, and *Peter Pan* (1912) by George Frampton commemorates the hero of J.M. Barrie's play for children, written in 1904—the boy who defied adulthood is depicted playing his pipes among fairies and woodland animals. Lancaster Gate exit is nearby. Head southwest from the Serpentine Gallery to visit the newly restored Albert Memorial (see panel); or go west to the Round Pond, where children and adults come to sail model boats at weekends, and from there to the more formal gardens of Kensington Palace.

**THE ALBERT MEMORIAL**
George Gilbert Scott's flamboyant monument to Prince Albert, husband of Queen Victoria, is a reminder of the values of the Victorian age. In the center is Albert himself, holding the catalog for the 1851 Great Exhibition, which he organized (see page 95). Completed in 1876, the memorial is crowded with 169 portraits of painters, composers, poets, and architects. Its corners illustrate the peoples of Asia, America, Europe, and Africa, while allegorical figures represent Albert's interests: Commerce, Manufacturing, Engineering, and Agriculture. Weather and pollution caused such serious deterioration that during the 1990s the whole monument was restored by skilled craftsmen (tel: 020-7495 0196, guided tours daily 9:30–1, whatever the weather; booking essential. *Admission charge).*

## ▶▶▶ Kensington Palace 106B3

*Kensington Gardens, W8 (tel: 020-7937 9561)*
*Open: May–Sep, daily 10–5; Oct–Apr, Wed–Sun 10–4.*
*Admission charge includes acoustiguide*
*Underground: High Street Kensington, Queensway*

The asthmatic William III was the first monarch to set up home in Kensington Palace, in 1689, escaping from the damp and smoke of riverside Whitehall Palace to the cleaner air and rural environment of Hyde Park. He purchased the existing house, built in 1605, and had it enlarged by Sir Christopher Wren. It was further extended, under George I, by William Kent in the 1720s. The result is a roughly rectangular brick building, which is arranged around three courtyards; architecturally it is surprisingly modest, more like a country house than a palace, although the interiors are more sumptuous, and the surrounding gardens are a great delight. Queen Victoria was born at the palace in 1819 and on her 70th birthday decided that the State Apartments should be opened to view. Several members of the present royal family still have apartments here, including Princess Margaret, Prince and Princess Michael of Kent, and the Duke and Duchess of Gloucester—you may catch a fleeting glimpse as they depart in their limousines to attend various public engagements in London.

Re-opened in 1998 after major refurbishment, the areas of the Palace open to visitors are the first-floor Ceremonial Court Dress Collection and upstairs, for the King's State Apartments and finally the Queen's State Apartments.

The largest of the Queen's State Apartments is Queen Mary's Gallery, a spacious paneled room hung with royal portraits and Kneller's forceful picture of Peter the Great of Russia, painted when the Czar visited England to study London's naval dockyards in 1698. A series of smaller private apartments is decorated with 17th-century furnishings and pictures, including the State Bed, in Queen Mary's Bedchamber, with its original hangings.

**FLOWERS FOR A PRINCESS**
When Diana, Princess of Wales died following a car accident in Paris in 1997, thousands of people paid tribute to her by laying flowers outside the gates of Kensington Palace, where she had lived. The bouquets lay thick on the ground outside the palace gates, and when they were removed it took a whole army of volunteers to salvage as many as possible of the cards and poems left by mourners.

*Kensington Palace: modest without but sumptuous within*

The King's State Apartments are very opulent. Italianate in style, the rooms have magnificent ceiling paintings by William Kent. The most magnificent of all is the Cupola Room, with its pillars, figures of Greek and Roman deities, and busts of Roman emperors and ancient philosophers. The Council Chamber displays objects associated with Prince Albert's great project, the Great Exhibition of 1851. Next comes the King's Drawing Room, which enjoys superb views over Kensington Gardens. Through Queen Victoria's bedroom, where a painting illustrates the Queen's marriage to Prince Albert in 1840, an anteroom leads to the King's Gallery. This has ceiling paintings of the adventures of Ulysses, and is decorated and furnished as it was during the palace's heyday. A curiosity is the wind-direction dial above the fireplace, turned by a weathervane on the roof

Courtiers and visitors would have arrived here up the King's Grand Staircase, designed by Wren, with its scrolled wrought-ironwork by Jean Tijou and its walls and ceiling coated in Venetian-style paintings by Kent, inspired by work at Versailles and Blenheim. The trompe l'oeil wall painting of a gallery crowded with figures includes many contemporary portraits of George I's courtiers and servants. One of them, known as Peter the Wild Boy, was discovered living like a wild animal in a forest near Hanover, Germany, and brought to England as a freak curiosity, although he has a central roundel depicting Apollo in his chariot. Finally, the Privy Chamber is painted with the figure of Mars (wearing the order of the Garter) symbolizing the military prowess of George I, and of Minerva, goddess of wisdom, accompanied by figures representing the Sciences and the Arts.

The Court Dress Collection presents a superb array of court finery. Visitors are taken through the elaborate process of dressing for court; from a replica of a store where materials were chosen, to a visit to the seamstress. Temporary exhibits display the garments of important royals such as Queen Mary and the Queen Mother.

**KENSINGTON PALACE GARDENS**

William III was a keen gardener and lavished much affection on the 25-acre garden he had laid out, in Dutch style, immediately around Kensington Palace. This has now gone, and in its place is the pretty sunken garden, made in 1909, surrounded by an alley of pleached lime trees on three sides, with flower beds framing the central lily pond (to which there is no public access). The north side of the garden is closed by the red-brick orangery of 1704. Facing south to catch the sun, this is where Queen Anne used to take tea, as visitors still can—part of the orangery serves as a restaurant. Beyond lies Kensington Gardens (see page 110). An attractive walk from the palace leads up the Broad Walk to Black Lion Gate and Queensway tube station, passing the playground, site of the Elfin Oak, a tree trunk carved by Ivor Innes in 1928 with elves, foxes, frogs, rabbits, and secret doorways.

*A glimpse through the gilded gates of Kensington Palace*

**NOTTING HILL CARNIVAL**
The Notting Hill Carnival was founded in 1966 as a local neighborhood festival but has since grown to be the biggest Caribbean-style carnival in Britain—perhaps in all Europe. In deference to the English climate it is held over the August Bank Holiday weekend (usually the last weekend in the month), rather than the traditional carnival date of Mardi Gras (Shrove Tuesday), which falls in chilly, wet February. Marred in the past by racial tension, the carnival is now a peaceful event, with processions of colorful floats, street stalls, steel-band music, and nonstop dancing.

## ▶▶▶ Linley Sambourne House 106A2

*18 Stafford Terrace, W8 (tel: 020-8994 1019)*
*Open: Mar–Oct, Wed 10–4, Sun 2–5. Admission charge*
*Underground: High Street Kensington*

Anyone interested in the Victorian period should make an effort to see this excellent museum; alternatively, rent the videos or see the Merchant-Ivory films based on E.M. Forster's novels, *A Room with a View* and *Maurice*, for many scenes in both were shot in this house. It is named for Edward Linley Sambourne, the chief political cartoonist for *Punch* magazine who also produced the illustrations for Charles Kingsley's *The Water Babies*, published in 1885. Sambourne bought the house in 1874, soon after it was built, and lived here until his death in 1910. His family continued to use it until 1980, when it was opened as a museum, and throughout the intervening years the house and its furnishings remained almost totally unaltered. The museum is a time capsule, preserving its over-furnished, cozy, late Victorian and Edwardian appearance and atmosphere. The rooms still have their original William Morris wallpapers, and the walls are hung with a mass of paintings, cartoons, and photographs. These combine to create a sense of cluttered richness, so beloved by the Victorians, which is further enhanced by the Oriental rugs, the stained-glass windows, and the heavy, Gothic-inspired furniture.

Among much that is undistinguished in the house, there are some gems on the walls, including paintings by Sambourne's friends—such as Watts, Millais, and Alma-Tadema—and drawings by other well-known book illustrators, such as Kate Greenaway and Sir John Tenniel. Vintage fixtures can be seen in the bathroom and lavatories, and one of the most charming rooms is that of "Roy" Sambourne, the artist's son, which is complete with pinup pictures of popular Edwardian actresses and his former girlfriends.

*The drawing room, Linley Sambourne House*

### ▶▶▶ Portobello Road Market *106C1*

*Portobello Road, W11 and W10, and surrounding streets*
*Open: Antiques Sat 7 AM–6 PM; general Mon–Wed 9–5, Thu 9–1, Fri, Sat 7–6; organic market Thu 11–6; clothes and bric-a-brac Fri–Sun 9–4; Golborne Road market Mon–Sat 9–5*
*Underground: Notting Hill Gate/Ladbroke Grove*

Portobello Market is more than just one market; it is a collection of smaller markets, each with its own character. Furthermore, the antiques shops spill over through Notting Hill and down Kensington Church Street. It is a far cry from its origins at the end of the 19th century, when gypsies traded horses and herbs along the track leading down to Porto Bello farm, named for the Caribbean city of Puerto Bello. Ironically, after World War II,

as the British Empire was disbanded and people from former colonies chose to take up their option of British citizenship, it was the Caribbeans who settled in this area. Meanwhile, the market had thrived, and when Caledonian market in north London closed, its antiques dealers came west to trade here instead.

Today, Portobello Road's Saturday antiques market combines stores and stalls, and is one of Britain's longest markets. This is the best day to come, and it is a full day's outing. At the top (Notting Hill) end, only the cleverest bargain hunters will strike lucky from the all-knowing antiques dealers. Down the hill, they may do better, and there are plenty of pubs and cafés, such as Tom's and Café 206 on Westbourne Grove, where you can pause to consider which of your finds might be worth buying. Here, too, are collectibles such as records, antique clothes and toys, and walking sticks. Along the side streets are contemporary art and ceramics stores, and designer clothes and jewelry outlets (Ledbury Road and Westbourne Grove). The best way to enjoy it is simply to poke about, keeping eyes sharp for attractive and unusual souvenirs.

Further down, find fruit and vegetables in Golborne Road, together with bicycles, household goods and new clothes. Here, too, is a favorite local institution, Lisboa Patisserie, a bustling Portuguese café. Alternatively, recover in the Brasserie du Marche aux Puces, Galicia or the Japanese Canteen, all in this stretch of Portobello.

**KENSAL GREEN CEMETERY**

Kensal Green Cemetery (on Harrow Road, reached from Kensal Green tube station) is, like Highgate Cemetery, full of interesting tombs beside tree-lined avenues. This was the first private cemetery in London (1833) and became fashionable after two of George III's children were buried here. Other notable tombs are those of Thackeray and Trollope, the novelists; Isambard Kingdom Brunel, the engineer; and the tightrope-walker, Blondin. Here too is the grave of James Barry who, after a successful career as an army surgeon, was made Inspector General of the Army Medical Department; only after "his" death in 1865 was it discovered that James Barry was actually a woman.

*Art meets junk in the Portobello Road*

The Royal Borough of Kensington and Chelsea
PORTOBELLO
ROAD W11

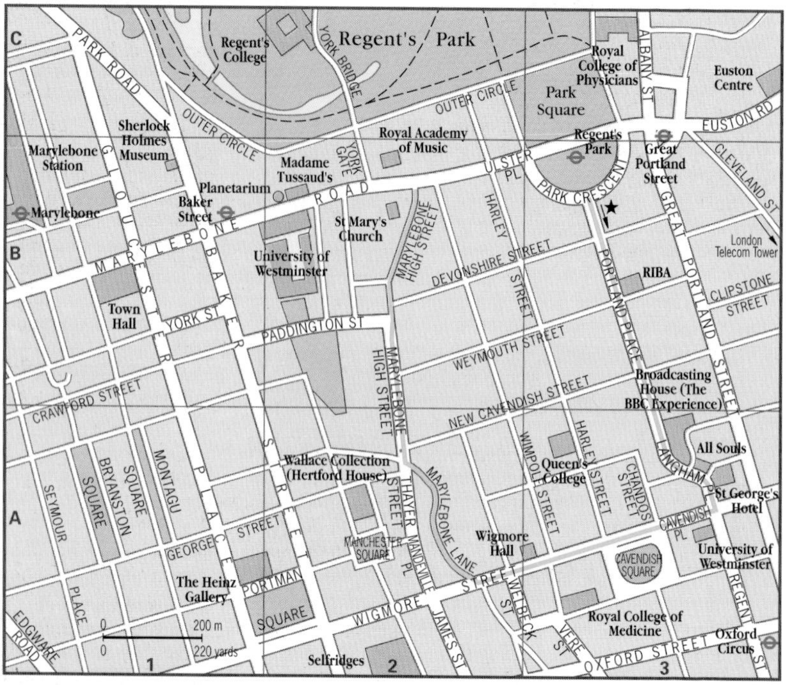

**ELIZABETH BARRETT**
No. 50 Wimpole Street (parallel to Portland Place) was the home of Elizabeth Barrett, whose *Poems* (1844) attracted the attention of the younger poet, Robert Browning. A correspondence and a meeting followed, and the two fell in love. Elizabeth's tyrannical father disapproved, so she married Robert secretly in St. Marylebone Church, and the pair later escaped to Italy in one of literary history's most romantic elopements.

**REGENT'S PARK AND MARYLEBONE** In 1812 work began on a bold scheme to transform the West End of London and remodel the Crown-owned lands of Marylebone Park. John Nash, the Prince Regent's architect, cut a swathe through the heart of the metropolis, from Carlton House Terrace north via Regent Street and Portland Place, to Park Crescent. Beyond, he laid out the huge Regent's Park and intended to build a whole garden city of Italianate villas and grand terraces. The project, although never completed, gave the city a new focus, and extended smart London northward. The benefits of Nash's great project are enjoyed by north Londoners today. Regent's Park is their back garden, used for walks, sport and picnics. It is a place to meet friends, to go boating, to delight in the roses, to exercise and play games, and to relax after visits to the Zoo.

**MARYLEBONE WALK** The contrasts of Marylebone are sampled on this tour, which starts with Georgian elegance and ends with stores and cafés.

Take the tube to Regent's Park station, near **Park Crescent**, a daring 1821 design by John Nash, who intended it to be completely circular, in contrast to the squares that characterize Georgian London. Only half of the circle was built, but the curving terrace, with its impressive colonnade of Ionic columns, hints at what Nash envisaged—to change the axis from the already busy east–west Marylebone Road to a south–north one running uninterrupted into Regent's Park; however, the builder of the circle went bankrupt, which was why it was never completed.

# Regent's Park and Marylebone

*The elegant semicircular sweep of Park Crescent*

In James Adam's speculative **Portland Place** (1776–1780), the best of the original houses lie between Weymouth and New Cavendish Streets. Beyond are **Broadcasting House** and **All Souls Church** (see page 118), then **St. George's Hotel**, whose rooftop restaurant offers extensive views over London.

Turn right onto Cavendish Place, which leads to Cavendish Square. Lord Nelson lived for a time at No. 5 Cavendish Square, but the best buildings are on the north side (**Nos. 11–14**), built in 1770 and originally designed as part of a mansion for the Duke of Chandos. The archway between the two has a large bronze *Madonna* by Jacob Epstein. In Chandos Street, running north from the square, **Chandos House** (1771) is one of Robert and James Adam's finest private town houses. **Harley Street**, which also leads off Cavendish Square, has been synonymous with medicine since the mid-19th century. Medical practitioners, dentists, psychiatrists, and plastic surgeons have their prestigious consulting rooms here, for the reception of private clients. On the same street (No. 64) the artist Turner lived from 1804 to 1808, and Queen's College (No. 43) was founded in 1848 as the first college of higher education for women in England.

Leave the square via Wigmore Street, which has interesting shops, as well as beautiful **Wigmore Hall** (1901), originally built by the piano maker Friedrich Bechstein next to his showrooms and still a place to hear fine recitals. Farther on, to the right, the rigid grid pattern of Marylebone's streets is broken by the serpentine shape of **Marylebone Lane**. This once threaded through the heart of the original medieval village of St. Mary by the Bourne (the River Tyburn). The lane leads to Marylebone High Street, lined with shops and galleries. Try **Pâtisserie Valerie et Sagne** (No. 105), a café that has changed little since it opened in the 1920s.

**▶▶▶ REGION HIGHLIGHTS**

**London Planetarium** *page 121*

**London Zoo** *page 125*

**Regent's Park** *page 122*

**Wallace Collection** *pages 126–127*

**TELECOM TOWER**
Of all the spires and towers that pierce the London skyline, the Telecom Tower is one of the most dominant. It was completed in 1964, attracting crowds of tourists and Londoners who came to enjoy superb views from the revolving restaurant near its 580-ft.-high summit. After a terrorist bomb exploded in the restaurant in 1975, public access was prohibited; too much is at stake to risk another such incident. The tower is used to transmit and receive satellite phone calls between the City and other financial markets. It also handles London's radio and T.V. signals.



*The Telecom Tower, below; the spire of All Souls, right*

## ▶ All Souls 116A3

*Langham Place, W1 (tel: 020-7580 3522)*
*Open: 10–6. Donation*
*Underground: Oxford Circus*

All Souls Church was built in 1822–1824 by John Nash—his only church—to provide a focal point for the view up Regent Street, and a means of turning the road to join it on to Portland Place, already built. This is a job it has done supremely well. The curving portico both arrests the eye and guides it to the left. The church was ridiculed in its time because Nash mixed together a classical portico with a Gothic spire and was therefore accused of breaking all the rules of architectural propriety, despite the fact that the combination works so well. The silhouette of the spire once dominated the skyline, but bigger buildings, notably Broadcasting House, have since diminished its impact. The interior is used by the B.B.C. for broadcasting live lunchtime and evening concerts, and for religious services. There is a bust of Nash on the exterior south wall.

## ▶▶ Broadcasting House (B.B.C. Experience) 116A3

*Portland Place, W1 (tel: 020-7580 4468)*
*Open: daily 9:30–5:30. Admission charge*
*Underground: Oxford Circus*

Broadcasting House, built in 1931, echoes the shape of All Souls Church, although its curving facade is topped by a radio mast rather than a spire. G. Val Myers's elegant building of Portland stone bears a sculpture by Eric Gill over the main door, showing Shakespeare's Prospero sending his ethereal creation Ariel out into the world (see panel, page 119). Ariel was chosen in the early days of the B.B.C. as an appropriate symbol for the new medium of radio broadcasting. The original 22 studios, from which the B.B.C. began broadcasting in May 1932, are housed within the core of the building to be insulated from noise, while the outer shell consists of offices where the Director General and the governors of the B.B.C. meet. The studios, which were quickly inadequate for the growing company, are now the site of the **B.B.C. Experience**, created in 1997 to celebrate the corporation's 75th birthday (see panel, page 119).

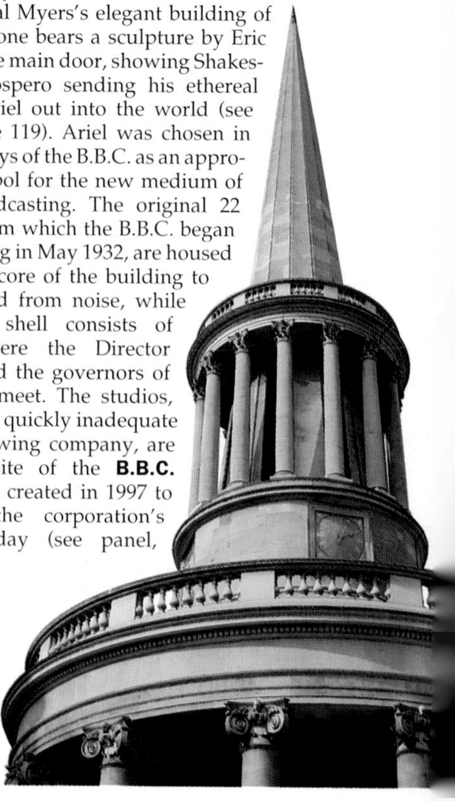

*The British Broadcasting Corporation (B.B.C.) is one of Britain's best-loved institutions and, at the same time, one that is much criticized. It is known affectionately as "Auntie Beeb" because of its tendency to take a high moral tone, sometimes at the expense of the preferences and tastes of the license-payers. This attitude is very much in the tradition of its founders.*

The B.B.C. was set up in 1922 in a deliberate government plan to prevent radio broadcasting in Britain from developing along commercial lines, as it had in the U.S. The B.B.C.'s first Director General, Lord Reith, was a dour figure with strong views about the B.B.C.'s missionary role; Christian morality and serious culture were the keynotes. As the "voice of the nation," B.B.C. announcers and presenters were trained to speak "formal" English and regional accents were looked down upon as the products of simplemindedness. High seriousness was pushed to ridiculous extremes. In the early days of the B.B.C., radio announcers and newsreaders were expected to wear full evening dress when in front of the microphone.

Despite this, the B.B.C. won the heart of the nation and continues to set high standards of journalistic integrity. Until the coming of television, almost everybody in Britain listened to the B.B.C., was entertained and educated by it, and many had their lives, ideas, and thoughts shaped by it. The wireless gadget was hugely popular. Nine million licenses were held by 1939, and the following year Bush House at Aldwych became home to the globe-encompassing B.B.C. World Service. Television followed, and B.B.C. T.V. Centre is in West London.

Today the B.B.C. no longer has a monopoly over broadcasting, and British audiences can choose from hundreds of channels thanks to digital, cable, and satellite stations. (Following historical tradition, the B.B.C's digital service is exceptionally good.) The B.B.C. is currently funded by the revenue from selling T.V. licenses to every television owner in the country, rather than from advertising, and is thus free to produce programs "in the public interest." This principle never fails to arouse passionate debate.

**B.B.C. EXPERIENCE**
The B.B.C.'s visitor center, at its Portland Place headquarters, offers a glimpse behind the scenes of program-making and reveals the complexities of broadcasting. Visitors can see *Titanic*'s last-known wireless message, direct an episode of a soap opera, commentate on great sporting occasions, deliver a weather forecast, select Desert Island discs, or create a radio play in a specially designed studio. Visits are structured as tours, about 1½ hours long, starting every 15 minutes. It is best to reserve a slot (tel: 0870-603 0304. *Open* Mon 1–4:30, Tue–Fri 9:30–4:30, Sat, Sun 9:30–5:30. *Admission charge*).

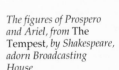

*The figures of Prospero and Ariel, from* The Tempest, *by Shakespeare, adorn Broadcasting House*

### ►► Jewish Museum 123C3

*129 Albert Street, NW1 (tel: 020-7284 1997)*
*Open: Mon–Thu, Sun 10–4. Admission charge*
*Underground: Camden Town*

Exhibits and an audiovisual program impart the long history of the Jewish community in England. Jews have been here since Norman times, sometimes treated with suspicion. Some ostensibly converted to Christianity. Many became wealthy as wool merchants and one, Rodrigo Lopez, became Queen Elizabeth I's physician.

The museum's outstanding collection of Jewish ceremonial objects mostly date from the end of the 17th century, when Oliver Cromwell removed the prohibitive laws on Jewish settlement, although there are earlier objects, such as the 13th-century bankers' tallies and 16th-century hardwritten scrolls. There is a second Jewish Museum in Finchley, North London (tel: 020-8349 1143).

*The foggy Victorian London of Jack the Ripper comes to life at Madame Tussaud's*



**ROYAL INSTITUTE OF BRITISH ARCHITECTS**
Grey Wornum's Swedish-inspired building of 1932–1934 somehow finds sympathy with Adam's palatial mansions strung along Portland Place. Founded in 1824, the R.I.B.A., as it is fondly known, thrives on controversy, particularly when the coveted annual Gold Medal is awarded—Norman Foster, who won it in 1983, and Richard Rogers, in 1985, are both now dominant influences in London's biggest building projects. Past presidents have included George Gilbert Scott, Charles Barry and Edwin Lutyens. It is well worth visiting the current exhibition, the architecture bookshop and the upstairs café (tel: 020-7580 5533; *Open* Mon–Fri 9–9, Sat 10–1:30. *Admission free*).

### ► Madame Tussaud's 116B2

*Marylebone Road, NW1 (tel: 020-7935 6861)*
*Open: Mon–Fri 10–5:30 (last admission), Sat, Sun 9:30–5:30 (9 AM Easter and summer)*
*Underground: Baker Street*

Madame Tussaud (1761–1850) perfected her craft during the French Revolution by taking death masks of guillotine victims, including Louis XVI and Marie Antoinette. She was a friend of Louis XVI's sister, so the Revolutionary authorities must have derived some satisfaction in assigning her this gruesome task. In 1802 she fled Paris and arrived in Britain with her macabre collection, first touring the country, then setting up an exhibition of historic figures, living and dead, in London in 1835. In 1884 the collection moved to Marylebone Road, where it has remained to this day. The collection is continually extended to encompass famous figures from every age, but they are made using techniques that have changed little in 200 years. More recent additions include Tony Blair, Brad Pitt, and Naomi Campbell.

Madame Tussaud's also has a special ride called the "Spirit of London" experience. It uses audio-animatronic figures to help re-create the sights, sounds, and smells of the city, and there is a spine-chilling new Chamber of Horrors (see panel). The oldest figure on display is Sleeping Beauty, made in 1765, a portrait of Louis XV's mistress, Madame du Barry. Overall, Madame Tussaud's is great fun—a chance to meet and be photographed with your own personal hero, whether that be Arnold Schwarzenegger, the Queen, or even Madame Tussaud herself, whose self-portrait can be seen in the Great Hall.

Madame Tussaud's, a quirky eccentricity, is one of the capital's favorite attractions, and annually draws more than 2 million visitors. If you want to beat the lines, which are especially long in the height of summer, make a reservation in advance by credit card.

## ▶▶▶ London Planetarium *116B2*

*Marylebone Road, NW1 (tel: 020-7935 6861)*
*Open: Mon–Fri 10 AM, Sat, Sun 9:30 AM (9 AM Easter and summer). 45-minute-long show throughout the day, with the last show at 5 PM.*
*Underground: Baker Street*

Adjacent to Madame Tussaud's (and with a combined admission ticket), the London Planetarium explains the basic aspects of astronomy on the inside of its copper dome. On the way into the theater there are wax figures of astronauts and personalities such as Albert Einstein and Galileo, plus hands-on stations that deal with the planets, man-made satellites, black holes, and so on.

The show itself, "Planetary Quest", is an enjoyable romp through space with 3-D simulator action that helps to enliven some of the more educational aspects of the accompanying commentary on the cosmos.

**THE CHAMBER OF HORRORS**
Human fascination with death and criminality makes the Chamber of Horrors at Madame Tussaud's one of the most popular attractions, despite the gory nature of its subject matter. Exhibits include Vlad the Impaler (the "real life" Count Dracula); Joan of Arc, burning at the stake; Guy Fawkes, hanged, drawn, and quartered; genuine artifacts from London's brutal Newgate Prison; Jack the Ripper (see opposite); and a scene that Madame T. would have been all too familiar with—execution by guillotine. Sweet dreams!

*Welcome to the Universe at the Planetarium*

*"More like a work of general destruction than anything else." This was how one newspaper described the scene in 1817 as Regent's Park was being laid out. Soon, however, it was described as "among the magnificent ornaments of our metropolis," and so it remains to this day: a beautiful park of 465 acres, a fine place for a stroll at any time of year, but especially in summer, when the roses and flower beds are at their best.*

**CAMDEN LOCK**
Camden Lock lies just to the north of Camden Town tube station, off Chalk Farm Road, and is famous for its lively and atmospheric market. Here you can browse among stalls selling crafts, hand-knitted and period clothes, antiques, and secondhand books. The lock was built as a branch off the Regent's Park Canal, where barge owners could unload and store their cargoes of lumber, brick, and coal. Many of the original Victorian warehouses have been turned into crafts studios, cafés, and stores, while another has been converted into Dingwalls nightclub, offering live rock. The markets have spilled out from the Lock along neighboring roads, and at weekends this area rivals Petticoat Lane in size, scope, and jollity.



The York Gate entrance, which is served by Baker Street station, lies just beyond **Madame Tussaud's** and the **Planetarium**. As you walk up you will notice, on the right, the **Royal Academy of Music**, founded in 1822, where some of the world's finest musicians, singers and composers perfected their art.

On York Bridge, look back to see **St. Mary's Church**, on Marylebone High Street. When Nash laid out Regent's Park he deliberately aligned the York Gate axis to take in a view of the church, with its majestic Corinthian portico and circular tower. York Bridge continues past **Regent's College**, on the left, now a center for European studies and part of Rockford College, Illinois, but formerly part of Bedford College, founded 1849 and a pioneer of the women's education movement. Beyond lies **Queen Mary's Garden**. Here, Nash had intended a temple dedicated to the memory of all who had contributed to British history and culture. Instead, the 17-acre circle contains London's finest rose garden planted to honor George V's wife, Queen Mary, and the much-loved **Open Air Theatre**, founded in 1932 (*Open* June–August; tel: 020-7486 2431 for information).

To the west is the Y-shaped boating lake, and if you walk around the upper part of the lake you will come to **Hanover Gate**. Here are the park's newer buildings. The **London Central Mosque**, to the north, with its splendid dome and minaret, was designed by Sir Frederick Gibberd and opened in 1978 as the principal Islamic mosque in Britain. To the south, fronting the Outer Circle, you can see Quinlan Terry's new villas (completed in 1992), which are disappointingly nostalgic and unimaginative, and compare poorly to Nash's theatrical flair.

*The minaret and golden dome of the London Central Mosque*

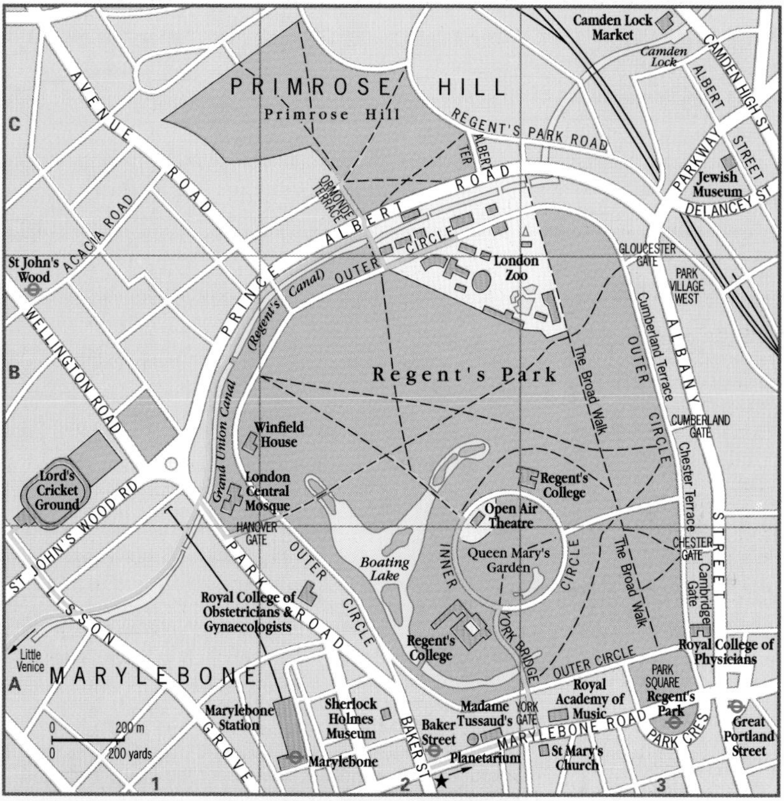

*Summer dreams, Regent's Park*

The towpath of **Regent's Canal** (a branch of the Grand Union Canal) leads around the northern perimeter of the Park to **London Zoo** (see page 125). From there you can cross over Prince Albert Road to Primrose Hill, whose summit has superb views. Alternatively, follow the canal westward to St. John's Wood. Star attractions are **Lord's Cricket Ground**, St. John's Wood Road, with a gallery of cricketing memorabilia (guided tours daily noon and 2 PM, except match days) and **Little Venice,** around Blomfield Road and Maida Avenue, with its waterside pubs, villas, and narrowboats.

**REGENT'S CANAL**
The Regent's Canal is a branch of the Grand Union Canal, cut between 1812 and 1820 through the north of London from the Paddington Basin to Limehouse, in the Docklands. Narrowboat cruises with commentaries, and trips to the Zoo from Little Venice or Camden, are run by the London Waterbus Company (*Open* year-round, but weekends only Nov–Mar; tel: 020-7482 2550).

*John Nash planned a utopian city for Regent's Park, with houses for the wealthy and for the working classes set in landscaped gardens around a lake. Most of that city's terraces remain, but only six of the villas. They can be seen on a stroll round the park's eastern fringes.*

*Regency fanlight*



**THE DIORAMA**
The Diorama, which opened in 1823, was the brainchild of Louis Jacques Daguerre, one of the early pioneers of photography. He was also a painter, skilled in creating vast *trompe l'œil* canvases, whose three-dimensional realism was enhanced by lighting and smoke effects, and by solid objects placed in the foreground. The Regent's Park Diorama showed the interior of Canterbury Cathedral. The audience would watch the scene change from daylight to candlelight to the accompaniment of ethereal music. Remarkably, the Diorama has survived, though it closed in 1854. It has been restored and is now used as the offices of the Prince's Trust, but sadly there is no public access to the building.

Great Portland Street and Regent's Park underground stations are both close to Park Crescent, a beautiful curving terrace built between 1812 and 1818 (see page 116). Opposite is Park Square, with two long terraces by Nash (1823–1825). Three houses on the eastern side of the terrace were built to house the Diorama, once a popular attraction (see panel).

Just beyond, on the right, is the Royal College of Physicians, in St. Andrew's Place, completed in 1964 to the designs of Sir Denys Lasdun. To the north is Cambridge Gate, built in 1876–1880 on the site of the famous Colosseum. This templelike structure displayed a circular view of the London panorama, painted by a Mr. Horner from the top of St. Paul's. The Colosseum was hugely popular at first, but Londoners soon lost interest, and it was demolished in 1875.

Continue north to Chester Gate; look for the bust of John Nash mounted on the left-hand wall. His Chester Terrace (1825) comes next, a handsome row of houses fronted by great Corinthian pillars, all in gleaming stucco. Nash intended the facade to be decorated by 52 statues but then decided that this would look too fussy. Cumberland Terrace (1826–1828) is slightly shorter but much more dramatic, and here Nash did place statues over the pediment of the central block.

Beyond Gloucester Gate you can leave the park, cross Albany Street, and turn right to look at Park Village West. Here, Nash embarked on his scheme for a series of villas set in gardens—notably Tower House, No. 12, once home to Dr. Johnson, physician to William IV.

*Corinthian capitals and gleaming white stucco*

*The London Zoological Gardens opened in 1828, the world's first institution dedicated to the study and display of animals. In its heyday in the 1950s, it received more than 3 million visitors a year. Today, study takes precedence over display, and visitors benefit from informed talks and hands-on demonstrations.*

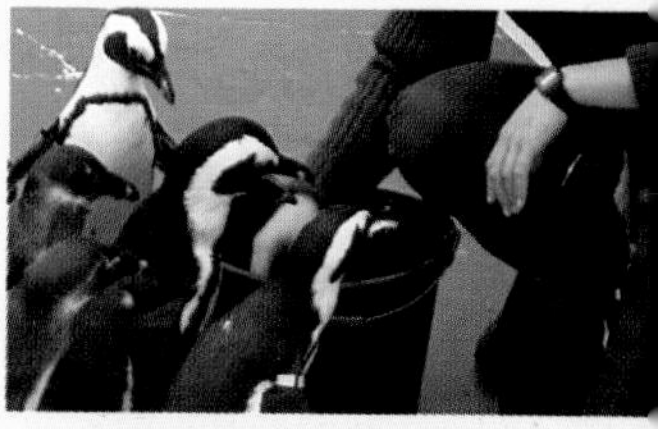

Before you start your tour look at the daily events program and try to be in the right place at the right time for feeding times and Animals in Action presentations. Across the road from the main entrance are the Cotton Terraces, where giraffes, zebras, okapi, oryx, and other African grazers may be seen. Behind is the landmark Snowdon Aviary, which you can walk through and share with a variety of birds. Adjacent are the charming small nocturnal inhabitants of the Moonlight World house.

Back on the main site, near the entrance, are the noisy primates, the silent and often beautiful world of the aquarium, and the reptile house. The Mappin Terrace (with sloth bears, monkey-like langurs, and muntjac deer) was designed by the radical architects Belcher and Joass in 1931; Joass had also designed a new Aquarium for the zoo in 1924. The Elephant and Rhino Pavilion is a favorite, even if its Brutalist architecture wins few friends—its rough surface deliberately reflects the coarse skin of its inhabitants.

The big cats are found beyond the children's zoo section. The Asian lions have their own open terrace, which is a nice contrast with most of the zoo where the animals are kept in sad, small barred enclosures. On either side are birds galore, including friendly wandering pelicans who happily (and harmlessly) munch on visitors' arms and feet! The penguin pool, always crowded at feeding time, was designed by Lubetkin and Tecton in 1931. Opposite, ponies offer their services to excited children on the Riding Lawn, where there are also displays and demonstrations.

**LONDON ZOO**
Back in the 1860s Jumbo the elephant gave children's rides, before he was sold to Phineas Barnum, the American showman. Today, the zoo's focus has changed: its Web of Life, opened in 1999, is a conservation and preservation center designed to encourage awareness of the world's fragile biological diversity and interdependence (tel: 020-7722 3333. *Open* daily, 10–5:30, Nov–Apr 10–4. *Admission charge*).



*The Elephant and Rhino Pavilion; a popular place at bathtime and weighing time*

## Sherlock Holmes Museum 116B1

*239 Baker Street, NW1 (tel: 020-7935 8866)*
*Open: daily 9:30–6. Admission charge*
*Underground: Baker Street*

This small museum, lovingly created by the Sherlock Holmes International Society, is dedicated to Sir Arthur Conan Doyle's famous sleuth. A re-creation of the detective's home is furnished with his personal possessions and memorabilia from his most important cases, and a "policeman" in period costume is posted outside the front door. Fans of the Sherlock Holmes stories will remember that the address of his house was 221b Baker Street. The address was pure invention—no such house ever existed—but the site where it would have notionally stood is marked by a plaque on the facade of the Abbey National bank. The Abbey National employs a full-time staff member just to deal with the extraordinary number of letters that arrive from all over the world addressed to Holmes.

*The famous fictional detective at home*

## ►►► Wallace Collection 116A2

*Hertford House, Manchester Square, W1 (tel: 020-7935 0687)*
*Open: Mon–Sat 10–5, Sun 2–5. Admission free*
*Underground: Bond Street*

The Wallace Collection has a world-class collection of art and yet remains little visited, leaving those who do make the trip free to enjoy the intimacy of a building that seems more like a private house than a museum; often the only sounds to be heard in the rooms are the tick tock and tinkling chimes of the fine French clocks.

The collection was largely put together by the Fourth Marquess of Hertford, a recluse in Paris. Helped by his illegitimate son, Richard Wallace, the Marquess avidly collected 18th-century French paintings, porcelain, and furniture, which he was able to buy cheaply in post-Revolutionary France because of its politically dangerous associations with the *ancien régime*. The Wallace Collection is especially rich in works by Fragonard, Boucher, Watteau, Lancret, and Poussin.

Richard Wallace inherited the collection at his father's death in 1870 and decided to bring it to England because of the unstable political situation in France. He added many fine examples of Renaissance ceramics, bronzes, armor, and jewelry, and his widow left the collection to the nation in 1897, on condition that it remain intact. The

126

**IN THE FOOTSTEPS OF SHERLOCK HOLMES**
Anyone hooked on *The Adventures of Sherlock Holmes* can eat and sleep with the ghost of their hero. The Sherlock Holmes pub, 10 Northumberland Avenue, is a shrine to the detective. Its walls are covered with Holmes memorabilia, and its upstairs room, next to the restaurant, has a re-creation of Holmes' study, with a model of the man himself seated in front of the fire studying a copy of *The Times*. Sir Arthur Conan Doyle used to drink here himself, and the pub features in *The Hound of the Baskervilles* (Chapter 4) under its old name, the Northumberland Hotel. The restaurant serves food with a Holmesian theme. After dinner here you could retire to the Sherlock Holmes Hotel, 108 Baker Street, part of the Hilton International chain, with plenty of decoration based on the Holmes stories.

*The collection of 18th-century Sèvres porcelain in the Wallace Collection is one of the finest of its kind in the world*

The Laughing Cavalier *(1624) by Frans Hals, much underrated in its day*

rooms are packed with all sorts of objects, from paintings, furnishings, and fittings originally made for the palaces of Fontainebleau and Versailles, to 18th-century saucepans and cabinets packed with guns, porcelain, or bejeweled baubles. Of particular note is the collection of European arms and armor, which is rich in decorated armor and 16th- and 17th-century swords. In a less warlike vein are the magnificent wardrobes and cabinets designed by André Charles Boulle, which are some of the finest surviving pieces of 18th-century French furniture.

Those on a quick tour should head straight upstairs for the Long Gallery (Room 24), one of London's finest picture galleries, which contains around 70 paintings from the 17th and 18th centuries. These include *The Laughing Cavalier* by Frans Hals (1624). The subject, whose identity remains unknown, wears an almost arrogant smirk beneath his carefully combed mustache, the sense of swagger emphasized by the hand on the hip and the rich lace collar. In the same room there is a touching portrait by Rembrandt of his son Titus (ca1657), the beautiful *Lady with a Fan* (1634–1636) by Velázquez, and Rubens's *Rainbow Landscape* (ca1636).

Here too is the Poussin painting, *Dance to the Music of Time* (1639–1640). It shows an allegory in which dancers represent Pleasure, Poverty, Riches, and Work, while the two-headed column on the left represents past and future; in the sky, Aurora (dawn) draws the chariot of Apollo (the sun), followed by the Hours.

In 2000, the Wallace celebrates the centenary of its public opening with four new galleries, a restaurant, and a glass roof for its courtyard.

**HERTFORD HOUSE**
The house that holds the Wallace Collection deserves as much study as the paintings. It was built in 1777 for the Duke of Manchester and acquired by the 2nd Marquess of Hertford in 1797. His flamboyant son, the 3rd Marquess, collected many of the 17th-century Dutch paintings in the collection and was able to do so because of his wife's wealth. She was illegitimate—more often than not a barrier to fortune, but in this case two very rich men claimed to be her father (the Duke of Queensberry and George Selwyn) and both left her vast sums of money. The house was refurnished when Richard Wallace moved the collection here. An important feature is the opulent white-marble staircase. This is flanked by a magnificent balustrade, made of wrought iron and bronze in 1723–1741 for Louis XV. It was originally installed in the Palais Mazarin (now the Bibliothèque Nationale) in Paris and was acquired by Wallace when it was sold for scrap in the chaotic world of mid-19th-century Paris.

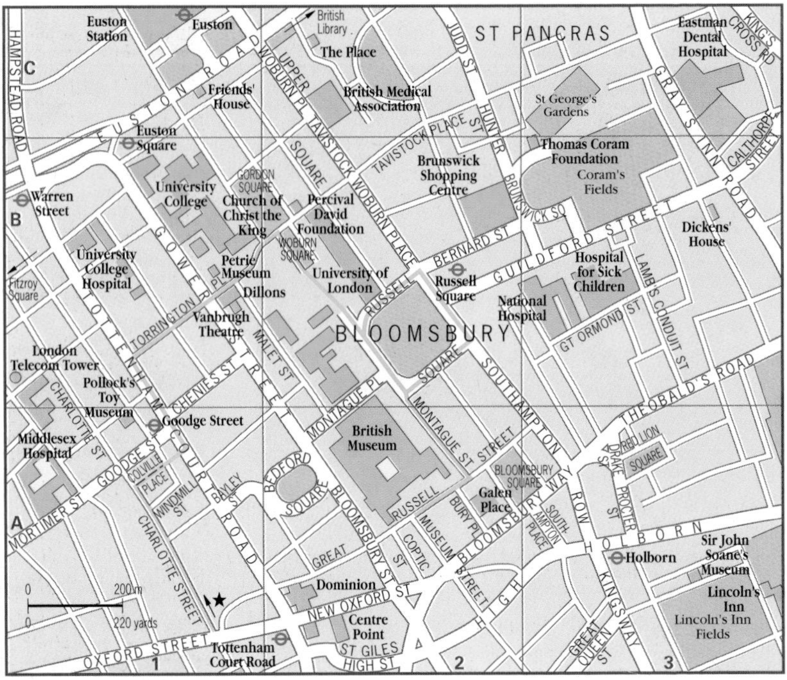

*Street entertainer*

**BLOOMSBURY AND FITZROVIA** Bloomsbury has the breeze of intellectual curiosity wafting through its leafy squares. The vast British Museum, Britain's most visited museum, is at its center. The University of London occupies many of the Georgian terrace houses, and students spill out from within, books in hand, to visit the British Library or relax in the public gardens and squares. While Bloomsbury is associated with early 20th-century writers Virginia Woolf, E.M. Forster, Lytton Strachey, and John Maynard Keynes, Fitzrovia, across Tottenham Court Road, was the haunt of hard-drinking Bohemian writers, journalists, and artists in the 1940s and 1950s, including Dylan Thomas, George Orwell, Cyril Connolly, and Anthony Burgess. They coined the name Fitzrovia to suggest the antithesis of genteel Belgravia.

**BLOOMSBURY AND FITZROVIA WALK** Charlotte Street, where this walk begins, is full of Bohemian atmosphere, with its pubs and inexpensive restaurants serving Greek, Turkish, Indian, and Italian food, and its sidewalk tables lending something of a Mediterranean feel to the area on sunny days.

Turn onto Colville Place, a Georgian alley that leads off Charlotte Street just south of Goodge Street; this threads through to Tottenham Court Road. To the right, leading south, **Tottenham Court Road** is lined with brash stores specializing in everything electronic at rock bottom prices and good after-sales service. To the north a number of design-conscious stores include **Paperchase, Habitat** and the more upscale **Heal's** (No. 196), with its big, curved windows (built in 1916). True to the philosophy of its founder, Ambrose Heal, the store specializes in top-

Bloomsbury and Fitzrovia

quality furnishings, including reproductions of its original Arts and Crafts designs.

Walk up Torrington Place, to the right beyond Heal's. This leads to **Dillons** bookshop (82 Gower Street), with a vast and comprehensive stock. Beyond Dillons, the tree-filled **Gordon Square** opens up on the left. Its garden is a favorite for students of the nearby Institute of Archaeology. Some of the square's rather dour houses were once centers of Bloomsbury intellectual life: No. 46, the home of Virginia Woolf, Vanessa Bell, and Clive Bell, was the meeting place of the Bloomsbury set, an elite circle that embraced Roger Fry, Duncan Grant, and E.M. Forster, among others. On the opposite, western side of the square is the Dr. Williams Library, where documents relating to the history of Nonconformity are preserved. On the southwestern corner, the University Church of Christ the King (1853) is a huge building with an ornate interior, whose intended spire was never built. Immediately south of Gordon Square is Woburn Square, lined with restrained Georgian-style terraces. Walking through **Woburn Square**, you will pass the more modern buildings of the **School of Oriental and African Studies**. (known as S.O.A.S.).

Continue to **Russell Square**, which was laid out in 1800 and is one of the largest in London. Do not miss Westmacott's statue of the 5th Duke of Bedford. The east side has two hotels: the **Russell Hotel**, of 1898, modeled on a French château, and the **Imperial**, the modern building that replaced the old Tudor Gothic-style hotel in 1966. The west side of the square has some of its original houses, designed by James Burton, and an entrance to the **Senate House** (begun in 1932), with its massive stone tower. The Senate is the governing body of the 50 or so colleges and faculties that together make up the University of London, Britain's largest university, with more than 95,000 students.

From the southwest corner of Russell Square, Montague Street leads to Great Russell Street and the front entrance to the British Museum (see pages 130–133).

The streets south of the museum (Coptic Street, Museum Street, Bury Place, and Galen Place) are worth exploring for their good bookstores and art galleries, as well as their cafés and pubs.

**▶▶▶ REGION HIGHLIGHTS**

**British Library**
*page 130*

**British Museum**
*pages 131–133*

**Dickens' House**
*pages 134–135*

**Percival David Foundation**
*page 138*

*The British Library*

**BRITISH LIBRARY ART**
The British Library's public spaces have a number of specially commissioned works of art. In the piazza, Eduardo Paolozzi's bronze statue of Isaac Newton was inspired by William Blake's image. It shows him seated and bending forward to plot the immensity of the universe with a pair of dividers, a symbol of the British Library's purpose: to preserve a record of man's endless search for truth. The entrance foyer has a more whimsical piece: Bill Woodrow's bronze and brass bench in the shape of an open book, titled *Sitting on History*. Here, too, is a facsimile of Louise Roubiliac's statue of William Shakespeare. Up the steps, find R.B. Kitaj's large tapestry, *If not, not*, incorporating a host of literary references on an idyllic background inspired by Giorgione's landscape paintings. Beyond it, four manuscript donors to the British Museum in its early years are remembered with busts: Sir Robert Cotton, Sir Joseph Banks, Thomas Grenwille and Sir Hans Sloane. Finally, the lower ground floor has the contemporary *Paradoxymoron* by Patrick Hughes, Matthew Noble's bust of Queen Victoria, and Peter Turnerelli's of Arthur Wellesley, Duke of Wellington.



## ▶▶▶ British Library

*96 Euston Road, NW1 (tel: 020-7412 7332)*
*Open: Mon, Wed, Thu 9:30–6, Tue 9:30–8, Fri, Sat 9:30–5, Sun 11–5. Admission free*
*Underground: King's Cross/St. Pancras/Euston*

Britain's national library, formed out of the British Museum's unwieldy manuscripts department in 1973, gained its own purpose-built complex in 1997. It houses a collection that has been growing since the early 18th century, and is now supplemented by the National Sound Archive. Professor Sir Colin St John Wilson's design has given Londoners a stunning new package of a welcoming, spacious piazza, three public galleries, new public art works, two restaurants, an excellent store and plenty of activities and tours. In all, it is a breakthrough in the British idea of the library. There is nothing fusty about the B.L.; manuscripts and books have been shown to be as exciting as they really are.

Before entering the galleries, go up the steps by the information desk and walk around the floor-to-ceiling central glass shaft to enjoy some of the beautiful bindings of the King's Library, George III's 65,000 volumes gifted by George IV in 1823. The outer walls store the British Library's stamp collection, the world's finest, and you can pull out the vertical trays of stamps to examine specimens more closely.

The John Ritblat Gallery displays more of the Library's treasures and houses the National Sound Archive. Here you can see the various editions of the Magna Carta, Shakespeare's First Folio, and the Gutenberg Bible, and listen to such sounds as rare bird song, or a Winston Churchill speech.

The Workshop of Words, Sounds and Images explains how books and newspapers are created and printed, and how sound is recorded. Finally, the Pearson Gallery of Living Words looks at the diversity of the British Library's collection, in children's books, scientific records, book illustration, and the story of writing.

Behind all this are the reading rooms, where those with passes have access to the whole collection, including every book printed since 1911, when the Copyright Act dictated that one copy of every book, periodical or newspaper published in Great Britain must come to the British Library. Currently, the B.L. has about 150 million items; some 8,000 are added each working day.

## ►►► British Museum *128A2*

*Great Russell Street, WC1 (tel: 020-7636 1555/7580 1788)*
*Underground: Holborn, Tottenham Court Road*
*Open: Mon–Sat 10–5; Sun 2:30–6. Admission free; donation*

This splendid museum, as its elaborate Grecian-style facade declares, is a temple to the arts and achievements of the world's civilizations. The British have always been avid collectors and this museum is the result of over 200 years of erudite collecting, kleptomania, excavation, or downright looting. It is unrivaled in the world for the variety and quality of its treasures.

The museum's origins go back to the "curiosities" that were bequeathed to the nation in 1753 by the wealthy physician, Sir Hans Sloane (see page 91). At the time it consisted largely of natural history specimens but also contained coins and trinkets that formed the nucleus of a historical collection. The museum's holdings grew rapidly as a result of the Napoleonic Wars: the victorious British seized many antiquities, including the Rosetta Stone, that the French had looted in Egypt. At the same time, the celebrated sculptures of the Parthenon and other important Greek works were sent to London by the 7th Earl of Elgin.

The main entrance hall is the place to take your bearings and study plans of the museum. By September 2000, this will be in the Great Court, whose redevelopment has released 40 percent more space for a museum whose 1,200 staff care for more than 4 million objects visited by more than 6 million people every year. Here in the newly roofed, 2-acre central courtyard of the museum, with its former reading room in the middle, visitors will be able to find out all about the museum. There will be on-screen information and images, stores, restaurants, and meeting places. If you pick up a map and choose what you want to see, you can set off to explore well prepared.

The museum covers an area of 13 acres, but some of the top attractions lie close at hand. Head for Room 8 to see if the Elgin Marbles are still in place. The most important of these sculptures is the Parthenon Frieze, carved between

**ASSYRIAN ART**

The rooms in the British Museum devoted to Assyrian art are less well known than the Greek antiquities but no less striking. Room 26 has a huge winged lion that once guarded the palace and temple complex at Nimrud, built around 880 BC, and the theme of the lion hunt features in several narrative friezes. These can be seen in Room 19, featuring sculptures from the throne room at Nimrud, and in Room 17, displaying magnificent carvings from the palace at Nineveh (7th century BC). These latter scenes seem almost modern in their clean, fluid lines, and their naturalistic portrayal of wounded lions writhing in agony.



*The Elgin Marbles*

*A fitting welcome to the world's greatest collection of antiquities: the frieze depicting the* Progress of Civilisation *on the museum's facade*



447 and 432 BC for the Temple of Athena, patroness of Athens. It originally ran around the interior wall of the temple colonnade, and it illustrates the procession that took place in the city every four years as part of a great festival in Athena's honor. The project was financed with money intended for the navy, overseen by the sculptor Phidias, and was just part of a civic plan to beautify Athens. But in the early 19th century, Lord Elgin rescued about half of the original frieze—over 247 feet in length—from the Parthenon ruins. Other parts had been shattered in 1687 when the Parthenon, used as an ammunitions store by occupying Turks, was hit by a shell and all but destroyed.

Two other rooms are worth seeking out nearby. Room 9 is known as the Room of the Caryatid, after the figure of a 5th-century BC maiden, one of a series of columns from the Erectheion in Athens (a shrine to the mythical king Erectheus). Room 12 contains what little survives of one of the Seven Wonders of the Ancient World, brought from Turkey: sculptural fragments from the Mausoleum of Halicarnassus, the great tomb built for Mausolus, Prince of Caria, by his wife in the 4th century BC. Mausolus himself is depicted, and possibly his wife, as well as a battle between the Greeks and Amazons.

The Sainsbury African Galleries, open in late 2000, are also easy to find. They display the British Museum's ethnographic collection.

The British Museum has the richest collections of ancient Egyptian art to be seen outside Cairo, and some of the best objects are displayed in Room 25. Among them is the Rosetta Stone, named for the town near the mouth of the Nile where it was found in 1799. The insignificant-looking slab unlocked the secret of ancient Egyptian hieroglyphs. Its inscription has a Greek translation alongside, allowing scholars to work from the known to decipher the unknown.

Not to be missed among all the other very fine tombs and statues is a naturalistic cat in bronze (wearing ear- and nose-rings) displayed in one of the central cases.

**CURIOSITIES**

Room 50, on the upper floor, holds the perfectly preserved 2,000-year-old body of Lindow Man, nicknamed "Pete Marsh" by the archeologists who found him in a waterlogged peat bog in Cheshire. Rooms 60 and 61 are filled with ancient Egyptian coffins and their contents: not just human mummies but also those of sacred animals—crocodiles, cats, dogs, fish, an ape, an ibex, and even a bull. You can compare the dice, mosaic gaming board, and counters in Room 55 (from ancient Ur, made around 2,600 BC) with the mid-12th-century Lewis chessmen, carved in ivory, in Room 42. Clocks, watches, and musical timepieces are shown in Room 44. Many are still working, and all chime together on the hour.

On the upper floor of the museum, a series of rooms tells the story of Europe and the British Isles from early prehistory to the end of the Middle Ages. Most important archeological treasures unearthed in Britain are displayed here, including some that throw light on the capital's early history. Among them is the superb Battersea Shield (Room 39), a fine example of Celtic art from the 1st century BC. Another is the tombstone of Julius Classicianus, who was the Roman official governing London from AD 61 to 65 (Room 40).

Nearby, the Mildenhall Treasure comprises a complete set of silver embossed tableware made in the 4th century, so magnificent that it must have belonged to a Roman governor or another high official. The finely carved, ivory Lewis Chessmen, found on the Hebridean island of Lewis, were possibly made in Scandinavia during the 12th century, and stand silent testimony to Scandinavia's medieval power.

Best of all is the Sutton Hoo Treasure (Room 41), consisting of bejeweled swords, helmets, buckles, bowls, drinking horns, and a bronze cauldron. They all come from a 7th-century ship burial discovered near Woodbridge in Suffolk, probably that of Redwald, King of the East Angles, and provide ample evidence that the raiders who settled in England during the Saxon period were not the uncouth barbarians of popular imagination, but highly skilled craftsmen.

In total contrast, the H.S.B.C. Money Gallery (Room 68) looks at 2,000 years of Britain's commercial history through something every society needs but often forgets to look at—its coinage.

**THE MUSEUM'S BACK DOOR**

Some of the British Museum's best galleries, covering prints, drawings, maps, and Oriental art, are among the quietest and least visited, because they lie farthest from the main entrance. If you want to concentrate on these you should slip into the museum by the back door, on Montague Place. Upstairs is Room 33, the Joseph Hotung Gallery, a vast room on the first floor which is devoted to Asian art, and ranges from Indian temple sculptures to Chinese grave horses. Some are gently erotic, some serenely mystic. Below is Room 34, the John Addiss Gallery, which displays treasures from all the Islamic world. There is brass from Syria, and jade from India. Look too, for 13th-century astrolabes and globes (both used by astronomers), and hookahs ("hubble-bubble" pipes), encrusted with precious stones.

*This beautiful piece of jewelry, made in the 1st century BC, is just one example of the Celtic craftwork to be found in Room 38*

*Bust of Charles Dickens*



**MEDICINE AND SALVATION**
There are two unusual museums in north Bloomsbury. The Wellcome Institute mounts fascinating science exhibitions, both historical and at the cutting edge of current knowledge (183–193 Euston Road, tel: 020-7611 8888). Nearby, the premises of the Salvationist Publishing & Supplies company has a small museum covering the origins of the Salvation Army, founded in 1878 by the Reverend William Booth to help the poor of London's East End (117–121 Judd Street, tel: 020-7332 0101).

## ▶▶▶ Dickens' House *128B3*

*48 Doughty Street, WC1 (tel: 020-7405 2127)*
*Open: Mon–Sat 10–5. Admission charge*
*Underground: Russell Square*

Charles Dickens (1812–1870), the great 19th-century novelist, is one of that handful of writers who have shaped and molded our vision of London. His descriptions of the fogbound haunts of torpid lawyers, of the criminal underworld of Fagin and his thieves, or the cramped and crooked home of Little Nell, the Old Curiosity Shop (see page 155), are as vivid now as they were 150 years ago. It only takes a little imagination to conjure up visions of Dickensian London as you wander the city's streets, and a visit to the house where Dickens wrote allows you to pursue the illusion further.

The house is the only surviving London home out of several in which Dickens lived and worked. He moved here in 1837, a year after his marriage to Catherine Hogarth. By 1839, such was Dickens's growing wealth that the family was able to move on to 1 Devonshire Terrace (since demolished), a more impressive house overlooking Regent's Park. In the time that Dickens lived here he was characteristically prolific: he completed the *Pickwick Papers,* wrote *Oliver Twist* and *Nicholas Nickleby,* and began *Barnaby Rudge* all in under three years. At the same time, his increasing fame enabled him to throw off his pseudonym, Boz.

His house, which was bought by the Dickens Fellowship in 1924, retains the heavy Victorian color scheme and the desk and chair where Dickens wrote surrounded by the hustle and bustle of family life (he possessed the

*The house where Dickens wrote* Oliver Twist

remarkable gift of being able to write even with the distractions of noise, visitors, and conversation all around him). Other Dickens memorabilia on display include first editions of his work, the copies he used for his public readings, marked with cues for gestures and intonation, and Lionel Bart's score for his musical version of *Oliver Twist*. A good store sells Dickens's work.

### ▶ London Canal Museum *182B1*

*King's Cross Basin, New Wharf Road, N1 (tel: 020-7713 0836)*
*Open: Tue–Sun 10–4:30. Admission charge*
*Underground: King's Cross*

A small but evocative collection housed in a Victorian warehouse pays tribute to one of the city's hidden (and so far wasted) assets: the extensive canal network that runs all the way around north London, and links the capital to the industrial cities of the Midlands, such as Birmingham, Leicester, and Nottingham. Some parts of the canal network—around Little Venice, Regent's Park, and Camden Lock—are very picturesque and attract many visitors. This museum, by contrast, is located in the rather scruffy area at the rear of King's Cross station, which is slowly being made more attractive by the local community. The warehouse was built around 1850 by Carlo Gatti, an Italian immigrant who made his fortune importing ice from Norway and storing it here in deep wells. Exhibits tell the story of Gatti and canal life. Developers plan to build a "model city of the future" in this area.

While the haggling goes on, local community groups, working with the London Wildlife Trust, have established a flourishing nature reserve at Camley Street, just west of the Canal Museum. The reserve (*Open* daily in summer except Fri) has attracted birds, butterflies, reptiles, and self-sown wildflowers. Its backdrop is formed by the brightly painted King's Cross gasholders, which have been declared listed buildings and are therefore protected from alteration or demolition.

**TRAIN STATIONS**
Euston, St. Pancras, and King's Cross stations stand almost side by side along the northern edge of Euston Road, each built in the 19th century by the independent railway companies that competed with each other until they were brought together to form British Rail. (Recently history has been reversed, with many lines sold back to the private sector.) Euston was wholly rebuilt in the 1960s; all that survives of the terminus are two lodge houses, part of the original formal entrance to the station. St. Pancras, by contrast, survives in its original form and is fronted by the Grand Midland Hotel, a magnificent monument of neo-Gothic architecture bristling with towers and spires, built in 1868–1872 by George Gilbert Scott. Long empty and disused, it is now under restoration. King's Cross is a much more utilitarian building, designed by Lewis Cubbitt and built in 1851–1852.

*Ornate barges on Little Venice canal*

*Sometimes it seems that there is no building or stretch of street in London that has not witnessed some historic event or been the home of an eminent person. Statues abound and hundreds of buildings bear blue commemorative plaques. Tracking these down can reveal a few interesting surprises—people you never knew lived in the city at all, for example—such as the Italian artist Canaletto (at 41 Beak Street) or the U.S. President John F. Kennedy (at 14 Prince's Gate).*

**BLUE PLAQUES**
The idea of placing plaques on the houses or sites where distinguished people once lived was devised in 1866 by William Ewart; the scheme was originally run by the Royal Society of Arts, then by the Greater London Council. The first was placed on the birthplace of Lord Byron in Holles Street. The person commemorated by a blue plaque must have been dead for over 20 years and born more than 100 years ago. He or she must also have made "some important contribution to human welfare or happiness."



*Charlie Chaplin in Leicester Square, right*

In total, London has more than 1,700 statues and 400 blue plaques, originally chocolate-brown but now standardized to a present-day Wedgwood blue with white lettering (see panel).

**Alfred the Great** In front of Holy Trinity Church (now the Henry Wood Hall) in Trinity Church Square (SE1) is a 14th-century statue of the 9th-century King of England; this is London's oldest commemorative statue.

**David Ben-Gurion** Israel's first prime minister lived at 75 Warrington Crescent, Maida Vale (W9).

**Simon Bolivar** The Latin-American revolutionary is commemorated by Hugo Daini's 1974 statue in Belgrave Square (SW1).

**Boudicca (Boadicea)** The rebellious queen of the Iceni tribe, who burned down Roman London in AD 60, is depicted in a stirring bronze statue by Thomas Thornycroft on Westminster Bridge (west end).

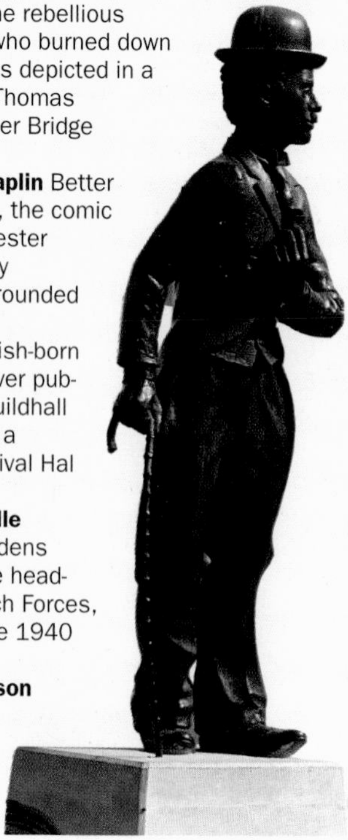

**Sir Charles Spencer Chaplin** Better known as Charlie Chaplin, the comic star, has a statue in Leicester Square by John Doubleday (1987), appropriately surrounded by movie theaters.

**Frédéric Chopin** The Polish-born composer gave his last ever public concert at London's Guildhall and is commemorated by a statue alongside the Festival Hal on the South Bank.

**General Charles de Gaulle** A plaque at 4 Carlton Gardens declares that this was the headquarters of the Free French Forces, led by de Gaulle from June 1940 until the end of the war.

**Elizabeth Garrett Anderson** The first woman ever to qualify as a doctor in Britain had her home at 20 Upper Berkeley Street.

*Captain Robert Scott, Antarctic explorer*

**Wolfgang Amadeus Mozart** The child prodigy composed his first symphony at 180 Ebury Street.

**Florence Nightingale** A statue of the pioneer of nursing, who was christened "the lady with the lamp" by her soldier patients, is part of the Crimean Memorial on Waterloo Place; the house in which she lived and died is at 10 South Street (off Park Lane).

**Captain Robert Scott** Scott of the Antarctic set off for his last fateful expedition from his house at 56 Oakley Street, Chelsea. Scott is portrayed, wearing the clothes he wore for the trip, in a bronze statue made by his widow, Lady Scott, in Waterloo Place.

**Princess Pocahontas** The Algonquin Indian princess, who saved the life of Captain John Smith in 1602, is remembered with a bronze statue in Red Lion Square (off Holborn). She married John Rolfe, came to England in 1614, and was a great success at the Jacobean Court, but lacked immunity to western diseases and died in 1617, aged 22.

**Bertrand Russell** Also in Red Lion Square is a bust of the philosopher, who lectured in nearby Conway Hall.

**Sun Yat Sen** The father of Chinese republicanism, who led the Kuomintang to overthrow the Qing dynasty in 1911, spent his time in exile in a house on the site of 4 Gray's Inn Place.

**Oscar Wilde** Maggie Hambling's statue, opposite Charing Cross station, unveiled in 1998, confirms the Irish writer's long-awaited reacceptance.

**Voltaire** A plaque recalls the fact that the writer and philosopher whose ideas inspired the Enlightenment once lodged at a house on the site of 10 Maiden Lane, in Covent Garden.

**POSTMAN'S PARK**
The churchyard of St. Botolph's Church, Aldersgate, is locally known as Postman's Park, since this is where workers from the nearby Postal Sorting Office come to enjoy their lunchtime sandwiches. The park was laid out in 1900 as a national memorial to ordinary men and women whose heroic deeds might otherwise have been forgotten. A long wall contains memorial plaques telling the stories of just a few of those people. One records that Alice Ayres, a laborer's daughter, gave her own life to save three children from a burning house; another commemorates Thomas Simpson, who died of exhaustion in January 1885, having rescued scores of skaters from drowning when the ice broke at Highgate Ponds. Michael Ayrton's symbolic sculpture, the *Minotaur*, has recently been acquired for the park.

**CORAM'S FIELDS**
The Thomas Coram Foundation fronts onto Coram's Fields, a 7½-acre garden full of trees where the children of the Foundling Hospital used to play until the institution moved to more rural premises in Berkhamsted in the 1920s. The garden is entered by the original gates of 1752, and a sign warns that no adult may visit the gardens unless accompanied by a child. Immediately south is the delightful Lamb's Conduit Street, a traffic-free precinct with many stores, pubs, and restaurants. The Lamb (No. 94) is an unspoiled Victorian pub with original woodwork and glass screens and photographs of music-hall stars on the walls, and The Sun (No. 63) stocks a great range of beers made by small independent breweries.



### ►►► Percival David Foundation of Chinese Art — *128B2*

*53 Gordon Square, WC1 (tel: 020-7387 3909)*
*Open: Mon–Fri 10:30–5. Admission free; donations*
*Underground: Russell Square*

One of London's most wonderful small museums lurks in an anonymous Bloomsbury terraced house. It is devoted to a permanent exhibition of Chinese ceramics which date from the Sung (10th century) to the Qing (19th century) dynasties and are consumate in their craftmanship. The collection of more than 1,500 pieces was assembled by Sir Percival David (1892–1964) and is the finest outside China. Very early pieces include a Tang dynasty hare. Ru and Guan pieces are especially fine, as are the two David vases made in the 14th century. In all, this is a feast of the finest craftsmanship whose perfect shapes and rich colors create a serenity that transports the visitor far from the teeming city.

### ► Petrie Museum of Egyptian Archaeology — *128B1*

*Department of Egyptology, University College, London, Malet Place, WC1 (tel: 020-7387 7050)*
*Open: Mon–Fri during university termtime 10–noon, 1:15–5. Admission free*
*Underground: Goodge Street, Russell Square, Euston*

The Petrie Museum of Egyptian Archaeology, well worth the effort of finding, comprises Egyptian antiquities collected by Amelia Edwards and Sir Flinders Petrie (1853–1942). Its sequence of Predynastic pottery provided the means of dating Egyptian ceramic styles. In the rows of traditional glass cabinets, curious visitors can seek out charming displays of cat figures, notable relief carvings and a child's linen dress dating, incredibly, from around 2800 BC. Other exhibits include a burial pot complete with skeleton inside, and a mummy with eyebrows and lashes still intact.

*Pollock's toy theaters as once sold by Benjamin Pollock; "a penny plain, twopence coloured"*

### ►► Pollock's Toy Museum *128A1*

*1 Scala Street, W1 (tel: 020-7636 3452)*
*Open: Mon–Sat 10–5. Admission charge*
*Underground: Goodge Street*
Robert Louis Stevenson wrote: "If you love art, folly, or the bright eyes of children, speed to Pollock's." He was referring to the store (since gone) where Benjamin Pollock sold printed sheets that Victorian and Edwardian children stuck to wood or cardboard to create miniature theaters. This small museum (upstairs), with a store below, is crammed with Pollock's theaters, as well as other toys, some from the 18th century. The museum is designed for children, with eye-level displays. Reproductions of toys from around the world are sold.

*Captain Thomas Coram, granted a royal charter in 1739 to care for London's abandoned street children (foundlings)*

### ►► Thomas Coram Foundation *128B3*

*40 Brunswick Square, WC1 (tel: 020-7278 2424)*
*Currently rebuilding; open by appointment only*
*Underground: Russell Square*
The Thomas Coram Foundation (or Foundling Hospital) was set up to provide shelter and an education for orphaned and abandoned children. Its founder was the remarkable Captain Thomas Coram, shipbuilder and master mariner, who played an important role in the colonization of Massachusetts, Georgia, and Nova Scotia. Returning to London in 1732, he was appalled by the sight of abandoned children and infants "left to die on dung hills." He devoted the remainder of his life to working on their behalf, establishing the Foundling Hospital. George II was a patron, Handel gave a copy of *The Messiah* score, and Hogarth, Gainsborough, Reynolds and others gave pictures. Many of the works are on charitable themes and are now displayed in the present, 1930s building whose governors' courtroom is a replica of the original.



**GREAT ORMOND STREET HOSPITAL**

In 1851, philanthropist Dr. Charles West established London's first Hospital for Sick Children in Great Ormond Street. He was, quite rightly, appalled by the child-mortality rate in 19th-century London (of 50,000 deaths recorded annually in the city, 21,000 were children under 10). The hospital was set up to remedy the situation and still receives an important part of its income from the legacy of writer Sir James Barrie. In 1929 Barrie made a gift of the copyright of *Peter Pan* to the hospital, which benefits from royalties every time the book is sold or the play performed on film, stage, television, or radio. Although the royalties expired in 1987, 50 years after Barrie's death, a special Act of Parliament was passed in the following year to ensure that the hospital would continue to benefit from them in perpetuity. Of the original Victorian hospital buildings, the chapel survives, decorated with mosaics and touching memorials.

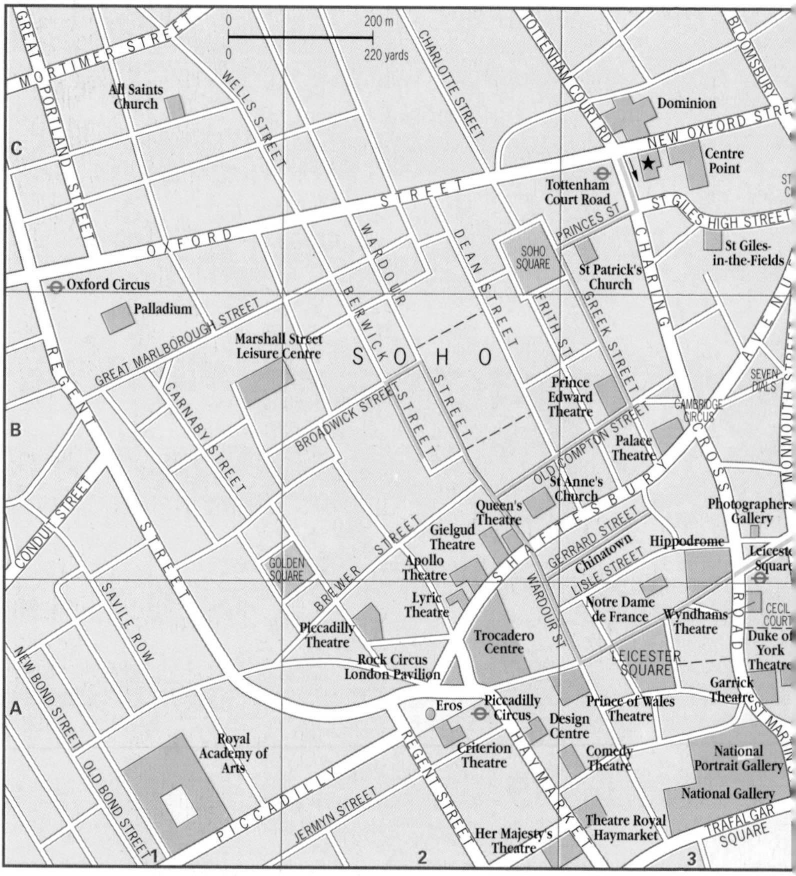

*A corner of London's Chinatown*

**SOHO AND COVENT GARDEN** Until the 1970s, Soho was a byword for sex clubs and sleaze, and Covent Garden was the run-down haunt of vegetable and flower traders. When the wholesale market moved to Nine Elms in 1974, the local community ensured that the market halls were converted into small stores and stalls. They still watch over the street performers and sidewalk cafés in the pedestrianized Piazza. Meanwhile Soho was cleaned up and blossomed, too, and the large Chinatown quarter at its heart was turned into a pedestrian district. Today, Soho is once again the heart of London nightlife, where people meet in large bars, eat in the many restaurants, dance the night away in clubs and, in summer, simply promenade.

**SOHO AND COVENT GARDEN WALK** From Tottenham Court Road tube station, walk south down Charing Cross Road. Off to the right is pretty **Soho Square**, where office workers from the film, advertising, and design companies of nearby Dean Street and Wardour Street come to eat lunchtime sandwiches. Executives are more likely to be consuming expense-account lunches in the restaurants of **Greek Street**, which leads southward out of the square.

Follow Greek Street to **Old Compton Street**, another gourmets' haven. Turn right at the end of Old Compton

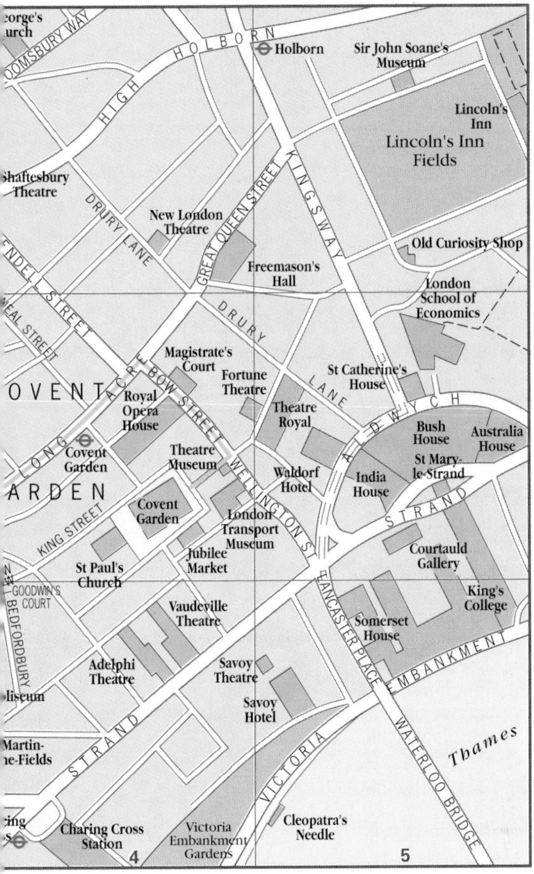


# Soho and Covent Garden

Street on Wardour Street, then take the third left into Broadwick Street for **Berwick Street market**, the best in central London for fresh fruit and vegetables.

To the left at the end of Old Compton Street, Wardour Street continues south of Shaftesbury Avenue and leads to **Gerrard Street**, the heart of London's Chinatown. Chinese restaurants line Wardour Street, which leads to the movie theaters of **Leicester Square**. The mechanical clock on the facade of the **Swiss Centre** is a popular attraction when it performs on the hour.

From Leicester Square, cross Charing Cross Road into Long Acre, Covent Garden's main thoroughfare. The second right turn is **Bow Street**. It was from here that the Bow Street Runners, London's prototype police force, operated in the early 19th century. Across the street, the **Royal Opera House** is home to the Royal Opera, Royal Ballet and the Chorus and Orchestra of the Royal Opera House. Dixon Jones BDP are the architects who have transformed not just the 1858 theater—where working conditions had improved little since that time—but added new and neighboring buildings as well, to create one of the world's greatest modern lyric theaters (see page 146). Sidewalk views of the old and new buildings from Bow Street and Covent Garden Piazza are stunning.

## ▶▶▶ REGION HIGHLIGHTS


**Covent Garden Central Market** *page 142*

**London Transport Museum** *page 146*

**Neal Street and Neal's Yard** *page 143*

**Royal Opera House** *page 146*

**Theatre Museum** *page 147*

*Covent Garden is a relatively peaceful oasis in the heart of London. The central Piazza and its side streets are pedestrian zones, so people are free to roam without the noise, pollution, and danger of traffic. The many stores and market stalls are small, personal, and sell a wide range of interesting products, from buttons and bows to books and works of art.*

**SEVEN DIALS**
Seven Dials stands at the junction of seven streets in a corner of Covent Garden that was once the haunt of prostitutes and thieves. A Doric pillar erected here in 1694, topped by seven sundials, was knocked down in 1773 because of a rumor that a large sum of money was buried at its base. It was later rebuilt on the green at Weybridge in Surrey. A replica, paid for by local residents and carved by trainee masons, was unveiled in 1989. It actually has only six sundials; the seventh is the column itself, which casts its shadow onto the pavement, where the hours are marked by iron posts.

The focal point of Covent Garden is the Central Market. This elegant building, designed by Charles Fowler, was completed in the 1830s, although the iron-and-glass roof over the central arcade was added in the 1870s. The wholesale fruit and vegetable market that operated here closed in 1974 and moved to Nine Elms, in south London. The market building was then converted to provide space for the small specialty stores and cafés that now line the arcade, itself filled with market stalls selling antiques, crafts, toys, jewelry, and clothing. The other Victorian market halls lining the Piazza have also enjoyed new leases: the London Transport Museum is in the old Flower Market, as is the Theatre Museum; Floral Hall is the spectacular foyer of the rebuilt Royal Opera House. The **Punch and Judy** pub, on the southwestern corner of the market, opened in 1980, but its name is a reminder that the first Punch and Judy puppet show was performed in the square below on May 9, 1662—Samuel Pepys was one of those who came to watch the antics of Pietro Gimonde's marionettes. Mr. Punch's birthday is still celebrated on the second Sunday in May, as part of the Covent Garden May Fayre festival.

Entertainment takes place here all week from 10 AM to dusk. The space in front of St. Paul's Church is used by all kinds of street performers—clowns, fire-eaters, musicians, acrobats. The church railings frame the entrance to the Victorian public rest rooms built below the square, an attraction in their own right.

**St. Paul's Church** is the oldest surviving building on the square. It was built by Inigo Jones in the 1630s, inspired by the cathedral in Livorno, Tuscany, which Jones had helped to design as an apprentice to the Renaissance architect Buontalenti. His client, the Earl of Bedford, was a low churchman, and told Jones to make the church as simple as a barn. Jones is said to have replied: "You shall have the handsomest barn in England." St. Paul's is known as "the Actors' Church" because, located near the Theatre Royal, Drury Lane, and the Royal Opera House, it is much frequented by playwrights, performers, and impresarios. Ellen Terry, Charlie Chaplin, Vivien Leigh, and Noel Coward are buried here or commemorated on the wall plaques.

To the north of Long Acre, Covent Garden's main thoroughfare, lies a maze of little streets. Some are lined with warehouses once used to store fruit and vegetables, now converted to dance studios, such as **Pineapple Dance Studios** (7 Langley Street), art galleries, and specialty

stores such as the **Kite Shop**, the **Bead Shop**, the **Astrology Shop**, and the **Comic Showcase**, all on Neal Street. Turn left off Neal Street onto Short's Gardens and look above the Neal's Yard Wholefood Warehouse to see a fascinating water clock. Close by at No.17 is Neal's Yard Dairy, one of England's best dairy shops, selling cheeses made by small producers all over Britain and Ireland. Just around the corner (look for the narrow passageway) is Neal's Yard, a wholefood haven set in a small pretty courtyard, festooned with windowboxes. This is one of London's most charming, bohemian spots and on a sunny day it is a joy to sit outside at one of the Yard's cheap-and-cheerful cafés, and escape the bustle and traffic. Excellent snacks and meals (eat in or take out) are served at Neal's Yard Bakery and Dining Room, and World Food Café, where photographer Chris Caldicott's images of his worldwide travels complement the food.

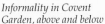

*Informality in Covent Garden, above and below*

**PUBS AND CAFÉS**
Covent Garden has scores of pubs and sidewalk cafés, offering a cosmopolitan range. Nothing could be more English than the Lamb and Flag (33 Rose Street), a 300-year-old pub serving homemade food, where you are in constant danger of banging your head on the low ceiling beams. That is not why the pub was once known as the Bucket of Blood; bare-knuckle boxing bouts once took place in the upstairs rooms. The Rock Garden, on the Piazza, serves American burgers and ribs, and there is live music in the converted banana warehouse every night. The informal Calabash (38 King Street) restaurant is one of a handful in London specializing in African food.

*Book lovers should have little trouble keeping themselves occupied in the West End of London. For a feast of good bookstores—eccentric, specialist, antiquarian—head straight for Charing Cross Road. But beware of wasting too much time in a fruitless search for No. 84. Helene Hanff's book* 84 Charing Cross Road *was based on her correspondence with the owners and staff of Mark's and Co.'s secondhand bookstore—but the original store is no more.*



**OTHER SPECIALIST BOOKSTORES**
Books for Cooks, 4 Blenheim Crescent, Notting Hill, is the largest store in the world devoted exclusively to the culinary arts of every nation. You may also find rare or out-of-print editions among its range of secondhand stock. A short step away is the Travel Bookshop (1–3 Blenheim Crescent), which inspired the setting for the movie *Notting Hill*, selling antiquarian and secondhand titles, as well as all the latest travel literature and practical guides. Another great travel bookstore is Daunt Books for Travellers (83 Marylebone High Street). The only bookstore devoted to publications on London is in the City, at Guildhall (Gresham Street); others with an especially good stock on London include Selfridges (in the basement) and Hatchards. For books and magazines in European languages other than English, Grant & Cutler (55–57 Great Marlborough Street), is the place to go; if they don't have what you want, try the European Bookstore (5 Warwick Street): both stores stock titles from the main French, Italian, Spanish, German, and Portuguese publishing houses.

One of the most enjoyable ways of spending a wet London afternoon is by browsing in a bookstore, and of all the bookstores, **Hatchards** is one of the most pleasant in which to while away a few hours—if the books you buy are too heavy to carry, they can be mailed home. John Hatchard opened his shop in 1797 and made it so inviting that Gladstone, Macaulay and other customers would spend mornings here in front of the fire, reading newspapers and new books. Today, the well-informed staff can, between them, advise usefully on almost any subject.

Nearby, **Waterstones**' Piccadilly store is the flagship of its chain, a book emporium filling what was the upscale, long-established Simpson's fashion store. Here and at **Books etc**., opposite, the in-house cafés transform book-buying into a leisurely experience. Both chains have further stores dotted about central London. This new approach to book-buying is well-established at **Borders** on Oxford Street, whose café and foreign newspapers make it an international meeting place.

Near here, down Charing Cross Road, you will find stores with specific themes. **Murder One** (No. 71), as its name suggests, has a huge stock of crime and detective stories. **Zwemmers** (Nos. 7 and 80) sells books on art, architecture, film, advertising, and design. There is scarcely an art book published that they do not stock, although the prices can be as staggering as the sheer weight of some of the

*Secondhand book bargains on sale in Cecil Court*

*Art books in Charing Cross Road*



beautifully bound and printed volumes. Close by on Caxton Walk (94–96 Charing Cross Road) is **Sportspages**, Britain's best sports bookstore. Little stores in between sell secondhand and antiquarian volumes. A word of warning: pickpockets operate here—they know how easy it is to relieve preoccupied browsers of their wallets or purses.

There is one particularly good enclave of antiquarian bookstores on Cecil Court (the narrow alley next to 24 Charing Cross Road, see panel, page 146). From here you can continue up to New Row and the entrance to another branch of Waterstones, this one with a very large and well-organized stock, as well as a good children's section.

The back door opens onto Garrick Street where, across the road in Floral Street, you can go in the back door of **Stanfords**. In this store, one of the best for travel books, maps, and navigational charts, you are quite likely to stumble across well-known explorers and travelers either signing copies of their latest books or buying maps for the next trip. Almost next door, on Long Acre, the clientele at **Dillons Arts Bookshop** is made up of artists, architects, and designers. Dillons has a much bigger store with a vast general stock at 82 Gower Street (the nearest tube station is Goodge Street), worth seeking out if you have not yet found the right book.

**A GOOD READ ON LONDON**

For hard information, the weekly *Time Out* magazine provides the most comprehensive listing of all that is going on in London—although it may take time to find your way round it, and its reviewers may not share your opinions. To find views that perhaps have more in common with your own, read the quality newspapers and the *Evening Standard;* first nights of major shows will be reviewed within a day or two of opening. Time Out also publishes *Kids Out* (monthly) and *Time Out Eating & Drinking Guide* (annually).

Many visitors to London like to read novels set in the city. To evoke past history, try some Dickens, Thackeray, Galsworthy, Conrad, P.G. Wodehouse, Virginia Woolf and Peter Ackroyd; for more modern fiction, there are Martin Amis, Julian Barnes Michael Moorcock and Iain Sinclair. London diaries abound, the most notable by James Boswell, Samuel Pepys, John Evelyn, Charles Lamb, Norman Collins, and Cecil Beaton.

*London buses: you wait for ages then three come at once!*



**THE COURTS OF COVENT GARDEN**

Although called "courts," the little lanes that run down from Covent Garden to Charing Cross Road are no more than narrow alleyways, with many a twist and bend where you would have risked a mugging in 18th- and 19th-century London. One example is Goodwin's Court, linking Bedfordbury to St. Martin's Lane, with a row of restored 17th-century houses on one side. Attractive as they look now, this and other courts were known as rookeries because of the sheer number of people who lived in their squalid ghettos. Straight across St. Martin's Lane is Cecil Court, now an enclave of excellent secondhand bookstores where you can buy rare first editions, maps, prints, and illustrated children's books. Cecil Court runs parallel to St. Martin's Court, the home of Sheekey's Restaurant and Oyster Bar, where diners come to enjoy fish dishes in a setting that has scarcely changed since 1892, when the restaurant opened.

### ▶▶▶ London Transport Museum *141B4*

*39 Wellington Street, WC2 (tel: 020-7379 6344)*
*Open: Mon–Thu, Sat, Sun 10–6, Fri 11–6. Admission charge*
*Underground: Covent Garden*

Housed in the old Flower Market (built in 1870), this is a far more enthralling museum than its title suggests. Children can climb aboard the historical buses, drive the underground train simulator, play on the new Fun Bus, and get involved in one of the special events (story telling, model making, face painting, etc.). Adults can meanwhile contemplate the sheer immensity and complexity of London's public transit system. Over 6 million passengers a day are carried on bus, train, and underground journeys that encompass more than 500,000 miles.

### ▶▶▶ Royal Opera House *141B4*

*Bow Street, WC2 (tel: 020-7240 1200/7304 4000)*
*Foyer and Amphitheatre Bar open by day. Admission free by day; admission by theater ticket in the evening*
*Underground: Covent Garden*

A combination of restoration, rebuilding and building from scratch by the architects Dixon Jones and B.D.P. has produced central London's most exciting new arts theater. The Royal Opera, Royal Ballet, and the Chorus and Orchestra of the Royal Opera House now present high-quality programs in modern theaters to wider audiences. The complex has three parts. There is the restored original theater, designed in 1858 by E.M. Barry and decorated with Flaxman's reliefs, which survive from an earlier building that burnt down. The 19th-century Floral Hall, built as a flower market and subsequently used for storing scenery, is now a spectacular foyer. An entirely new building houses more public areas, a rehearsal studio and scenery storage. The public can enjoy up to three performances a day in the main theater, and attend concerts and educational events in the Studio Theatre, and performances and workshops in the Studio Upstairs. Finally, a pedestrian walkway connects Bow Street to the Piazza.

### ▶▶▶ Theatre Museum *141B4*

*Tavistock Street, WC2 (tel: 020-7836 7891/2330)*
*Open: Tue–Sun 11–7. Admission charge*
*Underground: Covent Garden*

This splendid museum is an exhibition of all the major performing arts and really works hard to involve visitors (especially children) in the magic of the theater, with a program of activities and special exhibitions covering everything from makeup demonstrations (get yourself a hideous scar!) to dressing up in theatrical costumes. Permanent displays trace the history of the stage since the 17th century using models, props, and costumes, bringing the subject right up to date with a look at the glamorous world of rock music. The collection is arranged chronologically—one of its oldest exhibits is Hindu Cups, an ancient version of the card trick "Find the Lady," which is believed to be the earliest sleight of hand trick, dating back over 3,500 years. In a more conventional theatrical vein you come face to face with Hamlet, the great actors who have starred in the role, their costumes and historic set designs. You can see the dressing table where the great 18th-century actress, Sarah Siddons, used to apply her makeup before entrancing audiences in the role of Lady Macbeth, or admire Noel Coward's crimson monogrammed dressing gown and slippers. Other striking exhibits include the costumes worn by dancers in the innovative ballets choreographed by Diaghilev, and the wheelbarrow that was used by the famous acrobat Blondin in his daring tightrope acts. The museum also has a well-stocked shop. You can buy tickets for shows at all the main London theaters from the booking (reservations) office in the entrance hall.

**ELIZA DOOLITTLE AND NELL GWYN**

Two of the best-known names associated with Covent Garden both began as street traders. The Cockney heroine of Shaw's play *Pygmalion* (and of the musical based on it, *My Fair Lady*, by Alan Jay Lerner and Frederick Loewe) was Eliza Doolittle, a flower trader. The play opens with Eliza selling violets to pedestrians sheltering from the rain under the portico of St. Paul's Church. Eliza was, of course, a fictional creation, whereas Nell Gwyn really did exist, even if the events of her rags-to-riches life sound like a fairy tale. She started her career selling oranges to the patrons of the Theatre Royal, Drury Lane, then became an actress herself, making her stage debut in the same theater in Dryden's play *The Indian Queen* in 1665. Although, by some accounts, not a greatly gifted actress, she succeeded in charming King Charles II, becoming his mistress and bearing several of his children, one of whom was made Duke of St. Albans by the King. Her portrait can be seen in the National Portrait Gallery.

*Behind the scenes at the Theatre Museum*

*Some 40 theaters are packed into the area of London known as the West End, consisting of the Haymarket, St. Martin's Lane, Shaftesbury Avenue, Charing Cross Road, and the Strand. This area floods with life after dark, as the audiences arrive to enjoy the illuminated facades, glittering interiors, and intimate atmospheres of its Victorian and Edwardian theaters.*



London theater has a clear structure. There are the state-subsidized theaters: the Royal National Theatre (three stages, plays and musicals), the Royal Shakespeare Company at the Barbican (two stages, plays and musicals), the Coliseum (opera and ballet), and the Royal Opera House (three stages; opera, ballet and related events). Then there are the commercial theaters, located mostly in the West End, stretching from Aldwych to Piccadilly Circus (popular plays and musicals); Shakespeare's Globe is also a commerical theater. Standing apart from these are the more innovative, avant-garde theaters, which are nonetheless commercial, including the Almeida, Royal Court, Riverside Studios and Donmar Warehouse. This exciting theater is further explored in the small fringe theaters dotted around London; they include the Bush, Hampstead, Greenwich, King's Head, and the Old Red Lion, whose successful shows sometimes transfer to West End theaters.

To find out what's hot, consult the critical reviews in the daily newspapers; for a comprehensive listing refer to *Time Out*. To buy seats, either telephone the theater direct, or use a reliable agency such as Ticketmaster (tel: 020-7344 4444) or First Call (tel: 020-7497 9977); check surcharges. It is best to avoid all ticket touts; if desperate for specific tickets, try Harrods' ticket agency (tel: 020-7730 1234) who almost never fail, even if the surcharge is high. Also, some theaters (such as the R.N.T. and R.S.C.) keep some tickets back for sale on the day of

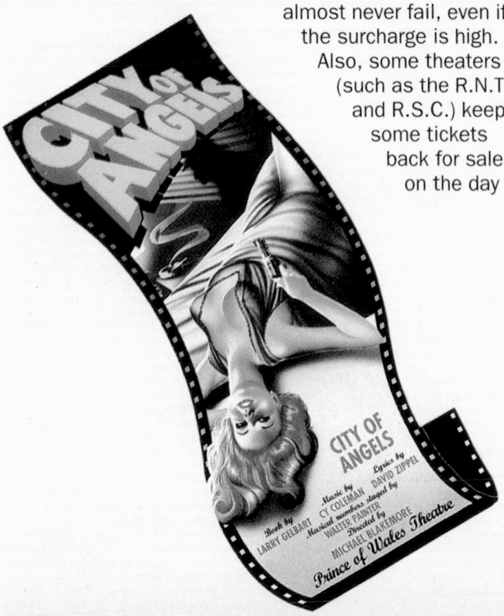

CITY OF ANGELS
CITY OF ANGELS
Book by LARRY GELBART
Music by CY COLEMAN
Lyrics by DAVID ZIPPEL
Musical numbers staged by WALTER PAINTER
Directed by MICHAEL BLAKEMORE
Prince of Wales Theatre


**REVIVED AND NEW THEATERS**
London may seem to have enough theaters, yet there are often new ones opening. Some are renovations of fine old theaters. Andrew Lloyd Webber picked up The Palace Theatre and returned Collcutt and Holloway's 1888–1889 extravaganza of gilding, marble, alabaster, and Doulton terra-cotta to its original sumptuousness. The Old Vic, originally built in 1816–1818 and once home to the National Theatre under Laurence Olivier, had its interior rebuilt in 1982. The Savoy Theatre, built in the 1880s to stage Gilbert and Sullivan operas, then refurbished in dramatic art deco in the 1920s by Basil Ionides and Frak Tugwell, was painstakingly rebuilt after a fire gutted it in 1990. In the East End, where music halls rocked to full audiences until movies killed them off in the 1930s, Franck Matcham's Hackney Empire and Theatre Royal Stratford East have re-opened for music and theater. Meanwhile, impresario Sally Greene and others have rescued Richmond Theatre, The Criterion Theatre, and are currently reviving Collin's Music Hall in Islington—where the Almeida Theatre was created in a disused literary institute, and Sadler's Wells was entirely rebuilt in the late 1990s.

performance. Matinee tickets are often easier to obtain. For half-price tickets, go to the Society of London Theatres' ticket booth on Leicester Square where tickets for some West End theaters are sold on the day of performance (*Open* Mon-Sat 2:30–6:30, on matinee days noon–6:30; cash only, four ticket maximum, small service charge). Beware of touts around the line.

**Historic theaters** The Puritans banned theaters from London in 1574, when Bankside, outside the city's precincts, became the entertainment center and the Globe, Rose and Swan were built. Thus, London's oldest theater is the **Theatre Royal, Drury Lane,** founded in 1663 after Charles II's restoration for Thomas Killigrew and The King's Servants. This and one other in Lincoln's Inn Fields were London's only legal theaters and theater companies until the great Victorian expansion of the 1840s—all others could be closed at a moment's notice. Rebuilt several times, David Garrick revived almost forgotten Shakespeare plays here in the 18th century. **Theatre Royal, Haymarket,** first built in 1720, was where Henry Fielding's crude satires caused the theater to be closed and the Lord Chamberlain's powers of censorship to be introduced in 1737, only finally lifted in 1968. Here, in the 1880s, J. G. Phipps built London's first proscenium (picture-frame) stage and converted the pit into the stalls. Manager Herbert Beerbohm Tree staged Oscar Wilde's *An Ideal Husband* here in 1895 before leaving to run **Her Majesty's Theatre** opposite, with huge success. This theater, which was founded in 1705 by architect-playwright John Vanbrugh, staged Handel's oratorios and operas for 40 years. Today, Andrew Lloyd Webber's *Phantom of the Opera* has played here since 1986.

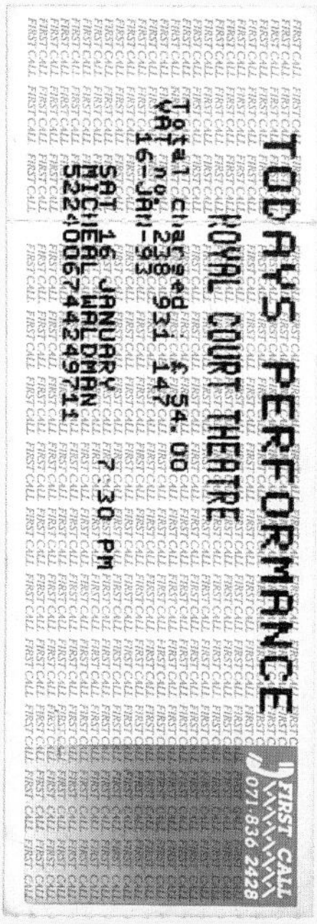


**ANDREW LLOYD WEBBER**

Andrew Lloyd Webber, the composer of several hit musicals, is one of Britain's most important economic assets. His productions attract so many visitors to Britain, who in turn spend money on hotels and restaurants, that he is single-handedly responsible for a large chunk of Britain's foreign currency earnings. *Cats*, which opened in 1981, is the longest-running musical in theater history, and other hits, such as *The Phantom of the Opera*, *Aspects of Love*, and *Sunset Boulevard*, are rarely off the stage. The secret of Lloyd Webber's success is to write tunes that, instead of sounding new, are instantly familiar. The dividing line between what is and is not genuinely original music is very thin. When Lloyd Webber composed the theme tune for the 1992 Barcelona Olympics he hired lawyers and researchers to ensure that it did not infringe any existing copyright—in other words, to check that he had not subconsciously copied someone else's work.

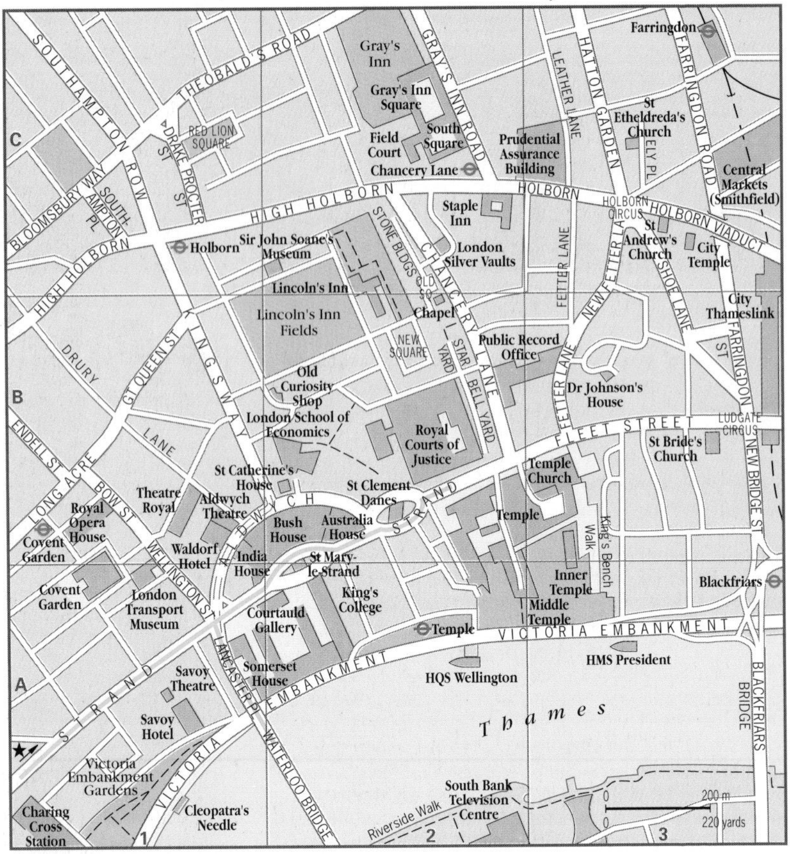

*Above: Silver dragons on the City of London's coat of arms*
*Opposite: St.-Mary-le-Strand*

**HOLBORN AND THE STRAND** Holborn and the Strand form the two main routes linking the City to the West End. The character of this district is heavily influenced by the medieval Inns of Court, with their collegiate buildings and noble open spaces providing a haven of tranquility a short step away from some of London's busiest thoroughfares. The west end of the Strand is dominated by Charing Cross station, where trains disgorge well over 100,000 commuters into the city every day. The Strand's east end meets Aldwych, where half-a-dozen theaters stand near some of London's most luxurious hotels—the Savoy, the Waldorf Meridien, Number One Aldwych. Here, too, is revived, palatial Somerset House.

**HOLBORN AND THE STRAND WALK** This route starts at Charing Cross station, which was opened in 1864 and is fronted by the Renaissance-style **Charing Cross Hotel**. Behind it, all is new, however: the station building, with its shopping malls and offices, was rebuilt in postmodernist style in 1990–1991.

Turn right outside the station and walk along **the Strand**. With the coming of the railway, many of the Strand's older riverside mansions were demolished to make way for palatial hotels. One of these is the **Savoy**, near the end of the Strand on the right. The epitome of luxury, it was completed in 1889 by Richard D'Oyly Carte, the impresario who produced the operettas of Gilbert and Sullivan. A striking feature is the hotel's stainless steel art-deco frontage, designed by Basil Ionides. D'Oyly Carte's Savoy Theatre, designed by Ionides and Tugwell in 1929 and meticulously rebuilt after a fire in 1990, stands in the hotel entrance court.

Just beyond, on the right, Lancaster Place leads to **Waterloo Bridge**. The original bridge, built to commemorate Wellington's victory at Waterloo in 1815, was replaced in 1945. Even so, the views to St. Paul's Cathedral and downstream to Canary Wharf, and upstream to the Houses of Parliament are among the city's best. Return down Lancaster Place and continue along the Strand. Opposite the main entrance to Somerset House is an island bounded by the Strand and the great arc of the **Aldwych**. On it are three notable buildings: Herbert Baker's fine **India House** (1928–1930), decorated with India-inspired friezes, **Bush House** (1923–1935)—headquarters of the B.B.C. World Service, and **Australia House** (1912–1918). These huge buildings dwarf the tiny church of **St. Mary-le-Strand**, stuck in the middle of the road, but an exquisite early 18th-century building, designed by James Gibbs. Its counterpart, a little farther along, is **St. Clement Danes**, built by Christopher Wren in 1680, with a steeple added by Gibbs in 1720. It was bombed in 1941 but beautifully restored and is dedicated to the Royal Air Force. Its floor is covered in crests carved in Welsh slate, one for each R.A.F. unit. Within the spired and turreted **Royal Courts of Justice** (1874–1882), the last major building on the Strand, judges hear some of the most important civil cases in the land; the public is admitted to the viewing galleries and to the Central Hall (*Closed* Aug–Sep).

**REGION HIGHLIGHTS**

**SIR FRANCIS BACON**
The most famous member of Gray's Inn, Sir Francis Bacon was a remarkable polymath—philosopher, scientist, statesman, and man of letters. He was part of Shakespeare's literary circle and it is frequently claimed (though never proven) that he was the true author of Shakespeare's plays. His death was no less colorful than his life. While conducting one of the country's first experiments in freezing food (on Highgate Hill in 1606) he caught a chill and died of pneumonia.

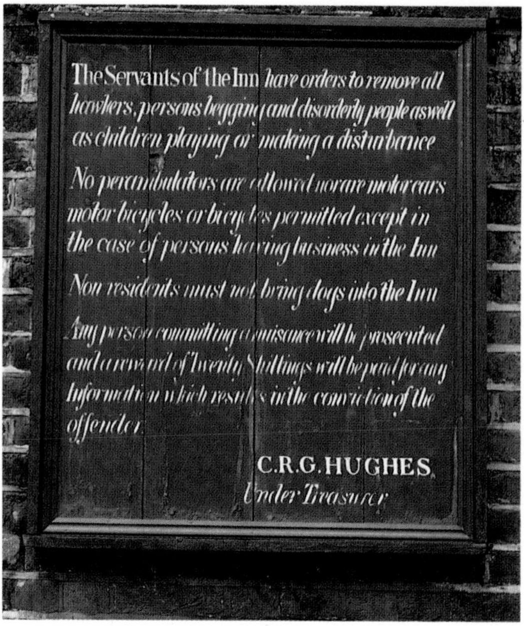
The Servants of the Inn have orders to remove all
hawkers, persons begging and disorderly people as well
as children playing or making a disturbance
No perambulators are allowed nor are motor cars
motor bicycles or bicycles permitted except in
the case of persons having business in the Inn
Non residents must not bring dogs into the Inn
Any person committing a nuisance will be prosecuted
and a reward of Twenty Shillings will be paid for any
Information which results in the conviction of the
offender
C.R.G. HUGHES
Under Treasurer



**THE ROYAL COURTS OF JUSTICE**
These cathedral-like buildings, known as the Law Courts, stand at Aldwych, where the Strand and Fleet Street meet. Together they form London's last great Gothic public building, and they solved the old problem of judges and lawyers having to dash around London to various little courts. The campaign for a central court was launched in 1841. Eventually, Parliamentary Bills were passed and the design competition announced in 1866. George Edmund Street won, but the first brick was not laid until 1874. By the time it was completed in 1882, Street had died of a stroke the year before, brought on by the exhausting complexity of the project—it had demanded almost 3,000 drawings.

## ▶ Gray's Inn

150C2

*High Holborn, WC1 (tel: 020-7405 8164)*
*Open: Mon–Fri 10–4. Admission free*
*Underground: Chancery Lane, Holborn*

Gray's Inn is one of four Inns of Court established in the 14th century to provide accommodations for lawyers and their students. The layout of the Inns resembles that of an Oxford or Cambridge college: each has a dining hall, chapel, and library, and the buildings that house the lawyers' chambers are grouped around courtyards and gardens. Of all the Inns, Gray's Inn suffered most from wartime bombing, but the most important buildings have been well restored. These include the 17th-century entrance gateway, on the north side of High Holborn (at No. 21 and near to the Cittie of York pub, a favorite lawyers' haunt). This leads into South Square, with its statue of Sir Francis Bacon (by F.W. Pomeroy, 1912), who was a member of Gray's Inn from 1576 until his death in 1626 (see panel). The Hall, on the north side of the square, is where Shakespeare's *The Comedy of Errors* was first performed in 1594. Passing through Gray's Inn Square and Field Court, you will reach the extensive gardens. These were laid out by Sir Francis Bacon in 1606, and the catalpa trees are said to have been planted from cuttings brought back from America by Sir Walter Raleigh. The raised terrace was a favorite place to walk during the 17th century and, as Samuel Pepys recorded in his diary, a good place in which to "espy fine ladies."

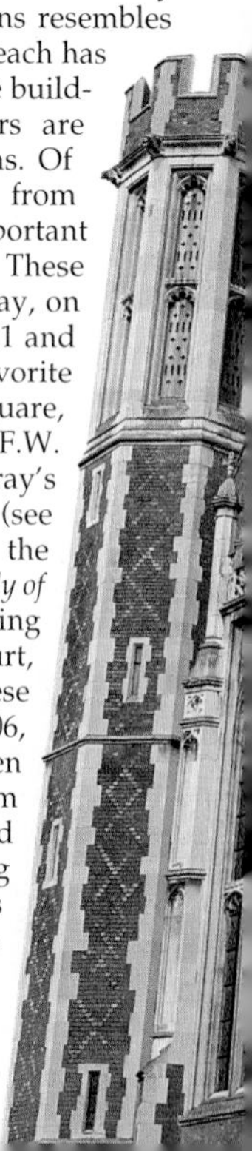

### ▶▶▶ Lincoln's Inn 150B2

*Chancery Lane, WC2 (tel: 020-7405 1393)*
*Open: Chapel Mon–Fri noon–2:30; grounds Mon–Fri 9–6. Admission free, donations*
*Underground: Chancery Lane, Holborn*

To explore Lincoln's Inn, which has the finest gardens of any of the 14th-century Inns of Court, it is best to start at the brick gatehouse, on Chancery Lane. This dates from 1518 and bears the coat of arms of Henry VIII above the original doorways of stout oak.

The narrow pedestrian entrance leads to Old Buildings. To the right is the **chapel** and its stone vaulted undercroft, paved with 18th-century tombstones. Steps lead up from here to the chapel itself, completed in 1623; John Donne, the poet, preached "a right rare and learned sermon" at its consecration. The east window contains 228 coats of arms of former Treasurers of Lincoln's Inn. To the right is Old Square, leading to **Stone Buildings**, built of crisp, white Portland stone in Palladian style. A low gate to the left leads to **Lincoln's Inn Fields**, a large green area of manicured lawns and statuesque trees. Straight ahead are the **hall** and **library**. They look perfectly medieval but were built by Philip Hardwick in 1845. To the left is New Square, where fig trees and wisteria climb over the late-17th-century buildings. If you walk down the left-hand side of New Square you will reach Lincoln's Inn Archway, sandwiched between the windows of Wildy & Sons, booksellers specializing in legal texts. The windows exhibit fascinating Victorian cartoons and engravings.

The archway leads into Carey Street, once the site of the bankruptcy courts—hence the archaic expression "heading for Queer Street" ("Queer" being a corruption of Carey) to describe someone in financial trouble. To the right is a pub popular with lawyers, the Seven Stars. To reach Temple (see pages 158–159) turn left on Carey Street, then right into Bell Yard, which leads to Fleet Street. Temple is opposite.

**AROUND HOLBORN CIRCUS**

Holborn Circus marks the busy meeting point of several roads leading into the City of London. To the north, Hatton Garden and its side streets are the traditional haunt of jewelers and diamond merchants: many of the stores here were founded by Jewish refugees fleeing persecution elsewhere in Europe. Leather Lane, running parallel to the west, has an entertaining street market on weekdays where stallholders call out their wares and perform all sorts of antics to attract trade. To the east, in Ely Place, is St. Etheldreda's Church, built around 1290 and well worth a visit for its tracery and stained glass.

## ▶ Lincoln's Inn Fields 150B2

*Underground: Holborn*

One of the earliest mentions of Lincoln's Inn Fields records that in 1150 this was a jousting ground for the Knights Templar (see Temple, pages 158–159). State-sanctioned violence continued to be a theme of this green and pleasant space for the next five centuries. Many executions were carried out here, most notably in 1586 when Anthony Babington and his 13 co-conspirators were found guilty of plotting against Queen Elizabeth I. A plaque in the bandstand in the center of the park (now usually frequented by down-and-outs) records the last execution here in 1683, of Lord William Russell, beheaded for treason.

The square of elegant buildings around the park began construction in the 1630s. It is the oldest surviving square in London, and also its largest public square, at just under 7 acres.

From the 17th century onward Lincoln's Inn Fields became a very fashionable place to live, though the only original house still standing is No. 59–60. It is a handsome structure, accredited to the great Inigo Jones, and from 1790 to 1807 was the home of Spencer Perceval, the only British Prime Minister ever to be assassinated.

## ▶ Prudential Assurance Building 150C3

*Holborn*

*Underground: Chancery Lane*

Alfred Waterhouse's huge redbrick-and-terra-cotta building was constructed in 1879, concurrently with his other London masterpiece, the Natural History Museum, which it closely resembles externally. The building occupies the site of Furnival's Inn, one of the Inns of Chancery (preparatory schools for the Inns of Court), which were dissolved in 1817. Just inside the courtyard a plaque and a bust commemorate Charles Dickens, who had lodgings in Furnival's Inn from 1834 to 1837. He wrote most of *The Pickwick Papers* here.

## ▶▶▶ Sir John Soane's Museum 150C2

*13 Lincoln's Inn Fields, WC2 (tel: 020-7405 2107)*

*Open: Tue–Sat 10–5. Admission free*

*Underground: Holborn*

Sir John Soane (1753–1837) was one of those brilliant architects that Britain produces from time to time, whose buildings are so quirky and original that they defy classification. Examples of his work in London include the Bank of England (see pages 162–163), the Dulwich College Picture Gallery (see page 214), and this remarkable house. The house was originally two—he bought No. 13 in 1812 and its neighbor No. 14 in 1824 and remodeled the interiors to serve as his home and as a museum for his paintings, sculpture, architectural models, and drawings. Recently the museum has been extended further by the purchase of No. 12, which has been converted to form a gallery for displaying drawings from Soane's massive collection of over 30,000 items. Soane's interior remodeling was brave and experimental: split-level flooring creates a strange and disorienting experience and anticipates, by 100 years or more, one of the favorite devices of modernist architects. The rooms are crammed with

**STAPLE INN**

Staple Inn, on Holborn, is one of London's oldest surviving timber-framed buildings (*Open* Courtyard only, Mon–Fri 8–8. *Admission free*). Built in 1545 as a hostel for wool merchants, the gabled building has projecting upper stories with oriel windows, while the store fronts below date from the 19th century. As you walk through the archway, note the sign on the left saying that the porters have orders to prevent "Old Clothes Men" and "Rude Children" from entering. Beyond is a peaceful brick courtyard and a rose garden, a favorite place for office workers to eat their lunchtime sandwiches.

**CHANCERY LANE**

If you are interested in antiques you should pay a call to the London Silver Vaults, 53–65 Chancery Lane (tel: 020-7242 3844). Originally this was set up in 1885 as a place where valuables could be stored in stout underground vaults, secure from the threat of fire or theft. Today the subterranean warren contains London's biggest concentration of antiques dealers specializing in silverplate and jewelry. Not far away is a curious sight that only male visitors get to see. In Star Yard, up against the high walls of Lincoln's Inn, is an ornate cast-iron urinal which looks as if it has been transported here from Paris. There are several good secondhand bookstores nearby in the alleys linking Star Yard to Chancery Lane.

*Bizarre but fun—Sir John Soane's Museum*

objects and made more bewildering still by the use of mirrors. It's fun just to explore the labyrinthine house and make chance discoveries, but you can also join a lecture tour given every Saturday at 2:30 PM. Not to be missed is the Picture Room, where two of Hogarth's series of paintings are displayed. *A Rake's Progress* (1732–1733) traces the career of Tom Rakewell in eight canvases, from his life as a happy young man about town to his imprisonment for debt and final home in the Bedlam insane asylum (see page 200). *The Election* (ca1754) presents an equally cynical view of bribery and corruption in British politics illustrated in a series of four pictures.

The fascinating basement is a little like a horror-movie set, with views through the windows to the Monk's Cloister, built in the garden from architectural fragments that Soane rescued when the Houses of Parliament were being rebuilt. Another star exhibit is the Sepulchral Chamber containing the Sarcophagus of Seti I (who died around 1300 BC).

**THE OLD CURIOSITY SHOP**

On the opposite side of Lincoln's Inn Fields to Sir John Soane's Museum is another rambling old building, the Old Curiosity Shop (13–14 Portsmouth Street). Whether it really is the building that Dickens immortalized in his novel of the same name doesn't really matter—it certainly looks the part. The timber-framed building, with its overhanging upper floor, dates from 1567, and until its recent closure could fairly claim to be London's oldest surviving store. Its neighbor is another colorful store selling all sorts of junk, from old books and comics and antique teddy bears to colonial pith helmets and dress uniforms.

*Manet's* Bar at the Folies-Bergère *(1882)*

**SOMERSET HOUSE**
Somerset House still contains an odd mix of government departments. One of them is the Inland Revenue, responsible for collecting income tax, as well as inheritance tax, home purchase tax, and land duty fees—an organization that everyone in the country loves to hate. Here too is the Principal Probate Registry, which holds copies of every will registered since 1858. The public is entitled to see any they choose—but you have to pay a fee. Immediately to the east of Somerset House is King's College, founded in 1828 by the Duke of Wellington, then Prime Minister, and the Archbishop of Canterbury. It was set up as a reaction to the founding of University College in 1826, called "the godless institution" because divinity was not on the syllabus; in contrast, King's put religion at the core of its teaching.



## ▶▶▶ Somerset House (Courtauld Gallery) *150A2*

*The Strand*
*Underground: Temple*
Some of the world's most famous Impressionist paintings can be seen in the treasure-filled Courtauld Gallery. The core of this collection was put together by the textile magnate Samuel Courtauld (1876–1947). He gave the pictures to the Institute that bears his name in 1931, aiming to provide students of art history with outstanding works that they could study in close detail. His gift was expanded when the art critic Roger Fry and other major patrons donated their private collections as well. In 1990 the whole collection was moved to the rooms of the Strand Block at Somerset House,

where they are hung to advantage beneath the ornate plaster ceilings.

You enter Somerset House through a triple-arched gateway facing onto the Strand. Facade sculptures symbolizing oceans and rivers, the Cardinal Virtues, and the Genius of Britain reinforce the building's monumental stature. Within is a courtyard and more facade sculptures of the Arms of Britain, the tritons and the Continents, and George III with the River Thames at his feet. The key to all this grandiloquence is the fact that William Chambers designed Somerset House in 1776–1776 to house important offices of state—among them the Navy Office, the Exchequer, and the Audit Office, the forerunners of today's government ministries.

Today, the civil servants have been ousted and the whole building is gradually being transformed into an arts complex. Riverside rooms are to contain the Gilbert Collection (see panel) and restaurants, the central courtyard is used for open-air opera and other events, and the restored Strand Block is home to the Courtauld Gallery. It originally contained the Royal Academy, the Royal Society, and the Society of Antiquaries, and their classically inspired fittings have remained, including the elegant staircase and the ceiling decorations. The ceiling of the first gallery has the initials R.A. (for Royal Academy) worked into it, along with pairs of paintbrushes in the corner. Among the 15th- and 16th-century paintings here are Renaissance masterpieces such as Botticelli's *Holy Trinity with Saint John and Mary Magdalen* (1490–1494). Parmigianino's *Virgin and Child* (1524–1527) is an example of the High Renaissance or Mannerist style, characterized by brilliant coloring and contorted figures.

Gallery 2, the former Royal Academy Council Room, has the best ceiling and several masterpieces.

**THE GILBERT COLLECTION**

In 1996, the Gilbert Public Arts Foundation in the United States donated £75 million worth of British gold and silver pieces (dating from the early 16th century onward), micro-mosaics, and gold boxes, all to be displayed in Somerset House. Arthur Gilbert left Britain in 1949, and it was deemed to be a serious loss to the nation when part of the collection went with him. It is hoped that the exhibition will be on view before the Millennium.



**THE ROMAN BATH OF STRAND LANE**

Strand Lane runs down the east side of King's College; halfway down, at No. 5, you can peer through a window at a curious plunge bath, built of red brick, with a rounded end and measuring about 13 ft. by 6½ ft. The bath is fed by a spring that delivers 2,000 gallons of icy water every day, then drains into the Thames. David Copperfield used to come here for a dip in what Dickens referred to as "the old Roman bath." The name has stuck, though nobody is quite sure whether it really is Roman; its first recorded mention was in 1784, and the best that archeologists can say at this stage is that although it might be Roman in origin, much of the brickwork dates from around 1588.

**MIDDLE TEMPLE HALL**
When exploring the Temple it is well worth checking whether Middle Temple Hall can be visited (tel: 020-7427 4800. *Open* Mon–Fri 10–11:30, 3–4. *Admission free*). This noble building is said to have been opened by Queen Elizabeth I in 1576 and has one of the finest hammerbeam roofs in England. Just as spectacular is the original Elizabethan oak screen at the east end, carved with big bold figures and statues in niches. The serving table, according to legend, is made from the timbers of Sir Francis Drake's ship, the *Golden Hinde*. In this room William Shakespeare took part in a performance of his own *Twelfth Night* on February 2, 1601.



Rubens's *Descent from the Cross* (1611) is a *modello*, or trial piece, for his most famous work, the great altarpiece in Antwerp Cathedral known as the *Antwerp Descent*.

In Gallery 3 the initials of the Society of Antiquaries have been worked into the ceiling. More paintings by Rubens hang here, notably the mysteriously poetic *Moonlit Landscape* (1635–1640).

Gallery 4 is devoted to 18th-century Italian art, Gallery 5 was the Royal Society Meeting Room, with plaster portraits of the Society's founder, Charles II, and George III. The great Gallery 8 holds the gorgeously colored works of Manet, Degas, Renoir, and Pissarro. Manet's *Bar at the Folies-Bergère* (1882) is the most eye-catching, and his *Déjeuner sur l'Herbe* (1863) is a smaller version of the painting in the Musée d'Orsay in Paris. Here too is Van Gogh's *Self-portrait with Bandaged Ear*, a reminder of the quarrel that the artist had with Gauguin (Van Gogh threatened his friend with a knife, and then cut off part of his own ear in remorse).

Until 1836 this room was used for Royal Academy summer exhibitions (see page 82). The "R.A. Line" runs around the room, a molding set 6½ feet or so above the floor. Works favored by the R.A. Hanging Committee, to give them more prominence, were hung below the line.

The remaining rooms display Postimpressionist works, changing exhibitions, and works by 20th-century British artists such as Roger Fry, Duncan Grant, Graham Sutherland, and Ben Nicolson.

## ▶▶▶ Temple *150B3*

*Inner Temple, EC4 (tel: 020-7353 1736)*
*Open: Wed–Sat 10–4 and Sun for services. Closed Aug.*
*Admission free*
*Underground: Temple (closed Sun), Covent Garden*

The Temple takes its name from the Knights Templar, the crusading order whose 12th-century round church survives at the heart of this network of alleys and courtyards.

The Temple actually consists of two Inns of Court (the Inner Temple and the Middle Temple), but they are so physically intertwined that they seem like one large collegiate campus, where lawyers in black gowns stroll between their chambers and the Royal Courts of Justice (see page 152), on the opposite side of Fleet Street. Between the Temple and the Royal Courts, in the middle of Fleet Street itself, **Temple Bar Monument**, marks the boundary between Westminster and the City. It guards the City's western boundary where, by tradition ever since 1558, the sovereign has stopped and sought permission of the Mayor to enter the City. Erected in 1880, it is topped by a bronze dragon (the symbol of the city), but is far less imposing than Sir Christopher Wren's gateway, which originally stood here. Wren's gateway was built in 1672 but became an impediment to traffic and was taken down in 1888.

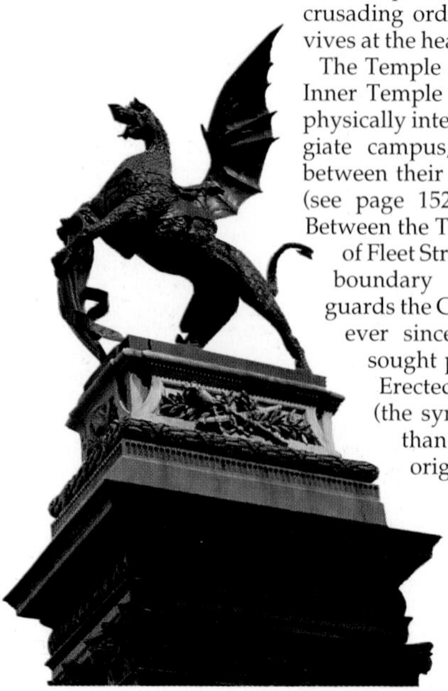

*A dragon's welcome to the City of London at Temple Bar Monument*

Near here, on the south side of Fleet Street, a timber-framed gatehouse leads from busy Fleet Street to the calm of Inner Temple Lane. This leads down to the **Temple Church**, past the elaborately carved Romanesque west door, which is

*The Middle Temple, whose past members include Drake, Raleigh, Dickens, and Fielding*

no longer used; the entrance is now from the south. The Temple Church's circular nave is known as "the Round." It was completed in 1185 and, in common with all the churches built by the Knights Templar, the shape is modeled on the Church of the Holy Sepulcher in Jerusalem. A remarkable series of effigies is set into the floor of the Round. These three-dimensional figures of sleeping knights, dressed in crusading armor, all date from the late 12th and early 13th centuries. The Round was built at the point of transition between Romanesque and Gothic architecture. Looking up, you will see that the triforium has Romanesque intersecting arches, but the arches themselves are pointed, in the Gothic style, rather than rounded. The chancel, known as "the Oblong," has the same slender Purbeck marble shafts as the Round, but the style is Early English. Added in 1240, the Oblong has been described as "one of the most perfectly and classically proportioned buildings of the 13th century in England."

Leaving the church and turning left past the pretty **Master's House**, you enter **King's Bench Walk**, a fine open space bordered by a handsome terrace designed by Wren in 1677. To the right, in Crown Office Row, is another leafy garden, but this one is strictly for the use of members of the Temple. An archway links Crown Office Row to the cobblestone alley of Middle Temple Lane.

Turn right, then left, to arrive in **Fountain Court**, where a huge plane tree and ancient mulberry dwarf the tiny circular fountain itself. Steps lead up on the right to **New Court**, flanked by ornate gas lamps that are topped by the lamb and flag symbol of the Middle Temple. Turn right beyond the steps to pass through an arch into Essex Court, then left onto Middle Temple Lane. This brings you to Fleet Street, passing a row of 17th-century timber-framed (but plastered) buildings on the right, whose jettied-out upper story forms a covered arcade at street level.

**LAWYERS' HAUNTS**
The Wig and Pen (Dining) Club, No. 229 Strand, is a favorite haunt for off-duty lawyers. With its political and legal cartoons in the window, it is set in a tiny timber-framed building of 1625, the only one on the Strand to have survived the Great Fire of London. Nearby, at Nos. 222–225, the Law Courts branch of Lloyd's Bank has a surprisingly ornate interior: Egyptian-style tiles cover the entrance lobby, and the banking hall is decorated with Doulton-tile pictures of flowers, cherubs, and historic figures under stucco-work ceilings. All this dates from around 1883 when the building, originally a restaurant, first opened.

*Effigy of a crusading knight in the Temple Church*

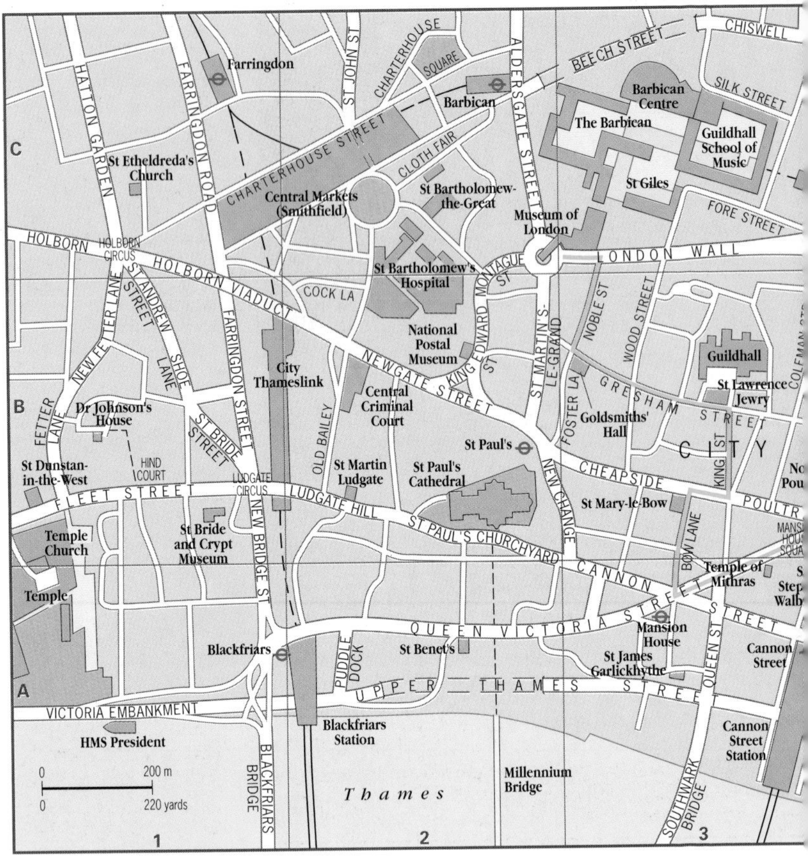

*The City's new face*

**WEEKEND GHOST TOWN**
To enjoy the City's architecture in peace, take a walk through its streets at the weekend. Most churches and public buildings are closed. Exceptions include St. Paul's Cathedral, Broadgate Centre, the Museum of London, and the Barbican Centre.

**THE CITY** The City today still roughly covers the area of the trading city founded by the Romans in AD 43, when Emperor Claudius needed a Thames crossing between his ports in Kent and the new Roman province's capital, Colchester. Here, almost 2,000 years later, the City remains the tiny, compact financial heart of Britain. Its soaring modern buildings stand next to medieval lanes and Wren churches; its international businessmen are subject to the rules of the stoically traditional Corporation of London and its Lord Mayor.

**THE CITY WALK** Starting from Liverpool Street Station, explore the buildings and art of **Broadgate,** with its centerpiece amphitheater and restaurants. Walking down Bishopsgate, turn left into St. Helen's Place to find **St. Helen's Bishopsgate,** London's largest surviving medieval church, with fine memorials, all restored after an I.R.A. bomb in 1992. Cutting through to St. Mary Axe, turn right down it and onto Lime Street to see Richard Rogers's **Lloyd's** building (1981–1986), where the marine insurance market founded in the 1680s now insures anything, including a U.S. space rescue operation. Turn right into Leadenhall Place to find busy **Leadenhall Market** and walk through it to Fenchurch Street. Turn left, then right onto **Lombard Street,** with its decorative banking signs.

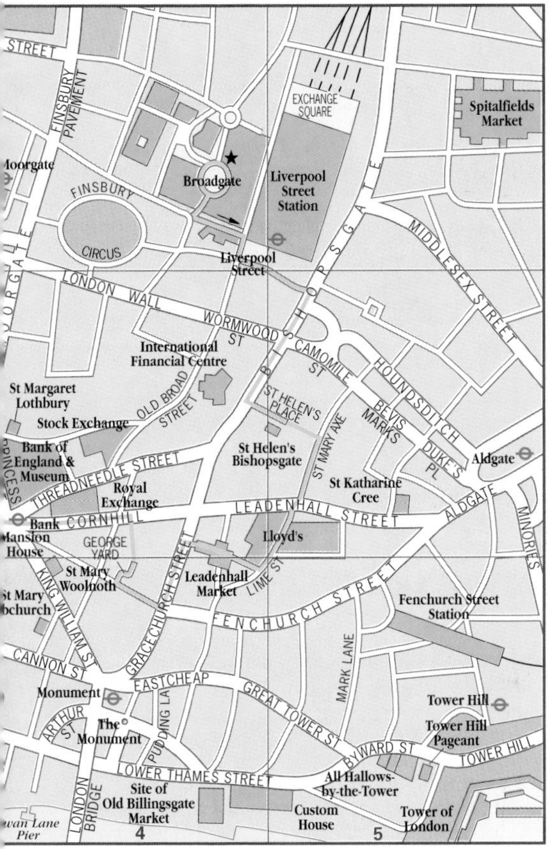


# The City

Here, find George Yard on the right and amble through a knot of old lanes, passing the Jamaica Wine House, where the Baltic Exchange began in the 17th century. Turn left onto Cornhill and walk to the junction, **Mansion House Square.** When Britain had an empire, this spot was considered its center. Here are Nicholas Hawksmoor's beautiful **St. Mary Woolnoth** (1716–1727), Sir William Tite's **Royal Exchange** (1841–1844), and Sir John Soane and Sir Herbert Baker's **Bank of England** (1788–1808 and 1921–1937) with its fascinating little museum round the back, opposite Wren's lovely **St. Margaret Lothbury** (1686–1690). On round Mansion House Square, you can see Stirling and Wilford's controversial rebuilding of **Number One Poultry,** with rooftop restaurant, and George Dance the Elder's **Mansion House** (1739–1752).

Continue by going down Queen Victoria Street, pausing to see the mosaics of the **Roman Temple of Mithras.** Then cut up Bow Lane to Wren's **St. Mary le Bow** (1670–1683), and through King Street to **Guildhall,** whose medieval hall (1411–1440), church of **St. Lawrence Jewry** (Wren, 1670–1687) and clock museum can be visited. Finally, walk along Gresham Street, past lavish **Goldsmiths' Hall** in Foster Lane and some chunks of remaining **London Wall** in Noble Street, to find the **Museum of London** at the roundabout where Aldersgate and London Wall meet.

### ►►► REGION HIGHLIGHTS

**Broadgate Centre** *page 165*

**Guildhall** *page 164*

**Museum of London** *pages 166–167*

**St. Bartholomew-the-Great** *page 173*

**St. Helen Bishopgate** *page 171*

**St. Paul's Cathedral** *page 168–169*

**Temple of Mithras** *page 167*

*Bank is to the City what Trafalgar Square is to the West End: a chaotic junction of several roads, surrounded by magnificent public buildings. At the weekend the streets are deserted, but during the week you can stand on any corner at Bank and feel the pulse of this frenetic world of high finance, where international bankers and traders work the investment and money markets worldwide.*



**DR. JOHNSON'S HOUSE**
Tucked behind Fleet Street, tiny Gough Square is a remnant of days when Fleet Street, the artery of information running between the City and Westminster, was alive with printers, publishers, pubs, writers, and gossip. Here, between 1749 and 1759, lived the genius Dr. Samuel Johnson (1709–1784). And it was here that he compiled his *Dictionary*, employing six amanuenses to help him. Five of them were Scots, and they all worked in the garret on the top floor. When the house fell into disrepair, the press baron Lord Harmsworth bought it in 1911, and it is now a simple tribute to one of London's greatest and most idiosyncratic men, who defined the literary and moral values of his age and is perhaps the greatest English man of letters. Inside, the simple furnished rooms have Johnson's friend Boswell's coffee cup, a tea set from another friend, Mrs. Thrale, and portraits of Johnson, Wesley and the actress Mrs. Siddons. There is also a portrait of Lord Chesterfield, patron of the *Dictionary*, and a copy of the book itself.

A good spot for people-watching and admiring the architecture is the triangular space in front of the Royal Exchange, in the angle formed by Threadneedle Street and Cornhill, where there is a statue of the Duke of Wellington (1844). Here stands the **Royal Exchange** (built 1843–1844), true temple to commerce. The figures carved in the pediment depict Commerce, attended by merchants of all nations, holding the charter granted by Elizabeth I in 1570. This was when the Exchange was first set up, in rivalry with that of Antwerp. Until recently this was where traders in the largest futures market outside the U.S. would operate, dressed in colored waistcoats and using mysterious hand signals and coded shouts. Dealing has now moved to nearby Cannon Bridge Station, Cousin's Lane (no public access) and the Royal Exchange is closed.

With the Royal Exchange behind you, the building on the left is the **Mansion House**, the official residence of the Lord Mayor of London, although today the Lord Mayors use their own homes. Designed and built by George Dance the Elder in 1739–1752, its pediment carvings show London trampling on the figure of Envy (in other words, commercial competitors) and leading in the figure of Plenty. Inside—you can write to Mansion House and reserve a place for the free tours—pictures from the City Corporation's impressive collection hang in the grand rooms. The triangular plot, to the west, on the corner of Poultry and Queen Victoria Street, has been redeveloped. Amid controversy, the Flemish Gothic Mappin & Webb building (1870) was demolished in 1994, to be replaced by James Stirling's landmark office building with an upscale rooftop restaurant called No. 1 Poultry.

On the right-hand (north) side of Bank is the vast bulk of the **Bank of England**, after which this whole area is named. The building resembles a fortress: at street level there are no doors or windows in the massive stone walls (except for the main entrance). Sir John Soane' walls (1788–1808) survive surrounding Sir Herbert Baker's rebuilding (1921–1937). Founded in 1694 to fund wars with France, the Bank's role has always been central to the British economy. The Bank is responsible for issuing paper money, raising funds for the government, managing the nation's foreign exchange reserves, setting interest rates, and regulating the banking system of the country as a whole. The story of its work is told in an excellent museum in the rebuilt Soane rooms (Bartholomew Lane,

EC2, tel: 020-7601 5545. *Open* Mon–Fri 10–5. *Admission free*). Farther down Threadneedle Street, Old Broad Street leads left to the **Stock Exchange**. Little did anyone suspect, when this building was opened in 1972, that 20 years later it would have become obsolete. The dealing floor, where jobbers once traded shares in an atmosphere of tense excitement, is empty, since buying and selling is now done by telephone and computer in the offices of brokerage firms.

For a complete contrast, cross Threadneedle Street to explore the alley behind the Royal Exchange leading to **Cornhill**, **Birchin Lane**, and **George Yard**. These little lanes preserve the City's medieval street pattern and are lined with pubs and wine bars. They are a reminder of the days when traders used to do deals in the crowded and congenial coffeehouses, before the markets were institutionalized. Something of the original atmosphere can still be savored in the oak-paneled upstairs bar of the **Jamaica Wine House**, St. Michael's Alley, Cornhill; this stands on the site of the coffeehouse where traders specializing in West Indian goods, such as rum and sugar, used to meet.

**THE LORD MAYOR**
The City of London has its own local government, headed by the Lord Mayor since 1192, when Henry Fitzailwyn was installed. Today the mayor is elected to serve for just one year. The election takes place on Michaelmas Day, September 29, and the mayor is installed in the Guildhall on the Friday preceding the second Saturday in November. The next day the mayor drives through the streets leading the Lord Mayor's Show, a colorful pageant with lavish floats. At the Lord Mayor's Banquet, on the following Monday, the Prime Minister makes an important speech on government policy. The Mayor spends much of the rest of the year attending ceremonial events to raise funds for charity.

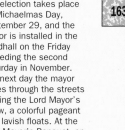

*The Bank of England*

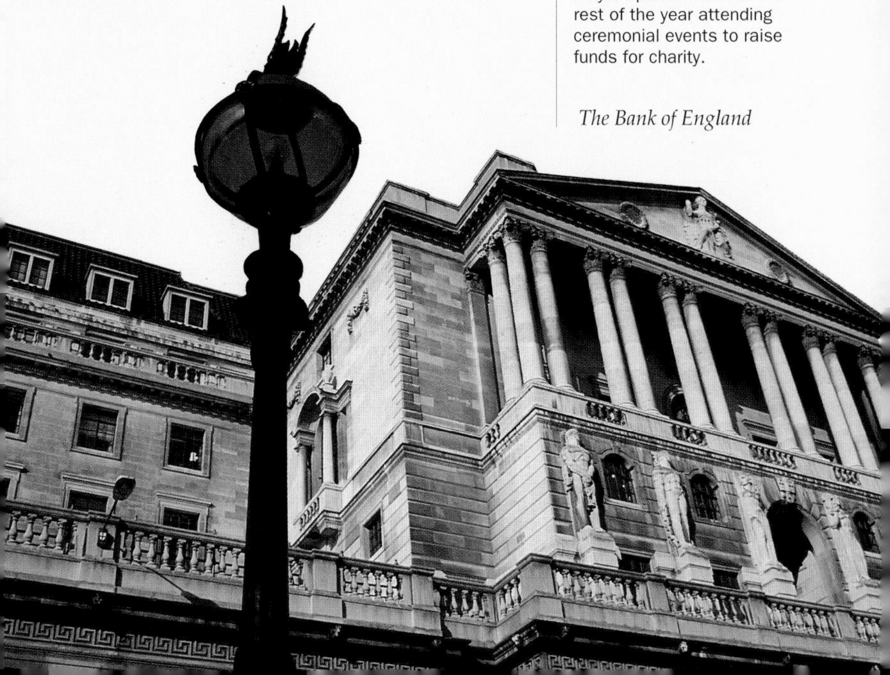

**SKYSCRAPERS**
The City does not have many skyscrapers. One of the few examples is the International Finance Centre, formerly known as the Nat West Tower (Old Broad Street). At 604 ft., it was Britain's tallest building when it was completed in 1981. Now it is second to the soaring tower of the 1990 Canary Wharf development (see page 190). These buildings are too far apart to make a brave statement. The English are deeply suspicious of tall buildings, and many rejoiced when the developers of Canary Wharf went bankrupt, killing the plans for two further towers.



*Lloyd's of London started life in a humble coffee shop*

## ▶▶▶ Guildhall *160B3*

*EC2 (tel: 020-7606 3030)*
*Open: Guildhall daily 9–5; Clock Museum Mon–Fri 9:30–4:45. Admission free*
*Underground: Bank*

The Guildhall was built in 1411 and, despite severe damage during the Great Fire of London (1666) and the Blitz, its stout medieval walls and impressive undercroft have survived intact. The roof was carefully reconstructed with stone arches by Sir Giles Gilbert Scott in the 1950s. The stained-glass windows incorporate the names of more than 600 past Lord Mayors, and the walls and roof are decorated with the coats of arms and embroidered banners of the City Livery Companies. These are the modern equivalent of the medieval trade guilds, who built the Guildhall for their meetings and ceremonies. The guilds were a powerful force in medieval London, responsible for fixing prices and wages and preventing nonmembers from setting up stores. Today the Livery Companies support the industries they represent (from brewers to weavers) by funding research and education. From their ranks, the Sheriffs and Lord Mayors are chosen to run the City's affairs, and the Guildhall is where they are installed, amid great ceremony. Looking down from the Guildhall's west gallery are two strange figures: Gog and Magog, the mythical giants supposed to be the founders of Albion (Britain). Also in the Guildhall, do not miss the Clock Museum, where 700 finely crafted clocks, watches and clock keys are on show.

*Broadgate's hanging gardens, the more acceptable face of 1980s "Big Bang" architecture*

## ▶ Leadenhall Market *161A4*

*Gracechurch Street, EC3*
*Open: Mon–Fri*
*Underground: Bank, Monument*

Amid all the markets dealing in stocks, shares, gold, insurance, and currencies, Leadenhall Market is a charming oddity that has nothing to do with finance. Traders here sell meat, fish, and poultry from stores and stalls on either side of a graceful Victorian arcade designed by Horace Jones in 1881, with highly ornamented facades and a roof of iron and glass. Stallholders mount impressive displays, which could have come straight out of a picture of Victorian or Edwardian London.

## ▶▶ Lloyd's of London *161B5*

*Lime Street, EC3*
*Underground: Monument*
*Currently closed to the public*

The Lloyd's building, completed in 1986, is one of London's most exciting and controversial modern buildings. Designed by Richard Rogers (also responsible for the Pompidou Centre in Paris), it is a daring building all of glass entwined in steel ventilation shafts, cranes, gantries, and staircases. The building is especially thrilling to see at night, when it glows a strange green and purple from concealed colored spotlights, creating a space-age effect. Ironically, this futuristic building houses one of London's most traditional institutions. Lloyd's evolved in the 1680s as a marine insurance market based at Edward Lloyd's Coffee House on Tower Street.

## ▶ Monument *161A4*

*Monument Street, EC2 (tel: 020-7626 2717)*
*Open: Apr–Sep, Mon–Fri 9–5:40, Sat, Sun 2–5:40; Oct–Mar Mon–Sat 2–5:40. Admission charge*
*Underground: Monument*

The Monument commemorates the Great Fire of London and was co-designed by Christopher Wren. The column, completed in 1677, is 203 feet high; as the inscription at the base of the column explains, the fire broke out in Pudding Lane, 202 feet away. The gilded bronze urn at the summit symbolizes the flames of the fire. Below the bronze urn is a viewing platform, reached by a dark, spiral staircase of 311 steps. On a clear day, views stretch to the chalk downlands of Kent and Sussex.

**THE BROADGATE CENTRE**

The Broadgate Centre, which wraps around Liverpool Street station at the top of Old Broad Street, is more than just a good example of modern office development. It is (or was) a political *cause célèbre*. Begun in July 1985, the first phase of the massive 9-acre development was officially opened just two years later. The speed of construction was highly unusual for Britain, whose construction industry was dogged by strikes and industrial relations disputes that constantly interrupted work. The complex, inspired by Chicago office architecture, is well worth exploring for its elevated walkways, outdoor sculptures, gardens, and the amphitheater used as an ice rink in winter and for open-air entertainment in summer.

**LONDON WALL**
The road called London Wall is so named because of the surviving section of the city's 3rd-century Roman wall that runs along its northern edge, visible below street level. There is a particularly well-preserved stretch alongside the Museum of London and another in St. Alphege Garden. The site of the wall can still be traced just by looking at a map of the city—to the east of London Wall, Houndsditch, the Minories, and Tower Bridge Approach perfectly preserve the course of its curving route down to the river. The stretch along London Wall was uncovered after World War II bombing flattened the area, leading to its wholesale redevelopment in the late 1950s. Six different architects were involved in the project, each given responsibility for one of the huge office buildings that line the route. Instead of exciting variety, what London Wall got was six of the dreariest buildings imaginable, featureless lumps of concrete and glass—so bad, in fact, that some of them were pulled down again in the late 1980s to be replaced by Terry Farrell's postmodern buildings that now span London Wall like a great monumental arch.

*The Roman Gallery*

## ▶▶▶ Museum of London *160C3*

*150 London Wall, EC2 (tel: 020-7600 3699)*
*Open: Tue–Sat 10–5:50, Sun noon–5:50. Admission charge; ticket valid for one year; entry after 4:30 free*
*Underground: St Paul's*

This highly entertaining collection is the largest city museum in the world, and traces over 2,000 years of London history through imaginative displays and reconstructions. The first gallery tells the story of human occupation in the London area from around 500,000 BC until the Roman invasion of AD 43. Recent archeological excavations have provided a wealth of new objects and information, now included in both this and the next gallery on Roman London (don't miss the detailed, large models of Roman London and its port, or the little leather swimming trunks found at the bottom of a 1st-century London well!). If short on time, visitors may want to fast forward on the museum's new Catwalk (named after Dick Whittington's famous, but fictional, feline). This is a new high-tech trail which snakes around the museum and provides interactive computer displays and object handling points en route. It's a great way to make progress through the museum with restless children in tow.

Moving on through the centuries, the Early Stuart period (1603–1666) is perhaps the most dramatic time in London's history. The English Civil War, the execution of Charles I, the restoration of the monarchy, the Great Plague, and the Great Fire of London are all recalled by relevant pieces: the death mask of Oliver Cromwell; a contemporary painting of the procession of Charles II; an actual plague bell, rung to announce the collection of

*The art of firefighting: an example of an appliance used on the London streets in the 1860s*

corpses ("bring out your dead"); and the Fire Experience, an audio visual model of London burning, to the accompaniment of a reading from the diary of Samuel Pepys, who witnessed the conflagration.

For many visitors, however, the best of the museum's displays cover more recent London history—store interiors, kitchen furnishings, and toys. Children will enjoy exploring the dank depths of a 1940s air-raid shelter or the reconstructions of dismal Georgian prison cells, complete with the graffiti scratched by inmates. Less chilling are the 18th- and 19th-century costumes, dolls' houses, and Valentine's Day cards. Keep an eye out too for the magnificent wrought iron and bronze decorated elevators used by Selfridges in the 1920s.

The growth of the London suburbs is illustrated by 1930s posters and advertisements—many of them art deco exhibits in their own right—extolling the delights of newly built housing subdivisions in the rural-sounding retreats of Golders Green and Hampstead Garden City.

Bringing the story right up to date is the London Now gallery, where a wide range of exhibits, photographs, and memorabilia transport visitors through the last 50 or so years; the London of ration books, new tower blocks, Mary Quant and Biba, Ford Cortinas, punk rockers, poll tax riots, and the transformation of Docklands.

Finally (near the exit, where it can be taken out for ceremonial occasions) there is the Lord Mayor's state coach, made in 1757 and still used for the Lord Mayor's Show (see page 163). Its painted sides show allegorical scenes set against the background of old London.

Before leaving the museum it is worth visiting the well-stocked bookstore, which also sells models and toys, and checking on the extensive program of special events and lectures that is on offer.

**THE TEMPLE OF MITHRAS**

On the raised sidewalk in front of No. 11 Queen Victoria Street, EC4, is a group of sculptures depicting Mithras, the god of heavenly light, whose adherents promoted chastity, honesty and courage. Mithraism was the main rival religion to Christianity in the 3rd and 4th centuries AD. The Temple of Mithras was mistaken for an early Christian church when it was discovered in 1954. The true nature of the building was realized when diggers came across sculptures of Mithras (now in the Museum of London), deliberately hidden to save them from members of the rival cult, the Christians.

**MONUMENTS**
Wren did not want his masterpiece cluttered with memorials, but its symbolic importance made this inevitable. One of the most imposing memorials is to Wellington, on the north side of the nave—a huge four poster topped by an equestrian statue. On the opposite side hangs *The Light of the World*, a much-loved painting by Holman Hunt. The tomb of the poet John Donne, on the south side of the choir, shows Donne wrapped in his shroud. It was the only monument to survive the fire that destroyed the medieval cathedral.



## ▶▶▶ St. Paul's Cathedral *160B2*

*Ludgate Hill, EC4 (tel: 020-7236 4128)*
*Open: Cathedral Mon–Sat 8:30–4; Galleries, crypt, ambulatory Mon–Sat 10–5. Admission charge, except for Sun services*
*Underground: St. Paul's*

St. Paul's Cathedral is one of the most awe-inspiring sights in London. Its dome, one of the world's largest, dominates the City skyline. The building also manages to communicate a sense of serenity, most notably in the famous (and fabricated) image of 1941 of the dome untouched but wreathed in the smoke and flames of the Blitz. This montage symbolized the undaunted spirit of Londoners during the darkest moments of the war and carried echoes of the cathedral's origins—born out of the flames of the Great Fire of London in 1666.

Wren's English Baroque cathedral mixes High Renaissance ideas of a Greek Cross centralized plan with a traditional long nave demanded by the clergy for their processions—it was a considerable compromise on his original design, a model of which is in the Crypt. It is Wren's dome that gives the cathedral such a wonderfully uplifting atmosphere.

On entering the church it is natural to head for the crossing beneath the dome, with its windows filtering down a

Gibbons' choir stalls

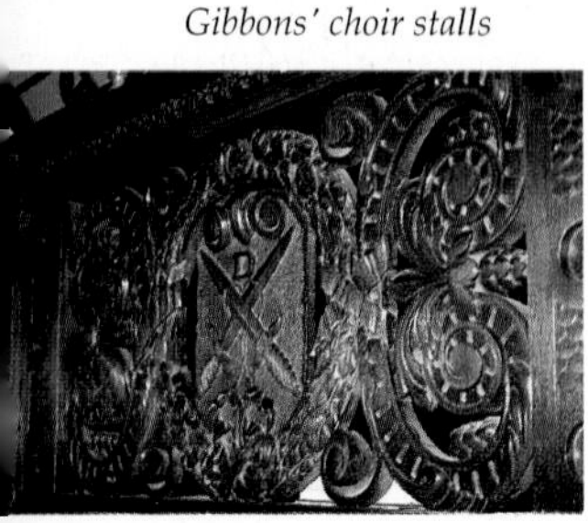

strangely ambiguous golden light. On the sidewalk below its very center is a memorial to Wren, composed by his son, which reads *Si monumentum requiris, circumspice* ("If you are seeking his monument, look around you"). The marvelous choir stalls and organ case near John Donne's tomb (see panel) were carved by Grinling Gibbons as part of Wren's original decorative scheme.

Next it is best to visit the crypt, where you can see Wren's actual tomb, a simple black slab, and an audio-visual program explaining the history and construction of the building, from the laying of the foundation stone in 1675 to the placing of the last stone on the lantern above

*Enjoy the view from the choir to the high altar with its splendid canopy featuring massive twisted oak pillars*

the dome in 1708. The crypt is massive, extending beneath nearly the whole of the church. In Painters' Corner, for example, the monuments read like a roll call of great artists, from Van Dyck to Constable. George Frampton's memorial is particularly charming and includes a small replica of the Peter Pan statue he made for Kensington Gardens (see page 111). In the center of the crypt are the ponderous tomb of Wellington and the Renaissance sarcophagus of Nelson. This last was actually made by Benedetto da Rovezzano for Cardinal Wolsey, then confiscated by Henry VIII but never used by him. Instead it remained empty until 1805, when Nelson's body was laid to rest within it, having been brought back from the Battle of Trafalgar pickled in spirits in a barrel. In the Treasury, at the west end of the crypt, you can see Wren's "Great Model," a scale model in wood of the original design.

After the descent into the crypt the next and most exciting part is the ascent to the dome. In Wren's England the concept of a dome was revolutionary and even today St. Paul's is still the only domed English cathedral. There are 259 steps to the Whispering Gallery. The circular gallery carries sound around so that someone standing on the opposite side will hear your whispers quite clearly after several seconds' delay—though only early visitors will have the peace to test these acoustics properly. There are fine views down to the nave below and up to the frescoes of the dome above, where the scenes from the *Life of St. Paul* were painted by Sir James Thornhill in 1716–1719.

Continue upward to the Stone Gallery, which runs around the exterior of the base of the dome. Climbing higher still you pass through the timberwork that rests on the inner dome, supporting the wooden skin of the outer, lead-covered dome. Between these two domes is a third: the brick cone supporting the elegant lantern crowning the whole structure. This can be viewed from the Golden Gallery. There is one last stairway up to the ball, added in 1721, surmounted by a golden cross and looking over the city from more than 366 feet above the cathedral floor. A hole in the floor of the Golden Gallery lets you look straight down to the cathedral floor.

**AROUND ST. PAUL'S**

Although St. Paul's itself miraculously escaped major damage in the Blitz, the surrounding area was flattened and then redeveloped in the 1960s with a series of dreary, windswept buildings. These are due to be razed and replaced, but there are several competing and equally controversial designs. They range from the highly modernistic (accused of being out of sympathy with Wren's masterpiece) to the more traditional (accused of being backward-looking), based on Wren's own plan to surround his church with a series of Italianate piazzas and boulevards. Most Londoners favor the latter approach, which will give St. Paul's the setting it deserves and open up views of the facades, now rather hemmed in by busy roads or bad buildings and difficult to see properly. The south facade would benefit especially if the road in front of it were closed. Here Wren had the word *Resurgam* ("I shall rise again") carved above the door and a phoenix rising from the fire carved in the pediment to symbolize the birth of the new church from the ashes of the old. The main (west) facade is the most richly decorated. The baroque twin towers, flanking rows of gigantic columns, are a quirky but successful piece of design to which Wren's gifted pupil Nicholas Hawksmoor may well have contributed.

*The Great Fire of London broke out at a bakery on Pudding Lane on September 2, 1666. Four days later, when the fire's rage was finally quelled, four-fifths of the City's buildings had been destroyed, including more than 13,000 houses and over 50 churches. The great rebuilding that took place after the fire provided the architects of the day with a wonderful opportunity to create a new city. The churches built by Christopher Wren and his assistants remain one of the great lasting legacies of that age, their spires, towers, and domes as much a symbol of the City as the skyscrapers of today's financial institutions.*



*The mighty bells of Bow, which, according to legend, called Dick Whittington back to the City*

**THE GREAT BELLS OF BOW**

The bells of St. Mary-le-Bow (Cheapside) are of great symbolic importance to Londoners. Only those born within the sound of the "Great Bells of Bow" qualify as true Cockneys. When the church was hit by a bomb in 1941, sending the bells crashing to the ground, the pieces were saved; in 1962 they were rehung, having been recast, and the church was restored. Of the original Wren church (built 1670–1680), the tower and splendid steeple survive, and below, in the crypt, restorers found remains of an 11th-century staircase.

**St. Martin Ludgate** (Ludgate Hill). Built in 1677–1687, this church stands within a short step of Wren's masterpiece, St. Paul's Cathedral. Its spire and portico seem designed to echo the twin towers fronting St. Paul's. Notable features of the interior are the galleries, reached through richly carved doors, and the pulpit.

**St. James Garlickhythe** (Garlick Hill). Wren was continually adding spires and towers to his churches in order to improve the London skyline. This church is an example: it was built between 1676 and 1683, but Wren decided to add the graceful spire in the early 18th century. In fact, some architectural historians think the spire may have been the work not of Wren himself but of his assistant, Nicholas Hawksmoor.

**St. Stephen Walbrook** (Walbrook). Some consider this to be the most majestic of all Wren's parish churches; it is one in which the architect experimented with ideas later used for St. Paul's, notably the large central dome. Henry Moore's stone central altar was placed below the dome in 1987.

**St. Mary Woolnoth** (King William Street). This astonishing building is the work of Nicholas Hawksmoor and was built between 1716 and 1724. Fronted by the powerful west tower, it is a strange and daring building that looks more like a pagan temple than a Christian church. Inside, do not miss the monument to a former rector of the church, John Newton, who died in 1807 having devoted many years of his life to campaigning for the abolition of the slave trade. He also wrote the perennially popular hymn *Amazing Grace*.

**St. Mary Abchurch** (Abchurch Lane). This is one of the few Wren churches to have remained virtually unaltered, complete with its woodwork. The chief glory is the huge reredos behind the altar, carved by Grinling Gibbons—all the more remarkable when you consider that it was carefully pieced together by restorers in 1948–1953, having been shattered into over 2,000 pieces by a bomb that fell during the Blitz.

**St. Helen Bishopsgate** (Great St. Helen's). St. Helen is one of the few City churches not to have been destroyed by the Great Fire. Fashionable during the Elizabethan and Jacobean periods, it preserves a remarkable series of 15th-century tomb effigies, including the fine recumbent figures of John and Mary de Oteswich and the wool merchant, Sir John Crosby. A later monument (1636) by Nicholas Stone commemorates the grandly named Sir Julius Caesar Adelmare, a judge in the Court of Admiralty.

**St. Katharine Cree** (Leadenhall Street). This is another church that escaped the Great Fire, and it is a very rare example of the transition from Gothic to classical, having been built around 1628. The nave arcades are supported on splendid Corinthian columns, but the vaulting is Gothic, as is the splendid rose window, symbolizing the wheel on which St. Katharine was martyred.

**SIR CHRISTOPHER WREN**
Sir Christopher Wren (1632–1723) was an extraordinary man. In his youth he was regarded as a brilliant mathematician and appointed Professor of Astronomy at Oxford at the age of 29. With little formal architectural training he launched himself on a glorious career by designing the Sheldonian Theatre in Oxford: he was appointed surveyor general and principal architect for rebuilding the City after the Great Fire, on the strength of a comprehensive plan he drew up. Apart from St. Paul's Cathedral, Wren personally designed 52 churches for the City, of which 23 survived the bombs, Blitz and developers. He also inspired a generation of artists and architects, including Grinling Gibbons, the great woodcarver, and Nicholas Hawksmoor, creator of the English baroque style.



**CITY LUNCHTIME MUSIC**
Many City churches open at lunchtime and stage relaxed, informal concerts played by professionals or students. The City Information Centre, by St. Paul's Cathedral (tel: 020-7332 1456) has a list.

*St. Mary-le-Bow, built by Wren, but gutted in 1941. The interior was rebuilt in the 1950s*

*Vegetarians and the squeamish should be warned that Smithfield is a raw, rough, and bloody place—London's main market for meat and poultry. Even those with strong stomachs have been known to blanch at the sight of porters in bloodied aprons running around with great sides of beef or whole pig carcasses slung across their backs. You will also be sworn at in resounding terms if you get in the way—this is a no-nonsense place; visitors are welcome provided they keep in their place.*

*Above: Rahere's tomb, church of St. Bartholomew-the-Great*



**CLOTH FAIR**
Cloth Fair is a quiet little street lined with timber buildings, antiques stores, and pubs running down the north side of St. Bartholomew-the-Great. It preserves something of the appearance of pre-Fire London, because the Great Fire died out finally at nearby Cock Lane. No. 43 Cloth Fair was for a long time the home of Sir John Betjeman, Poet Laureate and campaigner for the conservation of Victorian monuments. The house now belongs to the Landmark Trust, an organization that restores historic buildings and rents them as holiday homes (details from The Landmark Trust, Shottesbrooke, Maidenhead, Berkshire SL6 3SW, tel: 01628 825925). The wine bar below and the adjacent pub have walls decorated with Betjeman memorabilia and old photographs of Smithfield. Another excellent pub farther down the lane is the tiny Hand and Shears, on the corner of Middle Street, whose wood-paneled rooms, some no bigger than corridors, are usually packed with doctors from St. Bartholomew's.

Smithfield is the last remaining wholesale market operating in Central London, and it offers a unique example of a sight that was commonplace to Londoners until the 1970s, when cramped working conditions and the difficulties of truck access to London's narrow and congested streets drove long-established markets (such as Billingsgate for fish and Covent Garden for fruit, vegetables, and flowers) to new sites built on the edges of London. Smithfield (from "Smooth Field") was a livestock market at least as early as 1173, but the sale (and slaughter) of live animals was banned in the 1850s because of the squalor of the streets full of filth and entrails and because the drovers who brought their sheep, cows, and horses to the market delighted in terrorizing Londoners by making their charges stampede down the narrow streets. Smithfield has survived on this site because the meat market has declined in recent years, so there is space enough for the traders. This may yet change as a result of European Union regulations on the sale of meat or else because of development pressures—the market occupies a prime site, and the glorious cast-iron and glass hall that houses the market (built 1857–1866 and modeled on Joseph Paxton's Crystal Palace) would make a good shopping center.

Smithfield's decline is due to the large number of butchers' chains that now buy direct from producers, but the market still supplies many top restaurants and specialist butchers, whose buyers come here at the crack of dawn. The market is all but finished by 9:30 AM, so you have to be an early riser to see it in full swing. As a concession to its hours, pubs in the area open at 6:30 AM and serve gargantuan breakfasts to the hungry and exhausted porters.

Alongside the market is **St. Bartholomew's Hospital**, one of the City's four great teaching hospitals. It was founded in 1123 by Rahere, Henry I's court jester, in gratitude for his recovery from malaria, contracted while on a pilgrimage to Rome. The older buildings, including the baroque Great Hall and staircase (decorated with paintings by William Hogarth of *The Good Samaritan* and *The Pool of Bethesda*) can only be seen on a guided tour. You can admire, however, the figure of Henry VIII over the gateway, the inner courtyard laid out by James Gibbs

*Smithfield porters still use traditional barrows*

**CHARTERHOUSE SQUARE**
Charterhouse Square was originally a burial ground for victims of the Black Death, the bubonic plague that decimated London's population in the 1340s. A Carthusian monastery was set up where the monks prayed for the souls of plague victims. The name is an anglicization of Chartreuse, where the Carthusian order was founded. In 1611 the buildings were purchased by Thomas Sutton, who founded the Charterhouse School. The educational tradition lives on: the buildings behind the Charterhouse now house St. Bartholomew's Hospital Medical School, well worth visiting for their tranquility (guided tours Apr–Jul, Wed 2:15 from main gate).



(1730–1759), and the hospital church of St. Bartholomew-the-Less at any time. (Guided tours mid-Apr–Nov, Fri 2 PM from main gate.)

Just to the east of the hospital entrance is a 13th-century stone archway topped by a timber-framed gatehouse dated 1559. This leads to the quiet, flower-filled churchyard surrounding London's oldest surviving church, **St. Bartholomew-the-Great**, also founded by Rahere, for the Augustinian canons who maintained the hospital. At the Dissolution of the Monasteries, under Henry VIII, the nave was torn down (it stood in the present churchyard and extended to the gatehouse), but the lovely Romanesque choir was allowed to survive, serving as the district's parish church. Rahere himself, who died in 1143, is buried here beneath the canopied tomb on the north side. On the opposite side, high up on the nave wall above the massive Norman pillars, is an oriel window, installed by Prior Bolton at the beginning of the 16th century so that he could observe the monks who were in his charge. The window is carved with a rebus (a pictorial pun) on Bolton's name, consisting of a crossbow bolt and a tun (barrel).

*The half-timbered 16th-century gate-house leading to St. Bartholomew-the-Great*

*London has an extraordinary range of pubs. Some offer live music or theater, some offer top-quality food at a fraction of the price of a restaurant meal, some have waterside gardens, and many have historical associations and the decor to match.*

*The pub where Dr. Johnson drank*



The only surviving galleried inn in London is the **George Inn** in Southwark (77 Borough High Street), now owned by the National Trust. The rambling timber-framed coaching inn dates from 1676 and is unique in preserving its external galleries; Dickens mentions it in *Little Dorrit*. For warm days there is outdoor seating in the courtyard and in summer this is turned into a stage, where excerpts from Shakespeare's plays are performed. The **Black Friar** (174 Queen Victoria Street), on the other side of the river, is worth a visit for its splendid Arts and Crafts decorations (come in the early evening, when it is not too crowded). The interior is a riot of marble, mosaic, and woodwork, the walls covered in reliefs of monks at work and play above beautifully lettered mottos exhorting the oblivious drinkers below to reform and improve their dissolute lives. The whole pub is a charming and elaborate joke.

Another wonderful piece of fun is **Jack Straw's Castle** (North End Way) in Hampstead. The name commemorates one of the leaders of the 1381 Peasant's Revolt, an uprising that was sparked off by the imposition of a poll tax that everyone in the country was expected to pay, no matter how poor. The pub is built on the site of an encampment set up by Straw's followers and looks every inch an 18th-century coaching inn (in some guides you will find it described as just that!). In reality it was designed by Raymond Erith in 1962–1964, and is an exact contemporary of London's skyscrapers.

A pub that does not require such an effort to reach is the tiny **Olde Mitre** (1 Ely Court, Ely Place), which was founded in 1546. It proudly displays the trunk of a cherry tree around which Queen Elizabeth I is supposed to have danced with one of her favorites, Sir Christopher Hatton, in nearby Hatton Garden. Equally, **The French House** (49 Dean Street) in Soho is easy to visit. A haven for the Free French during World War II, including De Gaulle, it later began to attract writers such as Dylan Thomas and continues its literary associations today.

No historic pub crawl would be complete without a visit to **Ye Olde Cheshire Cheese**, just south of here at 145 Fleet Street. Built in 1667, it is the least altered 17th-century pub in London, a rambling building of low beams, intimate rooms, and sawdust-covered floors. Not all of its original decorations are on display, however. Archeologists researching the fabric of the pub in the 1970s discovered a blocked fireplace in an upper room, which was decorated with a series of 17th-century pornographic tiles.

**MUSIC PUBS**

Many pubs have music nights when live bands provide entertainment. Listings magazines provide a comprehensive guide, but the following pubs have well-established reputations for the quality of their acts. The **Half Moon** (93 Lower Richmond Road) in Putney has entertainment every night, usually blues and rock music. The **King's Head** (115 Upper Street) in Islington offers live music as well as adventurous theatrical performances. Jazz lovers in general are very well served, but rarely is good music and good food combined so well as at the **Bull's Head** (373 Lonsdale Road) in Barnes, a huge Victorian pub by the Thames; it is wise to reserve in advance. (tel: 020-8876 5241).

Moving closer in to the West End, the **Cittie of York** (22 High Holborn) has several times been voted "Pub of the Year" by readers of London's *Evening Standard* newspaper. The pub is both huge and intimate, but the drinking area is divided into lots of small, cozy cubicles, designed, it is said, so that lawyers from the nearby Inns of Court can hold confidential discussions with their clients. The large open fireplace intrigues most visitors because it has no chimney (the smoke is carried away by means of a vent in the floor).

A short walk away from the Cittie of York is the **Museum Tavern** (49 Great Russell Street), yet another pub in which you never quite know what famous bottom once occupied the seat you have chosen. As it was so close to the old Reading Room of the British Museum, it was a particularly convenient place for scholars to seek a spot of light relief from their mental labors; even Karl Marx used to slip in here for the odd drink from time to time while writing *Das Kapital*.

**FIRKIN PUBS**
London's "Firkin" chain of pubs was started by an entrepreneur named David Bruce, who set out to revive the tradition of brewing beer on the premises. Pubs in the chain are instantly recognizable by the use of the word Firkin (a small barrel or cask) in their name—hence the Frog and Firkin, 41 Tavistock Crescent (near Portobello Market), or the Fusilier and Firkin, 7–8 Chalk Farm Road (opposite Camden Lock market). In each pub you can watch the beer being brewed through glass observation windows and sample the result knowing that you are drinking a unique beer, rather than one originating in a factory that produces several million gallons a day.

*Liquid lunch*

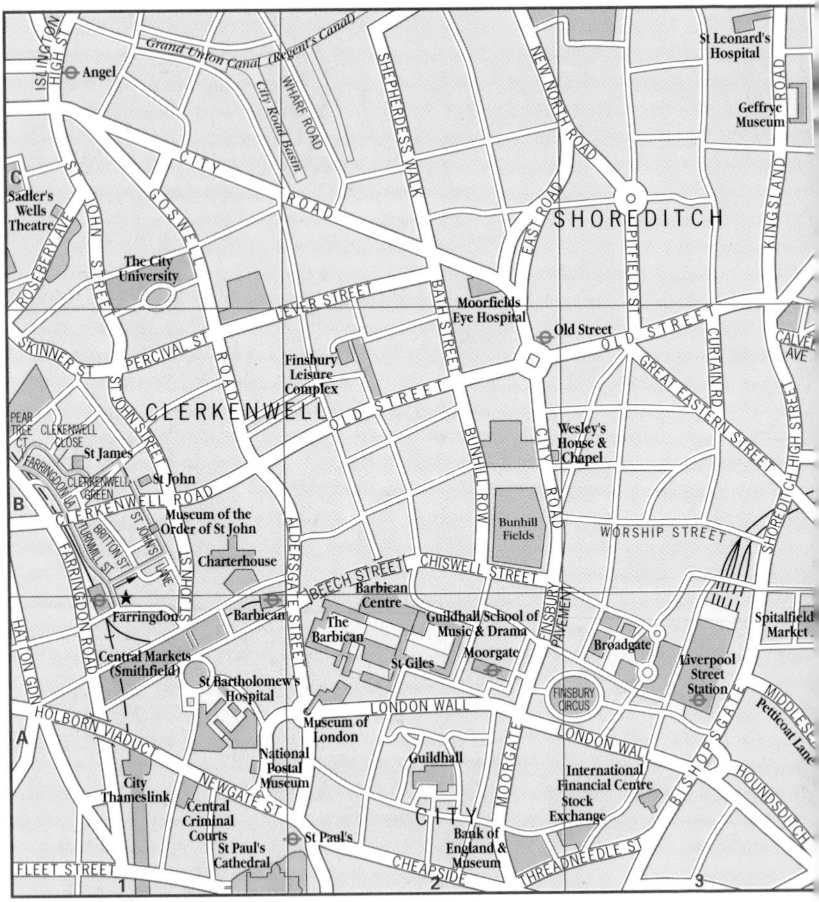

**CLERKENWELL, ISLINGTON, AND THE EAST END** Wrapped around the City to the north and the east are several small communities such as Clerkenwell, Islington, Spitalfields, Whitechapel, and Bethnal Green. Each began as a small village with a parish church, a manor house, and cottages around a green. Rapid population growth in the 19th century turned them into one vast metropolitan sprawl. Today, pioneering Londoners have rescued and restored the fine buildings, given these distinctive communities new life, and made them centers for fringe theater, craftsmen and artists, adventurous restaurants and avant-garde lifestyles.

**CLERKENWELL WALK** Start at **Farringdon Underground** station, the first Underground station to open in London, on January 10, 1863. Nearby, on Farringdon Road, a Dickensian street market specializes in old books and newspapers. Walking straight up Benjamin Street to Brittan Street, you will see a rare and interesting London addition: a purpose-built townhouse completed in 1987. Designed by Piers Gough for the flamboyant Janet Street-Porter, then Head of Youth and Entertainment Features at the B.B.C., the house has received rave reviews from

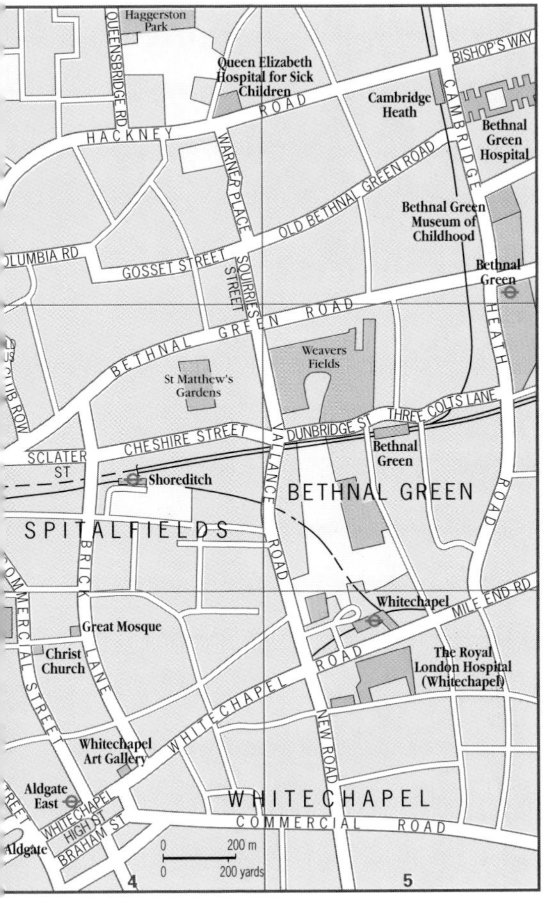


architects but has excited strong reactions from the public for its blue pantiles, brown brick, and steel lattice grilles thrusting up from the roof.

Continue up Albion Place, turning left on St. John's Lane to see **St. John's Gate** (1504), the gatehouse of the Priory of St. John of Jerusalem, the English base of the Knights Hospitallers, which evolved into the St. John's Ambulance Brigade. Across Clerkenwell Road is a small **museum** (tel: 020-7253 6644. *Open* Mon–Fri 10–4, Sat 10–4. *Donation*) about the Order.

Jerusalem Passage, a narrow alley, links St. John's Lane to Aylesbury Street; turn left to reach **Clerkenwell Green**, where the Palladian-style **Middlesex Sessions House** was built as a court of law in 1779–1782.

Clerkenwell Close winds northward from the green and leads past another splendid Palladian building: the parish church of **St. James**, built in 1788–1792.

Take the first left, into Pear Tree Court, and left again, to **Farringdon Lane**. Between Nos. 14 and 16, a window reveals the remains of the medieval **Clerk's Well**, after which Clerkenwell is named. The quality of its water accounts for the presence of Booth's gin distillery farther down on Turnmill Street, established in the 18th century.

*Outdoor terrace at the Barbican*

## ▶ Barbican Centre 176A2

*Aldersgate Street (theater entrance on Silk Street), EC2*
*(tel: 020-7638 4141)*
*Open: daily 9 AM–midnight*
*Underground: Barbican*

The Barbican Centre is one of London's most important arts locations. It is the London home of the Royal Shakespeare Company and the residence of the London Symphony Orchestra, and it mounts important art exhibitions and film seasons. Quite apart from all this there is a full program of free lobby exhibitions and musical entertainment, weekend activities especially for children, and an excellent bookstore specializing in the arts. The Centre stands on the northern edge of a massive housing complex that is an important example of postwar planning in its own right. In 1956, the government proposed that the 35-acre area, left a wasteland as a result of the Blitz, should be developed for housing rather than office buildings. The architects, Chamberlain, Powell, and Bon, produced a plan that was very forward-looking in its use of textured concrete. Some 6,500 people now live in the Barbican (which was not finally completed until 1981), many in high-rises over 402 feet high. The buildings are beginning to show their age, with the concrete facing now stained and dirty. It is difficult to imagine how enchanting and futuristic the complex looked when it first opened, with tier upon tier of cascading plants and bright crimson trailing geraniums spilling over every balcony, softening the brutal outlines of the concrete. Most residents have simply given up gardening because of the winds and because so many of them are temporary residents whose main homes are out of London. This gives a certain forlorn, unloved atmosphere to the complex, though the area right around the arts center is enlivened by sculptures, water gardens, fountains, and trees. The best spots to view the Barbican are from the Waterside Café (level 5) or the plant-filled conservatory (levels 8 and 9).

178

**THE BARBICAN MAZE**
The Barbican's various buildings are linked by a confusing maze of tunnels, elevated walkways, and staircases in which it is all too easy to get lost. To improve the situation, yellow markers have been placed on the sidewalks, leading eventually to the Barbican Centre arts complex. Alternatively you can use the church of St. Giles, Cripplegate, for orientation. This Tudor church was left a roofless ruin by the bombing that flattened the surrounding district but was rebuilt in 1952–1960. Surrounded by water, it appears to float on its own island, detached from the massive concrete structures all around. Inside are memorials to people associated with the church: a bust of John Milton, author of *Paradise Lost*, marks the approximate position of his grave. South of the church are remains of the Roman and medieval city walls.

*Toys for children of all ages at Bethnal Green*

### ▶▶▶ Bethnal Green Museum of Childhood *177C5*

*Cambridge Heath Road, E2 (tel: 020-8983 5200/5201)*
*Open: Mon–Thu, Sat 10–5:30, Sun 2:30–5:50. Admission free*
*Underground: Bethnal Green*

This museum of childhood holds the largest collection of toys in the world, so there is plenty to justify the trip out to a slightly off-beat area of the East End, perhaps following it with a visit to the nearby Geffrye Museum (see page 184) and Spitalfields (see pages 186-187). A branch of the Victoria and Albert Museum, this collection is housed in an interesting iron-and-glass building that originally stood on the V&A's South Kensington site, but was reerected here in east London in 1872 and clad in brick with sgraffito (scratched) designs illustrating the Arts, Sciences, and Agriculture.

A wonderful collection of 50 doll's houses is displayed in the museum's Central Hall. You can peer into the tiny world of a grand late-19th-century country house, stuffed with heavy furniture, or envy the lifestyle of the tiny inhabitants of Whiteladies, a stylish 1930s modernist house complete with tennis court, swimming pool, and veranda for cocktails.

The lower galleries are used to display a huge toy collection, grouped by type (dolls, trains, teddy bears, optical and musical toys, for example). The earliest exhibits are 17th-century, and there are toys from every corner of the world, including puppets from India, China, and Japan.

The upstairs galleries include displays that illustrate the history of childhood and the process of growing up, through exhibits such as baby equipment, nursery furniture, children's clothes, and teenage fads and fashions. There is also a collection of children's books from the last three centuries.

On most Saturdays and during school vacations the museum mounts a program of activities for children.

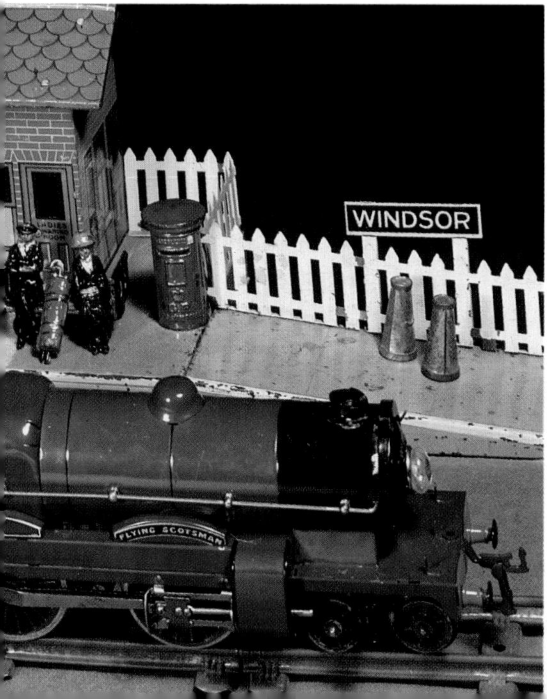


**▶▶▶ REGION HIGHLIGHTS**

**Bethnal Green Museum of Childhood** *page 179*

**Geffrye Museum** *page 184*

**Islington Walk** *pages 182–183*

**EAST END PHILANTHROPISTS**

Bethnal Green, along with neighboring Shoreditch and Whitechapel, was notorious in the 19th century for its overcrowded slums and for the poverty of its working-class population. Many attempts were made to improve the quality of life in the East End, not all of them successful or even appropriate. One was the setting up of the Bethnal Green Museum in 1875, in an attempt to bring art and culture to the masses. Another was the model housing built at great expense by Miss (later Baroness) Burdett-Coutts, whom Charles Dickens nicknamed Lady Bountiful, after the character in Farquhar's comedy *The Beaux' Stratagem*. These dwellings of the 1860s were themselves condemned as slums a century later and demolished. Model houses of a later period can, however, still be seen in the western part of Bethnal Green. The Boundary Estate, centered on Arnold Circus (just off Shoreditch High Street), was built in Arts and Crafts style and completed in 1900. The buildings were of such high quality that they inspired urban planners to construct similar complexes to house the poor in Paris, Amsterdam, Berlin, and Vienna. A good day to see them is Sunday; the trip can be combined with a visit to the Columbia Road flower market, definitely one of London's most colorful street markets and a place where you can buy top-quality houseplants and flowers at rock-bottom prices (*Open* Sun, 8–1).

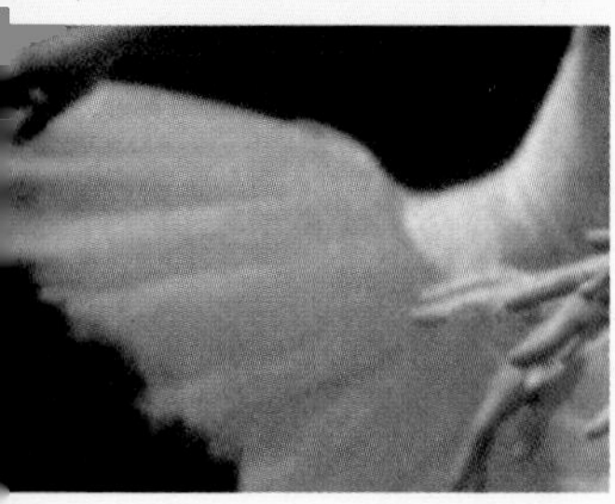

*In addition to hit musicals and popular dramas staged in the West End, London offers a wealth of quality entertainment for lovers of music, theater, opera, and dance. Two of the principal sites for the performing arts are the Barbican Centre and the South Bank Centre; both have resident companies. Other venues range from the huge Royal Albert Hall to intimate Wigmore Hall.*

The Barbican Centre is the London home of the **Royal Shakespeare Company**. It houses two stages, the large, proscenium Barbican Theatre and the intimate, flexible Pit. Here, some of Britain's most impressive actors and directors continue to explore new interpretations of Shakespeare's plays, to revive forgotten playwrights and introduce new ones.



Sharing the Barbican Centre with the R.S.C. is the **London Symphony Orchestra**—not only London's oldest orchestra but also the first to be run by its members. The L.S.O. was formed in 1904 by 50 musicians from Henry Wood's Queen's Hall Orchestra, who walked out after a dispute and formed their own self-governing body. Guest conductors are chosen by the orchestra members. The L.S.O. tries to include new or rarely performed works in its Barbican concerts, along with the more popular pieces that are considered essential for attracting large audiences.

On the South Bank, the Royal Festival Hall is the place to go for large-scale classical music performances. Top orchestras such as the **Royal Philharmonic** and the **London Philharmonic** perform here regularly. Next door, the Queen Elizabeth Hall's wide-ranging program includes the **Opera Factory**, a deliberately iconoclastic company, while the intimate **Purcell Room** is the ideal place for piano and song recitals.

The **Royal National Theatre**, also part of the South Bank complex, has three stages and enjoys similar status to the R.S.C. The building was planned to allow a great variety of production styles, ranging from experimental drama staged in the intimate and flexible Cottesloe Theatre to more traditional productions on the proscenium stage of the Lyttleton, and the large-scale productions in the Olivier Theatre, where the stage projects forward.

The huge Royal Albert Hall is used

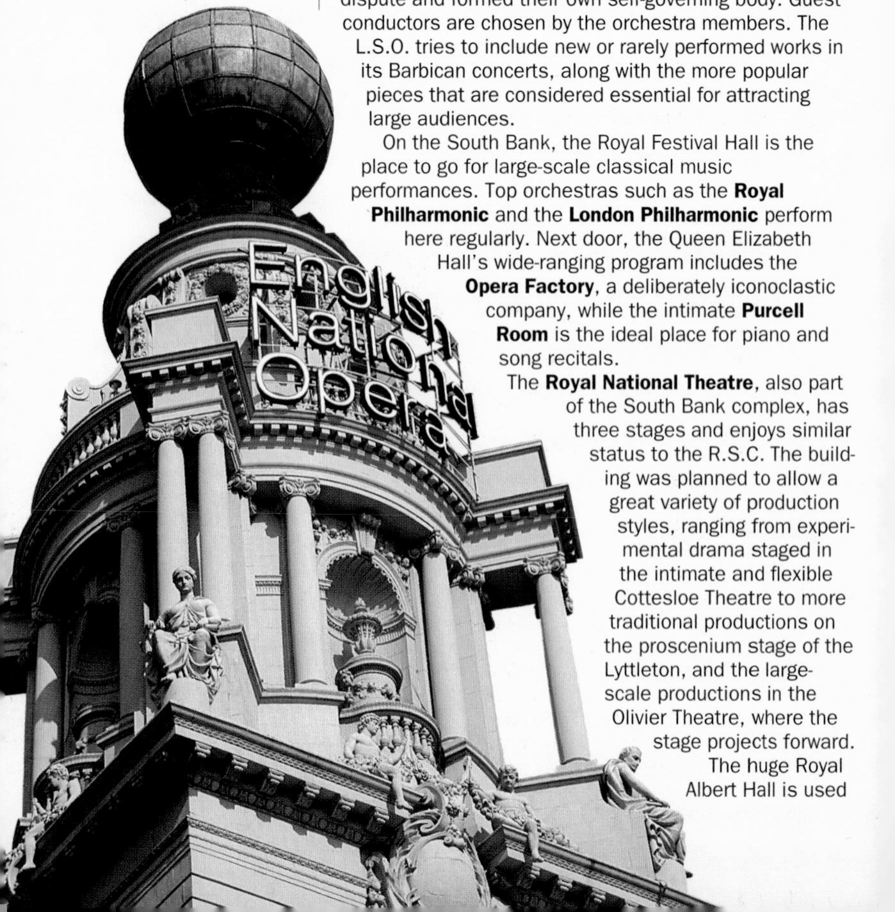


*The Coliseum, in St. Martin's Lane, home of the English National Opera*

for a wide variety of programs, ranging from rock and pop spectaculars to mime, ballet, Christmas carol concerts and, most famously, the summer long season of Henry Wood Promenade Concerts, when tickets at all prices, some sold on the day, fill the auditorium with music lovers every night. In contrast, Wigmore Hall was built in 1901 by Friedrich Bechstein, adjoining his piano showrooms and—apart from the churches—is probably London's most sympathetic setting for chamber music and recitals. For ballet lovers the **Royal Ballet**, usually based at the Royal Opera House, Covent Garden, may be the best known London company with the most glittering stage (and audience), but it faces healthy competition. The **English National Ballet** sometimes performs at the London Coliseum, St. Martin's Lane, during the summer months and at the Royal Festival Hall, where its *Nutcracker* (staged every January) is perennially popular. The **Sadler's Wells Theatre** (Rosebery Avenue) reopened in 1998 in a newly built theater. It presents touring international dance companies such as Momix, NDT2, Compania Antonio, Gades, and Kodo, as well as home-based talent such as the Rambert Dance Company, the City Ballet of London, and the British Youth Opera.

The **London Contemporary Dance**, at The Place (17 Duke's Road), has helped to put London in the forefront of modern dance, and the annual Dance Umbrella season (October and November), now has a worldwide reputation. The event is run by Riverside Studios (Crisp Road, Hammersmith), which is itself a busy and youthful arts center specializing in new work in all media. Opera has two principal venues: the Royal Opera House (see page 148), re-opened in 2000; and the Coliseum where performances are in English. Visiting companies use these and splendidly grand Hackney Empire, a Victorian music hall that was revived in 1987.

London also stages a wide variety of festivals. Some districts use them to reinforce local community spirit (see panel). Other events indulge fans of a particular medium: among the best are the London Film Festival, hosted by the National Film Theatre in November (South Bank, tel: 020-7928 3232) and Capital Radio's Music Festival (jazz, rock, and folk), held in June and July at locations all over London (see listings magazines). Several London theaters run back-stage tours, including the R.S.C., R.N.T., Shakespeare's Globe, and the Theatre Royal, Drury Lane.See also **Nightlife**, pages 244–245.

**ARTS FESTIVALS**

One of the most impressive of London's many arts festivals is the City of London Festival (tel: 020-7377 0540), when music, poetry, drama and other arts fill remarkable City buildings often closed to the public at other times. Other festivals include Kenwood Lakeside Concert season (tel: 020-7973 3427); Covent Garden May Fayre (tel: 020-7375 0441); Greenwich Festival in June (tel: 020-8305 1888); Richmond's July festival (tel: 020-8831 6138) and the Almeida Contemporary Music Festival (tel: 020-7359 4404) at the end of June and beginning of July.

*Musical treats*

*Islington has become a chic address for young Londoners. For those who can afford them, its terraces of late 18th- and early 19th-century houses offer elegant living in spacious well-proportioned rooms relatively close to the City and central London. As a result, Islington has a lively atmosphere, with street markets, theaters, restaurants, and pubs.*

**ISLINGTON THEATERS**
Half-a-dozen quality fringe theaters include **The King's Head**, 115 Upper Street, one of London's oldest and most vibrant-pub theaters, a Victorian gem. The **Almeida Theatre**, Almeida Street, is at the forefront of avant-garde theater, while puppets of all sizes star at the unique **Little Angel Puppet Theatre**, 14 Dagmar Passage, on Saturday and Sunday. At the **Tower Theatre**, Canonbury Place, Shakespeare and other classics are the specialty.



From King's Cross Road, a walk up Vernon Rise soon brings you to the elegant stucco-fronted houses of Percy Circus, developed from 1819, where Karl Marx lived for a time. More genteel houses in the same mold line the streets and squares to the south, such as Prideaux Place and Lloyd Square. Across Amwell Street, Myddelton Square, with its gardens surrounding St. Mark's Church, stands at the heart of the New River Estate. This was developed in the 1820s from the profits generated by the New River Company, which had brought fresh water to London from the River Lea in Hertfordshire, over 40 miles away since 1613, and still supplies this part of London with drinking water today. It was the brainwave of Sir Hugh Muddleton, a Welsh goldsmith who became a jeweler to James I.

From Myddelton Square, Mylne Street leads north to busy Pentonville Road where the Crafts Council has lively exhibitions. A detour here, down to Rosebery Avenue,

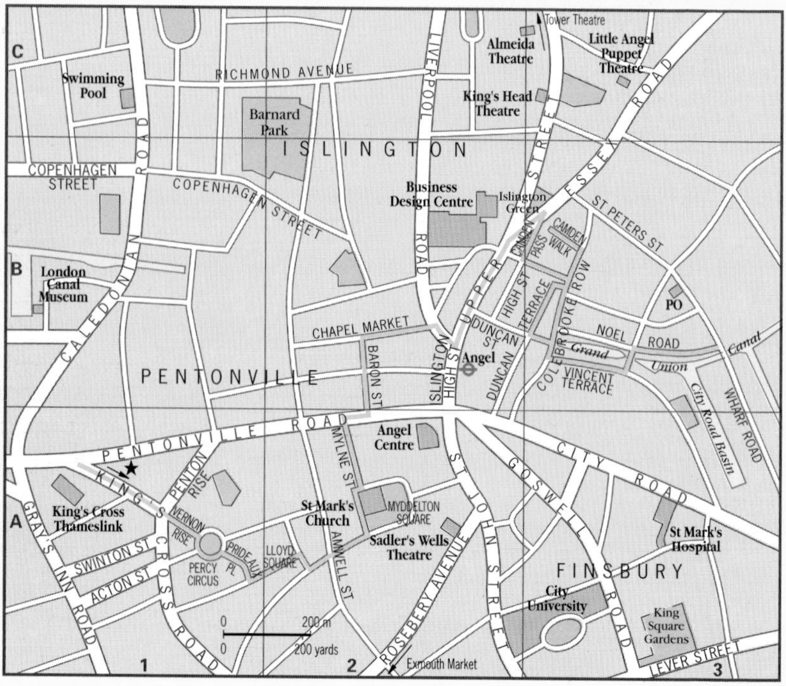

reaches Sadler's Wells Theatre, whose entirely new building opened in 1998, designed by Renton Howard Wood Lewis Partnership. Up Baron Street, you will find Chapel Market, a traditional local street-market where stallholders sell top-quality fruit, vegetables, flowers, and fish. Upper Street leads northward to Islington Green. On the left, the cast-iron and glass structure built in 1861–1862 as the Royal Agricultural Hall, a wholesale market for livestock, is now the **Business Design Centre**, a permanent showcase for British design, and usually open to the public.

Across the street, on a more intimate scale, **Camden Passage**, is lined with antiques stores tucked into Georgian houses. On Saturdays and Wednesdays, street stalls also set up here, selling a mix of antiques and collectables, including jewelry, toys, clothing, books, and records. Nearby is the Camden Head (2 Camden Walk), a busy, friendly Victorian pub with a patio for outdoor drinking in summer.

Camden Walk leads to Colebrooke Row and the parallel Duncan Terrace, two long rows of town houses, built from 1768 onward. Halfway down Colebrooke Row, on the left, Vincent Terrace is another pretty spot. It sits alongside the Grand Union Canal at the point where it emerges from the Islington Tunnel. The tree-filled gardens of Noel Road, backing onto the opposite bank of the canal, gives this attractive residential district an almost rural feel, and there are several good pubs serving food nearby, including the Narrow Boat, near Wharf Road Bridge, and the Island Queen, 87 Noel Road.

Those keen on contemporary art should walk northward along Upper Street for five minutes, to Canonbury, to visit the Estorick Collection of Modern Italian Art (Northampton Lodge, 39a Canonbury Square, N1; tel: 020-7704 9522, *Open* Tue–Sat 11–6) and enjoy pictures by Balla, Boccious and Carra, plus an excellent garden café.

**LITTLE ITALY**

Rosebery Avenue, leading south from Islington, cuts through the district once known as Little Italy because of the large community of Italians that lived here in the 19th century, many making their living as entertainers and ice-cream manufacturers. Exmouth Market, with its Italianate Church of the Holy Redeemer, its delicatessens, and its market, still has a Little Italy flavor. It was here, at No. 8, that Joseph Grimaldi, one of the most famous pantomime clowns of the 19th century, once lived; he first appeared on stage as a child dancer at the Sadler's Wells Theatre on Rosebery Avenue.



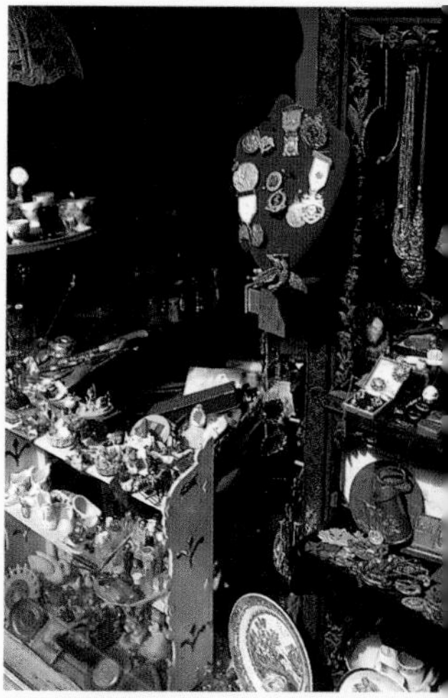

**BUNHILL FIELDS**
Bunhill Fields, on City Road across from Wesley's House, is the burial place of several Nonconformists, including the author of *Robinson Crusoe*, Daniel Defoe, the poet William Blake, the hymn writer Isaac Watts, and the author of *The Pilgrim's Progress*, John Bunyan. Originally the cemetery was a plague pit, opened up during the Great Plague that hit London in 1665, when people were dying in such numbers that their remains were simply dumped into one huge mass grave. Because it was never consecrated, the burial ground was later favored by Quakers, Methodists, and other Nonconformists, who could be buried according to their own rites rather than those of the established church. Today the cemetery is a delightful tree-shaded spot full of wildflowers.

**THE RAGGED SCHOOL MUSEUM**
If you are interested in the social history of the East End, pay a visit to the Ragged School Museum (44–48 Copperfield Road, E3; tel: 020-8980 6405. *Open* Wed, Thu 10–5. *Admission free*).
Ragged Schools were philanthropic Victorian institutions that provided education and two meals per day to children who could not pay their way. This particular school accommodated more than 1,000 pupils and functioned between 1877 and 1908.

### ▶▶▶ Geffrye Museum *176C3*

*Kingsland Road, E2 (tel: 020-7739 9893)*
*Open: Tue–Sat 10–5, Sun 2–5. Admission free*
*Underground: Liverpool Street then bus: 22A, 22B or 149*

Despite its out-of-the-way location, this treasure of a museum is well worth seeking out. It is like the Victoria and Albert Museum on a very much smaller scale, containing a series of rooms dating from 1600 to 1950, decorated in period style. It was created in 1914 to inspire crafts students in an area that had long been associated with furniture-making. The museum is housed in a row of handsome brick almshouses grouped around a courtyard, built in 1715 with money bequeathed by Sir Robert Geffrye. At the entrance is a gallery that gives a brief introduction to the displays. Beyond lies the Elizabethan Room, with its rush floor and handsome paneling, beginning a chronological sequence of galleries that covers every major period in English history.

The later rooms are the most fascinating, especially if you are looking for decorating ideas for your own home. The Mid-Victorian Room, with its bold color schemes, richly ornamented objects, and busy wallpapers and textiles, may be a little too cluttered for modern living. By contrast the Voysey Room, named after C.F.A. Voysey, the Arts and Crafts architect and designer, is furnished with simple and honest pieces whose style has had a major influence on the current generation of furniture designers. Last of all, the extension completed in 1999 includes a fashionable 1990s loft apartment. After the period rooms, explore the Reading Room, restaurant, store, exhibition gallery and design center. Don't miss the museum's award-winning walled herb garden where culinary, aromatic, and medicinal plants highlight the traditional past domestic use of herbs. In summer, there are outdoor concerts.

### ▶ Wesley's Chapel, House, and Museum *176B2*

*47 City Road, EC1 (tel: 020-7253 2262)*
*Open: Mon–Sat 10–4, Sun after the 11 AM service until 2.*
*Admission charge; Sun free*
*Underground: Old Street*

John Wesley, the founder of Methodism, lived in this Georgian house from 1779 until his death in 1791, along with several fellow preachers. Methodists from all over the world come here to see the relics of their founder, but the museum is also of interest as a monument to non-conformity. It is interesting to note, for example, that former Prime Minister Margaret Thatcher was married in the chapel attached to the house—as many commentators have noted, the enterprise culture which she espoused during her premiership is a direct product of non-conformist values and the Puritan work ethic. This chapel was designed by Wesley himself and completed in 1778 in a style that he summed up as "perfectly neat, but not fine." In the crypt you can watch a video on the history of Methodism, before touring the house. Here you can see portraits of Wesley, his clothes, furniture, pens, annotated books, and the prayer room in which he used to kneel at 4 AM every morning awaiting his daily orders from God. You can also see the electrical shock machine that Wesley used in an attempt to cure his bouts of melancholia.

### ▶▶ Whitechapel Art Gallery *177A4*

*80–82 Whitechapel High Street, E1 (tel: 020-7522 7888/7878)*
*Open: Tue, Thu–Sun 11–5, Wed 11–8. Admission free*
*Underground: Aldgate East*

This gallery in the East End has an international reputation for its provocative exhibitions of modern art. It also stages quality exhibitions of Asian art, reflecting the local Bengali immigrant population. The vibrant bi-annual Whitechapel Open is unique: an exhibition that spreads art from the gallery to include the studios of many of the estimated 10,000 artists living in the area. The building itself is a fine example of the Arts and Crafts style. The gallery was founded in 1901 by the social reformer and ardent missionary, Canon Samuel Augustus Barnett, whose avowed aim was to "decrease not suffering but sin." He mounted exhibitions of paintings here that were extremely popular with East Enders. He would probably approve of the fact that the café is a popular place for local people to meet, many of them struggling, young and idealistic artists.

**WHITECHAPEL**
Whitechapel was named for its whitewashed parish church and was the place where church bells were cast for parish churches up and down the land. The Whitechapel Bell Foundry, 32 Whitechapel Road, moved here in 1738 and made such notable bells as Big Ben and the original Liberty Bell. The firm now repairs historic bells. In the 19th century Whitechapel was flooded with Jewish refugees from Eastern Europe. Some of their children went on to make a fortune (including Alfred Marks, cofounder of the Marks and Spencer chain). Most moved on to less crowded suburbs, such as Golders Green.

*The splendid art nouveau building of the Whitechapel Art Gallery, designed in 1899 by Charles Harrison Townsend*

*A visit to Spitalfields lets you sample the surprising contrasts of London's East End. This neighborhood has long been a home to refugees. Its character was formed by Huguenot weavers. Their houses, many of them still standing today, had skylit attics where weavers worked to produce fine silk cloth. Then came Jewish refugees from Russia and Poland, who specialized in furs and leather. These were followed in the 1970s by Bengali immigrants, who now toil over sewing machines and steam irons, producing garments for sale in London's clothes stores and street markets. Meanwhile, discerning Londoners have restored many of the East End's elegant Georgian houses.*



**JACK THE RIPPER**
In modern parlance, Jack the Ripper would be called a serial killer. His six victims were murdered over an eight-week period beginning on August 7, 1888, when the first horribly mutilated body was found by a Spitalfields Market porter in nearby Gunthorpe Street. The Ten Bells pub, near Christ Church on Commercial Street, has a window engraved with the full list of his victims. The police's failure to find the notorious murderer led to the resignation of the London Police Commissioner. The celebrated case stimulated the public's appetite for crime and detective stories, such as *The Adventures of Sherlock Holmes*, which Sir Arthur Conan Doyle began to pen in 1891.

The Spitalfields area begins outside Liverpool Street Station, recently restored to its full Victorian splendor. Cross Bishopsgate to Artillery Lane, a narrow alley where No. 56 preserves a rare example of an 18th-century store front. Turn left and you will reach **Spitalfields Market**, where fruit, flowers, and vegetables were sold from the 1680s until 1991, when the market moved to Leyton, a suburb of East London.

The area was once earmarked as the "Covent Garden of the east." It currently houses a crafts market (*Open* daily except Sat), a food market, and a large Sunday market.

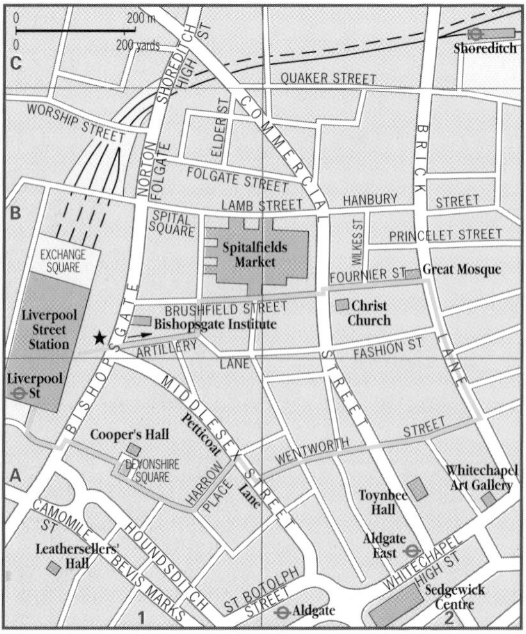

Redevelopment plans hope to emulate Broadgate's success, mixing new offices with refurbished market buildings and leisure facilities. Christ Church, towering above the eastern end of the market, may become the focal point of the development. Built in 1714, this is Nicholas Hawksmoor's masterpiece, and it provokes much debate because of its mixture of classical, Renaissance and baroque elements. Long neglected, and even threatened with demolition, it is now used both as a church and as a concert hall. Some of the gravestones in the churchyard have epitaphs in French, marking the graves of Huguenot refugees who found a haven here after 1685 when the Edict of Nantes, which had guaranteed their right to religious freedom, was revoked. Some grew wealthy as master weavers in the manufacture of silks, damasks, and velvets. Their houses can be seen in **Fournier Street**, to the north of Christ Church. Built between 1718 and 1728, several have been restored by their owners with an almost exaggerated respect for authenticity, rescuing what were regarded as slum properties in the 1970s, faced with the threat of demolition.

**Brick Lane** is now the heart of a large community of Bangladeshis, who fled their homeland after the demise of East Pakistan. Lined with stores selling exotic groceries, brightly printed fabrics, and saris, the simple restaurants serve some of the most authentic Bengali food to be found in London.

On Sundays, this whole area seems like one huge street market. At the northern end of Brick Lane, stalls are set up at dawn. Farther south and west, Commercial Street, Wentworth Street, and Middlesex Street are crammed with the stalls of Asian, Cockney, and Jewish traders on the weekend.

On the way back to Liverpool Street, it is worth seeking out Devonshire Square where, cheek by jowl with the bustling markets, is an office development sited within a group of warehouses dating from the late 18th century and originally built for the East India Company.

**THE NEW GEORGIANS**
The battle to save the Georgian houses of Spitalfields began in the late 1960s, when young Londoners took up residence in the buildings to save them from demolition. The Spitalfields Trust was then formed to buy run-down properties and make repairs before selling them. New owners had to sign agreements to preserve their historic integrity. Some researched Georgian life in minute detail and attempted to live in 18th-century style, without electricity or modern plumbing.

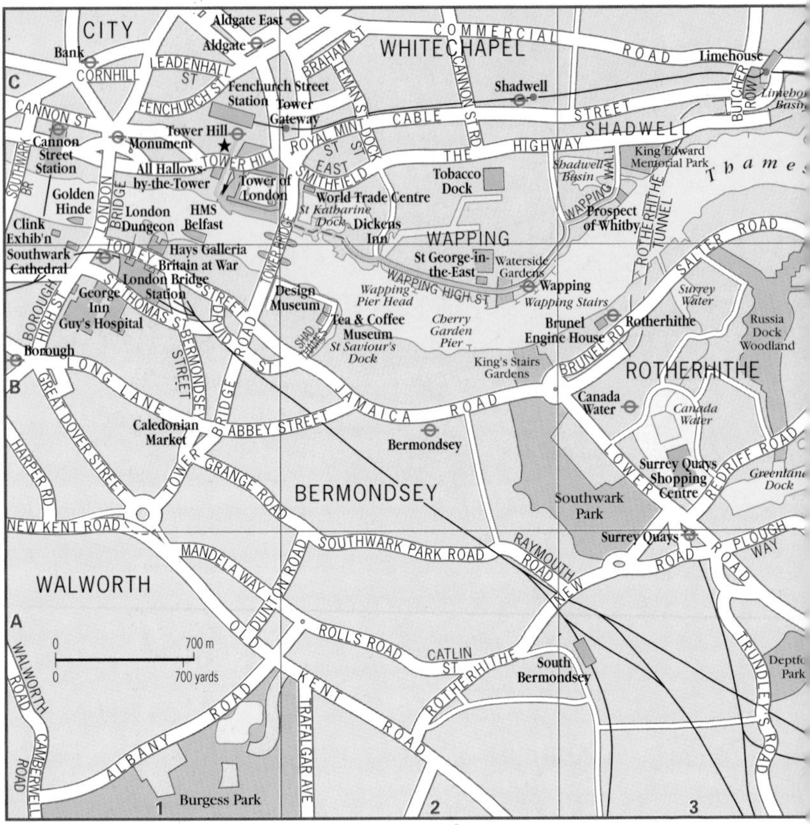

*Above: St. Katharine Dock*
*Right: Canary Wharf Tower*

**DOCKLANDS** London's former docklands lie to the east of the City, covering an area equal to the rest of central London. When the docks fell silent, a massive project backed by the government started in 1981 to create an infrastructure that would encourage the development of new apartments, offices and leisure facilities. Almost a generation later, despite relentless criticism, this new Docklands is maturing. Set on London's most beautiful natural site, the Thames snaking through land cut with a patchwork of water-filled docks, it houses 83,000 people, 2.1 million people visit annually and the occupation rate of the offices is an average of 95 percent. Canary Wharf, with Cesar Pelli's soaring tower, is the centerpiece, but many other architects have contributed notable buildings. The high-level Docklands Light Railway skims past these and past urban farms, parks, sports marinas, waterside restaurants, and restored dock buildings, including the Museum in Docklands, opening in 2001.

**DOCKLANDS WALK** This walk takes in old Docklands, as well as the remodeled buildings and brand new ones.

From Tower Hill tube station exit to your left and walk toward Tower Bridge. Just before it, steps lead down to the Tower Thistle Hotel. St. Katharine Dock, beyond, opened in 1828 and closed down in 1968. It then became the first chunk of Docklands to be restored, complete with

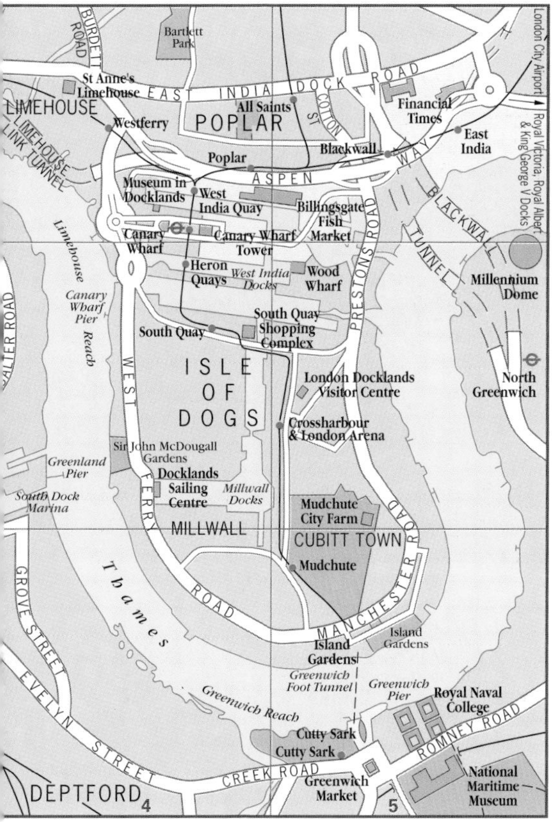


the boat basins and the Dickens Inn, converted from an 18th-century brewery (see page 194).

St. Katharine's Way leads south from the Dock, providing a link to Wapping High Street. This stretch of the route is lined with warehouses built to store tropical spices and valuable hardwoods. Now they have been made into chic loft apartments, although prices have fallen since the 1980s, when a Docklands apartment was the ultimate coveted symbol of success. Farther on, **Wapping Pierhead** is lined with Georgian houses, once the homes of wealthy wharf owners. Beyond this, **Waterside Gardens** has views toward Hawksmoor's baroque church, **St. George-in-the-East**. Continue down Wapping High Street, past the Wapping tube station, and turn right on Wapping Wall for the **Prospect of Whitby** pub, once a haunt of Samuel Pepys and artists such as Turner and Whistler, who came to paint the river views.

To enjoy views of Docklands without walking, take a ride on the elevated ▶▶▶ **Docklands Light Railway (D.L.R.)**. It runs from Tower Gateway Station (by Tower Hill Underground station) through the heart of Docklands to Island Gardens Station, at the tip of the Isle of Dogs. Extensions opening in 2000 take it under the Thames to Greenwich, Deptford and Lewisham, and to Docklands City Airport. From Island Gardens you may like to walk through the Foot Tunnel to Greenwich (see page 217).

*Tug in retirement in front of the The Museum in Docklands*

## ►► Canary Wharf *189C4*

*Canada Square, E14*
*D.L.R.: Canary Wharf station*

In 1988 the master planners, Skidmore, Owings & Merrill Inc., began to develop this huge site, believing that City buildings were difficult to remodel for modern financial needs and fresh ones would create a new financial center. They designed a self-contained mini-city covering 70 acres, with more than 3 million square feet of office space. A new railway (the D.L.R.) and airport (London City Airport) were part of the plan. Today, almost complete and under new ownership, Canary Wharf is the centerpiece of the revived Docklands, and its success can begin to be assessed. Certainly, it is less controversial, and one yardstick of its achievement is that office occupancy is 98 percent. It is well worth a look.

No. 1 Canada Square, Cabot Place and D.L.R.'s Canary Wharf station are all designed by Cesar Pelli. Its landmark tower, Britain's tallest, soars 800 feet high, described by the architect as "a square prism with a pyramidal top in the traditional form of the obelisk—this is the essence of the skyscraper." The first skyscraper to be clad in stainless steel, it reflects light bounced off the surrounding water. Around it are a number of small squares, with stores, restaurants and buildings designed by Troughton McAslan (25 North Colonnade), Terry Farrell (15 Westferry Circus) and Foster and Partners (33 Canada Square and 8–16 Canada Square). There are music and arts events in the public spaces, landscaped gardens and parks, and the art commissions include Bruce McLean's Watercourt railings, Richard Chaix's Cabot Square fountain, Guisseppe Lund's Westferry Circus screens and gates, and Rod Wales's benches for Wren Landing.

Other big projects in Docklands include Royal Albert Dock Regatta Centre, the Royal Arsenal at Woolwich, with its centerpiece, the Royal Artillery Museum, and the nearby Museum in Docklands (see panel).

**MUSEUM IN DOCKLANDS**

The Museum (Warehouse No. 1, West India Quay, E14, tel: 020-7515 1162. *Admission charge*) opens in 2001 and celebrates the story of London and its river, port and people from Roman times until today. Exhibits displayed in the Georgian warehouse that once stored sugar and rum include objects found during the Docklands redevelopment.

### ▶ H.M.S. *Belfast* 188C1

*Morgan's Lane, Tooley Street, SE1 (tel: 020-7407 6434)*
*Open: daily 10–6; Nov–Feb 10–5. Admission charge*
*Underground: London Bridge*

H.M.S. *Belfast* is one of the largest warships ever built for the British Navy. Saved from the scrap yard in 1971, the ship is now moored on the Thames and run as an outpost of the Imperial War Museum. On November 21, 1939, just after going into service, the ship was almost destroyed by a German mine and had to be substantially rebuilt. It played an important part in the D-Day landings, as one of the ship's several small exhibitions reveals. Other exhibits include a collection of 60 paintings by the war artist John Hamilton. The ship is popular with small children who love scrambling up and down its narrow steep ladders and exploring its warren of rooms.

### ▶ Limehouse 189C4

*D.L.R.: Limehouse station*

Limehouse, once a ship-building area notorious for its Chinese-run opium and gambling dens, retains some of its original character. Some Georgian buildings are found on Narrow Street, where the locks at Limehouse Basin link a branch of the Grand Union Canal with the Thames. Warehouse conversions here in the early 1980s set the tone for the loft apartment lifestyle that dominates the riverside revival. The Grapes pub, at No. 76 Narrow Street, was immortalized by Dickens in *Our Mutual Friend*.

*Canary Wharf, a monument to market optimism*

**▶▶▶ REGION HIGHLIGHTS**

**Canary Wharf** *page 190*

**Design Museum** *page 193*

**Docklands Light Railway** *page 189*

**Tower Bridge** *page 196*

**Tower of London** *pages 196–197*

**ROTHERHITHE**

The docklands on the southern side of the Thames, across from Limehouse, have none of the glamor and cachet associated with the redeveloped areas of Wapping or the Isle of Dogs, but they have seen their fair share of history. You can get to Rotherhithe by train from Wapping station, passing beneath the river in a tunnel that was first opened in 1843 as a footpath to enable dockers living on the south bank to walk to their places of work in the north. The engineer was Marc Brunel (father of Isambard Kingdom). The Brunel Engine House, a short walk north of Rotherhithe station on Tunnel Road, was built to pump water out of the tunnel during its construction. Now it is a small museum of local history (Tunnel Road, SE16, tel: 020-7252 0059. *Open* first Sun of the month, 12–4. *Admission charge*). Immediately to the west is the Mayflower pub (117 Rotherhithe Street). Near here, the Pilgrim Fathers set sail in the *Mayflower* bound for Plymouth, Massachusetts, in 1620. The pub sells special American postage stamps commemorating the *Mayflower* for the benefit of U.S. visitors. The captain of the *Mayflower*, Captain Jones, is buried in the nearby church of St. Mary the Virgin, among other fine monuments to local merchants, shipbuilders, and sailors.

*London Bridge City is the redeveloped strip of waterfront on the south bank of the Thames, stretching from London Bridge eastward to Tower Bridge and beyond, into Shad Thames. It is part of Bermondsey, stretching inland, which gained Victorian importance when wharves were built on the south bank to ease shipping congestion. Here, such longstanding institutions as New Caledonian Market survive amid the spunky revival of one of the last areas of inner London to be smartened up.*



**NEW CALEDONIAN MARKET**

Something of the shadowy world of Dickensian London lives on in the New Caledonian Market (confusingly, this is also known as the Bermondsey Antiques Market—it is located at the junction of Long Lane, Bermondsey Street, and Tower Bridge Road). The market, which claims to be the biggest of its kind in Europe, opens to the public at 7 AM every Friday, but long before the ordinary buyers arrive, a huge amount of trading will already have taken place between the stallholders themselves and the professional dealers who swoop at the crack of dawn to snap up the prize pieces. Everyone involved in the market denies that this is where thieves and burglars dispose of their stolen goods, but the suspicion lingers. This should not stop anyone interested in antiques and bric-a-brac from visiting, if only to savor the atmosphere and see the vast array of *objets d'art* on sale. The terms are strictly cash, and persistent haggling is essential if you do not want to pay an exaggerated price. By 11 AM most of the serious business will be over for the day.

Modern, sleek towers of glass in London Bridge City stand hard by survivors from docks days, including several giant warehouses now transformed into fashionable, airy loft apartments.

Starting at London Bridge (see map on pages 188–189) and following the riverside path, called St. Martin's Walk, you will come to **Hay's Galleria**, a stylish if somewhat contrived shopping center. The original Hay's Wharf has been filled in to create a courtyard for sidewalk cafés and gift stalls, sheltered from the elements by a glass atrium supported on iron columns. The blend of old and new works extremely well. Passing through the Galleria to Tooley Street you will find the art-deco facade of St. Olaf's House to the right (west), built in 1931 as the Hay's Wharf Company Offices by the architect H. S. Goodhart-Rendel. The jazzy stripes of this extraordinary building, now restored, look exotic among the dark alleys and utilitarian architecture of the warehouses that surround it.

Going back through Hay's Galleria and turning right (east), it is possible to follow the newly created riverside walk up to Tower Bridge. On the east side of the bridge, is **Shad Thames**, land once owned by the Knights Templar (its name is a corruption of St. John at Thames). Here warehouse walls rise sheer as cliffs, linked, high above, by a network of metal gangway bridges formerly used by warehouse workers to move loads to and from the inter-

*Market-style barrows at Hay's Galleria*

connecting buildings. Despite the dark and gloomy alleys, the apartments here (which were formerly spice warehouses) are highly prized because of their proximity to the City.

The area between Shad Thames and the river is known as **Butler's Wharf**. It is a huge, exemplary development (1987–1989) by Conran Roche, combining revitalization with conservation to preserve the historical spirit of the spice warehouses. Sir Terence Conran, style guru since the 1960s and founder of Habitat Stores and The Conran Shop, masterminded it, and his first-floor restaurants (marginal river views) and delicatessen open onto the wide riverside promenade.

Right on the bend, where Shad Thames curves round St. Saviour's Dock, is the **Design Museum** (Butler's Wharf, SE1; tel: 020-7403 6933. *Open* daily 11:30–6. *Admission charge*), another brainchild of Sir Terence Conran. The core of the museum, itself a modernist warehouse conversion, examines how design affects our lives. Exhibits include everyday objects, from typewriters and kettles to automobiles, selected as classics of modern design and permanently displayed as a study collection. This is augmented by stimulating temporary exhibitions. The museum has a very good bookstore, and reference library, and the upstairs Blueprint Café (an upscale restaurant) boasts wonderful river views. In all, the developers' mixture of dynamic conservation and exciting new buildings on this bank constrasts strikingly with the area east of the Tower, directly opposite.

**BERMONDSEY OLD AND NEW**

Plans to rejuvenate the Bermondsey embankment of the Thames, from Tower Bridge eastward, include the creation of an uninterrupted riverside walkway all the way to Cherry Garden Pier. This pier is traditionally the point at which ships passing upstream would sound their horns if they needed the central span of Tower Bridge lifted to let them pass through. Near the pier is one of the area's best-kept secrets, the Angel pub (101 Bermondsey Wall East), a 15th-century inn with a balcony built out on timber piles enjoying views of the City and the river. Past customers included Samuel Pepys and Captain Cook, while prints on the walls recall the appearance of old Bermondsey. The pub was once a notorious haunt of smugglers and thieves—before the River Police were founded to patrol the river in 1769, and it is estimated that nearly half of all the cargo landed on these shores simply disappeared; many port workers and stevedores were allegedly involved in the racket.

*Sculptural fantasy on the theme of the sea in Hay's Galleria*

## ►► London Dungeon 188B1

*28–34 Tooley Street, SE1 (tel: 020-7403 0606)*
*Open: Apr–Sep 10–6:30; Oct–Mar 10–5:30. Admission charge*
*Underground: London Bridge*

Horrific sights that would send a chill up the spines of most sensitive adults seem to have the opposite effect on children, as you will discover if your offspring demand to be taken to the gruesome London Dungeon. They will shriek with delight at the realistic portrayals of executions and torture, while adults squirm uncomfortably. The most appalling aspect of this hugely successful attraction is that nearly every display is based on reality—the working models of instruments of torture, the painful scenes of martyrdom (particularly St. George), of hanging, flogging, boiling alive, burning at the stake, and disemboweling simply reflect the extraordinarily cruel punishments that human beings have devised and inflicted upon each other. Perhaps children can derive pleasure from the spectacle because they know (or think they know) "it is not real," whereas adults know only too well that it is.

*One of the less grisly displays in the London Dungeon*

**WINSTON CHURCHILL'S BRITAIN AT WAR EXPERIENCE**

This museum (64 Tooley Street, SE1; tel: 020-7403 3171) re-creates the experience of the Blitz (see page 36) through documentary films, and mock-ups of an underground air-raid shelter and a newly bombed street, complete with choking heat and dust. Exhibits include ration books and gas masks.

## ►► St. Katharine Dock 188C2

*St. Katharine Way, E1 (tel: 020-7481 8350/ 488 0555)*
*Open: daily 6 AM–8:30 PM. Admission free*
*Underground: Tower Hill*

St. Katharine Dock was built in 1824–1828 by Thomas Telford and is the closest of all London's docks to the City of London, nestling up against the Tower of London. This proximity to the financial center made the dock a prime target for redevelopment when it became obsolete in 1968, and the 19th-century warehouses have been converted to luxury flats for boat lovers, whose yachts are moored in one of the two main basins. Mingled in among them are historic vessels, including Thames sailing barges that are available to rent (with crew) and the lightship *Norse*, which once operated in the Thames estuary. The dock is a peaceful spot, popular for pub food served at the Dickens Inn, artfully restored from an 18th-century timber-framed brewery.

### ▶ Southwark Cathedral *188B1*

*Montague Close, Borough High Street, SE1 (tel: 020-7407 3708)*
*Open: daily 8–6, including all services. Donation*
*Underground: London Bridge*

Southwark Cathedral, originally a grand Augustinian priory church, became thoroughly down-at-heel after the Reformation and might have disappeared entirely when the railways criss-crossed this deprived area in the 19th century. But it was saved, first by devoted 19th-century restoration and then by being given the status of cathedral in 1905. Until then, it was called St. Mary Overie (a corruption of St. Mary Over the Water, so called because of its position on the south bank of the Thames). Its fine choir, chancel and east-end chapels mix French, English and revival Gothic styles and can be enjoyed during quality lunchtime concerts and services. So can the fine monuments, some of which have been gilded and brightly painted as was originally intended. One commemorates John Harvard, who emigrated to Massachusetts in 1637 and died there within a year, leaving his wealth and his library for the founding of Harvard University. John Gower, the poet and friend of Chaucer, has a splendidly painted effigy, as has the great Jacobean preacher, Lancelot Andrewes. The monument in the north transept, to one Joyce Austin, was carved by Nicholas Stone in 1633. It uses the harvest as a metaphor for death—flanking the central figure are two girls sleeping in straw hats and flowing robes after a hard day's toil in the fields.

*Historic vessels moored in St. Katharine Dock*

*John Gower's tomb*



**THE INNS OF SOUTHWARK**

Talbot Yard, on Borough High Street, a short way south of Southwark Cathedral, is where the Tabard Inn, of Geoffrey Chaucer's *The Canterbury Tales*, once stood. It was one of a cluster of inns. Others were the White Hart, mentioned by Shakespeare in *Henry VI* and by Dickens in *The Pickwick Papers*, and the Queen's Head, which John Harvard sold in 1637 when he emigrated to Massachusetts (see Southwark Cathedral). Only one of Southwark's coaching inns has survived in its original form: the George Inn (1677), by Southwark Cathedral (see page 174). In 1999, a new kind of inn opened, Vinopolis (tel: 020-7645 3700). Housed in the Victorian vaults under the railway lines by Southwark Cathedral, 20 halls are devoted to wine regions of the world, complemented by river-facing restaurants and bars, a wine school, and a store selling wines.

**TOWER TRADITIONS**
The Tower has many ancient traditions. One is the nightly Ceremony of the Keys, when the Chief Yeoman Warder locks the main gates of the Tower at 10 PM, after which a bugler sounds the Last Post. This ceremony has scarcely changed in more than 700 years, except that it now takes place under floodlights with an audience (make a reservation well in advance by writing to: The Ceremony of the Keys, Queen's House, H.M. Tower of London, EC3N 4AB, enclosing a stamped, self-addressed envelope). Eight ravens live in the gardens, well cared for by the official Ravenmaster; legend has it that the Tower will collapse if they fly away. On May 21 members of Eton College and King's College, Cambridge put white roses and lilies in Wakefield Tower in memory of Henry VI, who founded both institutions, and who was murdered here in 1471.



## ▶▶▶ Tower Bridge *188B1*

*SE1 (tel: 020-7407 0922)*
*Open: daily 10–6:30; Nov–Mar 9:30–6. Admission charge*
*Underground: Tower Hill. D.L.R.: Tower Gateway*

Tower Bridge is among London's most famous landmarks even though it was only completed in 1894. It became the last road bridge in central London, famous for its bascule (seesaw) bridge operation which allowed cargo ships into the Upper Pool of London just to its west.

It was hailed in its day as one of the engineering wonders of the world, and visitors can take the Tower Bridge Experience tour to see just how it was constructed. Whether or not you take the tour, however, walk out to the bridge's huge pier to enjoy (free of charge) one of London's finest river views. The tour ascends the north tower, moves along the glassed-in high-level walkways (which offer more wonderful river views) and descends the south tower. En route, chirpy Cockneys and bewhiskered Victorian entrepreneurs (in animatronic and film form) give an entertaining guided tour. The tour ends in the impressive original Victorian engine rooms where there are also hands-on exhibits to pull and push.

## ▶▶▶ Tower of London *188C1*

*Tower Hill, EC3 (tel: 020-7709 0765)*
*Open: Mar–Oct, Mon–Sat 9–5, Sun 10–5; Nov–Feb, Tue–Sat 9–4, Mon, Sun 10–4. Admission charge*
*Underground: Tower Hill. D.L.R.: Tower Gateway*

In summer the Tower of London can be one of the most crowded spots in London, so get there early to avoid the lines inside; to save waiting in line outside, buy your tickets in advance from any Underground station. The

*The style of Tower Bridge echoes that of the Tower of London*

Tower, Britain's best surviving medieval fort, is important to London today for two reasons; it has a long and bloody history and it is home to the British Crown Jewels. In fact only seven people have been privately executed inside the fort; but more than 300 others suffered publicly on Tower Hill just outside the Tower. Henry VIII's second and fifth wives, Anne Boleyn and Catherine Howard, and Lady Jane Grey, who was proclaimed Queen of England

in 1553 but deposed after nine days, were all executed inside the Tower, while Sir Thomas More and Sir Walter Raleigh were imprisoned here before their final journeys. Prisoners were brought in and out of the Tower by boat through the Traitor's Gate, still visible from the embankment. Several dark deeds were committed in the tower (the "Little Princes," Edward V and his brother Richard, were murdered in the Bloody Tower, possibly by their uncle, Richard III, in 1483), but the pace of execution really stepped up under Henry VIII. The site of the block was on Tower Green, in front of the Chapel of St. Peter ad Vincula, whose floor was raised in 1870 to reveal a pile of beheaded skeletons, including those of Anne Boleyn and Catherine Howard. Not surprisingly the Tower is the most haunted building in London, famous for sightings of the ghosts of Anne Boleyn and Sir Walter Raleigh.

Of course, the Tower was not just a place of execution. It also served as a royal fort and palace. William the Conqueror began its construction in 1078, building the central keep, known as the White Tower which contains the exquisite 12th-century Chapel of St. John. Henry III kept his menagerie here, including three leopards, given to him by the Holy Roman Emperor, and a polar bear.

Most of the Crown Jewels, which are kept in the Jewel House, date from the period after 1660; earlier regalia were melted down after Charles I's execution in 1649. The Imperial State Crown includes the 317-carat Second Star of Africa diamond; the Queen Consort's Crown contains the Koh-i-Nur diamond mined in India. An excellent visual story of the jewels entertains those waiting in line, and it is possible to repeat the circuit round the actual jewels immediately for a second look at no extra cost; just ask. There are many other attractions within the Tower including the Fusiliers Museum, the fascinating Medieval Palace, the amazing Royal Armouries, and the Wall Walk.

The fancily dressed Yeoman Warders ("Beefeaters") have looked after the tower since their appointment by Henry VII in 1485. Today, they conduct tours and are a mine of information about the Tower's history.

*Beefeaters have been guarding the Tower since 1485*

**ALL-HALLOWS-BY-THE-TOWER**

The church that stands a short way west of the Tower, on busy Byward Street, is one of the oldest and most interesting in London (Byward Street, EC3; tel: 020-7481 2928. *Open* Mon–Sat 9–6, Sun 10–5). Its medieval crypt contains a Roman floor and a small museum tracing the church's history from its foundation in the 7th century. Upstairs, the church has fine furnishings including a font cover probably by Grinling Gibbons. Pepys watched the Great Fire of London from the tower of this church in 1666.

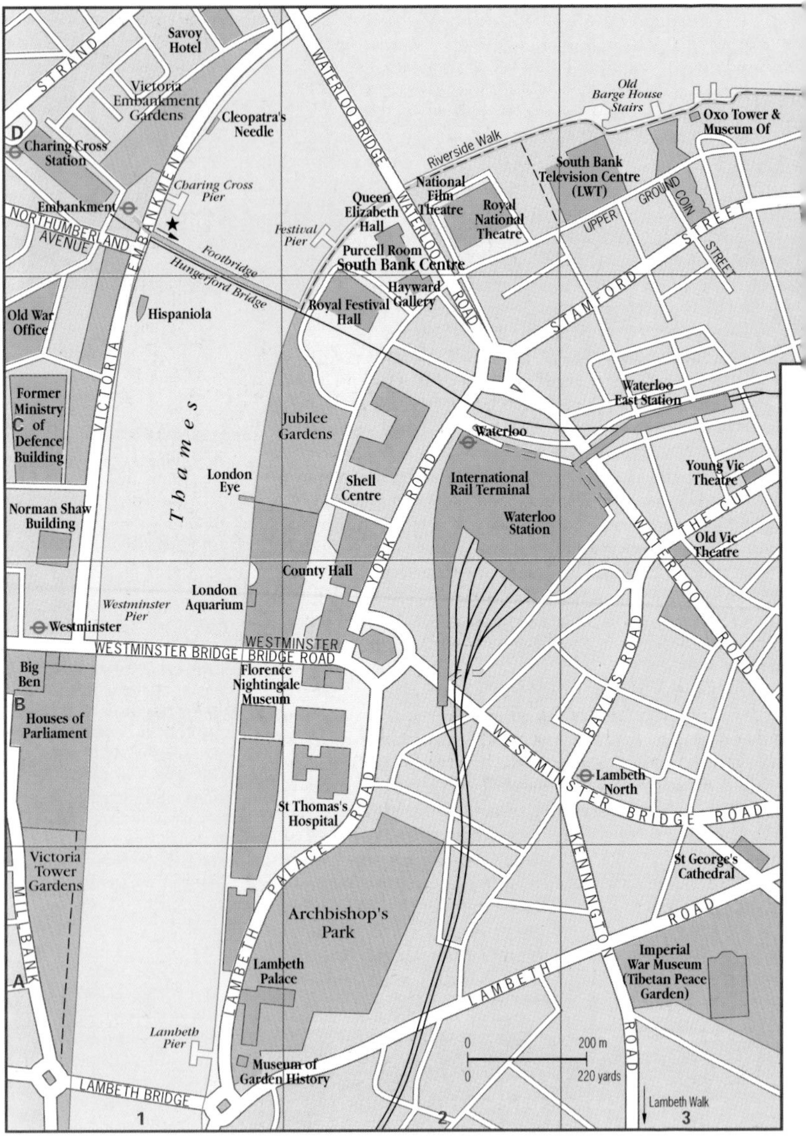

**BANKSIDE** London's south bank has a long association with the theater. Theaters, bear pits, and brothels were banned from the City because authorities felt that apprentices spent too much time playgoing, so the actors moved to the south bank, out of the City's jurisdiction. Today, a long stretch of riverside from Westminster Bridge to London Bridge, and including Bankside, has been regenerated to become a traffic-free boulevard, dotted with museums, galleries, concert halls, theaters, restaurants, and stores—and its own new bridge over the Thames.

**BANKSIDE WALK** From Charing Cross or Embankment Underground stations, on the north side of the river, an

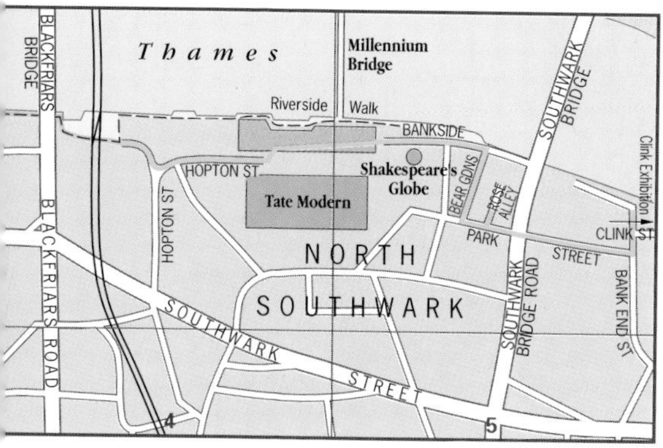


# Bankside



elevated walkway leads across the rebuilt Hungerford Bridge (completed 2000), with good views of Somerset House and the City beyond. Steps descend from the bridge on the south bank to pass in front of the Royal Festival Hall and the South Bank complex (see pages 202–203). Here you will find street musicians, exhibitions, and a crafts market, or you can slip into the Festival Hall for free foyer exhibitions and musical recitals.

The Riverside Walk continues under Waterloo Bridge, past the **National Theatre**, the **National Film Theatre**, and the headquarters of **London Weekend Television**. It then runs under Blackfriars Bridge to join Hopton Street. Farther along, the walk passes **Tate Modern,** and the **Millennium Bridge** (see pages 204–205 for details on both new developments). Next comes Bankside, where a replica of Shakespeare's **Globe Theatre** has been built as faithfully as possible (see page 202).

Bear Gardens leads right (south) from Bankside. In the adjacent Rose Alley, the foundations of the **Rose Theatre** of 1587, which once hosted the plays of Shakespeare and Marlowe, were discovered in 1989. Its remains will be preserved in a gallery beneath a new office development.

Walk down Park Street, past the site on the eastern side of Southwark Bridge Road, where Shakespeare's original Globe Theatre stood. Turn left on Bank End. Here you will find a recently restored pub dating back to the 15th century, the **Anchor Inn**.

Set midway between Southwark and London Bridges, **Clink Street** was the site of a notorious prison, used from the 16th century on to detain heretics, and later thieves, vagabonds, and ruffians. The name is said to derive from the "clinch" irons that were used to pin prisoners to the wall or floor, and "the clink" has become a slang term for any prison. The Clink Exhibition, nearby, reveals the gruesome nature of prison life. Close by is the St. Mary Overie Dock. Look up and you can marvel at the survival of the tall stone wall and rose window frame of Winchester Palace's Great Hall built in the 14th century; archeologists have found traces of Roman villas beneath it. Farther along, the **Golden Hinde** is moored. It is a full-scale replica of the ship in which Sir Francis Drake circumnavigated the world in 1577-1580. In fact the replica has traveled farther than the original, twice around the globe before coming to rest in London. There are five decks, and guides in Elizabethan costume.

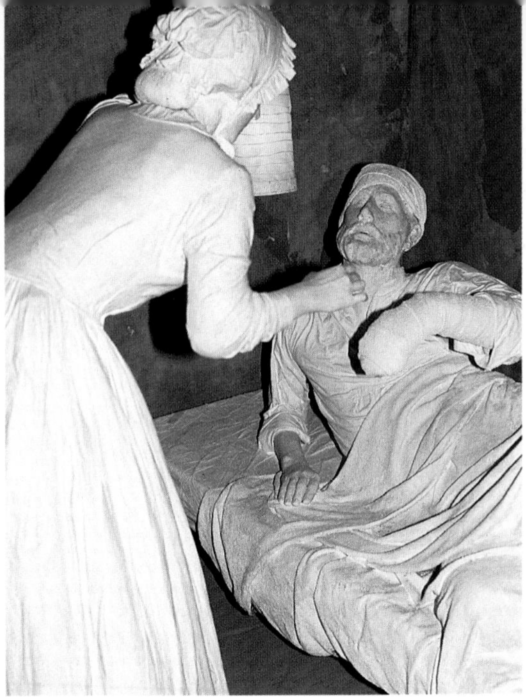

*Britain's most famous nurse, Florence Nightingale, tends the Crimea wounded*

**BEDLAM**

The building that houses the Imperial War Museum was originally built to house the Bethlehem Royal Hospital, an asylum for the mentally ill, popularly known as Bedlam. The original hospital was founded in 1247 as the Priory of St. Mary Bethlehem, situated outside Bishopsgate. In the 17th century it moved to Moorfields and became a popular tourist attraction. Visitors were allowed in to watch the patients, who were placed in caged cells like animals in a zoo (the last of the paintings in the *Rake's Progress*, by Hogarth, depicts the scene—see page 155). The cruelty of such treatment was not appreciated until the late 18th century; the fact that King George III suffered from mental illness helped to bring about a more humane attitude. The asylum moved to this site in Lambeth in 1816 as part of an overall reform of the treatment of patients with serious psychiatric problems. Criminal patients were then moved from here to Broadmoor in 1864, and in 1930 the remaining patients were moved to new premises in Surrey.

*Machines of war, from World War I biplanes to modern missiles*

### ▶ Florence Nightingale Museum *198B2*

*St. Thomas's Hospital, 2 Lambeth Palace Road, SE1 (tel: 020-7620 0374)*
*Open: Tue–Sun 10–5, last admission 4*
*Underground: Westminster*

St. Thomas's Hospital, founded in Southwark in 1213, moved to this site, in 1868, inspired by hospital reforms recommended by Florence Nightingale. She set up the first school of nursing at St. Thomas's and this museum traces the story of her life using audiovisuals and a series of realistic reconstructions. One of these recreates the barrack hospital at Scutari, in the Crimea. The famous lamp that earned her the nickname "the Lady with the Lamp" is on display.

### ▶▶▶ Imperial War Museum *198A3*

*Lambeth Road, SE1 (tel: 020-7416 5000)*
*Open: daily 10–6. Admission charge for adults; children free*
*Underground: Lambeth North*

The title could mislead you. This is one of London's most interesting museums for the whole family. Telling the story of 20th-century conflict from every social, domestic and military viewpoint, there are several excellent permanent exhibitions.

Several displays in the basement take a thematic look at the horrors of the two World Wars. You can tramp through the misery and discomforts of a trench from World War I, then relive the Blitz of 1940–1941 among street scenes littered with the rubble of collapsed and burned-out buildings, complete with the acrid smells of charred wood and the sound of air-raid sirens. The displays also cover war as experienced by concentration camp victims living under Nazi tyranny, Royal Air Force pilots, and members of the armed services fighting on various fronts, in Europe, Africa, and the Far East.

Excellent use is made of audiovisuals and documentary film footage, and the human side of war is also conveyed through the recorded words of war poets and the vivid pictures and sculptures of artists as diverse as David Bomberg, Henry Moore, and John Piper. The *Conflicts Since 1945* exhibition brings events right up to date; from Korea and Vietnam, to Bosnia,and Northern Ireland.

On the first floor the mechanical and technical aspects of war are explored, with huge exhibits of military hardware. The more insidious weapons of germ and chemical warfare are represented, and the display includes John Singer Sargent's large and nightmarish picture of 1918–1919, simply entitled *Gassed*.

Aerial warfare is one theme of the third-floor gallery. There is also an exhibition devoted to clandestine operations and the role of the SAS (Special Air Service) and élite special forces.

The top floor is devoted to works of art by official war artists, including some of the most important painters and sculptors of our time.

In the third stage of the museum's redevelopment, a permanent exhibition on The Holocaust opens in 2000. It examines the persecution and murder of European Jewry and other groups from 1933 to 1945, using original documents and objects, photographs, film, maps and graphics to create a narrative display. A second gallery looks at the impact of war on humanity.

### ▶ Museum of Garden History *198A1*

*St. Mary at Lambeth Church, Lambeth Palace Road, SE1 (tel: 020-7261 1891)*
*Open: Mar–Dec, Mon–Fri 10:30–4, Sun 10:30–5. Donation*
*Underground: Lambeth North, Waterloo*

John Tradescant, the intrepid botanist, introduced many plants, such as the apricot, lilac, and Virginia creeper, to

*The British naval guns that guard the Imperial War Museum were the most powerful weapons of their day*

**▶▶▶ REGION HIGHLIGHTS**



**LAMBETH AND VAUXHALL PLEASURES**

To the west of the Imperial War Museum lies Lambeth Walk, which inspired a song in the musical *Me and My Gal*, written in 1937. Here, Cockneys would come for Sunday afternoon strolls, a tradition dating back to the 17th century when Lambeth Wells was a popular spa with music, dancing and diversions. Other pleasure gardens included the infamous Vauxhall Gardens where sideshows, dancing and extravagant balls mixed pleasure and vice. Today, The London Balloon Company has revived Vauxhall as a place of pleasure (Spring Gardens, SE11, by Vauxhall Underground station, tel: 0345-023842, flights Mon–Sat 10–dusk, Sat, Sun 10–midnight, weather permitting. Tickets may be reserved in advance and are valid for one year in case of cancellation). Their tethered helium balloon, the first of its kind in Britain and world's largest, can lift up to 30 people to more than 400 feet to enjoy panoramic aerial views of London.

**THE PEDDLER'S WINDOW**
A stained-glass window in the south chapel of St. Mary at Lambeth Church depicts a peddler and his dog and is inscribed with the prayer: "May God prosper the land as he hath prospered me." Designed by Francis Stephens, the window commemorates an impoverished 16th-century peddler who took shelter with his dog in the porch of the church one dark and stormy night. Many years later the peddler died a very rich merchant, and he remembered the church in his will, bequeathing an acre of land that he owned not far from the parish on condition that they commemorate him and his dog in a window. Eventually that land was sold to the London County Council and on the site they built themselves a splendid new civic palace, the County Hall. This was the headquarters of London's local authority, a powerful elected body responsible for running everything in the city from public transportation to education, until 1986, when the government decided to abolish the council (see pages 12 and 205).

Europe as a result of expeditions to America, Africa, and the Mediterranean. His aim was to seek out novelties for the aristocratic gardens that he managed, including those of Charles I. He was buried in 1638 in this graveyard; when the church was closed down in 1977 a group of devoted horticulturalists set up the Tradescant Trust to convert it into a museum concerned with all aspects of garden history. The church is now used for temporary exhibitions, and has a stained-glass window of Tradescant and his botanist son. The churchyard is a place of peaceful retreat, full of plants and flowers that the Tradescants brought to Britain from overseas.

### ►►► Shakespeare's Globe *199D5*

*New Globe Walk, Bankside, SE1 (tel: 020-7902 1500)*
*Exhibition open: May–Sep, 9–noon; Oct–Apr, 10–5. Admission charge. Theater season: May–Sep, box office tel: 020-7401 9919)*
*Underground: Mansion House, London Bridge Riverboat: Bankside Pier*

The dream of Sam Wanamaker, the late American film and theater director, was finally realized in May 1997: an established likeness of Shakespeare's Globe Theatre (originally erected in 1599) was completed. Late 16th-century construction techniques were used and the circular building (known as "the Wooden 0") has the first thatched roof in central London since the Great Fire. As in Shakespeare's day, the central part of the theater is open to the elements, though all seats are covered.

A second (indoor) theater, the Inigo Jones Theatre, inspired by Inigo Jones's Cockpit Theatre in Drury Lane, awaits completion and currently houses the Shakespeare's Globe Exhibition. There is a good café, store and education program for all ages.

### ►►► South Bank Centre *198D2*

*South Bank, SE1 (tel: 020-7960 4242/633 0932)*
*Underground: Waterloo, Embankment*
*Open: daily 10 AM–approx 10:30 PM. Admission free*

Grouped along the Thames embankment, on either side of Waterloo Bridge, are the buildings of London's most

*Shakespeare's Globe*

*Bold but brutal—the South Bank arts complex*

important arts complex. Apart from the concerts, plays, and exhibitions held in the main buildings, the traffic-free riverside terraces and lobby spaces are used for exhibitions, book and music stores, cafés and restaurants, street markets, and pass-the-hat musical performances.

The first building on this site was the Royal Festival Hall, the centerpiece of the 1951 Festival of Britain, designed to cheer the nation after the years of rationing and austerity that followed World War II. The building itself is somber, but the acoustics are excellent, and the hall is often used for big choral works.

Alongside are the Queen Elizabeth Hall and Purcell Room, both used for smaller concerts, and the Hayward Gallery, which stages major art exhibitions. These windowless buildings of weather-stained concrete were built in the Brutalist style of the 1960s, as was the Royal National Theatre, beyond Waterloo Bridge, which stages excellent drama (the theater also offers behind-the-scenes tours; for more information, tel: 020-7452 3400).

The architecture of the whole of the South Bank complex has stirred controversy for over three decades. Architects admire the spacious and adaptable interiors and the unabashed use of modern materials, but the public complain about the unfriendliness of the building. The whole group is to be given a facelift inside and out, with particular emphasis on the Royal Festival Hall.

**LAMBETH PALACE**

Right next door to the Museum of Garden History is Lambeth Palace, the official residence of the head of the Church of England, the Archbishop of Canterbury. It has been the archbishop's home since 1190, but the main building visible to the public—the brick gatehouse—was built in 1501. Frequently the palace has been at the center of controversy and storm. In 1534 Thomas More found himself facing a tribunal in the guard room; despite attempts to persuade him, he refused to sign the Oath of Supremacy recognizing Henry VIII, rather than the Pope, as the head of the English church. For this he was hauled off to the Tower and from there to his execution for treason in 1535. From 1867 until recently the palace regularly hosted the Lambeth Conference, a meeting of all the bishops of the worldwide Anglican church, but the location has now moved as the palace is too small.

*Statue of Nelson Mandela on one of the South Bank Centre's walkways*

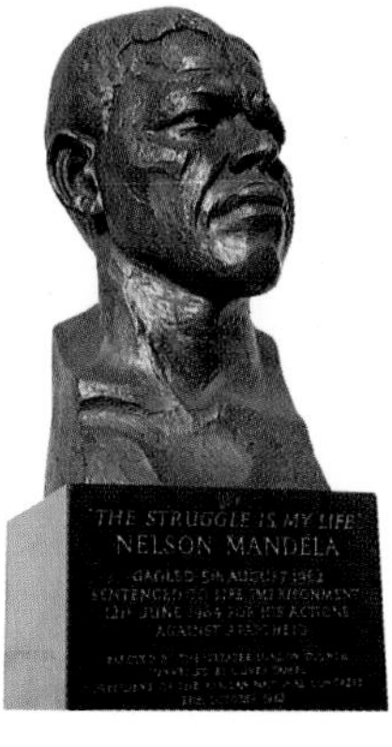

**COIN STREET, GABRIEL'S WHARF, AND OXO TOWER**
The section of river frontage just to the east of the South Bank arts complex has been regenerated by the dynamic Coin Street Community Builders. It comprises housing, Bernie Spain gardens, the riverside walkway, Gabriel's Wharf craft market, and the Oxo Tower. This is a splendid art deco tower built in 1930 for the Oxo company, with the letters "OXO" spelled out in geometrical windows as a permanent advertisement. The Harvey Nichols Restaurant Bar and Brasserie, a sandwich and deli bar, and a free public viewing gallery are at the top of the tower. Lower down, The Museum Of, a new concept, creates temporary museums in The Bargehouse (tel: 020-7401 2255, Wed–Fri 1–7:30, Sat, Sun noon–7:30. *Admission free. Closed* between exhibitions).

*Bankside Power Station has been transformed*



## ▶▶▶ Tate Modern

*Bankside, SE1*
*Open from mid-May 2000. Admission free*
*Underground: Southwark/Blackfriars*

This new museum is one of the world's leading museums of modern art, comparable to the Metropolitan Museum of Modern Art in New York. Its collection, one of the world's finest, could only be partly appreciated when it was housed with the national British Collection at the Tate Gallery (see pages 56–57). Now it is revealed in its full richness, diversity and glory, complemented by further collections at its two out-of-town sites in Liverpool and St. Ives, Cornwall.

The building is spectacular: George Gilbert Scott's monumental brick Bankside Power Station (1947 and 1963; closed from 1981), whose huge spaces are ideal for exhibiting large-scale works of art in an innovative way. So too is the site: standing on the south bank of the Thames, opposite St. Paul's Cathedral, right in the center of the capital.

A competition was held to transform the building from power station to international art gallery, and the winners were the Swiss architects Herzog & de Meuron, designers of the Goetz Gallery in Munich and others in Basel and Mulhouse. Their plan respects the old building while providing an appropriately contemporary setting; for instance, a glass structure spans the length of the roof, adding two floors for public facilities and superb London views, and providing extra natural light for upper floor galleries. Entry is by a ramp down to the former turbine hall; the main galleries of various shapes and heights fill three floors above; facilities include a movie theater, auditorium, café, and store.

Works exhibited in the galleries continue the story of art where the National Gallery leaves off. They are changed

A Bigger Splash,
*by David Hockney*

regularly, to allow visitors and Londoners to enjoy a wide range of exhibits, but always include works by the most influential artists of the 20th century, including Picasso, Matisse, Dali, Duchamp, Moore, Bacon, Gabo, Giacometti, and Warhol. Together, they cover all the significant artistic periods and movements of the 20th century, from Surrealism and Abstract Expressionism to Pop Art and Conceptual Art.

There are pieces by European artists, such as Brancusi's *Maiastra*, Picasso's *The Three Dancers* and Rodin's *The Kiss*. Works by Americans include Richard Hamilton's *The Large Glass* and Andy Warhol's *Marilyn Diptych*. And there are key works of modern British art, showing the different directions it has been developing in. There is Stanley Spencer's mystical painting, Francis Bacon's powerful canvases, Henry Moore and Barbara Hepworth's sculptures, David Hockney's strong draughtsmanship, and Howard Hodgkin's pure color, alongside seminal works by David Bomberg, Sir Anthony Caro, Ben Nicholson, and W. R. Sickert.

As if this were not riches enough, each annual program includes three special loan exhibitions and a number of mid-scale exhibitions focusing on a single artist, theme, or period, with plenty of related events for visitors of all levels of interest. Indeed, a day here is a hugely rewarding London experience, and you can break off to enjoy City and river views from the bankside terrace café or the upscale rooftop restaurant.

One more modern work of art sits outside the gallery. This is the pedestrian Millennium Bridge, which crosses the Thames from St. Paul's Cathedral, and whose southern anchor point is the riverside walk in front of the gallery. Designed by an unusual team (architect Sir Norman Foster, sculptor Sir Anthony Caro and engineers Ove Arup & Partners), this is London's first new bridge since Tower Bridge, opened in 1894, and the city's first dedicated pedestrian bridge.

**COUNTY HALL/ LONDON AQUARIUM**

County Hall, Ralph Knott's palatial riverside building, completed in 1933 as the headquarters of London's administrative body, the Greater London Council (abolished in 1986) is now home to two hotels and the London Aquarium (Westminster Bridge Road, SE1; tel: 020-7967 8000. *Open* daily 10–6. *Admission charge*). A subterranean wonderland of floor-to-ceiling tanks stocked with the world's aquatic life has as its centerpiece the three-story high Atlantic and Pacific displays. The latter has large sharks and stingrays that glide silently between giant sunken Easter Island heads. There are myriad colorful fish to enjoy in the Reef and Corals and Indian Ocean exhibits, and children get a real thrill out of stroking a stingray in the Discovery Zone. County Hall also houses the FA Premier League Hall of Fame and the British Airways London Eye, a 500-feet tall ferris wheel that offers vertigo-inducing views of London.

*Despite childhood memories of long, boring afternoons spent on cold, wet playing fields, a great many British people are obsessively interested in sports, which is why even the serious newspapers devote a large number of pages (usually the last section) to the subject. On Saturday afternoons, the climax of the sports week, a big segment of the population will be sitting in front of the television watching rugby, cricket, track and field, or horse racing.*



**OXFORD VS. CAMBRIDGE**
Twice a year London plays host to sporting events for Britain's two oldest universities, Oxford (the dark blues) and Cambridge (the light blues). One is the Varsity Rugby Match at Twickenham in December; the other is the Boat Race, held on a Saturday afternoon in Spring, when teams race along the Thames from Putney to Mortlake. Most of the spectators have no connection with the universities; many are not even interested in sports. The appeal is to attend a traditional event, and visit pretty riverside pubs.

Cricket was once the national game, but now interest has widened. Today, soccer commands the largest audiences and sports such as tennis challenge cricket for attention throughout the summer. Despite the climate, sport is taken very seriously by most people, whether they participate or merely watch. Currently, when Britain does badly in international games, the nation goes into a state of gloom, and questions are asked in parliament. Substantial funds raised from the sale of National Lottery tickets are to be devoted to providing new sports grounds, sports facilities and better training, with the aid of government money.

Visitors to London who want to watch sports have a wide choice. Football (soccer) and cricket are plentiful, with top-quality matches in the capital. Cricket fans should look for Middlesex (at Lord's) or Surrey (at the Oval); London's premier league football teams include Arsenal, Chelsea, Tottenham Hotspur (Spurs), West Ham, and Wimbledon. Alternatively you can visit a number of sports museums to learn about the record-breaking achievements of past players. One of the best is the award-winning **Lawn Tennis Museum** (Tue–Sat, Sun PM) at Wimbledon, which makes imaginative use of audio-visuals to explain the history of the game. There is a

*London Marathon*

display of tennis clothing and equipment that vividly shows that the speed and excitement of women's tennis in particular has improved as the players have discarded long skirts and hats (All England Lawn Tennis Club, Church Road).

Equally worthwhile are the guided tours. **Wembley Stadium**, completed in time to host the 1923 F.A. (Football Association) Cup final, is to be totally rebuilt between 2000 and 2002 as the core of England's bid for the 2006 World Cup. However, rugby fans can visit the stadium in Twickenham (see page 234).

For cricket lovers, **Lord's Cricket Ground** (St. John's Wood Road) is almost a place of pilgrimage. The ground is named for the property developer Thomas Lord and not, as is often supposed, because so many early players were aristocrats. Lord set up the first cricket field in what is now Dorset Square in 1787; when the site was developed for housing, he moved the turf of the original ground first to North Bank and finally to the present site in 1811. This and other intriguing episodes in the history of cricket are covered by the **M.C.C. (Marylebone Cricket Club) Museum** at Lord's (daily; guided tours of the museum and players' facilities are also available, daily, at noon and 2 PM, except on match days).

The prize exhibit here is the tiny urn containing the Ashes, the trophy awarded each year to the winner of the England versus Australia test series (the trophy stays at Lord's even when Australia wins). The "Ashes" are those of a bail symbolically burned by Australian supporters after their defeat at the hands of the Marylebone Cricket Club (M.C.C.) in 1883. Other exhibits include portraits of leading cricketers, such as W. G. Grace, and a stuffed sparrow killed by a fast ball bowled by Jehangir Khan on July 3, 1936. Lord's itself is particularly interesting from an architectural point of view: the tentlike structure which protects spectators who are seated in the Mound Stand is an innovative example of modern stadium design by Michael Hopkins and Partners (1986). The latest architectural contribution to the ground is the startlingly space-age Media Centre, the world's first building to be made of a single aluminum shell. When it was opened in May 1999, the Media Centre, designed by Future Systems, was described as resembling "a giant radio alarm clock on stilts."

*Wimbledon ball girl*



**THE LONDON MARATHON**
Another great annual event that perpetuates the spirit of amateurism is the London Marathon, held in April. The streets that form the route are closed off and thousands of spectators line the route to cheer on the many thousands of runners taking part in the biggest event of its kind. First run in 1981, it has rapidly become a major fixture in the city's calendar. Top international athletes cover the 26-mile course, from Greenwich/Blackheath to the Mall, in a little over two hours. It is the slower, amateur runners, however, who delight the crowds—celebrities, runners in outlandish costumes, children, senior citizens, and athletes with disabilities. Most of them raise substantial sums of money for charity, from the friends, families, and workmates who agree to sponsor them.

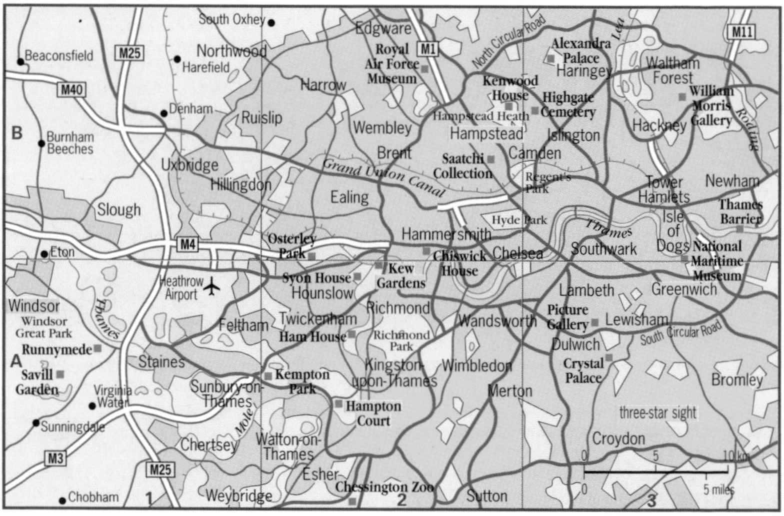




*Let the train take the strain*

**TRAVEL INFORMATION** Leaflets, tickets, and advice on a range of excursions and options for exploring the London area, can be obtained from the London Tourist Board Information Centre, in Victoria Station Forecourt (no telephone inquiries). The British Visitor Centre, 1 Regent Street, Piccadilly Circus, SW1 (no tel. inquiries. *Open* Mon–Fri 9–6:30, Sat, Sun 10–4, except Jul–Sep, Sat 9–5) has information on the whole of Britain.

**▶▶▶ HIGHLIGHTS**

**Bath** *page 210*
**Cambridge** *page 211*
**Greenwich** *pages 216–219*
**Hampstead** *pages 220–221*
**Hampton Court Palace** *pages 222–223*
**Highgate** *pages 224–225*
**Kew Gardens** *pages 226–227*
**Oxford** *page 211*
**Syon House and Park** *pages 232–233*
**Windsor** *pages 236–237*

**EXCURSIONS** Inner London holds enough attractions to keep most visitors happy and entertained for weeks on end, but sometimes it is worth escaping for a day to explore delights farther afield.

This section highlights the best of the villages, parks, river walks, museums, and stately homes within easy reach of central London, from the royal palaces of Hampton Court and Windsor to the botanical riches at Kew Gardens, or the absorbing account of Britain's sea faring history at the Greenwich Maritime Museum. All these sites are well served by public transportation and if you buy a one-day Travelcard, from any Underground or British Rail station, you can enjoy unlimited travel by bus, tube, or rail in the London area. A two-day Travelcard covering Saturday and Sunday at a 25 percent discount is also available, as is a family ticket Travelcard, offering a 20 percent discount.

London is also at the heart of the nation's rail and road network, which means that many other historic towns and cities are within easy reach of the capital. Tour operators offer well-planned day trips to Oxford, Stratford-upon-Avon, Canterbury, or Cambridge, and these can often be reserved through your hotel.

Alternatively, you may prefer to travel independently: InterCity Rail services will take you to far-away towns such as as Bath, York, or Edinburgh in a few hours, or to Oxford and Cambridge, which are much closer. There is also a useful express bus service to Oxford. It is wise to book tickets and reserve seats in advance, if possible.

Renting a car is perhaps the least attractive option because of England's congested road system and the difficulty of parking in London (and other major cities). On the other hand, a car is essential if you want to see some of England's gardens, stately homes, and rural back roads. In this case you should consider taking a train to the region that you want to explore and renting a car locally to avoid the traumatic experience of driving in London.

In any event, remember that London's roads are busiest during the rush hours (8–10 and 4–7), and long traffic jams are common on the roads that lead out of London on Friday evenings and on routes into the city on Sunday evenings and Monday mornings, as people travel to and from the country. The M25, London's "beltway," is almost always crowded.

**INTERCITY RAIL SERVICES**

The following mainline stations in London serve the main cities and regions of Britain:
Paddington for Oxford, Bath, and the West Country.
Euston for Stratford-upon-Avon, the Midlands, and Glasgow.
King's Cross for Cambridge, York, and Edinburgh.
Liverpool Street for Cambridge, Colchester, Ipswich, and Norwich.
Waterloo for Winchester, Salisbury, Bournemouth, and Portsmouth.
Victoria for Gatwick, Brighton, Canterbury, and Dover.
For all rail enquiries tel: 0345-484 950.



*Early morning mists give King's College Cambridge (founded in 1441) a timeless feel*

*Two of Bath's great attractions, its 16th-century abbey and the adjacent Roman Baths*

**THE NATIONAL TRUST**
Many of England's stately homes, castles, gardens, and landscapes are owned by the National Trust—including such London properties as Ham House (see page 231), Osterley Park (see page 228), and Carlyle's House (see page 90). The National Trust was set up in 1895 and has rescued many buildings, threatened areas of countryside, and antiquities that might otherwise have suffered from neglect or destruction. Members gain free admission to most of its properties, and receive a comprehensive directory. Details from any National Trust property, from its London Information Centre and store at Blewcoat School, 23 Caxton Street, SW1 (tel: 020-7222 2877) or from The National Trust, Membership Department, P.O. Box 39, Bromley, Kent BR1 3XL (tel: 020-7315 1111 for credit-card membership by phone).

## Days out from London

Here are a few suggestions for day trips out of town that could easily be extended with an overnight stop.

**Bath▶▶▶** The train ride from Paddington station to Bath takes just under two hours. The magnificent Roman baths and the spa town's elegant Regency buildings, crescents, and gardens evoke the age of Beau Nash and the high-society gatherings that took place in the Pump Room, Theatre Royal, and Assembly Rooms in the early 19th century. Additional attractions are excellent stores and the American Museum at Claverton Manor.

**Brighton▶** An hour by train from Victoria station, Brighton was the favored seaside resort of aristocratic Londoners including the Prince Regent (later King George IV), who built the extraordinary Pavilion, with its Oriental domes and Chinese-style state rooms. Nearby, the stores of the Lanes are a great place to browse. Walk along the Victorian Palace Pier promenade to enjoy the sea air.

**Cambridge▶▶▶** An hour's train journey from King's Cross or Liverpool Street takes you to Cambridge—a wonderful place to see in spring, when the college gardens backing on to the River Cam are a mass of daffodils, or in summer, when you can rent a boat along the river, enjoying views of Kings College Chapel, the Bridge of Sighs, or the self-supporting Mathematical Bridge, built of wood, without the help of nails.

**Canterbury▶** Chaucer's pilgrims, heading for the shrine of St. Thomas à Becket, expected to take several days to journey from London to Canterbury, but now the cathedral city is an hour away by train from Victoria. The cathedral, with its stained glass, sits within the city's surviving Roman walls and not far away from the ruins of St. Augustine's abbey, founded in AD 598, when Augustine was sent from Rome to bring Christianity to the British Isles. If you rent a car, Canterbury also makes a good base for exploring Leeds Castle, set on an island surrounded by parkland, and Sissinghurst's magnificent garden, created by Harold Nicolson and Vita Sackville-West.

**Oxford▶▶▶** Just over an hour's journey from Paddington station, Oxford was described by the poet Matthew Arnold as "that sweet city with her dreaming spires." The university town is crowded with ancient collegiate buildings of honey-colored Cotswold limestone, many of which have lovingly tended gardens. It is also famous for its many good bookstores, its river walks, and its lively student atmosphere. If you decide to stay overnight, you could take a bus tour of Stratford-upon-Avon, to see Shakespeare's birthplace, Ann Hathaway's cottage, and the poet's grave in Holy Trinity Church, alongside the River Avon.

**Salisbury▶** Salisbury's glorious 13th-century cathedral has changed remarkably little since John Constable painted its needle-sharp spire rising out of the surrounding water meadows. The cathedral, restored in the 20th century, offers intriguing tours of the roof. Salisbury is just over an hour from London, by train from Waterloo. The 5,000-year-old stone circle at Stonehenge is only 10 miles outside the city (there is a bus that passes the site and leaves from Salisbury railway station).

*Gliding along the tranquil River Cam in Cambridge*

**ENGLISH HERITAGE**
English Heritage is funded by the government and responsible for properties such as Chiswick House (see pages 212–213), Kenwood (see page 225), and Marble Hill (see page 234). Membership benefits include free admission to all properties and a comprehensive guide. For details, ask at any property or write to English Heritage, Membership Department, P.O. Box 1BB, London W1A 1BB (tel: 020-7973 3434).



**THE COTSWOLDS AND BLENHEIM PALACE**
You won't be able to see much of the Cotswolds by just taking a day trip out of London, but trips do run from Oxford and Stratford-upon-Avon, which are both on the edge of this area of outstanding natural beauty. Better still, you can rent a car and explore for yourself. Places within easy reach and well worth a visit include Chipping Campden, Broadway, The Slaughters, Snowshill Manor, and Burford. Just north of Oxford is one of England's great palaces, Blenheim, where Churchill was born.

*Simple domesticity at William Hogarth's House, featuring a picture of the artist and dog*

**THE HOUSES OF CHISWICK MALL**

Chiswick Mall's houses betray the wealth of their original owners, able to afford that rare commodity in London, uninterrupted views of the River Thames and gardens that sweep down to the water's edge. One of the best buildings is Walpole House, a rare example of Restoration-period architecture, built around 1700 for Barbara Villiers, the Duchess of Cleveland, one of Charles II's mistresses. In the 19th century it served as a school, said to be the one on which Thackeray modeled Miss Pinkerton's Academy for Young Ladies in his novel *Vanity Fair*. Another building of note is Kelmscott House, on the Upper Mall, the home of William Morris from 1878 to 1896 and named for his country house in Oxfordshire. It was at the nearby Sussex House that Morris set up the Kelmscott Press to produce beautifully hand-printed, illustrated and bound books.



## ►► Chiswick *209B2*

In the 18th and 19th centuries, Chiswick was a favorite place of residence for artists such as William Hogarth, and it was here that Lord Burlington built Chiswick House, the most perfect example of a Palladian country villa in England. Those interested in Arts and Crafts housing should take a stroll around Bedford Park, designed by E.W. Godwin and Norman Shaw in the 1870s.

The best way to reach Chiswick is by train from Waterloo. From Chiswick station, turn right and follow Burlington Lane for about half a mile to reach the entrance to Chiswick House, with its fine Italianate gardens and the long, sweeping avenue that leads up to the house.

**Chiswick House►►►** (Burlington Lane, tel: 020-8995 0508. *Open* Apr–Oct, daily 10–6; Nov–Mar, Wed–Sun 10–4. *Admission charge.* Gardens open daily dawn to dusk, free). This delightful villa was built in 1725–1729 by Lord Burlington, a patron of the arts and an accomplished architect in his own right; he had already commissioned Colen Cambell to build his townhouse, Burlington House (now home to the Royal Academy of Arts, see page 82). His inspiration was Palladio's Villa Capra, near Vicenza in northern Italy, but the building is far from being a slavish copy. The main east front, for example, has an elaborate double staircase leading to the two-story portico, unlike any Palladian prototype. Flanking the staircase are fine statues carved by Rysbrack around 1730, representing Palladio and Inigo Jones, the English architect who did so much to introduce the ideals of classical architecture to England.

There is another homage to Inigo Jones in the obelisks on the roof that surround the central dome. These are, in fact, disguised chimneys and are copied from designs made by Jones for the Queen's House at Greenwich, as are some of the magnificent chimney pieces inside the villa. The upper floor is richly decorated with gilded cherubs, swags and scrolls, statues of classical deities, and ceiling paintings by William Kent.

The garden, also designed by Kent, makes a romantic setting for the villa. Although Italian in style, and dotted with temples, statues, and obelisks, it marks a departure from the strict geometric Renaissance form to a safer, more idealized version of the Roman Campagna as found in the landscape paintings of artists such as Claude and Salvator Rosa.

**Chiswick Mall▶** An underpass leads from beneath the busy Hogarth Roundabout to Church Street and St. Nicholas Church, the burial place of several artists and architects, including Hogarth, William Kent, Colen Campbell, and James McNeill Whistler. From the church you can walk for over a mile along Chiswick Mall, Upper Mall and Lower Mall, admiring some of London's finest 18th-century houses and perhaps stopping at one of several riverside pubs. At the end of the Lower Mall, Hammersmith Bridge Road leads north to Hammersmith tube station for the journey back to central London.

**Hogarth's House▶** (Hogarth Lane, tel: 020-8994 6757. *Open* Apr–Sep, Tue–Fri 1–5, Sat, Sun 1–6; Oct–Mar, Tue–Fri 1–4, Sat, Sun 1–5. Some closures. *Admission charge*). Today, Hogarth's House stands to the north of Chiswick House on Hogarth Lane, close to a busy traffic circle. The scene was very different when the "little country box by the Thames" stood in open fields. Hogarth used it as his summer residence between 1749 and 1764, and the simple rooms are hung with copies of his satirical engravings, including *Marriage à la Mode* (1745) and *A Rake's Progress* (1735). In the tiny garden, an ancient mulberry tree, under which Hogarth used to sit, survives and bears fruit.

**RIVERSIDE PUBS**

As you stroll along the Mall you can choose from one of several historic pubs. The 16th-century **Dove Inn** (19 Upper Mall) is where Charles II and Nell Gwyn are said to have made secret rendezvous. A list of other famous customers (including Ernest Hemingway and Graham Greene) is displayed above the great fireplace. This pub earns an entry in the *Guinness Book of Records* for having the smallest public bar in England (a mere 5 feet by 8 feet). The **Old Ship** (25 Upper Mall) dates from the mid-17th century and is decorated with nautical relics, and the **Blue Anchor** (13 Lower Mall) is the popular wood-paneled haunt of members of the Amateur Rowing Association, whose headquarters are next door.



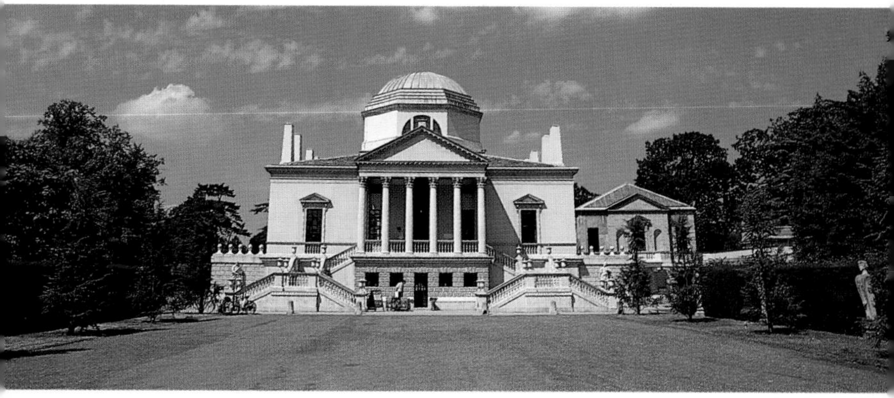

*Chiswick House: Palladian grandeur in a country setting just a few minutes by Underground from the center of London*

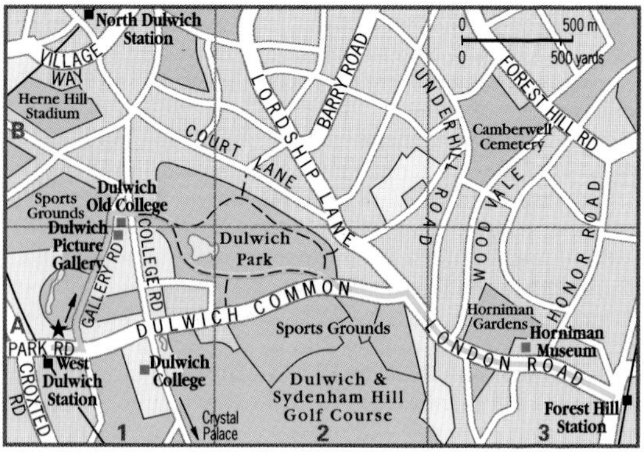


**THE HISTORY OF DULWICH GALLERY**
The remarkable collection of paintings housed in the Dulwich College Picture Gallery was put together by the art dealer Noel Desenfans. He was commissioned in 1790 by the king of Poland to buy paintings for a National Gallery that was planned for Warsaw. When the king was deposed, Desenfans offered the collection to the British government, suggesting that it could form the basis of a new National Gallery. The government refused (it finally got around to founding today's National Gallery in 1824), so in 1807 Desenfans left the collection to his friend, Sir Francis Bourgeois, who in turn bequeathed it to Dulwich College in 1811. As a result, an exceptionally fine collection of art, with major works by Rubens, Gainsborough, Van Dyck, Rembrandt, and Raphael, fit to grace any national museum, has ended up in a quiet south London suburb.



## ►► Dulwich

In 1605 Edward Alleyn, an actor-manager who amassed a considerable fortune by running bull- and bear-baiting entertainment as well as theaters, bought the manor of Dulwich. Here he built and endowed Dulwich College, a school for the poor, and ensured the survival of a large expanse of parkland in south London. The attractions in Dulwich today include the Dulwich College Picture Gallery, with its collection of Old Masters, and the Horniman Museum, which is renowned for its ethnography collection.

**Dulwich Gallery►►►** (College Road, tel: 020-8693 5254. *Open* Tue–Fri 10–5, Sat 11–5, Sun 2–5. *Admission charge*) reopens in May 2000 after refurbishment to include a café overlooking its five-acre garden. The collection, consisting of some 300-plus masterpieces, dating largely from the 17th century, hang in the refined neoclassical building designed by Sir John Soane in 1811–1814. This was the first purpose-built art gallery in England, and its highlights include Rembrandt's portrait of *Jacob III de Gheyn* (stolen several times from the gallery but, fortunately, recovered each time), Van Dyck's *Madonna and Child*, and Poussin's *Return of the Holy Family from Egypt*.

The gallery also serves as a mausoleum: at the rear of the building is the tomb of Noel Desenfans, who was responsible for putting the collection together, and Sir Francis Bourgeois, who bequeathed it to Dulwich College in 1811 (see side panel).

Alongside the Picture Gallery, **Dulwich Old College►** dates from 1619 and now serves as offices. This was the original school founded by Edward Alleyn; the main school today lies half-a-mile to the south, housed in Renaissance-style buildings designed in 1866–1870 by Charles Barry, the son of the architect who built the Houses of Parliament.

A path to the Horniman Museum leads through **Dulwich Park►** from the entrance just east of the Picture Gallery. The park is especially colorful in May, when the azaleas and rhododendrons are in full bloom, but there are fine trees to admire at all times of the year, including statuesque oaks, and a number of more exotic specimens, such as the Japanese pagoda tree.

The path takes you south of the boating lake, café, and aviary, and out by the lodge gates on Dulwich Common—once a royal hunting ground, now a golf course. Turn left, then right on Lordship Lane to reach the Horniman Museum on London Road.

**Horniman Museum▶▶** (London Road, tel: 020-8699 1872. *Open* Mon–Sat 10:30–5:30, Sun 2–5:30. *Admission free*) is very popular with children, not least because of its miniature zoo.

The entrance to C. Harrison Townsend's 1901 art nouveau building, has a large mosaic by Robert Anning Bell: *The Course of Human Life*. Inside, the exhibits reflect the quirky interests of Frederick John Horniman who, as head of his family's tea importing business, traveled widely in the 1870s and collected anything that appealed to his sense of curiosity: these include stuffed animals, fossils, musical instruments, masks, sculptures, and assorted tribal artifacts.

Objects representing different cultures have been arranged to illuminate a number of topics, including initiation rites, the use of narcotics, agriculture, crafts, fishing, and cooking. Do not miss African Worlds, a gallery dedicated to African, Afro-Carribean and Brazilian culture opened in 1999.

For the return journey to central London follow London Road left to Forest Hill railway station, where frequent trains depart for London Bridge.

*The art nouveau tower of the Horniman Museum*

**CRYSTAL PALACE**

Once it had served its purpose of housing the Great Exhibition in Hyde Park in 1851, the Crystal Palace Exhibition hall was re-erected on a high hill just to the south of Dulwich. The monumental glass-and-iron building, designed by Joseph Paxton, then became the centerpiece of a huge amusement park, opened by Queen Victoria in 1854. In 1936, the Crystal Palace went up in flames; 90 fire engines failed to quench the ferocious blaze. Today, all that remains of this vast Victorian Disneyland is the boating lake with some life-size models of prehistoric dinosaurs, made in 1854, set on a series of artificial islands. A small museum on Anerley Hill, near Crystal Palace station, covers the history of this fairy-tale building and its sad demise (Anerley Hill, tel: 020-8676 0700. *Open* Sun 11–5. *Admission free*).

The park now houses a city farm, major sports stadium and concert bowl where pop and orchestral concerts take place in summer (daily).

**GREENWICH PUBS**
In Greenwich you have plenty of choices when it comes to traditional pubs, many of which serve seafood and have outdoor terraces with river views. Perhaps the best is the **Trafalgar Tavern** (reservations advised for meals, tel. 020-8858 2437) in Park Row, which Dickens describes in *Our Mutual Friend*. The interior is like a ship, with nautical relics on display and large windows overlooking the Thames. Another shiplike tavern, the **Cutty Sark**, is reached by following the riverside path, via Crane Street and Highbridge, to Ballast Quay; it's well worth the walk just for the view northward up the vast expanse of the Thames to Blackwall. Within the center of Greenwich the choice includes the **Spanish Galleon Tavern** and the **Gipsy Moth**, both on Greenwich Church Street, or the **Coach and Horses**, built in 1730, in Turpin Lane alongside bustling Greenwich Market.

*Right: The* Cutty Sark.
*Below: Early telescope*

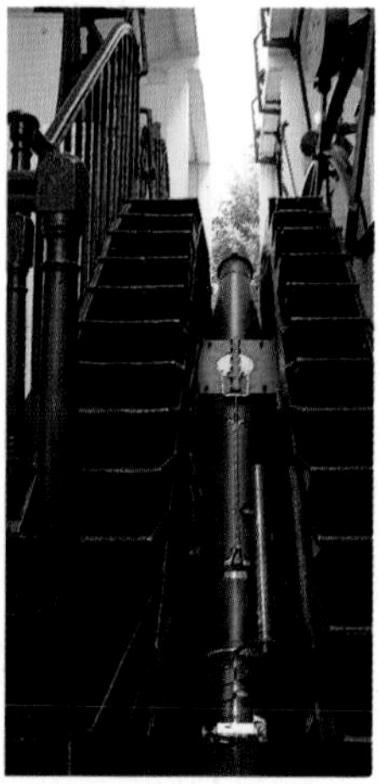

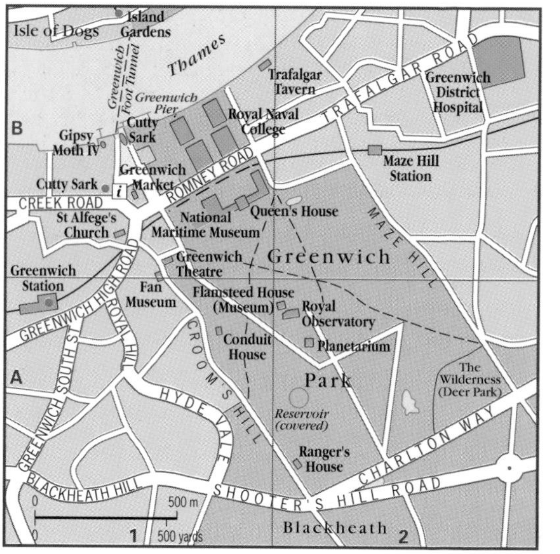


## ▶▶▶ Greenwich

Greenwich is every bit as beautiful as its name (a corruption of "green reach") suggests. Here, set in parkland that sweeps down to the river's edge, are some of London's most noble buildings: the Queen's House—built by Inigo Jones and now the National Maritime Museum, Wren's Royal Naval College alongside the Thames, and his Royal Observatory on the hill above. Add to this the attractions of the *Cutty Sark* and a delightful village, and you have all the ingredients for a full and varied day's outing from central London.

There are several ways to get to Greenwich: by train from London Bridge; by riverbus from Westminster, Charing Cross, or Tower piers; or by Docklands Light Railway to Island Gardens station. The advantage of this last route is that you will enjoy Christopher Wren's carefully planned view from Island Gardens across the river to the Royal Naval College, with the Queen's House beyond. It is then just a short walk under the Thames through the Greenwich Foot Tunnel to reach all the sights of Greenwich.

Both the foot tunnel and the riverbus bring visitors to Greenwich Pier, where the **Cutty Sark▶▶** (King William Walk, tel: 020-8858 3445. *Open* Apr–Sep, Mon–Sat 10–6, Sun noon–6; Oct–Mar, daily 10–5, Sun noon–5. *Admission charge*) lies moored in a dry dock, housing an exhibition of ships' figureheads below deck. This sleek and handsome ship, with its tall masts and intricate rigging, was built in 1869 as a tea clipper, carrying precious cargoes between Britain and the Orient. In 1871 she broke the world record for sailing between London and China, completing the trip in only 107 days, at her fastest covering 360 miles in a single day. Exploring the ship will give you some idea of the cramped living conditions that were endured by the 28-man crew.

Moored nearby is **Gipsy Moth IV▶** (King William Walk, tel: 020-8853 3589. *Open* Easter–Oct, Mon–Sat 10–6, Sun noon–6. *Admission charge*), the tiny yacht in which Sir Francis Chichester made the first single-handed circumnavigation of the globe in 1966–1967. Nearly 400 years before that, Sir Francis Drake had been the first Englishman to sail around the world. The sword used by Queen Elizabeth II to knight Sir Francis Chichester was the same one used by Elizabeth I to knight Drake in the 16th century.

Immediately south of the pier is College Approach, the route into the core village of **Greenwich▶**, lined with some early 19th-century buildings that flank the entrance to Greenwich Market. The covered market, built in 1831, is now only open on weekends and specializes in crafts. Another market, selling antiques, books, and period clothing, operates during weekends in the summer on Greenwich Church Street.

A short walk away, splendid wrought-iron gates on King William Walk form the main entrance to the **Royal Naval College▶▶** (West Gate, King William Walk, tel: 020-8852 2154. *Open* daily 2:30–4:45. *Admission free*), originally built as a hospital for infirm and aged seamen. These monumental buildings were begun in 1664, with a riverside wing for Charles II. Christopher Wren , brought in by William and Mary to create a sailors' hospital similar to his one in Chelsea (see pages 92–93), evened up the symmetry either side of the court to frame the impressive southward view of the Queen's House. This bold and brilliant design is best appreciated from the Isle of Dogs, at Island Gardens beside the Greenwich Foot Tunnel.

Two of the buildings are open to the public. The Painted Hall, created by Sir James Thornhill in 1707–1717, has some of the finest baroque paintings in England. They show William and Mary surrounded by allegorical figures symbolizing the triumph of virtue over vice.

The Chapel (1718-1725), which was originally designed by James Stuart but was rebuilt after a fire in 1779, is in neo-Grecian style and a vast altar painting by Benjamin West, *St. Paul Shaking Off the Viper*, is also displayed here.

**MILLENNIUM DOME**
Greenwich is London's Millennium Exhibition Site. The central dome (*Open* daily for two operating sessions. Admission by pre-booked ticket only. Current information on www.London\Town.com) is the largest structure of its kind in the world, with a diameter of more than 1,000 feet. Designed by a team which includes Richard Rogers, the Dome contains 14 attraction zones arranged in a circle around a central performance area (live shows daily). The themed zones celebrate British ideas and technology and address questions about 21st-century life

*The domed entrance to the Greenwich Foot Tunnel beneath the Thames to the Isle of Dogs*

*The Greenwich Meridian line, which visitors love to straddle: one foot in the east, one foot in the west*



The principal attraction in Greenwich is the **National Maritime Museum▶▶▶** (Romney Road, tel: 020-8858 4422/8312 6565. *Open* daily 10–5. *Admission charge*), entered from Romney Road. It occupies several buildings in Greenwich Park and tells the story of Britain's age-old relationship with the sea.

The museum's central building, the **Queen's House▶▶▶**, is an architectural monument in its own right—the first Renaissance building in England to be designed in the classical style, and the prototype for many subsequent public buildings and stately homes. Inigo Jones began the building in 1616 as a rural retreat for Anne of Denmark, James I's queen, but she died in 1619; it was Henrietta Maria, the French wife of Charles I, who presided over its completion in 1635. The finest feature of the interior is the Tulip Stair, named for the pattern on its balustrade (probably intended to represent fleurs-de-lis, the symbol of France). This leads to the Great Hall, its dimensions forming a perfect cube, with ceiling paintings showing the Muses, the Virtues, and the Liberal Arts. The original paintings were moved to Marlborough House, Pall Mall, in the 18th century; these are a computer-enhanced replica.

On either side are the State Apartments (the king's to the east and the queen's to the west), furnished in 17th-century style. One of the most intriguing rooms is the Queen's Presence Chamber, where original painted decorations survive, showing the lilies of France impaling the British arms and symbolizing the marriage of Charles I to Henrietta Maria.

Re-opened in 1999 after major refurbishment, the 16 new galleries and huge glass-roofed Neptune Court of the modern museum tell the 2,000-year history of Britain and the sea. Galleries focus on exploration, trade and empire,

**THE FAN MUSEUM AND THE RANGER'S HOUSE**
The Fan Museum, (Croombs Hill, tel: 020-8305 1441) is dedicated to the ancient and beautiful art of fan-making. More than 3,000 fans are housed in a superbly restored 18th-century town house. A short stroll away on Chesterfield Walk is the Ranger's House (tel: 020-8853 0035), a grand 18th-century villa where the fine Jacobean portraits of the Suffolk Collection hang.

luxury liners, naval heroes, and more. Among the huge collection of ships (both real ones and models), paintings, navigational instruments, and the relics of sailors and explorers, you can seek out the sumptuous state barge made for Frederick, Prince of Wales, in 1732, and the jacket Nelson was wearing when he was shot in the left shoulder and fatally wounded at the Battle of Trafalgar in 1805.

The **Royal Observatory Greenwich▶▶** (Flamsteed House, tel: 020-8858 4422/8312 6565. *Open* daily 10–5. *Admission charge*), situated high on the hill above Greenwich, is an annex to the Maritime Museum, consisting of several historic buildings.

The Greenwich Observatory was founded by Charles II in 1675; Flamsteed House was designed by Christopher Wren for John Flamsteed, the first Astronomer Royal. Today the house is furnished to give the impression that Flamsteed and his wife still live there. Early telescopes and time-measuring instruments are on display, there is an astronomy gallery, and the large red ball on top of one tower still drops down its mast at 1 PM each day, enabling the Thames navigators to set their chronometers.

From the start, the Observatory's job was to set standards of measurement for time, distance, latitude, and longitude—key components of navigation. The large Gate Clock measures Greenwich Mean Time, the standard by which time is set all round the world. You can stand astride the Greenwich Meridian, marked by a brass strip crossing the Observatory courtyard. This is the dividing line between the earth's eastern and western hemispheres. (If you wish, you can buy a computer printout recording the precise time of your visit.)

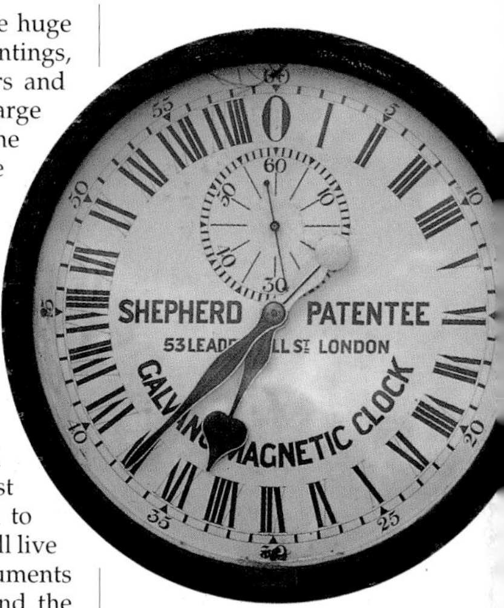


*Setting the standard—Greenwich Mean Time*



**THE MILLENNIUM EXPERIENCE VISITOR CENTRE**

To appreciate fully the engineering feat of the Millennium Dome, visit this hands-on exhibition in the Royal Naval College (King William Walk, tel: 020-8305 3456. *Open* Mon–Fri 11–7, Sat, Sun 11–6. *Admission free*). Models, graphics, interior plans, touch-screen displays and a multimedia room explain the wonder of the world's largest dome (see p. 217).

*The National Maritime Museum houses a huge collection of ships*

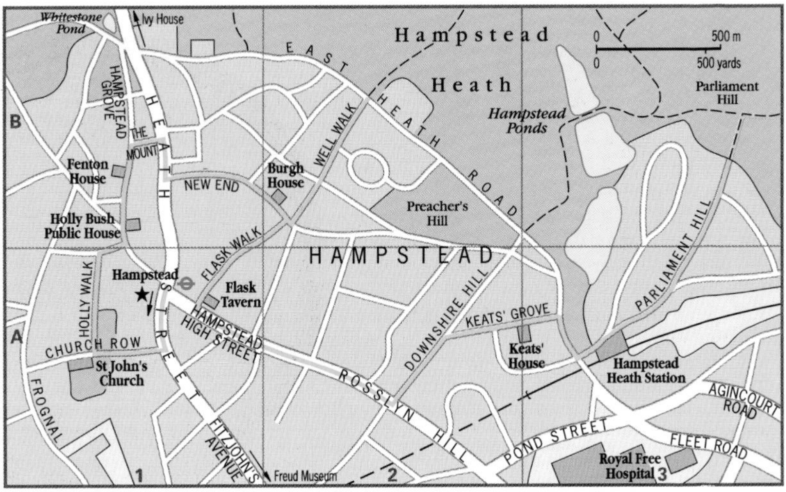




**HAMPSTEAD HEATH**
In 1829, Hampstead's Lord of the Manor, Sir Thomas Wilson, wanting to capitalize on the popularity of the village, produced a plan to build new houses all over the vast 815-acre expanse of sandy heath that he owned to the north of the village. This caused uproar, and opposition to the idea raged for 40 years until, at Wilson's death in 1869, conservationists finally won the battle to save the Heath for public enjoyment. The Heath is a vast nature reserve, as well as a public playground where Londoners come to walk, jog, ride their horses, enjoy picnics, fly their kites, and swim in the three ponds (Kenwood Pond for women, Highgate Pond for men, and Hampstead Pond for mixed swimming).

## ▶▶▶ Hampstead

Hampstead's pretty lanes and village atmosphere and its vast expanse of semirural heath have attracted many eminent writers, politicians, and intellectuals, past and present. The tone of the area today is still intellectual, prosperous, and liberal. Hampstead Heath is a fine place to walk and a popular place for families.

Hampstead Underground station, the deepest in the system, lies amid the intricate maze of attractive lanes that cluster around the High Street. Heath Street descends south to Church Row, with its Georgian houses fronted by iron railings. Halfway down the Row is the parish church of St. John, built in 1744–1747. Inside are memorials to many famous former Hampstead residents, including Keats, Norman Shaw, John Constable, and George du Maurier.

Holly Walk, off Church Row, leads north to Vernon Hill and Hampstead Grove, and so to 17th-century **Fenton House▶** (Windmill Hill, tel: 020-7435 3471. *Open* Sat, Sun, bank holiday Mon 11–5, Wed, Thu, Fri 2–5; Mar, Sat, Sun only 11–5. *Admission charge*). A William and Mary house built in 1695, Fenton House, with its walled garden, is one of the best of its kind surviving in London. The period furnishings are complemented by some of George Salting's fine ceramics collection. In addition, the Benton Fletcher Collection of 17th- and 18th-century keyboard instruments is kept here, and these are used for the regular concerts given in the house.

The little lanes that run around Hampstead Grove are worth exploring, and many houses display blue plaques honoring former residents.

Heading up Heath Street, you will come to New End, a street on your right. Here is **Burgh House** (New End Square, tel: 020-7431 0144. *Open* Wed–Sun noon–5. *Admission free*), a Queen Anne house built in 1703 by the physician Dr. Gibbons. Its rooms are now used for art exhibitions and local history displays.

Nearby, Flask Walk and Well Walk are reminders that Londoners once came here to take the waters at the Pump House, which has since disappeared. In Flask Walk, the

Flask Tavern was the meeting place in the early 18th century of the Kit-Cat Club, a political and literary group whose members included Britain's first prime minister, Robert Walpole; the essayists, Addison and Steele; and Vanbrugh, the playwright and architect. Flask Walk leads to Hampstead High Street, with its good bookstores, boutiques, and restaurants.

At the end of Hampstead High Street is Rosslyn Hill where, on the left, Downshire Hill leads to Keats' Grove (formerly known as Wentworth Grove) and the **Keats' House Museum▶** (Wentworth Place, tel: 020-7435 2062. *Open* Mon–Fri 10–1, 2–6, Sat 10–1, 2–5, Sun 2–5. *Donation*). John Keats came to live here in 1818, fell in love with his next-door neighbor, Fanny Brawne, and became engaged to her in 1819. In 1820 he left for Italy for health reasons and died there in 1821. During the short time he lived in this house he wrote some of his best-loved poems, including *Ode to a Nightingale*; the plum tree under which he wrote this poem has gone, but a recent replacement in the garden marks the spot. The rest of the house displays letters, manuscripts, and furnishings in period style.

It is worth returning to Willow Road to see London's only Modern Movement house (No. 2), complete with its original contents, that is open to the public (tel: 020-7435 6166, *Open* Apr–Oct, Thu, Fri, Sat noon–5. *Admission charge*). Designed by Erno Goldfinger, he and his family lived here until his death in 1987.

From Keats' Grove it is a short step to Hampstead Heath railway station, or you can walk up Parliament Hill for extensive views over central London—local legend claims that Queen Boudicca (Boadicea), the Iron-Age ruler who fought against the Roman conquest of Britain, lies buried beneath the hill.

*Summertime, and in Hampstead's leafy lanes the living is easy*



**NEARBY MUSEUMS**
Sigmund Freud lived at 20 Maresfield Gardens, in South Hampstead, from 1938, when he escaped from Vienna, until his death the following year. After his daughter, Anna, died in 1983, it opened as a museum (tel: 020-7435 2002/7435 5167. *Open* Wed–Sun noon–5. *Admission charge*). Freud's famous couch, along with books, letters, and personal relics, are on display. Just north of Hampstead, in Finchley, the Jewish Museum (80 East End Road; tel: 020-8349 1143. *Open* Mon–Thu 10:30–5, Sun 10:30–4:30. *Admission charge*), documents the social history of London's Jewish community. The fine objects and art complement the Jewish ceremonial objects displayed at the Jewish Museum in Camden (see page 120).

*Taking a well-earned breather at the Wells Tavern in Hampstead*

*Hampton Court's vivid mix of styles*

**THE HAUNTED GALLERY**
Ghosts are inevitable in a palace that has seen so much history, but one in particular is supposed to frequent Hampton Court's Haunted Gallery. It was here that Catherine Howard, the fifth wife of Henry VIII, is said to have broken away from her guards after being arrested for adultery and rushed screaming to appeal to the king who, oblivious to her cries, attended mass in the nearby Chapel Royal. Howard, who continued to protest her innocence, was sentenced to death and beheaded in the Tower in 1542. A figure in white has been spotted in the gallery on several occasions since, uttering an unearthly and exceptionally piercing scream.



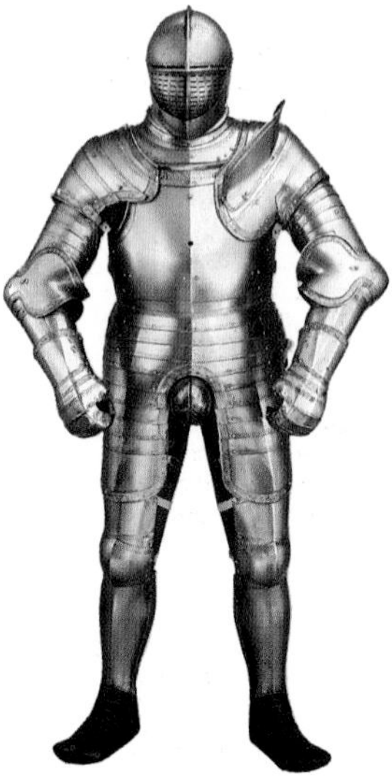

*Henry VIII's armor*

**►►► Hampton Court Palace** *209A2*

*East Molesey (tel: 020-8781 9500)*
*Open: Apr–Oct, Mon 10:15–6, Tue–Sun 9:30–6; Nov–Mar, Mon 10.15–4:30, Tue–Sun 9:30–4:30. Admission charge. Park open daily dawn–dusk. Admission free*

Hampton Court is one of the oldest and most interesting of London's royal palaces. Wren's south wing, badly damaged by fire in 1986, has been superbly restored, and the palace, in typical Tudor style, looks like a miniature town which has grown in an organic, unplanned way, unity provided only by the warm reds and browns of the brickwork. The fastest way to reach Hampton Court is by rail from Waterloo station (30 minutes), but a more leisurely journey (of three to four hours) can be made by riverbus in summer, departing from Westminster Pier (tel: 020-7930 4721 for details).

**The palace** Hampton Court is approached through the Trophy Gate, where its vast scale is immediately apparent. The palace was not merely a royal residence. It also housed a huge retinue of courtiers and followers and the warren of courtyards and buildings to the left used to contain "grace and favor" apartments, where Crown officials, retirees, and dependants of the royal family lived. The Landmark Trust also has two vacation homes here that can be rented by the week: Fish Court, which sleeps six, and the Georgian House, which sleeps eight. Details from the Landmark Trust, Shottesbrooke, Maidenhead, Berkshire SL6 3SW (tel: 01628 825925). Ahead is the Great Gatehouse, built by Cardinal Wolsey.

Set in the two side turrets are terracotta roundels depicting Roman emperors. These and Base Court, beyond, date from Wolsey's time. Anne Boleyn's gateway, opposite, is carved with the intertwined initials "H" and "A," for Henry and Anne, celebrating a marriage that lasted only four years before Boleyn was beheaded. Clock Court comes next, named for the astronomical clock on the gateway's inner side. On the left is Henry VIII's Great Hall, with its splendid oriel window and an impressive hammerbeam roof. Under the Great Hall are the Tudor Kitchens, with their vast fireplaces and ancient cooking utensils. Opposite is Christopher Wren's elegant colonnade. Wren planned to demolish the whole palace and build a new one as grand as Versailles. Luckily, William III could not afford this, and some Tudor buildings were left standing. But the State Apartments, which you enter here are rich indeed, decorated with paintings, furnishings, armor, and tapestries. Jean Tijou, the French blacksmith, made the ironwork balustrades of the staircases, Grinling Gibbons made the woodwork, and Verrio painted many of the ceilings. The more intimate queen's apartments look into Wren's lavish Fountain Court, while the public rooms look over the gardens, with their leafy avenues, canals, and fountains. Do not miss the dolls' house model that explains how these rooms were used.

**The gardens** Like the palace, the gardens are a mixture of styles. To the south, between the Thames and the palace, is the Privy Garden, designed for the exclusive use of the royal family and separated from the river by Tijou's handsome wrought-iron screen. The Privy Garden has been acurately restored to its appearance and planting of 1702 when it was completed for William III. Nearby are Henry VIII's Pond Garden and an Elizabethan Knot Garden of aromatic herbs. The Great Vine grows near the Banqueting House; planted in 1768, it still produces Black Hamburg grapes, on sale in season. To the north of the palace is the Wilderness, the Laburnum Walk, the Maze, planted in 1690, and the indoor royal tennis court, built in 1626. The game of royal (or real) tennis that is still played here resembles an amalgam of tennis and squash and was all the rage with the European aristocracy in the 16th century. Look in and you may find a game in progress.

*Extravagantly decorated Tudor chimneys*

**CARDINAL WOLSEY AND HAMPTON COURT**

Hampton Court started out in 1515 as an ecclesiastical palace, not a royal one, built by Cardinal Wolsey, the son of an Ipswich butcher who rose to fill the highest offices of church and state. As the confidant of Henry VIII he took a leading role in the king's complicated marriage affairs. He amassed great wealth and spent it extravagantly, intending Hampton Court to be the most splendid palace in the land. This spurred the King's envy, however, and Wolsey tactfully decided that it might be wise to present Hampton Court to Henry as a gift, which he did in 1525. This did not satisfy the king who, in 1529, had his former friend arrested on a charge of treason and then seized Wolsey's possessions, including the palace of Whitehall. Disgraced and rejected, the Cardinal soon fell ill, and died at York within a year.

*The hammerbeam roof of the Great Hall, built in 1532, is richly decorated with pendants, royal arms, badges, and a series of carved and painted heads*

*Memorial to Karl Marx, Highgate Cemetery*

**DICK WHITTINGTON**
On the left-hand side of Highgate Hill, about 275 yards up from Archway tube station, look for the Whittington Stone, set by the roadside. Here, according to legend, Dick Whittington rested with his cat on his way out of London, having failed to make his fortune in the city. Three times, as he rested, he thought he heard the Bow Bells chime "Turn again, Whittington, thrice Mayor of London," and the third time he decided to return. Thus goes the story; in reality, Richard Whittington was born the son of a Gloucestershire squire. He was, indeed, three times Mayor of London (in 1397, 1406, and 1419), but the fable of his rags-to-riches rise seems to have been invented in the 17th century, 200 years after Whittington's death.



### ►► Highgate *209B3*

Highgate still retains its village atmosphere, though since the early 19th century it has been swallowed up by London's northward expansion. The core of the village has many opulent 18th-century houses, which set the exclusive tone of the whole area.

To reach Highgate, it is best to take the tube to Archway station and walk up **Highgate Hill**. The ugly hospital buildings soon give way to elegant houses, on the right. On the left, a long wall separates the road from the peaceful oasis of **Waterlow Park** (Highgate Hill, tel: 020-8348 8716. *Open* daily dawn–dusk. *Admission free*), a hillside garden with fine views toward Regent's Park and central London. At the top of the park, you can visit **Lauderdale House**, built in

*Kenwood House and its paintings were bequeathed to the nation by the 1st Earl of Iveagh in 1927*

1645 and briefly the home of Nell Gwyn, who was Charles II's mistress.

Highgate village is grouped around **Pond Square**, which has a delightful mixture of Georgian cottages, grander houses, small stores, and restaurants. To one side is the **Flask** pub, so called because travelers used to stop here to fill their flasks for the journey ahead. More Georgian houses can be found in The Grove, a little to the north (the poet Samuel Taylor Coleridge lived at No. 3).

**Highgate Cemetery▶▶▶** (Swain's Lane; tel: 020-8340 1834. *Open* Apr–Oct, daily 10–5; Nov–Mar 10–4. *Admission charge.* No children). You can reach Highgate Cemetery by walking south from Pond Square, down Swains Lane. The lane divides the cemetery in two.

A number of interesting people are buried here, amid the Victorian landscaping and the fascinating variety of funerary architecture. More than 50,000 tombs, accommodating 166,000 people, lie within its 37 acres. It was opened in 1839 and became an immediate attraction.

In the Eastern Cemetery (open to individual visitors), the most famous grave is that of Karl Marx (who died in Hampstead in 1883), marked by a large head sculpted by Laurence Bradshaw (1956) and the inscription: "Workers of all lands unite."

**Kenwood House (The Iveagh Bequest)▶▶▶** (Hampstead Lane; tel: 020-8348 1286. *Open* Apr–Sep 10–6; Oct–Mar 10–4. *Admission free*) From the center of Highgate it is a 10-minute walk along Hampstead Lane to Kenwood House, gloriously situated in wooded grounds to the north of Hampstead Heath. This stately home was built in 1616 and remodeled by Robert Adam in 1764 for George III's Chief Justice, the Earl of Mansfield (see Adam's fine library ceiling). It was left to the nation in 1927 by the 1st Earl of Iveagh, along with its outstanding collection of paintings. Here you will find Rembrandt's brooding *Portrait of the Artist* (ca1665), Vermeer's *The Guitar Player* (ca1676), and Gainsborough's fine portrait of Lady Howe (ca1764), among many other important works by English and Dutch masters. Open-air concerts are given in the grounds, by the lake, on Saturday evenings in June, July, and August, with fireworks providing a spectacular finale to some performances.

*The grave of George Eliot, the nom de plume of Mary Ann Evans (1819–1880), whose novels include* Middlemarch, Mill on the Floss, *and* Adam Bede



**HIGHGATE CEMETERY**
Highgate Cemetery opened in 1839 as a commercial enterprise. The Cemetery was immensely popular but in time, with all the burial plots sold and no revenue for maintenance, it fell into neglect. Recently it has been rescued by the Friends of Highgate Cemetery. Tombs in the Western Section (accessible only on tours) include the physicist Michael Faraday (died 1867), and the poet Christina Rossetti (died 1894), and Dante Gabriel Rossetti's beautiful wife, Elizabeth Siddal (died 1862).

*The Palm House, guarded by the heraldic Queen's Beasts, which were carved in 1953*

**MARIANNE NORTH**
Kew has a superb collection of botanical paintings representing the life's work of Marianne North (1830–1890). These colorful pictures (mostly in oil) are crammed into a small gallery on the southeastern edge of the gardens. Marianne North traveled around the world to paint plants in their natural environment, before her forced retirement to Gloucestershire, caused by a tropical fever.



**KEW AND THE RUBBER TREE**
Kew has sent seeds all over the world and was actively involved in the introduction of rubber to Southeast Asia. The original rubber-tree seeds were smuggled from Brazil (which did not wish to share this profitable plant), propagated at Kew, and studied by Henry Ridley, who became the director of the botanic gardens in Singapore in the 1870s and persuaded many local landowners to develop new rubber plantations. Rubber is now a staple of Indonesian economies.

**KEW PALACE**
Within the gardens is delightful 17th-century Kew Palace, the summer home of George III. It reopens in 2000 after restoration.

## ►►► Kew Gardens (Royal Botanic Gardens) *209A2*

*Kew, Richmond (tel: 020-8940 1171)*
*Open: daily 9:30–shortly before dusk, phone for closing times. Admission charge*

Whatever time of year it is, there is something to see at Kew's Royal Botanic Gardens. Even in the gray depths of winter, the Victorian greenhouses are full of luxuriant tropical growth, while spring and early summer bring massed bulbs, frothing groves of Japanese cherries and magnolias, or swathes of colorful azaleas and rhododendrons. There are plants here from all over the globe and from every habitat, desert, swamp, and rain forest.

The gardens were created by combining two royal estates in 1772. Under the patronage of George III they developed into one of the world's foremost centers of horticultural research. The credit for this was largely due to Sir Joseph Banks, who became the king's adviser shortly after returning from a voyage around the world with Captain Cook on board the *Endeavour*. During this expedition Banks had recorded a huge number of hitherto unknown plants, which he now brought to Britain for the first time, growing them at Kew to assess their value, either as ornamental plants or as sources of food or medicines. The early botanic garden occupied a small part of the total area; the rest was landscaped by Capability Brown (his lake and Rhododendron Dell remain) and dotted with fanciful buildings for the amusement of courtly visitors. Of these, the oldest is the 10-story pagoda, built in 1761–1762 to the designs of William Chambers. Today, the vistas, royal palace, magnificent glasshouses, mature trees and glorious 300-acre gardens still entrance visitors.

**The Palm House** Kew began to change after 1841, when the gardens were handed over to the state, and several greenhouses were added. The Palm House, designed by Decimus Burton, opened in 1848.

**The Temperate House** The next to be built was the Temperate House, also by Decimus Burton, beginning in 1859; by the time it was completed, 40 years later, it was the world's largest greenhouse. It has an elevated gallery from which to enjoy views of brightly colored plants, including the Chilean wine palm, planted in 1846 and now claimed to be the largest greenhouse plant in existence.

**The Princess of Wales Conservatory** Opened in 1987, much of this conservatory is below ground level (for insulation) and lit by a series of low, tentlike glass roofs. Computer controls simulate several different environments in the one building, so you pass from arid desert at one end to the orchid-filled tropics at the other. Each climate zone has its own weird and wonderful creations, from the stonelike lithops of the dry regions to the carnivorous pitcher plants of the Asian rain forests. A crowd favorite is the giant water lily pads, up to 6½ feet across, grown annually from seed.

**Queen Charlotte's Cottage and Gardens** (*Open* May–Sep, Sat, Sun and bank holidays 11–5:30) British native wildflowers are the theme at this peaceful spot on the southwestern fringes of the site, where George III's queen had a rustic "cottage" built in the 1770s. This is now a woodland nature reserve, in accordance with the wishes of Queen Victoria; sheets of bluebells flower here in May.

**KEW VILLAGE**
The main gate to the Royal Botanical Gardens is on Kew Green, an immaculate triangle where long, lazy games of cricket are played on summer Sundays against a backdrop of late Georgian buildings, provided for members of George III's court. St. Anne's Church, built of yellow brick in 1714, stands on the southern edge of the green and is a quirky, attractive building with an octagonal cupola and Venetian windows. Thomas Gainsborough, the artist, is buried in the churchyard and two former directors of Kew Gardens, William and Joseph Hooker (father and son), both have unusual memorials of porcelain decorated with ferns and flowers. Two museums stand nearby, on the opposite bank of the Thames. The Kew Bridge Steam Museum (Green Dragon Lane; *Open* daily, but machines in operation on weekends only) houses several giant steam engines that once pumped millions of gallons of fresh water a day. Steam-powered boats, trucks, and traction engines are also on display, as well as a Victorian machine store and forge. Its near neighbor is the Musical Museum (368 High Street, Brentford; tel: 020-8560 8108. *Open* Apr–Jun, Sep, Oct, Sat, Sun 2–5; Jul–Aug, Wed 2–4, Sat, Sun 2–5. *Admission charge*), housed in a converted Victorian church. There are 200 or so mechanical instruments crowded into the building, all in working order, as the guides demonstrate when they show you around.

*The Temperate House is the largest of Kew's glasshouses and contains the huge Chilean wine palm, around 60 feet tall*

Above: Adam-style finery; below: Tudor turrets, Adam interior

**OSTERLEY STATION**
Osterley Park is reached by taking the Piccadilly Underground line to Osterley station; then follow the Great West Road to Thornbury Road. The station itself, a 1930s design by Charles Holden, was modeled on the town hall in the Amsterdam suburb of Hilversum. Other Underground stations by Holden have interesting architecture: he designed the circular concourse of Piccadilly Circus station in 1925–1928, but his best work is on the Piccadilly line from Holloway Road, with its pretty tilework, to Arnos Grove, which is frequently compared to a flying saucer.



## ▶ Osterley Park 209B2

*Jersey Road, Isleworth (tel: 020-8568 7714)*
*House open: Apr–Oct, Wed–Sun 1–4:30. Admission charge. Park open daily dawn–dusk, free*

Osterley Park, on the western fringes of London, was built in the 1560s for the wealthy City merchant Sir Thomas Gresham. After Gresham's death, the building was untouched. In 1711 Sir Francis Child, founder of Child's Bank, acquired the property to use the Elizabethan vaults to store quantities of money but never actually lived there. His grandsons, Francis and Robert Child, hired Robert Adam to transform the house along neoclassical lines, in 1761. Externally, the final result is a strange marriage of styles: the Tudor brick corner turrets were retained but linked together by a grand open portico with a carved and painted pediment supported by Doric columns and standing above wide, shallow steps.

Inside the house, the sequence of remodeled rooms is exactly as Adam intended, beautifully restored by the National Trust during recent years and furnished with superb examples of 18th-century tapestries, chairs, and pictures. The classical themes that give unity to the house and its decoration have been meticulously recreated following Adam's original, surprisingly brightly colored, designs. Even the furniture is arranged around the edge of some rooms, in the Georgian manner. Horace Walpole, the writer, whose own home at Strawberry Hill introduced the neo-Gothic style, found some of the rooms "too theatric." On the other hand, Walpole did take a liking to the rich pink, green, and gold ceilings of the Drawing Room, with its carpet of similar hues, describing the room as "worthy of Eve before the Fall"—a rather strange comment to make about such a sophisticated room, which is the exact antithesis of innocent naturalism. The description might perhaps have been more appropriately used for the tranquil garden, with its eye-catching bridge, its lakes, its stately trees, grazing cows, and its long and meandering paths.

*London has several small museums and galleries well worth investigating. Some of these are outside the city center, and may require a little extra planning to get to—but for those with a particular interest in their collections, or who like to wander away from the tourist track, they provide a refreshing alternative.*

**The Saatchi Collection** (98a Boundary Road; tel: 020-7624 8299, *Open* Thu–Sun noon–6) was built up by the advertising mogul Charles Saatchi and his wife, Doris. Richard Wilson's *20:20*, an installation on permanent view, reflects their robust contemporary patronage. There are three temporary shows each year.

The **William Morris House** (Water House, Lloyd Park, Forest Road, Walthamstow; tel: 020-8527 3782. *Open* Tue–Sat 10–1, 2–5 and first Sun of month) merits the effort to get there. The Georgian house was home to William Morris in 1848–1858 and now displays a collection of textiles, ceramics, stained glass, and furniture designed by Morris and his contemporaries, as well as a collection of paintings bequeathed by the artist Sir Frank Brangwyn, which is rich in Pre-Raphaelite works.

The **Royal Air Force Museum** (Grahame Park Way, Hendon; tel: 020-8205 2266. *Open* daily 10–6. Admission charge) is one of the finest collections of historic fighting aircraft in the world. It starts with early experiments with flight (from balloons to man-lifting kites) and comes up to date with high-tech displays on modern fighter aircraft, such as a Red Arrows flight simulator and a Fun'n' Flight interactive gallery. A whole section is devoted to the Battle of Britain. An art gallery shows works by Elizabeth Frink, Paul Nash, Graham Sutherland, and others.

**MARTINWARE**
The late 19th century was an age of lively experimentation in the pottery industry, and no products of the period are more humorous and grotesque than the stoneware birds and face jugs produced by the Martin brothers (Charles, Edwin, Robert, and Walter) between 1873 and 1923. The firm moved to Southall in 1877, and the Southall Library has a small museum devoted to their wares (Osterley Park Road, Southall; tel: 020-8574 3412. *Open* by appointment on Tue–Thu, Sat. *Admission free*).

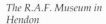

*The R.A.F. Museum in Hendon*

**RICHMOND BRIDGE**
Richmond Bridge dates from 1777 and holds the distinction of now being the oldest in London: all the other bridges were rebuilt at some stage in the 18th and 19th centuries to cope with an ever-growing traffic burden, but Richmond's elegant five-arch bridge survives in its original form. The design itself is even older—the architect, James Paine, used as his model a bridge designed by the great 16th-century architect Palladio for the northern Italian town of Vicenza.



## ►► Richmond

Richmond is a riverside village west of London, reached by Underground or by boat from Westminster Pier in summer. Its attractions include several good pubs, such as the White Cross on Water Lane or the Rose of York on Petersham Road, with good food and gardens overlooking the Thames. For the more energetic, there are walks along the leafy east bank of the river to Ham House, or up Richmond Hill to the 2,470-acre Richmond Park.

If you arrive by train, the river lies to the left as you leave the station, walking down the store-lined Quadrant to the Square. To the right, Duke Street leads to Richmond Green, an open space surrounded by 17th- and 18th-century houses. Northeast of the green is the Little Green, with its late Victorian Richmond Theatre and the Orange Tree theater pub, sites used for the Richmond Festival in June and July. South of the green, the four houses on Maids of Honour Row were built in 1724 for the ladies-in-waiting of the Princess of Wales. Behind this row, in Old Palace Yard, is the gatehouse of Richmond Palace, most of which was demolished by Parliamentarians after the execution of Charles I.

Little alleys full of antiques stores and boutiques lead south to the river itself, spanned by Richmond Bridge (see side panel). North of the bridge is **Richmond Riverside**, a group of 20 buildings in retro-classical style, arranged

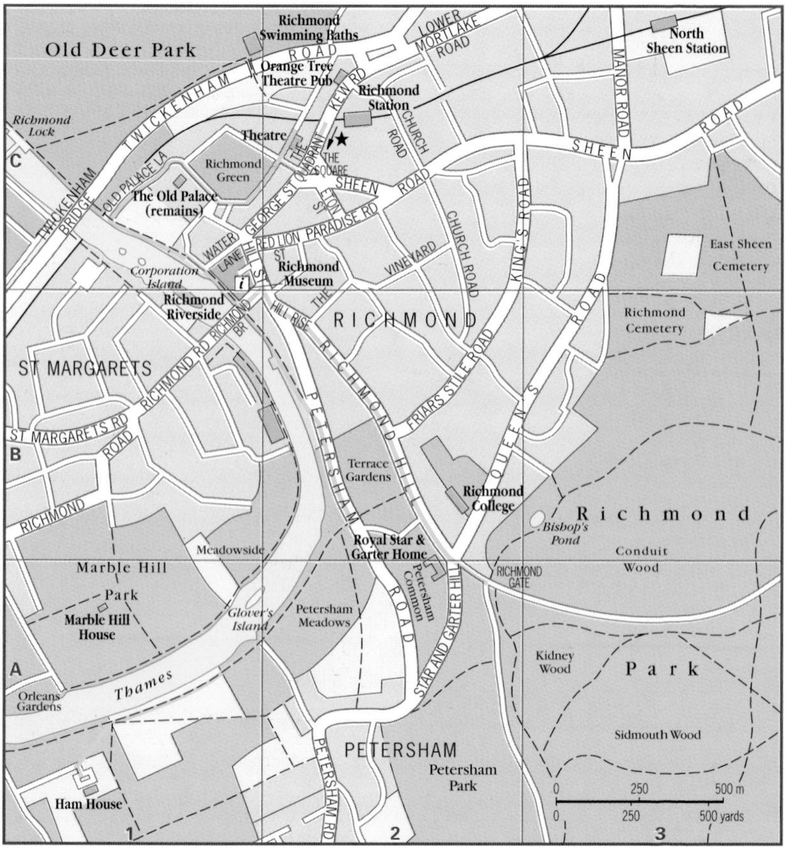

around four courtyards, with stores, a restaurant, and a tourist information center. The development (1988) is the work of Quinlan Terry, an architect who passionately believes in classical values.

A footpath leads south under Richmond Bridge (joining Petersham Road for a short stretch), following the course of the River Thames to **Ham House▶▶** (Ham Street, tel: 020-8940 1950. *House open* Apr–Oct, Mon–Wed, Sat, Sun 1–5. *Admission charge. Garden open* daily 10:30–6, or dusk. *Admission charge*) with good views of Marble Hill House (see page 234).

Ham House is a bold Jacobean building, dating from 1610, but remodeled in the 1670s. The sumptuous, grand rooms are remarkable for their ostentatious woodwork, plaster ceilings, and furnishings, and the walls are hung with paintings by Lely, Reynolds, and Constable. In the restored 17th-century gardens, find square lawns, hornbeam hedges, cherry trees and herbs; there is an orangery housing a café.

Richmond Bridge, Hill Rise and Richmond Hill lead upward for about half a mile to **Richmond Park▶** (tel: 020-8948 3209. *Open* 7 AM until 30 mins before dusk. *Admission free*); turn around for views of the river as you climb the hill, which is lined by attractive 18th-century buildings, including Wick House, where the artist Joshua Reynolds lived. The park was enclosed by Charles I in 1637 as a royal hunting ground, and red and fallow deer still wander freely around the grassland, which is dotted with oak trees (some of which are over 600 years old) and man-made ponds. One enclave, the Isabella Plantation, is spectacular in late spring when the azaleas and rhododendrons are in full bloom, and has many unusual and attractive flowering trees.

*Adding to the air of bygone elegance in Richmond*



**RICHMOND RIVERSIDE**

Quinlan Terry's classical design for the buildings of Richmond Riverside has proved surprisingly controversial. Many inhabitants of Richmond consider the buildings to be a pleasing addition to their handsome riverfront and a fine complement to the bridge. Architects, however, accuse Terry of being populist and backward-looking. They also claim the development is dishonest: behind the classical porticos and facades there are ordinary, steel-framed offices. It is an argument that is likely to continue for some time. Competing designs submitted for the redevelopment of the area around St. Paul's Cathedral and Spitalfields, in the City of London, have produced a similar conflict between the classical and the postmodernist approach.

*Richmond Theatre, built facing the green in 1899, has a beautiful interior and stages some top-quality productions*

**FROM SYON TO THE SCAFFOLD**
Several former inhabitants of Syon House ended up in the Tower of London or with their heads on a block. Before the house was built, it was the site of a convent, which Henry VIII seized at the Dissolution and gave to the Duke of Somerset. In 1541 Catherine Howard, the king's fifth wife, was imprisoned here, falsely accused of adultery, before her trial and execution. Next it was the turn of Somerset himself: he was appointed Protector to the boy king Edward VI at Henry VIII's death but was thought to exercise too much power; accused of conspiracy, he too was beheaded in 1552. Syon then became home to Lady Jane Grey, but only for a short while. Having been proclaimed queen in 1553 she was executed in 1554, one of the victims of the political maneuverings of the age.



*In the distinguished company of the ancient gods at Syon*

## ▶▶ Syon House and Park *209A2*

*Brentford (tel: 020-8560 0883/0881)*
*House open: mid-Mar–Oct, Wed–Sun 11–5. Admission charge. Gardens open daily 10–5:30 or dusk. Admission charge*

Syon House and Park is an excellent day out: a stately home by Robert Adam, grounds by Capability Brown, the London Butterfly House, the Aquatic Experience and arts and crafts exhibitions. To get there, take the tube to Gunnersbury or train to Kew Bridge, then bus 237 or 267; or go to Syon Lane station and walk down Syon Lane and Spur Road to the London Road entrance.

**Syon House** From the outside, this historic seat of the Dukes of Northumberland looks slightly forbidding, but the battlemented mid-16th-century building contains some of the most magnificently and elegantly decorated rooms in England. They are the work of Robert Adam, who remodeled the interior (1761–1768) using marble, gilded statues, and plasterwork to create a palace fit for one of the country's most powerful aristocratic families. As you explore the house you'll discover that some rooms were exclusively for the males of the family and others for the females, a fact reflected in the decoration and furnishings. The immensely long but narrow Long Gallery, for example, was designed, according to Adam, to "afford variety and amusement for the ladies" and is finished in pastel mauve and green with highlights of gold. Around the cornice of the same room, portrait medallions illustrate the lineage of the Dukes of Northumberland, beginning with Charlemagne, the first Holy Roman Emperor, from whom the family claims descent. Several rooms are hung with important family portraits, including works by Gainsborough and Reynolds.

**Syon Park** The grounds of Syon House were landscaped between 1767 and 1773 by Capability Brown, who transformed the land and created an idyllic version of the countryside, with lakes, lawns and fine specimen trees.

*Family portraits of the Dukes of Northumberland*

The centerpiece, linking lake and garden, is the Great Conservatory. It has a graceful central dome of glass and iron and two curving side wings and was built between 1820 and 1827. Charles Fowler, the architect of Covent Garden market, designed it, and it perhaps influenced Joseph Paxton's design for the Crystal Palace. The conservatory contains several different gardens, ranging from the damp fernery to the hot, dry cactus beds.

The Rose Garden, laid out between the house and river, was replanted in 1995. More than 8,000 roses, including some rare bushes, are now mature and at their most spectacular in June. Farther away, a stroll around the lakes will show you many moisture-loving plants, flowering shrubs, and unusual trees.

**Other attractions** For most visitors the main draw is the **London Butterfly House** with hundreds of large and colorful species flying freely in a jungle-like setting; there is also a display of giant spiders, scorpions, and other creatures that usually bring on a frisson of fear.

Syon's other wildlife attraction is the **Aquatic Experience** with fish, reptiles, amphibians, and birds in near-natural habitats. There is plenty more to see and do within the grounds, including a giant indoor adventure playground, and centers for art, wholefood, needlecraft, and gardening.

Syon has a café and a restaurant, although you can also picnic in the grounds.

**OLD ISLEWORTH**
The core of Old Isleworth lies just outside the gates to Syon Park. Here, Georgian houses have recently been restored as part of a major redevelopment program transforming a formerly run-down area. All Saints Church, by Michael Blee, dates from 1969 and incorporates part of a 14th-century church destroyed by fire during World War II. Nearby is a riverside pub, The London Apprentice (62 Church Street), dating in its present form from the mid-18th century and decorated with original Hogarth prints. Apprentices from London would line up here for a drink, which accounts for its name. The pub restaurant has good views over the river to Richmond Park and serves traditional English food.

**TWICKENHAM HOUSES**

**York House**, off York Street, is a late 17th-century mansion built by an Indian tea merchant, Sir Ratan Tata, with delightful gardens stretching toward the river. The building now houses local government offices, and the tourist information office in the adjacent Civic Centre provides details of tours that take place on Fridays. **Pope's Villa**, the villa built by the poet Alexander Pope, in which he lived from 1719 to 1744, has now been replaced by St. James's Independent School. But the mineral-lined grotto he created survives from his garden, and can be visited by written appointment (19 Crossdeep, Twickenham).

One of Twickenham's most famous houses is Strawberry Hill (tel: 020-8240 4114/4224. *Open* Easter Sun–mid Oct, Sun 2–3:30. *Admission charge*), now St. Mary's University College. Horace Walpole (novelist and letter writer) bought a simple cottage here in 1747 and, inspired by his studies of medieval buildings, spent the next 30 years turning it into a neo-Gothic castle. The building was enormously influential in reviving the Gothic style and led to the construction of many follies, churches, and even whole houses in the same picturesque Strawberry Hill style.



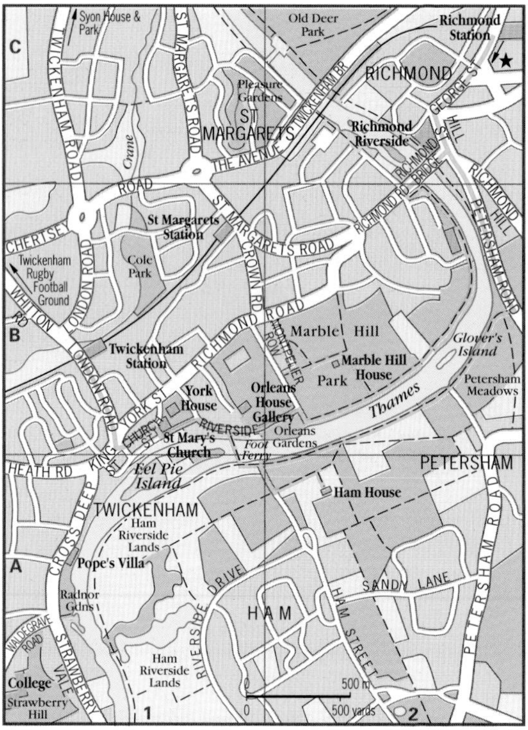


## ►► Twickenham

Twickenham, to sports fans, means the famous rugby stadium where international matches are held, as well as the Varsity match between Oxford and Cambridge. The stadium lies to the north of the village, with a museum on the history of the game (Rugby Road; tel: 020-8892 2000. *Open* Tue–Sat 10:30–5. *Admission charge*. Tours Tue–Sat, reservations possible). The village itself is best reached by taking the Underground to neighboring Richmond (see pages 230–231) or by riverboat, which sets off from Westminster Pier in summer.

From Richmond station, turn left and walk down the Quadrant, George Street and Hill Street to cross Richmond Bridge. Take the riverside path south to Marble Hill House, set in its spacious and leafy park.

**Marble Hill House►** (Richmond Road, tel: 020-8892 5115. *Open* Apr–Sep, daily 10–6; Oct–Mar, Wed–Sun 10–4. *Admission charge*) is an exemplary Palladian villa, built to make the most of the views over the river toward Richmond Hill. It was designed as a rural retreat for Henrietta Howard, mistress of the Prince of Wales (the future George II) in 1729; later it was given to another royal consort, Mrs. Fitzherbert, secretly married to the future George IV in 1785, then rejected by him in favor of Caroline of Brunswick. As with all Palladian villas, the main rooms are on the second floor, the *piano nobile*. The Great Room is a perfect cube, in keeping with the Palladian love of geometry. It is furnished as it would have been in Henrietta Howard's time, when regular visitors included the writers John Gay, Horace Walpole, and Alexander Pope—he advised on the layout of the garden, with its groves of statuesque trees and manicured lawns.

From Marble Hill, visit Montpelier Row, to the northwest, to take a look at one of the best surviving examples of early terrace housing (row-housing) in London, dating from 1720.

The riverside path continues upstream to the **Orleans House Gallery▶** (Riverside, tel: 020-8892 0221. *Open* Apr–Sep, Tue–Sat 1–5:30, Sun 2–5:30; Oct–Mar, Tue–Sat 1–4:30, Sun 2–4:30. *Admission charge*), built by James Gibbs in 1720 and beautifully framed by woodland. The gallery is all that remains of Orleans House, which was demolished in 1927. The Duc d'Orléans (later King Louis-Philippe of France) lived here from 1814 to 1817. Today, the gallery has commercial art exhibitions, art for sale and houses the Ionides Collection of Topographical Paintings of Richmond and Twickenham.

From the Orleans House Gallery, continue along Riverside toward **Twickenham Village▶**, passing two good waterside pubs that offer food and refreshment, the Riverside Inn and the White Swan. Beyond lie Church Lane, Bell Lane, and Water Lane, each lined with Georgian houses. The nearby church of St. Mary is an odd combination of medieval tower and classical nave, rebuilt in 1715. Inside are monuments to the 18th-century poet and satirist Alexander Pope, his parents, and his nurse, Mary Beach. Church Street, now pedestrianized, has good stores and is the site of a fair held in May during the Twickenham Week festival. London Road leads north toward the train station; otherwise, you might consider crossing the Thames by ferry from Riverside to visit Ham House (see page 231), and then walking back along the Thames to the tube station at Richmond.

*Twickenham ("Twickers") is the home of English rugby*



*The former home of a French king—the Orleans House Gallery in Twickenham*

**ETON**
Thames Street leads from Windsor Castle down to the river, where Windsor Bridge takes you to Windsor's twin town of Eton, on the northern bank. This is the home of Eton College, founded by Henry VI in 1440, the school that has produced 20 prime ministers. When school is in session you will see the students dressed in their distinctive tailcoats and wing collars. The impressive school buildings include a Museum of Eton Life (tel: 01753-671 177. *Open* daily mid-Mar–Sep, call for times), with displays on the school's history. The chapel has 15th-century wall paintings and stained-glass windows by John Piper and Evie Hone.

## ▶▶▶ Windsor *209A1*

England's largest castle, part of it painstakingly restored after the devastating fire of 1992, has been a royal home since 1070. The queen lives here for part of the year, usually around Easter and mid-June (when the State Apartments are closed).

A colorful Changing of the Guard ceremony is held outside the castle, May to mid-August daily at 11 AM, and on alternate days the rest of the year.

**Windsor Castle** (tel: 01753-868286/831118. *Open* Mar–Oct, daily 10–5; Nov–Feb, daily 10–3. *Admission charge*. Some sections may close for royal functions). The castle itself towers above the town on a chalk cliff. Its strategic site was first defended by William the Conqueror in 1070 and for the next 900 years the building was continually enlarged, growing from a medieval castle to a vast and complex royal palace. It took on its present appearance during the 19th century.

There are several buildings to visit. St. George's Chapel is a masterpiece of Perpendicular Gothic architecture, begun in 1478 and completed in 1511. Ten monarchs are buried here. The monument to Princess Charlotte (who died in 1817 in childbirth) in the northwest chapel shows her ascending to heaven with an angel carrying her stillborn child. The Chapel's ceiling is very beautiful; and elaborate 15th-century choir stalls are covered in vignettes (animals, jesters, the Dance of Death, and biblical stories) and surmounted by banners of the 26 Knights

*Above: castle guard*
*Left: Windsor Castle gatehouse, built by Henry VIII*



of the Garter, whose installation has taken place here since 1348. It was here that the Queen's youngest child, Edward, married Sophie Rees Jones in 1999.

The restored State Apartments are hung with works from the Royal Collection, the world's finest private art collection. Do not miss Queen Mary's Dolls' House, designed by Sir Edwin Lutyens and given to the nation in 1923. The furnishings are designed at one-twelfth life-size, the plumbing and lighting really work, and eminent writers and artists contributed handwritten books or miniature paintings to the library.

**Windsor town** After visiting the castle, it is worth exploring Windsor's stores and public buildings. The Guildhall on the High Street was completed in 1707 by Sir Christopher Wren. Its Tuscan columns, on the first floor, do not touch the ceiling; apparently, the town council insisted on having them, but Wren left the gap to prove that they were structurally superfluous. Continuing up the High Street you will pass the 19th-century parish church of St. John the Baptist; farther on and to the left, St. Albans Street leads to the Royal Mews and an exhibition of the Queen's horses, carriages, and state coaches.

**Windsor Great Park** You can continue from here up Park Street to the Long Walk, which skirts Windsor Great Park. This 3-mile avenue was laid out by Charles I and planted with elms, but the original trees died and had to be replaced in 1945 with chestnuts and plane trees.

**LEGOLAND**

Based on the original in Billund, Denmark, Legoland Windsor opened in 1996 (tel: 0990-040 404. *Open* mid-Mar–Oct daily 10–6, until 8 in school summer holidays. *Admission charge*). It's in a beautiful setting of landscaped and manicured grounds, with the entrance high on a hill in Windsor Great Park, enjoying magnificent views over Windsor Castle. Legoland is designed specifically for kids (ages 2–12) but all the family will love it. Miniland is a huge model village of European landmarks built with more than 20 million Lego pieces. Other activity zones include themed rides, drive-yourself boats and cars, dozens of ingenious working models, a dragon rollercoaster, a Legoland Driving School, and live shows.

On the negative side, lines can be long (so bring a back-pack of snacks and drinks to recharge the energy during the wait). On a sunny day this is undoubtedly the best day out of London for young children.

## Accommodations

The cost of hotel accommodations in central London is horrendously high. You can expect to pay $160 a night for a reasonable room, and the rates begin to soar if you stay at one of London's grand old hotels such as the Connaught, Claridges, the Dorchester, or the Savoy. Good value hotels and guest houses do exist, of course (a large number of them are listed in the Directory section at the back of this book). Rooms in these hotels are, however, very much in demand, and to get a room you must reserve well in advance—often two or three months prior to your visit.

Many hotels will ask you to confirm your reservation in some way and will charge you a fee if you cancel at short notice or fail to turn up. In some cases you will lose any deposit you have paid and some hotels will charge the cost of the room to your credit card, so advise your hotel as soon as possible of any change of plans.

**General tips** Here are a few general points to bear in mind when staying in London:

- For relatively cheap but central hotels and guest houses, concentrate on the Bloomsbury area (for example, hotels in Gower Street or Cartwright Gardens, off Russell Square), and the Pimlico–Victoria area.
- Remember that many hotels geared primarily to business travelers offer much cheaper rates on the weekend. It is worth checking to see whether big chains such as the Forte group or Thistle Hotels are offering one of their regular weekend-break discount offers. Some hotels also offer lower rates to guests staying for a week or more.
- London is a popular year-round destination, but rates can be cheaper during February and March, and October and November. London is also generally quieter and less hectic during these months.
- Consider alternatives to hotels, such as renting apartments or staying with a London family. The **London Tourist Board** has leaflets on these and other options, and publishes a selective guide to hotels, guest houses, apartments, and bed-and-breakfast establishments in the capital. This is called *Where to Stay in London* and is available from many bookstores or by visiting the L.T.B. information center on the forecourt of Victoria station (no telephone inquiries, however). There is also an Accommodation Booking Service here and at the L.T.B. desk at Heathrow airport.

**CHARGES**
When making a reservation, check what the room rate quoted includes: usually the price is inclusive of V.A.T. (Value Added Tax) and a service charge, but it is best to be sure, because these can amount to nearly a third of the bill. Breakfast is often included in the cheaper hotels; the more upscale you go, the more likely it is that breakfast will be charged as extra.

*If you want luxury in London expect to pay top prices*

**Hotel facilities** The biggest problem with London hotels is noise, as many are located on busy streets. Some have double or triple glazing to keep out the sound, but that can make rooms unbearably stuffy, especially since air-conditioning is by no means a standard facility. You should bear this point in mind when choosing a hotel and, if you value peace and quiet, look for hotels on side streets in residential areas; or request a room at the rear of the hotel or higher up in the building.

Most hotel rooms have a private bathroom, television, and direct dial I.D.D. telephone—but beware of very high markups on telephone calls. Laundry service is often slow and expensive. Increasingly hotels are supplying electric kettles and tea or coffee packets so that guests can make their own hot drinks. For other facilities, such as parking, 24-hour room service, gyms, and swimming pools, you can expect to pay a very high premium within central London.

*The Russell Hotel in Bloomsbury, a grand Victorian landmark convenient for the British Museum*

*The London Hilton on Park Lane may not be stunning from the outside, but inside guests can enjoy wonderful views*

*London's cafés and restaurants compare with the world's best*

## Food and drink

Eating and drinking in London underwent a revolution that began in the late 1980s and continued throughout the 1990s. Cafés smartened up. Pubs disposed of their smoke and became places to meet, eat and perhaps drink all day—some even do breakfast. Bars re-invented themselves into upbeat forums. Even in-house museum and gallery eating improved substantially. Meanwhile, restaurants increased in number and became fiercely competitive in setting (well-known architects and designers modeled many), service, and in the authenticity and creativity of their food and drinks. In essence, eating out became an enjoyable and regular experience.

Today, you can sample most of the world's cuisines in central London. Furthermore, their distinctive regional variants are cooked correctly and to a high level, be it north Italian, South Indian, Cajun or Californian. Alternatively, you can enjoy the highly creative cooking of young, imaginative chefs inspired by various countries round the world. Fresh ingredients imported into London from almost every country help ensure quality is maintained. There is no need to eat badly.

Finding the ideal restaurants for your needs may prove something of a challenge, however. You will almost certainly have a specific setting in mind to suit the mood of the occasion, be it romantic, informal, a family meal or business lunch. Furthermore, this restaurant will need to be in the right place; it is pointless to cross London from an Islington theater to a Kensington restaurant, only to return to a St James's hotel. The price must accord with your budget for the occasion. To add to the difficulties, restaurants open up and close down with alarming speed—more than a hundred restaurants varying from okay to excellent do so every year—and chefs move on. Thus, it is wise to start by doing some research (see panel page 241) and to take a few tips from experienced

*Snacking al fresco in Soho, one of central London's best places for quality casual dining*

**SUNDAY LUNCH**
This is a good way to enjoy fine food at a relaxed pace. It can also prove a bargain if you opt for the fixed-price menu. At the top end, try the Connaught or Savoy River Restaurant; The Ivy, Tamarind, Chor Bizarre down the price scale; or the cheaper Veeraswamy or Townhouse brasseries. Most hotels offer a fixed price traditional Sunday roast, too, to include extravagant desserts and a good cheeseboard.

*Food for the budget-conscious visitor*

Londoners—even they have to work to keep abreast of the whole scene.

**Finding the good deal** Meal deals abound in London. They make a huge difference to the bill, and not even the most comfortable purse will ignore them. Many of London's finest restaurants offer a fixed price menu at a substantial reduction on the same dishes selected à la carte. They are usually offered for weekday lunches. Some of the best include La Tante Claire, the Oak Room, La Porte des Indes, Veeraswamy, J. Sheekey, Lemonia, Lou Pescadou. There are also good fixed price menus for pre- or post-theater suppers, such as at the Savoy Grill, Bentley's, and Launceston Place.

**Reservations** Reserving a table is essential if you want to eat at a specific restaurant at a specific time—which most people do in London. Top chefs, fashionable restaurants and popular locals need to be reserved up well in advance. Some will be more likely to have a table at lunch than at dinner. Lunch is eaten from as early as 12:15 or as late as 1:45, and tends to end 2:15–3:00. If you are meeting for a drink before going to the theater or out to dinner, try the Meridien Warldorf, the American Bar in the Savoy, Mezzo, One Aldwych and the Dorchester. Some restaurants near the West End theaters—which stretch from Aldwych to Piccadilly, will be quiet and lack atmosphere during performance time; furthermore, they will expect people to leave in time for the restaurant's post-theater bookings, and this can make dinner more hurried than you might wish. If dinner after the theater ends very late, you can ask the staff to call a black cab for you.

**SPECIALIST GUIDES**
For an idea of the full range on offer, see the *Time Out Restaurant Guide*. For a more personal selection, see the *AA Guide to Britain's Best Restaurants* (of which a selection is listed on page 277–281), *Harden's London Restaurants* or the *Zagat Survey of London Restaurants*, all published annually.

*Fresh fruit ice cream at Neal's Yard in Covent Garden*

*Regent Street decked out for Christmas*



## Shopping

London offers shoppers a vast range, from mini-city department stores to wheelbarrow bargains and Dickensian specialty stores. Many people come to London just to shop, so Oxford Street and Regent Street can be crammed to bursting point in summer and in the Christmas shopping season, and particularly long lines can be expected at the most popular stores such as **Hamley's**. Remember, there are plenty of other quieter areas to shop.

**Opening hours** The worst crowds can be avoided by shopping early. Stores tend to open around 9 AM (though some do not open until 10 AM) and you will often find that service is more attentive during the slacker period before lunchtime shoppers begin to arrive. Stores have become increasingly flexible in their opening hours in recent years; it is now common to find them open until 9 or 10 PM in the main areas, though the big department stores have late-night opening on only one day of the week (typically Wednesday or Thursday). Increasingly, too, plenty of stores open on Sunday.

**Bargain time** Twice a year, London stores slash their prices in order to sell off the previous season's remaining stock: the January sales start immediately after Christmas and continue well into February. Determined bargain-hunters camp out in the streets for several days in advance to be first in the line when the sales open at Harrods, Debenhams, or Selfridges.

The summer sales begin in June or July and last to the end of August. Strict rules govern the way that sales operate in Britain, and the fact that you bought an item in a sale does not affect your statutory rights as a consumer; you are, for example, entitled to a full refund if the goods

*Summer temptations on display in Berwick Street market*

prove faulty (unless they were sold as damaged goods)—but you must retain your receipt as proof of purchase.

*The famous Harrods green livery extends to the doormen*

**Tax-free shopping** If the goods you buy are going to be exported to a non-European Union country you are exempt from Value Added Tax; this can be a considerable saving (but you have to spend a minimum amount which varies from store to store). Most leading stores have details of the tax-free shopping policy and can help with your claims.

**Street vendors** Beware of street vendors anywhere in London. The products they sell are often not what they claim to be, and while you are absorbed in watching their theatrical sales technique, their accomplices may well be picking your pockets.

**Markets** The same advice about pickpockets applies to crowded street markets, but otherwise London's markets are enormously fun—the sales banter of stallholders is refreshingly direct and there are real bargains to be found. Here is a selection of the best:
• **Berwick Street** (Soho): top-quality fruits and vegetables daily except Sunday.
• **Covent Garden**: antiques on Monday, crafts on Tuesday to Sunday, in and around the central arcade.
• **Camden Lock**: crafts, antiques, books, used clothes, and jewelry: Wednesday to Sunday.
• **Portobello Road**: fruit and vegetables, but antiques, used clothes, and jewelry; best by far on Saturday.
• **Camden Passage**: antiques and collectables on Wednesday and Saturday.
• **Petticoat Lane** and surrounding streets: a complete mixture serving City office workers and local East End residents—everything from silk saris to tacky ties, plus fruits and vegetables—daily.
• There is more of the same nearby at **Leather Lane** (weekday lunchtimes) and at **Brick Lane** (Sunday mornings only).

*Browsing among the market stalls is a favorite London pastime*

*London's club scene is a melting pot of constant, dynamic change*

**WORLD MUSIC**
If you're feeling homesick or just want to try another musical culture, the following venues are a good bet:
Africa Centre, 38 King Street, Covent Garden (tel: 020-7836 1973), live African bands most nights;
Cecil Sharp House, 2 Regent's Park Road (tel: 020-7485 2206), home to British folk music but also stages world roots bands;
Jazz Café, 5 Parkway London N1 (tel: 020-7344 0044), jazz, blues, soul, plus acts from all over the world.

## Nightlife

London has rich and varied nightlife, a fact that is immediately apparent when you flick through the pages of *Time Out* magazine—an indispensable guide if you want to know what is on where, and which clubs, nightspots, or discos are active that week. The magazine will also advise you on points of club etiquette, such as dress codes, so that you look the part—most clubs frown on casual jeans, T-shirts, and trainers. The preferred dress is smart but casual, although for theme nights you will be expected to dress with flair. Club venues come and go with bewildering speed, and some host different nightclubs or themes on each day of the week. Here are a few venues that have had some staying power:

**Camden Palace**, 1 Camden High Street (tel: 020-7387 0428); very popular with overseas visitors: vast and fun.
**The Gardening Club**, 4 The Piazza, Covent Garden (tel: 020-7497 3154). The name refers to the area, not a predilection with horticulture. As hip as they come; house, garage, trance, or whatever is the flavor of the month.
**The Hippodrome**, Charing Cross Road (tel: 020-7437 4311); disco with all the latest technological effects.
**Ministry of Sound**, 103 Gaunt Street (tel: 020-7378 6528); another club based on a New York prototype, the legendary Paradise Garage.

**Comedy, cabaret, and jazz**
**The Comedy Store**, Haymarket House, 1 Oxendon Street (tel: 020-7344 4444); founded in 1979, and still going strong as the place to see both new talent and the more established comedians.
**Dover Street Wine Bar**, 8–9 Dover Street (tel: 020-7629 9813); food and wine by candlelight with live jazz, blues, or soul (and dancing) Monday to Saturday until 3 AM.
**Jongleurs Battersea**, The Cornet, 49 Lavender Gardens, SW11 (tel: 020-7564 2500). This is the original venue for one of London's best and longest-running comedy companies. Also at Dingwalls, Camden Lock (tel: 020-7564 2500) and Bow Wharf, 221 Grove Road (tel: 020-7564 2500).
**100 Club**, 100 Oxford Street (tel: 020-7636 0933); live jazz or R&B, depending on which night you go. Drinks at pub prices. Very hot and smoky.
**Madame Jo Jo's**, 8–10 Brewer Street (tel: 020-7734 2473); often listed as part of the London gay scene, but it attracts a huge straight audience as well for scintillating cabaret performed by outrageously camp drag artists.
**Ronnie Scott's**, 47 Frith Street (tel: 020-7439 0747); famous for top-quality jazz—so it gets very crowded, especially on Saturday, when reservations are essential.

**Theater, music, and dance** See pages 148–149, 180–181.

**Film** Newspapers and listings magazines carry general movie information; foreign movies often experience a delay before being released in the U.K. A number of theaters show a changing schedule of art/classic/cult/kitsch or offbeat movies, usually with late-night screenings; try the following:
**Barbican**, Barbican Centre, Silk Street (tel: 020-7638 8891).
**Lumière**, 42–49 St. Martin's Lane (tel: 020-7836 0691).
**National Film Theatre**, South Bank (tel: 020-7928 3232).
**Screen on the Green**, 83 Upper Street, Islington (tel: 020-7226 3520).

*Stringfellows, the haunt of glitterati, paparazzi, and sun-baked wannabes*



*Bright lights, action, movies on Leicester Square: the place to catch the latest Hollywood blockbusters*

*Keep your eyes open for London's colorful old street furnishings, such as this Victorian mailbox*

## Itineraries

Here are some suggestions for making the most of your time in London.

### A weekend in London

Since every minute is going to be precious, do as much advance planning and reserving as possible. Reserve hotels, theater tickets, and restaurants well ahead so you do not have to worry about practicalities on arrival. Remember too that you can save time in lines by buying tickets in advance for some of London's most popular attractions, such as the Tower of London (see pages 196–197), Madame Tussaud's (see pages 120–121), and Buckingham Palace (see pages 64–65). Westminster Abbey, St. Paul's, and other major churches will be holding services on Sunday, and visits are thus restricted—if you want to see them, plan to do this on Saturday. Saturday is also an excellent day for sampling markets, such as Camden Lock and Portobello Road. Museums open later on Sunday, so use your Sunday morning for a stroll around some intriguing part of London, taking advantage of the relative quiet and lack of traffic to get a good look at the varied architecture.

### A week in London

With a whole week at your disposal in London, you'll have a better chance of getting right under the skin of the city. You will probably have your own personal priorities, but consider the following suggestions:

**Day 1**: Take a guided tour by bus (see page 40) or a river trip (see page 55) to get your bearings.
**Day 2**: Explore Covent Garden, with its stores, stalls, street performers, museums, and restaurants, for a truly varied day.
**Day 3**: Visit one of London's big museums—there are plenty to choose from—in the morning, but plan something different for the afternoon, such as a stroll around

*The National Gallery, on Trafalgar Square, is London's best free picture show*

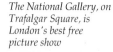

St. James's Park and shopping in the Piccadilly/Regent Street area.
**Day 4**: Hit the popular sights of London, but be prepared to make an early start: buy your ticket in advance but still arrive early at either the Tower of London or Madame Tussaud's; alternatively, skip Madame Tussaud's and pay a visit to the royal wax effigies in the undercroft at Westminster Abbey instead—perhaps combining this with the Changing of the Guard at Horse Guards or St. James's.
**Day 5**: Get out of town altogether and take a trip to Greenwich or Hampton Court, both very rewarding full day trips with lots to see.
**Day 6**: Visit some more museums. If you have not seen the Victoria and Albert or the British Museum, now is the time to do so—you will find so much to see that you will promise yourself a return visit.
**Day 7**: Your last day may well be spent shopping for presents in Liberty's or one of the huge department stores, such as Harrods and Selfridges; for something clearly related to London, find special products in the museum shops of the Tate, National Gallery, V&A, or British Museum, and take a walk along Bankside for some last memorable views of London.



*French-style cafés in Old Compton Street*

**Best sights for children**
**1 Natural History Museum** see pages 94, 98–99
**2 London Aquarium** see page 205
**3 London Zoo** see page 125
**4 Pollock's Toy Museum** see page 139
**5 London Transport Museum** see page 146
**6 Museum of London** see pages 166–167
**7 Bethnal Green Museum of Childhood** see page 179
**8 H.M.S. *Belfast*** see page 191
**9 B.B.C. Experience** see pages 118–119
**10 Imperial War Museum** see pages 200–201

**Away from the hustle**
**1 Chelsea Physic Garden** see page 91
**2 Leighton House Museum** see pages 108–109
**3 Linley Sambourne House** see page 114
**4 The Wallace Collection** see pages 126–127
**5 Sir John Soane's Museum** see pages 154–155
**6 Courtauld Gallery** see pages 156–158
**7 Syon House** see pages 232–233
**8 Dulwich Gallery** see page 214
**9 Fenton House** see page 220
**10 Kew Gardens** see pages 226–227

**FAMILIES COME FREE**
Most museums allow free admission to children under five years old and some to older children, too. However, the whole family can visit four of London's top fee-paying museums for free at the end of each day. At the Natural History Museum head straight for the excellent Dinosaurs exhibition, then onto Mammals. At the Science Museum children can exercise hands and minds at Launch Pad and in the basement at The Garden. The Museum of London is full of interest for children. The Victoria and Albert Museum is most child-friendly on Sunday when their Activity Cart is wheeled out.



## London for free

London can be one of the world's most expensive cities. But those who know better can seek out top quality entertainment without spending a penny.

• Not all museums charge visitors. The National Gallery, the National Portrait Gallery, the British Museum, the Tate galleries, the Wallace Collection, Sir John Soane's Museum, the National Army Museum, and many other, smaller museums are free. If you enjoy yourself, you may like to make a donation.

• It costs nothing to visit the Central Criminal Court (better known as the Old Bailey) or the Royal Courts of Justice (where civil cases are heard) where you can watch the English legal system at work—ask the ushers who guard the entrance to the public galleries which of the trials is likely to prove the most entertaining.

• Both of the major arts locations—the Barbican and the South Bank—have free lobby exhibitions, children's events, musical performances, and other entertainment. With a little bit of nerve you may also be able to get in to listen to orchestral rehearsals and see some of the world's finest musicians and conductors at work.

• If people-watching, clowning, acrobatics, puppetry, and sidewalk musicians are more to your taste, Covent Garden market is the place to go, especially at lunchtime and on weekends in summer. The quality of the street theater is very high—although you should, in all conscience, contribute a few coins, or more, as gratuities for the actors and performers.

• Go to Harrods or Liberty's or any other of London's great department stores and dream of what you might buy—and perhaps buy it.

• Go to an auction and watch others spend their fortunes—sales at Christie's, Sotheby's, Bonham's, or Phillips are fascinating to watch.

• Attend a free lunchtime concert. There is usually a choice of several, especially in City churches (for details ask at the City of London Information Center, across from St. Paul's Cathedral).

*Street entertainers*

# Travel Facts

## Arriving

**Entry formalities** European Union citizens have the right to enter the United Kingdom at will; in theory you need only to carry some evidence of identity, such as an I.D. card or driver's license. In practice the United Kingdom authorities are uncomfortable with the idea of open borders, arguing that checks are necessary to combat terrorism, smuggling, and illegal immigration. It is therefore advisable to bring your full passport.

Visitors from outside the European Union must have a valid passport to enter the U.K. Citizens of most Commonwealth countries, the U.S., Japan, and much of South America do not need a visa, but there are some exceptions (including Nigeria, Ghana, India, Bangladesh, Sri Lanka, and Pakistan). If in doubt, check with your travel agent or the British Embassy in your home country.



**Airports** Most visitors to the U.K. arrive at Heathrow or Gatwick airports where both have good facilities including tourist information, hotel reservations, and car rental services. See also information on telephone numbers on page 251.

• **Gatwick** From Gatwick, two train services operate to London. The Gatwick Express leaves every 15 minutes (less often at night) on its 30-minute ride to Victoria. Thameslink trains stop at London Bridge, Blackfriars, City Thameslink, Farringdon, and King's Cross. Flightline 777 buses run hourly by day; taxis run 24 hours.

• **Heathrow** Train is the fastest way to reach London; you can travel either by Underground on the Piccadilly Line (60 minutes to the center) or by Heathrow Express to Paddington, departing every 15 minutes from 5:10 AM–11:40 PM (the journey takes 15 minutes).

The Airbus service (which takes roughly an hour) picks passengers up from all terminals every half hour 5:40 AM–9:45 PM daily. Route A1 goes to Victoria train station with interim stops in Earl's Court, South Kensington, and Knightsbridge. The A2 service passes by Marble Arch and Baker Street to Euston and Russell Square. Black taxicabs or minicabs will take you direct to your hotel, but can be expensive.

• **London City** This airport, mostly used by business travelers, is closest to the city center. There is an Airbus service, to which the only alternative is a taxi.

• **Stansted** There is a good train service from London's third airport, Stansted, which departs every 30 minutes and takes 45 minutes to reach Liverpool Street station.

*Liverpool Street Station*

*London's distinctive black taxicabs are the most pleasant and convenient way to get about town, but can be expensive*

❑ **Airport information:**
Gatwick: 01293-535353
Heathrow: 020-8759 4321
London City: 020-7646 0088
Stansted: 01279-680500 ❑

**Arriving by Train** Eurostar trains (tel: 0990-186186) arrive regularly at Waterloo International Terminal from Paris and Disneyland Paris, Brussels and Lille.

National trains (tel: 0345-484950) mostly come in to Charing Cross, Euston, King's Cross, Liverpool Street, London Bridge, Paddington, Victoria, and Waterloo stations, or along the Thameslink line.

Long-distance bus services arrive at Victoria Coach Station (tel: 020-7730 3466). Major bus companies include National Express (tel: 0990-808080) and Eurolines (tel: 01582 404511).

**Other options** Visitors coming from other European countries have a wealth of options for getting to the U.K., such as shuttle flights, which operate between smaller regional airports, trans-European train and bus services (including the Channel Tunnel), and ferry, jetfoil, and hovercraft services.

It is well worth shopping around for the best deal—you may find that can save a lot of money. Inclusive packages, covering travel and hotel accommodations, often represent the best value.

**Car rental**
It is not worth the expense and worry of renting a car in London if you only intend to travel within the city. Using public transportation or taxis will cost you far less and save all the time spent looking for parking space and navigating unfamiliar roads. Even for trips out of London, it can be simpler to use train or bus services. If you do decide to rent a car, you will find a huge range of companies and options listed in the *Yellow Pages* telephone directory, and by phoning around you should get a competitive deal.

Some points to bear in mind:

• You must have a driver's license (an international driver's license is not required).

• You must be over 18 years old to rent a car (in fact, many companies have an age limit of 21); and you must also have at least 12 months' driving experience.

• Reserving in advance is essential on weekends, especially for the cheaper end of the range (and for cars at the very top end—Rolls Royces are much in demand at weekends for weddings).

• Car-rental firms prefer you to pay by credit card so that they can check your address and identity—expect to encounter problems if you want to pay by cash or check (usually a very large deposit is demanded if this is the case).



❑ **Leading firms—central reservation numbers**
Avis in U.K.—0990-900500
Budget—0800-181181
Holiday Autos in U.K.—0990-300400
Eurocar—0345-222525
Hertz—0990-996699 ❑

**Car repairs and servicing**
If you rent a car in London, the car-rental company will usually give you the number of its 24-hour breakdown service. Otherwise, there are two main organizations offering road service in the U.K.: the Automobile Association (A.A.) and the Royal Automobile Club (R.A.C.).

If you are a member of a similar organization in your own country, check before you travel to London whether you have the right to use the services of one of these organizations for free—and bring the necessary documentation.

**Automobile Association**: for membership information tel: 0800-919595. For emergency breakdown service tel: 0800-887766 (freephone).

**Royal Automobile Club**: for membership information tel: 0800-550550. For

*Many Londoners travel by tube*

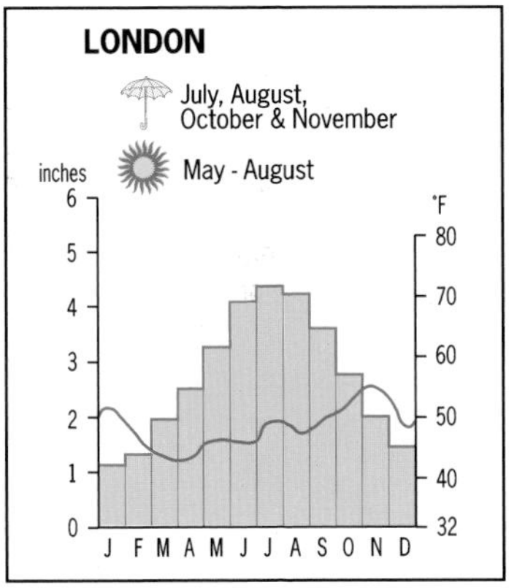


emergency breakdown service tel: 0800-828282 (freephone).

**Climate**

The British love to talk about the weather simply because it is so variable—changing hour by hour, if not minute by minute. All daily newspapers carry weather forecasts, as do all the T.V. and radio channels (usually just before or just after the main newscasts of the day) but as every Londoner will tell you, they are not always reliable. London has its own microclimate, because of the great number of heated buildings in the city, so frost and lingering snow are very rare. The temperature seldom falls below freezing point, although chilling northerly winds can make it feel cold in the winter. Rain is the biggest problem. Officially the wettest weeks are from late September to the end of November, but it can be just as wet in the middle of summer. As a rule of thumb, you can usually plan that if you carry full anti-rain gear—waterproof coat and hat, umbrella, boots—the day will probably be dry and sunny, but if you go out unprepared it will pour. Fortunately, you are never very far away from shelter in London—unless, that is, you decide to go for a hike across Hyde Park!

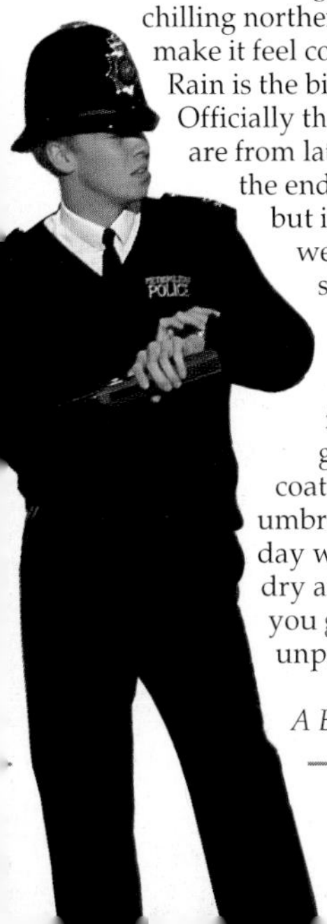

*A British policeman*

**Crime**

A substantial amount of petty crime takes place on London's streets by day and night, and visitors are particularly at risk from pickpocketing and theft of property from parked cars (which is another good reason for not driving in London).

Here are some tips to make your vacation safer:

• Make photocopies of important documents such as your passport, and keep notes of traveler's check numbers and credit-card details. This record should be kept separately from the original documents and will help you obtain replacements quickly if the originals are lost or stolen.

• Lock all your valuables in a hotel safe. Most good hotels will allocate you a safe with its own key where you can put your money, jewelry, camera, and so on.

• If you must carry valuables, conceal them in a money belt or something similar and keep a tight hold on your camera at all times.

• Be especially wary in crowded situations, such as in street markets, on a bus or subway, or in crowds crossing busy roads, like Oxford Street. Be alert at all times and try not to become so absorbed in window-shopping that you are oblivious to other people around you.

• Trust nobody and be wary of anyone who approaches you, no matter how innocently. Some people operate with accomplices who pick your pocket while you are distracted giving directions. Other thieves hang out wherever there are beggars or street musicians watching to see where you put your hand when asked for money—giving them a clue to where you keep your valuables.

If you are robbed you should do the following:

• Report the loss of your credit cards and travelers' checks to the issuing company as soon as possible.

• Make a report to the nearest police station and obtain a copy of your

Enjoying a rare spot of sunshine

statement so that you can make an insurance claim. They will issue you with a crime reference number.

• Report the loss of a passport to your embassy or consulate (see page 257).

• It is not sensible to be out in some parts of London late at night on your own. If you must be out, go as part of a group. Do not go to parks or commons after dark and keep to busy, well-lit streets. Buses, trains, and the Tube are relatively safe at night, but it is a sensible rule to stay with the crowds, rather than exposing yourself to the risk of attack by sitting in an empty train car. After the public transportation system closes down at night it is better to take a taxi, despite the expense, than risk being on the streets alone—especially if you are in the city suburbs.

**Customs regulations**

You will not normally have to pay duty on personal possessions brought into the U.K., but some goods, such as tobacco and alcohol, are liable to tax and duty. The amount that you are allowed to import without paying duty depends on where the goods were purchased. There are two different levels of duty-free allowance, as shown below, but you have to be over 17 years of age to qualify.

**Goods purchased outside the European Union (E.U.):**

Import Duty is payable on certain goods brought into the European Community; once paid, those goods may be moved from one European Community country to another without further payment. Excise Duty is payable on certain goods, such as alcohol and cigarettes, when they are brought from any country into the United Kingdom. In both categories, various restrictions cover a wide range of goods and are liable to change at any time. If you think you have goods to declare for duty, either go through the Red Channel at the port of entry (where you can pay any duty levied by credit card), or before you leave for London contact H.M. Customs and Excise Enquiries, Dorset House, Stamford Street, London SE1 9PY, tel: 020-7865 4400, fax 020-8346 9154 (Mon–Fri, 9–5).

**Goods brought into the U.S.**
Visitors aged 21 or over may import the following:
• 200 cigarettes or 50 cigars or 2kg of tobacco.
• 1 liter of alcohol.
• gifts to the value of $100.

**Domestic travel**
For travel outside London, see pages 210–211. For travel within London see Public transportation, page 265.

**Travelers with disabilities**
London is a better city than most for people with disabilities. As a general

*Clamping to deter illegal parking*

rule, it is a good idea to telephone in advance if you need special help or services so that the museum, restaurant, theater, or organization you are visiting can make arrangements.

An organization called **Artsline** (tel: 020-7388 2227) offers free information and advice for people with disabilities on all aspects of the London arts and entertainment scene, including museums, galleries, concert halls, theaters and movie theaters. For accommodations contact the **Holiday Care Service** (tel: 01293-774 535), which offers a free advisory service; for specific transportation advice, contact London Transport's Unit for Disabled Travellers (tel: 020-7918 3312).

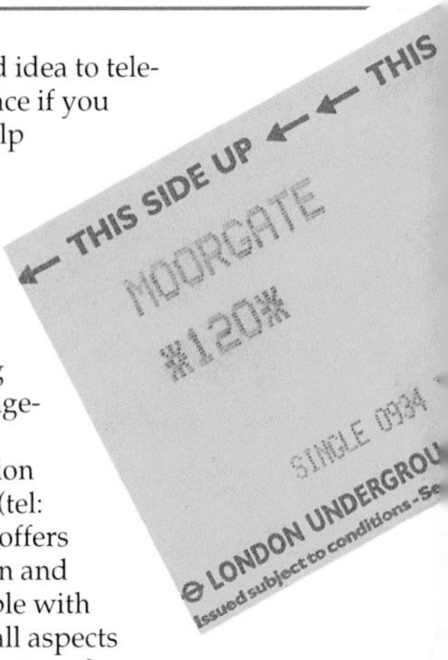


The most comprehensive specialist guide to London for people with disabilities is *Access in London*, published by Nicholson, and available from Access Project, 39 Bradley Gardens, West Ealing, London W13 8HE. It was written and researched by people with disabilities. For information on tour operators who cater specifically for travelers with disabilities, contact R.A.D.A.R. (the Royal Association for Disability and Rehabiliation, tel: 020-7250 3222).

**Driving tips**
The best tip for anyone contemplating driving in London is simple: don't. London already has too many vehicles and it will take you much longer to get around by car than by public transportation. Parking spaces are hard to find, meters are expensive, and your car will be clamped (a lock put on the wheel so you cannot drive) or towed away if you park illegally. Theft from cars is the commonest crime in the U.K. and is still on the increase. If you must drive, then:
• Carry lots of small change to feed parking meters (20p, 50p and £1

*Taking a rest from sightseeing*

coins). Do not overstay your allotted time; there are plenty of traffic police around to nab offenders, and the fines are expensive. Meter parking is usually free after 6:30 PM, after 1:30 PM Saturday and all day Sunday, but there are a few exceptions, so check what it says on the meter.

• Don't park on double yellow lines or in areas reserved for permit holders—to do so virtually guarantees that you will have your wheels clamped, or your vehicle towed—a very expensive inconvenience. You should avoid areas with double red lines and near crossings at all times.

• If you are leaving your car parked in London for any length of time, use a patrolled parking lot, staffed by attendants, despite the cost involved, rather than leaving your car on the streets, where it can be stolen.

❑ **24-hour parking garages in central London**

Park Lane (the biggest in central London, below Marble Arch traffic circle—there are usually spaces here even when all other car parks are full)
Brewer Street
Newport Place
Upper St. Martin's Lane

**24-hour gas stations in central London**

83 Park Lane
71 King's Cross Road
104 Bayswater Road ❑

**Car clamping** If your car is clamped, the notice posted on your windshield will explain how to get it released. If you do not have the time to wait around, you can pay someone else a fee to do it for you. Try the **Car Recovery Club** (tel: 020-8777 2287).

**Electricity**
The electrical current in the U.K. is 240 volts, 50 cycle A.C. Plugs are three-prong square. Most hotels also have two-pin 110-volt shaver sockets. To use most American or European appliances you will need an adapter.

**Embassies, consulates, and high commissions**
**Australia** Australia House, Strand (tel: 020-7379 4334)
**Austria** 18 Belgrave Mews West (tel: 020-7235 3731/visas 0891 600250)
**Belgium** 103 Eaton Square (tel: 020-7470 3700/visas 0891 600255)
**Brazil** 32 Green Street (tel: 020-7499 0877/visas 930 7055)
**Canada** 38 Grosvenor Street (tel: 020-7409 2071)
**Chile** 12 Devonshire Street (tel: 020-7580 6392/1023)
**China** 49 Portland Place (tel: 020-7636 5726)
**Denmark** 55 Sloane Street (tel: 020-7333 0200/visas 333 0265)
**Egypt** 24 South Street (tel: 020-7493 2649/visas 0891 88777)
**Finland** 38 Chesham Place (tel: 020-7838 6200)
**France** 21 Cromwell Road (tel: 020-7838 2000); visa section: 6A Cromwell Place (tel: 020-7838 2050)
**Germany** 23 Belgrave Square (tel: 020-7824 1300)
**Ghana** 102 Park Street (tel: 020-7235 4142/342 8686)
**Greece** 1A Holland Park (tel: 020-7221 6467/visas 0891 171202)
**India** India House, Aldwych (tel: 020-7836 8484)
**Ireland** 17 Grosvenor Place (tel: 020-7235 2171)
**Israel** 2 Palace Green (tel: 020-7957 9500)
**Italy** 14, Three King's Yard (tel: 020-7312 2200/visas 0891 600340)
**Jamaica** 1–2 Prince Consort Road (tel: 020-7823 9911)
**Japan** 101–104 Piccadilly (tel: 020-7465 6500)
**Kenya** 45 Portland Place (tel: 020-7636 2371)
**Luxembourg** 27 Wilton Crescent (tel: 020-7235 6961)
**Netherlands** 38 Hyde Park Gate (tel: 020-7590 3200/visas 0891 171217)
**New Zealand** New Zealand House, 80 Haymarket (tel: 020-7930 8422)
**Norway** 25 Belgrave Square (tel: 020-7591 5500)
**Pakistan** 35 Lowndes Square (tel: 020-7235 2044)
**Portugal** 11 Belgrave Square (tel: 020-7235 5331/visas 0891 600202)
**Saudi Arabia** 30 Charles Street (tel: 020-7917 3000)
**South Africa**, South Africa House, Trafalgar Square (tel: 020-7930 4488)
**Spain**,visas, 23 Manchester Square (tel: 020-7589 8989/0891 600123)

*The traditional home of the Prime Minister—No. 10 Downing Street*

## CONVERSION CHARTS

| FROM | TO | MULTIPLY BY |
|---|---|---|
| Inches | Centimetres | 2.54 |
| Centimetres | Inches | 0.3937 |
| Feet | Metres | 0.3048 |
| Metres | Feet | 3.2810 |
| Yards | Metres | 0.9144 |
| Metres | Yards | 1.0940 |
| Miles | Kilometres | 1.6090 |
| Kilometres | Miles | 0.6214 |
| Acres | Hectares | 0.4047 |
| Hectares | Acres | 2.4710 |
| Gallons | Litres | 4.5460 |
| Litres | Gallons | 0.2200 |
| Ounces | Grams | 28.35 |
| Grams | Ounces | 0.0353 |
| Pounds | Grams | 453.6 |
| Grams | Pounds | 0.0022 |
| Pounds | Kilograms | 0.4536 |
| Kilograms | Pounds | 2.205 |
| Tons | Tonnes | 1.0160 |
| Tonnes | Tons | 0.9842 |

**MEN'S SUITS**

| | | | | | | | |
|---|---|---|---|---|---|---|---|
| UK | 36 | 38 | 40 | 42 | 44 | 46 | 48 |
| Rest of Europe | 46 | 48 | 50 | 52 | 54 | 56 | 58 |
| US | 36 | 38 | 40 | 42 | 44 | 46 | 48 |

**DRESS SIZES**

| | | | | | | |
|---|---|---|---|---|---|---|
| UK | 8 | 10 | 12 | 14 | 16 | 18 |
| France | 36 | 38 | 40 | 42 | 44 | 46 |
| Italy | 38 | 40 | 42 | 44 | 46 | 48 |
| Rest of Europe | 34 | 36 | 38 | 40 | 42 | 44 |
| US | 6 | 8 | 10 | 12 | 14 | 16 |

**MEN'S SHIRTS**

| | | | | | | | |
|---|---|---|---|---|---|---|---|
| UK | 14 | 14.5 | 15 | 15.5 | 16 | 16.5 | 17 |
| Rest of Europe | 36 | 37 | 38 | 39/40 | 41 | 42 | 43 |
| US | 14 | 14.5 | 15 | 15.5 | 16 | 16.5 | 17 |

**MEN'S SHOES**

| | | | | | | |
|---|---|---|---|---|---|---|
| UK | 7 | 7.5 | 8.5 | 9.5 | 10.5 | 11 |
| Rest of Europe | 41 | 42 | 43 | 44 | 45 | 46 |
| US | 8 | 8.5 | 9.5 | 10.5 | 11.5 | 12 |

**WOMEN'S SHOES**

| | | | | | | |
|---|---|---|---|---|---|---|
| UK | 4.5 | 5 | 5.5 | 6 | 6.5 | 7 |
| Rest of Europe | 38 | 38 | 39 | 39 | 40 | 41 |
| US | 6 | 6.5 | 7 | 7.5 | 8 | 8.5 |



**Sweden** 11 Montagu Place (tel: 020-7724 2101)
**Switzerland** 16 Montagu Place (tel: 020-7616 6000/visas 0891 331313)
**Turkey** 43 Belgrave Square (tel: 020-7393 0202)
**U.S.A**. 24 Grosvenor Square (tel: 020-7499 9000)
**Zimbabwe** 429 Strand (tel: 020-7836 7755/visas 0891 600172)

### Emergency telephone numbers

Dial 999 and state whether you need Fire, Police, or Ambulance. All calls are free and you can use any telephone—you can dial from a card phone without inserting a card or from a pay phone without inserting any coins.

### Health and insurance

In the event of serious illness or injury you can seek medical help at the emergency room ("casualty department") of any hospital that has one, and you can call an ambulance by dialing 999. Most of the larger hotels have a doctor on call to deal with more routine problems, but a charge is often made for their services.

Free medical treatment is available to citizens of the European Union and some other countries with whom Britain has reciprocal arrangements. It is advisable to check the precise arrangements before you leave your own country because free treatment is usually only available to those who have completed all the necessary documentation in advance. All other foreign visitors (including those from the U.S. and Canada) are required to pay the full cost of the medical treatment they receive and you are strongly advised to arrange your health insurance before arriving in the U.K.

### Lost property

Any property left on the bus or Tube system will be taken to the **Lost Property Office** at 200 Baker Street, next door to the Baker Street tube station (Mon–Fri 9:30–2). You must stop by in person (or write a letter) since they won't take inquiries over the phone. If you left something in a black taxi cab contact the **Taxi Lost Property Office**, 15 Penton Street (tel:

*The world's news*

020-7833 0996). If you lose property on a train contact the station at which your train terminated (see telephone directories for station telephone numbers).

Insurance companies will expect you to report the loss of money or valuables to the nearest police station as soon as possible.

**Media**

**Overseas newspapers and magazines** To keep in touch with events back home through your own favorite newspaper or magazine, the following newsstands (newsagents) pride themselves on having all the leading international papers in stock: **A. Maroni & Son**, 68 Old Compton Street (tel: 020-7437 2847; Mon–Sat 7 AM–7:15 PM and Sun 7 AM–2 PM); **Grays Inn News**, 50 Theobald Road (tel: 020-7405 5241; Mon–Fri 4 AM–5:30 PM); **W.H. Smith's**, Sloane Square branch, **John Menzies** at 104 Long Acre, and **Capital Newsagents**, 48 Old Compton Street.

**British magazines and newspapers** The publication for all London information is the listings magazine *Time*

*Signs to look for*

*Out*. The British have an unusually large number of national daily newspapers, both broadsheet and tabloid. *The Times*, the *Daily Telegraph*, the *Guardian* and the *Independent* are all serious broadsheets with high standards of reporting on U.K. and international affairs, and good arts coverage. The *Financial Times*, printed distinctively on pink paper, covers world business news and market prices.

All the above papers have large Saturday editions with plenty of London arts news. In addition, the *Independent on Sunday*, the *Sunday Times*, and the *Observer* all bring out heavyweight Sunday editions.

London also has its own newspaper, the *Evening Standard*, which reviews restaurants and pubs as well as performing arts and exhibitions. Many individual areas of London, such as Islington, Hampstead, and Highgate, have their own weekly newspapers covering news and events of local interest.

There is an abundance of magazines. Among them, the satirical *Private Eye*, and the establishment *The New Statesman* (both weeklies) provide an entertaining read. Condé Nast has its own UK stable that includes *Vogue*, *Vanity Fair*, *GQ*, *Brides*, and *Condé Nast Traveller*.

*Currency dealers abound*

**Radio** London has several radio stations that are good sources of music and of information about events in the capital. These include:

**Capital Gold** 1548A.M.: golden-oldies 24 hours a day, aimed at a broad range of listeners, but mainly those old enough to remember the Top 40 hits of the 1960s, 1970s, and 1980s.

**Capital Radio** 95.8F.M.: pop music and news 24 hours a day, aimed at younger listeners—the station you are likely to hear playing in many stores and taxis.

**G.L.R. (Greater London Radio)** 94.9F.M.: London's best pop music station by a long way.

**London News Radio** 97.3F.M.: mainly news, interviews, and discussions, plus endless call-ins.

In addition there are several national stations. Of these, **Classic F.M.** (100.99F.M.) and **Virgin 1215** (1215M.W.) are the most important commercial stations. Classic F.M. broadcasts popular classical music, while Richard Branson's Virgin 1215 station promises "classic album tracks and the best new music." Otherwise the B.B.C. still dominates the airwaves with its five channels:

**Radio 1** 98.8F.M.: mainly pop geared for young people.

**Radio 2** 89.2F.M.: middle-of-the-road and easy-listening music.

**Radio 3** 91.3F.M.: classical music, including live concerts.

*Shop around for the best rates*

**Radio 4** 93.5F.M.: news, current affairs, talk shows, radio drama, and reviews (*Today* is the flagship news and current affairs program).
**Radio 5 Live** 693 and 909M.W.: mainly live commentary on major sporting events plus news reports and features.

**Television** London has its own independent television networks—Carlton and L.W.T.—which broadcast local news, while I.T.N. provides national and international news programs for this and all other I.T.V. areas. (This arrangement parallels the relationship between local U.S. television stations and the national broadcasting companies.) The other channels are B.B.C.1, aimed at mainstream audiences, B.B.C.2 and Channel 4, both of which show a very broad range of cultural and special interest programs, and Channel 5, whose output is taking time to get going. Most hotels supply guests with Cable T.V. which includes Sky; a few have digital T.V.

**Money matters**
**Local currency** Britain's currency is divided into pounds and pence (100p. = £1). Bills are available in denominations of £50, £20, £10, and £5. Coins now come in denominations of £2, £1, 50p., 20p., 10p., 5p., 2p., and 1p.

**Currency exchange** Banks give by far the best rates of exchange, whether you are changing currency or traveler's checks, and only in an emergency should you consider using any other service. Hotels will change money and traveler's checks but give a very poor rate, as do those shops that accept U.S. dollars and other currencies. There are plenty of bureaux de change in London's main tourist haunts, advertising rates that may look more attractive than those of the banks, but once you've paid their hefty commission fees you will usually find that you're actually getting less for your money. If, as a last resort, you decide to use a *bureau de change*, you should seek out a reputable organization like Thomas Cook or Chequepoint. Their 24-hour branches can be found at or near Piccadilly Circus, Leicester Square, Marble Arch, and Victoria Underground stations.

**Banks** There are four main banks in the U.K. and they have branches all over London: they are the National Westminster, Barclays, Lloyds, and the H.S.B.C. (formerly the Midland). Most of the major branches have a

*Credit cards can be used at ATMS*

separate foreign currency window; if not, you can use any window that is open. All branches will allow you to draw cash against your credit card or will cash Eurocheques (see page 262).

**Credit cards** You can use the four main credit cards (Visa, MasterCard, American Express, and Diners Club) just about anywhere in London, although retailers may not take kindly to, or disallow, your using them for small purchases—say, less than £10, and some major retailers, such as Marks & Spencer, do not accept them. One great advantage of using credit cards to pay for your purchases is the favorable exchange rate. Credit-card companies use the Interbank rate, which can be several percentage points better than the tourist rate, for their exchange calculations. Moreover, by using a credit card, you avoid paying commission on exchange transactions.

These advantages work only if you pay your credit-card bill in full when you receive it and only use your card for purchases, not for cash advances. The very high rates of interest charged on cash withdrawals and credit-card balances will more than wipe out any exchange-rate gains.

**Money savers** For traveling round London, use a Travelcard (see page 265). For trips out of the city, railways offer saver, weekend, and supersaver tickets, and hotels have good mid-week deals that may include the rail fare. For London culture, consider buying a London White Card (on sale at museums and tourist offices); joining English Heritage (tel: 020-7973 3434) or the National Trust (tel: 020-7222 9251); buying a South Kensington Museums' season ticket (on sale at the museums); or joining the National Art Collections Fund (tel: 020-7225 4800). All these offer cut-price or free admission to various museums and attractions.

**Travelers' checks** These are a safe and convenient method of carrying large amounts of money, since the checks can be canceled if they are lost or stolen and you can obtain replacement checks. Many stores, restaurants, and hotels will accept traveler's checks in payment for goods and services—but do make sure that you are being offered a favorable exchange rate. You can avoid the problem of exchange rates altogether by buying your checks in pounds sterling in the first place. It is also a good idea to buy some small-denomination checks so that you don't have to cash a big check if you

end of your trip. Eurocheques, which are widely used in several other European countries, are not quite so easy to use in London, although all major banks will allow you to exchange them for cash.

**National holidays**
Although banks and businesses close on public holidays, the trend in London is for tourist attractions and stores to remain open, except on Christmas, Boxing Day (the day after Christmas), and New Year, when almost everything shuts (and if any of these days falls on a Saturday or Sunday, the next weekday is an additional holiday).
New Year's Day (January 1)
Good Friday
Easter Monday
First Monday in May
Last Monday in May
Last Monday in August
Christmas Day (December 25)
Boxing Day (December 26)

**Opening hours**
In London the trend is increasingly for stores and sights to open later in the morning—at 10 AM rather than 9 AM—but to stay open later in the evenings—until 6 PM or later in the major tourist haunts. Late-night shopping, when all stores remain open until 8 PM, is on Wednesday in the Knightsbridge and Kensington area and Thursday in the Oxford Street and Regent Street area.

Museums are as a rule open Mon–Sat 10–6 and Sun 2–6, but there are exceptions—check the listings magazines or daily newspapers first. Some government-run museums are closed all day Monday, and some commercial museums remain open until as late as 10 PM.

**Pharmacies**
Remember that many drugs sold over the counter in other countries are only dispensed in Britain with a prescription from a doctor. If you are not eligible for National Health Service treatment, you will have to go to a doctor with a private practice for a prescription. **Medical Express**, 117a Harley Street (tel: 020-7499 1991), offers a private walk-in medical service; or you can ask your hotel to arrange for a doctor to attend to you if you need a prescription (it is also a good idea to know the generic name of any drugs you take regularly, since they may be sold under a different brand name in the U.K.).

If you have a simple ailment that can be treated with nonprescription drugs, go to a pharmacist and ask for advice. British pharmacists are highly trained and knowledgeable people who will do their best to help you. Pharmacies (chemists) are to be found all over London. At night, they post a small sign on their doors telling you the address of the nearest

*Westminster Abbey*

drugstore that is open late. The following centrally located chemists open longer hours than others: **Bliss Chemist**, 5 Marble Arch. Daily 9 AM until midnight (tel: 020-7723 6116)
**Boots the Chemist**, 44–46 Regent Street. Mon–Fri 8:30–8, Sat 9–8, Sun noon–6 (tel: 020-7734 6126).

**Places of worship**
For a full list of churches and their addresses, consult the "Places of Worship" section of the London Yellow Pages telephone directory.

**Church of England: St. Martin-in-the-Fields**, on Trafalgar Square (tel: 020-7930 1862), is a friendly and central church popular with overseas visitors. **Westminster Abbey**, Broad Sanctuary (tel: 020-7222 5152), has a fine choir and **St. Paul's Cathedral** is a good place for organ music (tel: 020-7246 8348).



**Islam: The London Central Mosque**, 146 Park Road (tel: 020-7724 3363), is the main religious center for London's Muslims. Further information is available from the **Muslim World League** (tel: 020-7636 7568).
**Jewish:** There are Orthodox, Liberal, and Reformed synagogues all over London (200 in total); for further information contact the Central Enquiry Desk, **Board of Deputies of British Jews**, Upper Woburn Place (tel: 020-7543 5400).

**Roman Catholic Westminster Cathedral**, Ashley Place (tel: 020-7798 9097), is the main Catholic church in Britain. **Brompton Oratory**, Brompton Road (tel: 020-7589 4811), has a wide reputation for its particularly good choral music and sung mass in Latin.

**Police**
The days of the friendly London bobby, ever willing to help tourists find their way, have not quite gone, but today's police, overstretched by a rising tide of crime, are often too busy to patrol the streets (although that is what most law-abiding citizens want them to do), and have less time or opportunity to be friendly and helpful. If you report a crime the chances of catching and prosecuting the perpetrators are very slim.

If you have your pockets picked or your bag snatched you will receive sympathy but little hope of getting your money back. Still, you should report the crime, if only because insurance companies insist upon it as a policy condition. Look up "Police" in the telephone directory to find the nearest police station. In an emergency, if you are in danger or

*The unconventional detective*

*Royal Mail mailbox*

under threat of any kind, dial 999 and ask for the police, who will usually respond rapidly.

**Post offices**
Many ordinary stores and newsstands sell postage stamps and phone cards. Post offices can also provide special services, such as parcel post, registered mail, or express deliveries. They are normally open Mon–Fri 9–5:30 and Sat 9–noon; many close on Wednesday afternoons. The branch near Trafalgar Square—24–28 William IV Street (tel: 020-7484 9307)—is open Mon–Sat 8–8. Poste restante may also be sent to this office.

**Public transportation**
The Underground, which dates back to the middle of the last century, is the biggest and busiest subway system in the world. The basic choice is between using the Underground system (generally known as the Tube, although strictly this only applies to the deep-dug tunnel sections) or taking a bus. The top deck of a bus is good for sightseeing, and you may actually get to talk to real Londoners. The Tube is usually faster, but it can be extremely crowded during rush hours (8–9:30 AM and 5–7 PM on weekdays).

**Travelcards** If you buy a Travelcard, you can switch between the bus and Tube system as you please, since the

*An artistic view*

cards are valid on both, and on the Docklands Light Railway and certain rail services. One Day Travelcards are very economic if you are likely to make more than two or three journeys a day; you cannot use them before 9:30 AM Mon–Fri and they are not valid on night buses—a slightly more expensive Travelcard permits pre-9:30 AM travel. They are on sale at all Underground stations and many newsagents. Weekly or monthly passes, on the other hand, can be used at any time of day, but to buy one you need a passport-size photograph. There are photo machines at

*Entrance to the tube*

the airport and at some stations in town. Further information on Travelcards can be obtained at any Underground station. An alternative to a Travelcard if you are simply shuttling back and forward on short rides within central London's Zone 1 is the Paris metro-style carnet or batch of 10 Zone 1 tickets at a 10 percent discount.

**Child fares** Children under five travel free on the tube and buses. Children up to age 16 qualify for reduced fares but 14- and 15-year olds must carry a Child Rate Photocard as evidence of their age, available free from tube stations (they'll need to have a passport-size photograph and proof of their age).

**The Underground** The Underground (Tube) runs daily (except Christmas Day). Trains start running at around 5:30 AM Mon–Sat and 7 AM on Sun, last trains run just after midnight on weekdays and 11:30 PM on Sun (the times of the first and last trains out of each station are posted in the station entrances).The system is divided into six zones, and you pay more for trips that pass through two or more zones. A table of fares is usually posted close to the self-service ticket machines. These take coins and will normally give change (if not, a message saying "exact money only" will be lit). You can also buy tickets from the station ticket office, but expect long lines. Most stations now have automatic turnstiles, which will not let you through if you have the wrong ticket—for example, if you traveled farther than you originally planned and have not paid the correct fare. In this case, seek help from station staff, but be prepared to be treated as a suspected fare dodger.

Smoking is prohibited everywhere on the Underground. Technically, playing music and begging for handouts are illegal as well. If you feel you are being harassed, report the incident to station staff or the transit police who patrol the Underground. Most platforms have strategically placed red panic buttons that you can press if you are in danger or feel threatened—you can use them to alert the transit police.

**Buses** Many people prefer to travel by bus in London, for a variety of reasons. Some people find the Tube too hot and claustrophobic, while others can't deal with the long walks that are often involved between ticket office and platform. Above all, buses offer views, a chance to get to grips with the complex geography of London, and social contact. Visitors to London getting onto a bus will often ask for help and directions

*Performing for the fare*

from the conductor or other passengers; conversations start and soon news, gossip, opinions, and family histories are being exchanged.

At main bus stops (signs show a red circle on a white background) you will find information on bus routes and times. The bus will stop here automatically. At request stops (white circle on a red background) you must wave your arm to stop the bus. Once on the bus, if you want to get off at a request stop, you must ring the bell located on the handrails well before reaching the stop.

Fares are set according to zones. If you do not have a Travelcard (see page 265), simply tell the driver where you want to go and he or she will tell you the fare (on old-fashioned buses with an open entrance at the back, a conductor will come and take your fare). Drivers and conductors prefer you to give them the precise amount of money but they will give change. Hold on to your ticket until the end of the journey because inspectors regularly

*Working out the route*



board the buses to check tickets and catch fare cheaters.

Daytime buses in London run Mon–Sat from around 6 AM to midnight and Sun from 7:30 AM to 11:30 PM. In theory, buses run at least once every 10 to 15 minutes in each direction along the route, and much more frequently on heavily used routes. In practice, because of the traffic conditions, you can wait for 30 minutes for a bus to arrive, and then three will all come at the same time.

Night buses run between 11 PM and 6 AM on main routes through London; all of them pass through Trafalgar Square. A leaflet (called *Buses for Night Owls*) is available from London Transport information centers (see below) detailing the routes and times.

**Docklands Light Railway** The computerized and driverless trains of the Docklands Light Railway (D.L.R.) serve the Docklands area to the east of the City. The D.L.R. is part of the Underground system, so Travelcards may be used.

The system operates between Tower Gateway station (near Tower Hill Underground) and south through the Isle of Dogs and Greenwich to Lewisham, north to Stratford, and east to Beckton. Mechanical and engineering faults have dogged the D.L.R., but it can usually be counted upon to run Mon–Fri 5:40 AM–9:30 PM with a more limited service at weekends (tel: 020-7222 1234 for information).

**River cruises** London's river, the Thames, is being revived as a transportation artery. New piers include those at Bankside and the Dome at Greenwich Peninsula. Riverbuses supply a regular service between Westminster and Greenwich, but one of the most pleasurable ways to travel on the Thames, enjoying London's skyline from a different perspective, is to use one of the tourist cruise services that operate from Westminster Pier (see page 55). They have commentary on sights you pass and there is usually a bar or café aboard.

**Travel information** The main London Transport Information Centre, at Piccadilly Circus Underground Station, is open daily 9–6 and supplies free route maps and schedules as well as information brochures in several languages. You can also phone for information (tel: 020-7222 1234). Travel information centers can also be found at Heathrow Airport (Terminals 1, 2, 3), Euston, King's Cross, Oxford Circus, St. James's Park, and Liverpool Street Tube stations and at Victoria train station.

**Student and youth travel**
If you have an International Student Identity Card you can get special deals on long-distance travel to the U.K., such as youth rail passes. Once in London, it is worth looking for the theaters, movie houses, and exhibitions that offer reduced rates for students. The listings magazine *Time*

*You see more by bus*

*Near antiques in Islington*

*Out* has good information about student discounts at museums, theaters and clubs, plus advice on getting the best out of the city's sights and entertainment at little cost.

**Telephones**
There are public telephone booths all over London—in the streets, in pubs and stores, in museums, and on many station platforms. Telephone boxes are provided by one of the two main telephone companies. B.T. (British Telecom) phones are still the most numerous, but you will also see Mercury call boxes, which have marginally cheaper charges for long-distance calls.

- **B.T. coin-operated phones**: These will only accept £1, 50p., 20p., and 10p. coins.
- **B.T. card phones**: These accept BT phone cards, which can be bought from post offices and newsstands in various denominations. More and

*The Docklands Light Railway*

more telephone booths will also accept credit cards.

• **Mercury card phones**: These accept both credit cards (minimum charge 50p.) and Mercury phone cards, sold at the same outlets as B.T. cards.

❑ Useful numbers
International lines 00 + country code
Operator (collect/reverse charge/ credit-card calls within U.K.) 100
International operator (collect/ credit-card calls outside U.K.) 155
Information: London 142; rest of U.K. 192; overseas 153
International telegrams: 0800 190 190 ❑

• **Dial tones**: When you lift the receiver you should hear a continuous dial tone. After you have dialed you will hear ring-ring-pause, ring-ring-pause to indicate that the number is ringing at the other end. A series of rapid bleeps means that the number is busy; a continuous note means the number is "unobtainable"—perhaps because you have misdialed, so try again.

• One way to keep the cost of calls down is to use public telephone services; hotel phones are horrendously expensive and calls are often charged at three or four times the official rate.

The cost of a call from a public phone depends on when you make it. The cheapest times for calls within the U.K. are Mon–Fri 6 PM–8 AM (evening rate) and on weekends. The most expensive time is Mon–Fri 8 AM–6 PM, during the Daytime Rate.

**Time**
Between October and March, Britain observes Greenwich Mean Time; during British Summer Time, from March to October, clocks are put forward by an hour.

**Tipping**
Rates and categories differ only slightly from what is expected in other Western countries. Taxi drivers should be given at least 10 percent of the fare as a tip. The usual tip in restaurants and cafés is 10 percent; check if it is added to the bill. Other people whom it is customary to tip are restroom attendants, hotel doormen, bellhops and room-service waiters, porters at train stations or airports, hairdressers and barbers, and sightseeing guides. Bartenders do not expect tips—although you can, if you wish, offer to buy him or her a drink—nor do theater or movie-house usherettes.

**Toilets**
Finding a toilet (restroom) in London is not usually too difficult. Museums, pubs, restaurants, department stores, theaters, and movie houses have them.

Toilets can also to be found on every major railroad station, but here you may need the correct change for the entrance turnstile. Aluminum "Loomatic" toilets are coin-operated.

**Tourist information**
The London Tourist Board (L.T.B.) runs the useful, constantly updated Visitorcall system. This is a series of prerecorded announcements (charged at premium call rate). Dial 0839-123 and add 400 for What's On This Week, 432 for River Trips, 483 for Houses and Gardens, and so on; tourist offices keep a full list, or tel: 020-7971 0026 to have one mailed; those with push-button phones can call 020-7971 0027 for full information.

L.T.B.'s faxback service is 0891 353 715/716; simply dial the number and after the tone comes press the start/receive button.

L.T.B.'s excellent website is www.LondonTown.com.

There are information centers at the following locations:

**Heathrow Terminals 1,2,3** Underground station, daily 8:30 AM–6 PM and Heathrow Airport (Terminal 3), daily 6 AM–11 PM.
**Liverpool Street** Underground Station, Mon–Fri 8–6, weekends 8:45 AM–5:30 PM.
**Victoria British Rail Station Forecourt**, Easter–Oct, daily 8–7; Nov–Easter Mon–Sat 8–6, Sun 8:30–4.
**Waterloo International,** daily 8:30–10:30.

*One of the city's younger visitors takes a relaxing look at London*

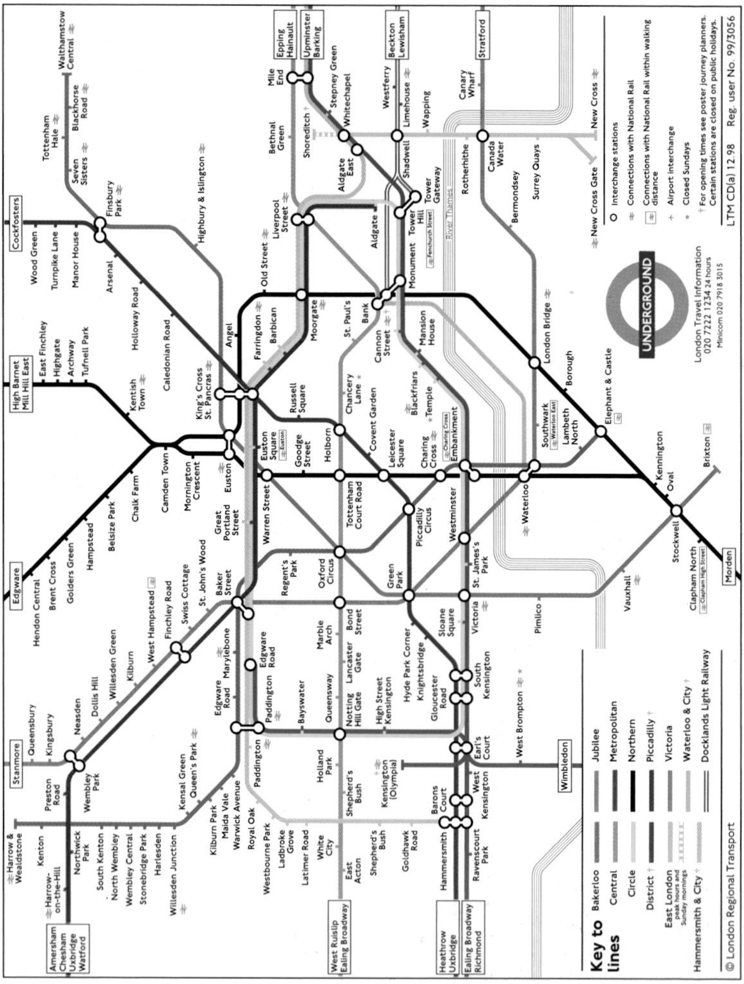


Other London tourist information centers can be found at the following locations:

**City of London** opposite south side of St. Paul's Cathedral, tel: 020-7332 1456;

**Southwark**, tel: 020-7403 8299;

**Greenwich** 46 Greenwich Church Street tel: 020-858 6376;

**Islington** 44 Duncan Street, tel: 020-7278 8787;

**Richmond** Old Town Hall, tel: 020-8940 9125;

**Twickenham** Civic Centre, York Street, tel: 020-8891 7272.

**British Visitor Centre**, 1 Regent Street, Piccadilly Circus. Mon–Fri 9–6:30, Sat, Sun 10–4; Jul–Sep, Sat 9–5.

## Women Travelers

Two organizations provide support in an emergency:

**Women's Aid** (tel: 020-7392 2092);

**London Rape Crisis Center** (tel: 020-7837 1600).

# Accommodations & Restaurants

# ACCOMMODATIONS

The following recommended hotels have been divided into three price categories:
**budget** ($): a double room for $65–$110
**moderate** ($$): a double room for $110–$225
**expensive** ($$$): expect to pay more than $225 for a double room

## MAYFAIR, PICCADILLY, ST. JAMES'S, AND THE MALL

**Athenaeum Hotel** ($$$)
*116 Piccadilly, W1 tel: 020-7499 3464*
Elegant hotel overlooking Green Park. Well-equipped bedrooms provide every comfort. Pool, jacuzzi, fitness suite, and beauty salon. Good food in Bullochs Restaurant.

**The Cavendish** ($$$)
*81 Jermyn Street, SW1 tel: 020-7930 2111*
Large, modern, and popular hotel with good amenities that are suited to the needs of a business clientele. The 81 Restaurant offers Mediterranean-style food cooked with skill.



**Claridge's** ($$$)
*Brook Street, W1 tel: 020-7629 8860*
This is the hotel where U.S. presidents, guests of the Queen, monarchs, and public figures from around the world all stay; it's one of the country's most prestigious hotels.

**Goring** ($$$)
*15 Beeston Place, SW1 tel: 020-7396 9000*
Just beside Buckingham Palace and often used to accommodate royal guests, this is a fine hotel, full of old-world charm.

**Le Meridien Piccadilly** ($$$)
*21 Piccadilly, W1 tel: 020-7734 8000*
Popular Edwardian hotel run by Granada-Forte with top-quality restaurants and within easy walking distance of West End theaters and movie houses.

**London Hilton on Park Lane** ($$$)
*22 Park Lane WI tel: 020-7493 8000*
Designed primarily to cater for the needs of business travelers, which it does superbly. Regular rooms are very comfortable, but the Executive floor offers access to a clubroom with private check-in and a host of complimentary facilities.

**The Ritz** ($$$)
*Piccadilly, W1 tel: 020-7493 8181*
A byword for stylish opulence and high living, the Ritz is the peak of mirrored and gilded splendor. Live cabaret, tea dances, and Palm Court afternoon teas provide ample opportunity for "putting on the Ritz."

**Stafford** ($$$)
*16–18 St. James's Place, SW1*
*tel: 020-7493 0111*
Intimate hotel with a club-like atmosphere and a restaurant serving modern British cooking to a loyal clientele of regulars.

**22 Jermyn Street** ($$$)
*22 Jermyn Street, SW1 tel: 020-7734 2353*
An elegant town house just minutes from Piccadilly and Leicester Square. There are some thoughtful extras in the rooms.

**The Washington Mayfair** ($$$)
*5–7 Curzon Street, W1 tel: 020-7499 7000*
Accommodations in this attractive and air-conditioned modern hotel range from state rooms and suites with spa baths to equally comfortable twins and doubles. A wide range of business services includes several private conference and board rooms.

**Wigmore Court Hotel** ($–$$)
*23 Gloucester Place, W1 tel: 020-7935 0928*
Superior class B&B, ideal for families, with large en-suite rooms and laundry and kitchen facilities available on request. Short walk from Oxford Street.

## SOHO AND COVENT GARDEN, BLOOMSBURY AND FITZROVIA, REGENT'S PARK AND MARYLEBONE

**Academy** ($$)
*17–21 Gower Street, WC1*
*tel: 020-7631 4115*
Stylish conversion of Georgian town houses in the heart of Bloomsbury.

**Blooms Hotel** ($$$)
*7 Montague Street, WC1 tel: 020-7323 1717*
This elegant 18th-century town house is just around the corner from the British Museum. Comfortable rooms complemented by antiques-filled public areas. Lovely garden terrace.

**The Bonnington in Bloomsbury** ($$)
*92 Southampton Row, WC1*
*tel: 020-7242 2828*
This late Edwardian Hotel maintains traditional standards in comfortable, modern surroundings. There are rooms suitable for families and for guests with disabilities, as well as designated rooms for nonsmokers.

**Four Seasons Hotel** ($)
*173 Gloucester Place, NW1*
*tel: 020-7724 3461*
Friendly, family-run hotel in the heart of the West End; comfortable, well-equipped rooms.

**The Hampshire** ($$$)
*Leicester Square, WC2 tel: 020-7839 9399*
This stylish period hotel, built within the existing shell of the Royal Dental hospital, has a prime location on Leicester Square. Rooms are very comfortable and fully equipped with modern facilities including access to the Internet. The team of staff is particularly friendly.

**Hotel Ibis Euston** ($)
*3 Cardington Street, NW1 tel: 020-7388 7777*
French chain-hotel offering comfort and reasonable prices in the Euston area, with good facilities for people with disabilities.

**London Regents Park Hilton** ($$$)
*18 Lodge Road, NW8 tel: 020-7722 7722*
Some of the rooms overlook Lord's Cricket Ground and a cricket theme continues in the lounge bar. Rooms are modern and spacious; two restaurants (one Japanese).

**Mentone Hotel** ($)
*54–55 Cartwright Gardens, WC1*
*tel: 020-7387 3927*
This friendly, family-run guest house features brightly decorated bedrooms.

**The Mountbatten** ($$$)
*Monmouth Street, WC2 tel: 020-7836 4300*
Situated at Seven Dials—well placed for theatergoers. Many rooms are small but pleasantly furnished and all have marbled bathrooms. Stylish public areas include a comfortable cocktail bar and restaurant.
**The White House Hotel** ($$)
*Albany Street, NW1 tel: 020-7387 1200*
One of London's best-kept secrets, this charming hotel—formerly an apartment building—is well-placed for the West End. The emphasis is on hospitality and comfort.

## HOLBORN, THE STRAND, AND THE CITY

**The Barbican** ($$)
*Central Street, EC1 tel: 020-7251 1565*
Well situated for the Barbican arts complex and the City, this is a large and modern hotel with friendly and helpful staff.
**Hotel Russell** ($$)
*Russell Square WC1 tel: 020-7837 6470*
Handy for the British Museum and the West End, this stately Victorian landmark offers public rooms that have great character. Good range of bars, restaurants, and lounges.
**Savoy** ($$$)
*The Strand, WC2 tel: 020-7836 4343*
Founded by Richard D'Oyly Carte, with the profits from staging Gilbert and Sullivan operettas, the Savoy is a majestic hotel, a contender for the title "best in the world." Rooms overlooking the river, with vast marble tubs, are very much in demand.
**Strand Palace** ($$)
*372 Strand, WC2 tel: 020-7836 8080*
Across the street from the Savoy, the Strand Palace is vast (800 rooms) but efficient and offers relatively inexpensive rooms. Very convenient for the West End and Covent Garden.

## WESTMINSTER, BANKSIDE, AND DOCKLANDS

**Thistle Royal Horse Guards** ($$$)
*Whitehall Court, SW1 tel: 020-7839 3400*
In the heart of central London territory and close to tourist sights. This has refurbished bedrooms and good public areas.
**Thistle Tower** ($$$)
*St Katharine's Way, E1 tel: 020-7481 2575*
Modern hotel enjoying spectacular views of the Tower of London, Tower Bridge, and St. Katharine's Dock. Very convenient for the City.

## CHELSEA AND KNIGHTSBRIDGE, KENSINGTON AND NOTTING HILL, HYDE PARK

**Abbey Court** ($$)
*20 Pembridge Gardens, W2*
*tel: 020-7221 7518*
Gracious Victorian mansion in Notting Hill, furnished with antiques in country-house style.
**Basil Street Hotel** ($$$)
*8 Basil Street, SW3 tel: 020-7581 3311*
Old-fashioned charm, not far from Harrods.
**Beaufort** ($$$)
*33 Beaufort Gardens, SW3*
*tel: 020-7584 5252*
Top-class small hotel (28 rooms) with homey personal touches, located on a quiet square in the heart of Knightsbridge.
**Berkeley** ($$$)
*Wilton Place, SW1 tel: 020-7235 6000*
Splendid hotel on Hyde Park Corner with a rooftop pool like a Roman bath and elegant period rooms.
**Capital** ($$$)
*22 Basil Street, SW3 tel: 020-7589 5171*
This very elegant hotel in the heart of Knightsbridge boasts an award-winning restaurant and a tastefully furnished interior.
**Comfort Inn** ($$)
*22–32 West Cromwell Road, SW5*
*tel: 020-7373 3300*
A cheerful modern hotel conveniently placed for Earls Court. Bedrooms vary in size, but are well equipped and some are air-conditioned; public areas are bright and cozy.
**The Executive Hotel** ($$)
*57 Pont Street, Knightsbridge, SW1*
*tel: 020-7581 2424*
The Executive Hotel reflects the ambience of a Victorian London town house. Bedrooms are attractively decorated, comfortably furnished and equipped with modern facilities.
**Five Sumner Place** ($$)
*5 Sumner Place, SW7 tel: 020-7584 7586*
Part of a pretty row of townhouses on a fine street in South Kensington. A great bed-and-breakfast hotel—perhaps because breakfast is served in the flower-filled conservatory.
**Halcyon Hotel** ($$$)
*81 Holland Park, W11 tel: 020-7727 7288*
The elegant foyer gives a splendid first impression with fresh flowers, fine pictures, and antique furniture. Rooms are individually decorated and spacious with sizeable marble bathrooms. Good food in the restaurant.
**Hyatt Carlton Tower Hotel** ($$$)
*Cadogan Place, SW1 tel: 020-7235 1234*
A busy international hotel with health club and swimming pool. Rooms, including a range of suites, are air-conditioned and well equipped.
**The Lowndes Hyatt** ($$$)
*21 Lowndes Street, SW1 tel: 020-7823 1234*
This chic air-conditioned hotel provides bedrooms and suites with every modern facility. Good food in the Lowndes Brasserie 21.
**Mandarin Oriental Hyde Park** ($$$)
*66 Knightsbridge, SW1 tel: 020-7235 2000*
Palatial public rooms, luxurious décor, and extensive views across leafy Hyde Park are the hallmarks of this stately hotel.
**Melbourne House** ($)
*79 Belgrave Road, SW1 tel: 020-7828 3516*
Another good choice on the Belgrave Road, this is a small, family-run place. Most rooms are ensuite and the lounge is very pleasant.
**The Millennium Chelsea Hotel** ($$$)
*17 Sloane Street, SW1 tel: 020-7235 4377*
Surrounded by exclusive designer houses, with Harrods and Harvey Nichols nearby. All the rooms have a full range of modern facilities.

**Parkwood Hotel** ($)
*4 Stanhope Place, W2 tel: 020-7402 2241*
This pretty hotel in a quiet street facing onto Hyde Park is popular with families, as the paintings by visiting children, hung in the "artists' gallery," demonstrate.
**Pembridge Court Hotel** ($$)
*34 Pembridge Gardens, W2*
*tel: 020-7229 9977*
Victorian town house in a quiet road. Well-appointed rooms include one with a four-poster. Parking meter spaces usually available around the square.
**Rembrandt Hotel** ($$)
*11 Thurloe Place, SW7 tel: 020-7589 8100*
The ornate architecture of the Rembrandt Hotel reflects that of Harrods farther along the road—bedrooms vary in size, but offer real comfort and style.
**Swiss House** ($$)
*171 Old Brompton Road, SW5*
*tel: 020-7373 2769*
Although more English-country-house than Swiss in atmosphere, this hotel in the Gloucester Road area has scarlet geraniums and ivy cascading from its window boxes. Very comfy and popular; reserve well ahead.
**Willett Hotel** ($$)
*32 Sloane Gardens, SW1 tel: 020-7824 8415*
A fine Victorian house that has been tastefully restored to maintain many of the original features. Bedrooms vary in size, but are thoughtfully decorated and furnished.



## OUTSIDE THE CENTER

**La Gaffe** ($$)
*107–111 Heath Street, NW3*
*tel: 020-7435 4941*
A warm Italian welcome is assured at this friendly family-run guest house. Rooms are compact and modestly furnished but well equipped. There is a popular Italian restaurant.

### Y.M.C.A.s and Y.H.A.s

**Y.M.C.A.** ($)
*National Council for Y.M.C.A.s, 640 Forest Road, E17 tel: 020-8520 5599*
You can write to the above address for details of all 18 Y.M.C.A. hotels in London; they are extremely good value, and it is vital to reserve at least two months ahead. One of the best is the Barbican Y.M.C.A., 2 Fann Street, a purpose-built hotel with good sports facilities.
**Youth Hostels** (Y.H.A.) ($)
*8 St. Stephen's Hill, St Albans, Herts, AL1 2DY*
*tel: 01727 855215*
Write to the above address for details of the seven youth hostels in London and reserve at least three months ahead for summer. The City of London Youth Hostel is excellent, located near St. Paul's, while the Holland House Hostel is converted from the remains of a Jacobean mansion, set in Holland Park gardens. The other hostels are at Oxford Street, Earls Court, Highgate, Hampstead, and Rotherhithe, some of which are very new and expressly built.

# RESTAURANTS

The following recommended restaurants have been divided into three price categories. Prices are for a three-course meal per person excluding drinks:
**budget** ($): under $18
**moderate** ($$): $18–$24
**expensive** ($$$): over $24
All the restaurants listed here have vegetarian dishes on the menu, unless otherwise stated. See pages 88–89 for additional restaurant selections.

## MAYFAIR, PICCADILLY, ST. JAMES'S, AND THE MALL

**Bice** ($$$)
*13 Albemarle Street, W1 tel: 020-7409 1011*
Offspring of a famous Milanese establishment, this is an upscale Italian with a wide choice for every course.
**Le Caprice** ($$)
*Arlington House, Arlington Street, SW1 tel: 020-7629 2239*
Reservations are essential at this very chic restaurant favored by celebrities, where the choices range from traditional English dishes to classic brasserie fare.
**Caraffini** ($$$)
*61–63 Lower Sloane Street, SW1*
*tel: 020-7259 0235*
Simple, well-executed Italian food with no pretensions to modernity. Portions of vegetables are charged separately. All-Italian wine list.
**Chez Nico at Ninety Park Lane** ($$$)
*90 Park Lane, W1 tel: 020-7409 1290*
Nico Ladenis' restaurant remains immaculate in every sense with great, albeit formal, service. This is haute cuisine; sophisticated and classic.
**Chor Bizarre** ($$)
*16 Albemarle Street, W1*
*tel: 020-7629 9802/7629 8542*
Crowded Indian "thieves market" look and some unusual regional dishes among the tandooris and thalis.
**The Criterion** ($$)
*224 Piccadilly, W1 tel: 020-7930 0488*
Marco Pierre White's opulent restaurant at the heart of Piccadilly Circus is stunning and the place just heaves from 5.30pm till late. Fast-paced service and modern brasserie dishes draw the crowds.
**Le Gavroche Restaurant** ($$$)
*43 Upper Brook Street, W1*
*tel: 020-7408 0881/7499 1826*
The feel of a discreet, English gentleman's club with service to match. Michel Roux jnr has really made his mark here, his modern French cooking showing skill and discretion.
**Green's Restaurant and Oyster Bar** ($$)
*36 Duke Street, St James's, SW1*
*tel: 020-7930 4566*
A stylish arrangement of eating and drinking areas (plus a famous oyster bar) where the fish and seafood dishes are excellently prepared.

**Langan's Brasserie** ($$)
*Stratton House, Stratton Street, W1*
*tel: 020-7491 8822*
Reservations essential. The boisterous founder of Langan's Brasserie has passed on, but the glitterati still flock here for live jazz in the bar and the food, which ranges from the famous bangers-and-mash to the more delicate seafood dishes.

**Mirabelle** ($$$)
*56 Curzon Street, W1 tel: 020-7499 4636*
Firmly established once again as one of the most fashionable haute cuisine restaurants in London. Top chef Marco Pierre White displays his first-class classic French cooking; lunch is good value. Reservations essential.

**Mulligans of Mayfair** ($$)
*13–14 Cork Street, W1 tel: 020-7409 1370*
Mulligans is decorated like a Dublin bar (all brown walls and woodwork), and the food is based on Irish home-cooking. If the prices in the restaurant seem a bit high, try the upstairs bar with its cheaper menu.

**Nobu** ($$$)
*Metropolitan Hotel, 19 Old Park Lane, W1*
*tel: 020-7447 4747*
New York's Nobuyuki Matsuhisa brings his pan-American Japanese cooking to the cool confines of the Metropolitan Hotel. A haunt of A-list celebrities. Reserve well in advance.

**The Oak Room, Marco Pierre White** ($$$)
*21 Piccadilly, W1 tel: 020-7437 0202*
The grand-scale room is a fitting setting for Marco Pierre White's astonishing version of classic haute cuisine.

**Porte des Indes** ($$$)
*32 Bryanston Street, W1 tel: 020-7224 0055*
Dramatic, beautiful establishment with a wide selection of the sub-continent's finest cuisine. Intriguing French Creole dishes from the Pondicherry area are a specialty.

**Quaglino's** ($$–$$$)
*16 Bury Street, W1 tel: 020-7930 6767*
Skeptics scoffed when Terence Conran converted this vast ballroom into a 500-seat restaurant, yet diners flock here (advance reservations are vital). Outstanding food and wine and impeccable service, with less expensive snacks at the bar an alternative to a meal.

**Rasa W1** ($$)
*6 Dering Street, W1 tel: 020-7629 1346*
Das Shreedharan's inspired Keralan vegetarian dishes make a brilliant introduction to this exciting regional Indian cruisine.

**Ristorante L'Incontro** ($$$)
*87 Pimlico Road, SW1 tel: 020-7730 3663*
The setting is glamorous and the food has a price tag to match. The cooking is based on that of Venice and northeastern Italy, with dishes such as bean and pasta soup. Pasta is made on the premises.

**The Sugar Club** ($$)
*21 Warwick Street, W1 tel: 020-7437 7776*
Peter Gordon's philosophy remains the same at the ultra-fashionable Sugar Club, at least when it comes to hot, powerful spicing. This is cutting-edge fusion food, some of the most imaginative in town.

**Suntory** ($$$)
*72 St. James's Street, SW1*
*tel: 020-7409 0201*
The oldest Japanese restaurant in London and highly regarded. In view of this you would expect the prices to be steep, but the quality is worth it (set lunch is not that expensive).

**Tamarind** ($$)
*20 Queen Street, W1 tel: 020-7629 3561*
The most fashionable of London's Indian restaurants, noted for Atul Kochhar's imaginative regional cooking. The use of specially imported herbs and spices creates some quite memorable flavors.

**Veeraswamy** ($$)
*99-101 Regent Street W1*
*tel: 020-7734 1401*
London's oldest Indian restaurant with a smart new face lift. Classical regional Indian food has a modern twist to suit Western palates.

**Wiltons** ($$$)
*55 Jermyn Street, SW1 tel: 020-7629 9955*
Very formal and sophisticated, with M.P.s, aristocrats, and royalty among the regular clients. Renowned for its outstanding fish dishes and traditional desserts, such as summer pudding.



### Cafés and bars

**Coffee Republic** ($)
*2 South Molton Street, W1*
*tel: 020-7629 4567*
Lots of metal and dark wood predominate at this the most stylish of a small chain of cafés. Good cakes and pastries, and excellent espresso.

**Fortnum & Mason** ($$)
*St. James's, 181 Piccadilly W1*
*tel: 020-7734 8040*
Anything from breakfast to afternoon tea is a treat at this upscale food-lovers' emporium. Popular with Londoners and tourists alike, so be prepared for a line, especially for lunch and afternoon tea.

**Richoux Coffee Company** ($)
*171 Piccadilly, W1 tel: 020-7629 4991*
Spacious café that has benefited from a much-needed makeover. Imaginative food ranges from salads, sandwiches, and quiches, to good cakes and pastries.

## SOHO AND COVENT GARDEN, BLOOMSBURY AND FITZROVIA, REGENT'S PARK AND MARYLEBONE

**Alastair Little Soho** ($$$)
*49 Frith Street, W1 tel: 020-7734 5183*
Good food firmly influenced by Italian cuisine. Informal, and reasonably priced set lunches.

**Belgo Centraal** ($)
*50 Earlham Street, WC2 tel: 020-7813 2233*
An unlikely success—a restaurant serving Belgian food (huge platefuls of mussels and fries) washed down by Belgium's legendary fruit beers. Be sure to make a reservation (on busy days, you will be allocated one of three two-hour sittings). Branch (Belgo Noord) at 72 Chalk Farm Road tel: 020-7267 0718.

**Bertorelli's Restaurant/Café Italien** ($–$$)
*19–23 Charlotte Street, W1 (020-7636 4174*
Bertorelli's (upstairs) is an institution; a popular Italian restaurant with affordable prices. The Café Italien downstairs is great for people watching, with sidewalk tables in warm weather. Branch at 44A Floral Street tel: 020-7836 3969

**The Birdcage** ($$)
*110 Whitfield Street, W1 tel: 020-7383 5036*
A striking, idiosyncratic Thai-inspired setting for Michael von Hruschka's unique, ultra-modern interpretation of Far Eastern cuisine.

**Café du Jardin** ($$)
*28 Wellington Street, WC2*
*tel: 020-7836 8769/7836 8760*
Buzzing, cosmopolitan brasserie in the heart of the West End with excellent pre- and post-theater menus. The cooking has an up-to-date European appeal, and a pianist plays most evenings.

**Café Pacifico** ($)
*5 Langley Street, WC2 tel: 020-7379 7728*
Mexican restaurant, located in a cavernous Covent Garden warehouse. Superb range of beers and cocktails.



**Calabash** ($)
*The Africa Centre, 38 King Street, WC2*
*tel: 020-7836 1976*
Relaxed basement-restaurant just off the Covent Garden piazza with dishes from all over Africa, explained by the helpful menu; meals are washed down with Nigerian beer or wine from Zimbabwe.

**Christopher's** ($$)
*18 Wellington Street, WC2*
*tel: 020-7240 4222*
This is a popular Covent Garden spot for the classic East Coast Sunday brunch. At other times the All-American menu majors on char-grills. The café does a good line in salads and sandwiches.

**L'Escargot** ($$)
*48 Greek Street, W1 tel: 020-7437 6828*
This recently revamped Soho institution features in a number of novels and counts well-known writers and their publishers among its clientele. Classic French food and the choice of a lively brasserie downstairs or a formal restaurant above.

**Fung Shing** ($$)
*15 Lisle Street, WC2 tel: 020-7437 1539*
Popular restaurant, highly regarded by local Chinatown residents.

**Gay Hussar** ($$)
*2 Greek Street, W1 tel: 020-7437 0973*
An unchanging pool of calm in the maelstrom of Soho, this popular Hungarian restaurant is noted for its good value and old-fashioned cooking.

**The Ivy** ($$)
*1 West Street, WC2 tel: 020-7836 4751*
Very much a place to be seen, with stylish 1930s décor and the work of well-known contemporary British artists on the walls. Popular dishes are eggs Benedict and the Ivy mixed grill. Reserve tables several weeks in advance to be sure of getting in.

**J Sheekey** ($$)
*28-32 St Martin's Court, WC2*
*tel: 020-7240 2565*
One of London's best-known seafood restaurants, now owned by the team that is responsible for The Ivy and Le Caprice. Expect traditional English fish dishes and old-fashioned puddings.

**Justin de Blank** ($)
*120 Marylebone High Street, W1*
*tel: 020-7486 5250*
Modern brasserie with considerable easygoing charm. Saturday brunch is recommended.

**Lemonia** ($)
*89 Regents Park Road, NW1*
*tel: 020-7586 7454*
Popular Greek Cypriot restaurant, more stylish than most. Start with the *meze* hot and cold selection (for two), then try a charcoal grill such as chicken shashlik, lamb or pork souvlaki; or ordikia—quails in olive oil and oregano.

**Lindsay House** ($$)
*21 Romilly Street, W1 tel: 020-7439 0450*
Irish chef Richard Corrigan is unique. His Celtic roots are still very evident in a gutsy, almost robust style. This is inspired cooking from one of London's top chefs.

**Neal Street Restaurant** ($$$)
*26 Neal Street, WC2 tel: 020-7836 8368*
This temple dedicated to the finest Italian foods, with décor by David Hockney, attracts the seriously wealthy and those who share the owner's passion for mushrooms (which feature prominently on the menu and which are sought out from all over England).

**New World** ($$)
*1 Gerrard Place, W1 tel: 020-7434 2508*
The triple-floored, 600-seater Chinatown restaurant is the place for dim sum. Waitresses parade the floors with steaming carts of delicacies. Get there early on a Sunday as tables are hard to come by after midday.

**O'Connor Don-Ard-Ri Dining Room** ($$$)
*88 Marylebone Lane, W1 tel: 020-7935 9311*
In this simple dining room in a popular family-run pub you get traditional Irish dishes (beef and Guinness casserole) and a great atmosphere.

**Orso** ($$)
*27 Wellington Street, WC2*
*tel: 020-7240 5269*
If you do not fancy the trek to Clapham for the Osteria Antica Bologna (see page 281), try Orso instead, conveniently located in Covent Garden and popular (noisily so) for its modern Italian food.

**Le Palais du Jardin** ($$)
*136 Long Acre, WC2 tel: 020-7379 5353*
Good value *fruits de mer*, plus other French favorites at reasonable prices (it is the wines that send your check soaring.) Professional service.

**Purple Sage** ($)
92 Wigmore Street, W1 tel: 020-7486 1912
Bright, airy restaurant offering a functional interior, great pizzas from the wood-fired oven, pastas and risottos. The short list of predominantly Italian wines is also recommended.

**RK Stanley** ($)
*6 Little Portland Street, W1*
*tel: 020-7462 0099*
Informal restaurant with a menu built around beer and sausages: an impressive selection of both with beers including smoked, fruit and honey brews, and sausages ranging from Thai to vegetarian Glamorgan.

**Rules** ($$)
*35 Maiden Lane, WC2 tel: 020-7836 5314*
One of London's oldest eating places and a favorite with actors and theater-goers, drawn by traditional British fare, notably excellent game. Pre-theater dinners are good value for money.

**Sarastro** ($$–$$$)
*126 Drury Lane, WC2*
*tel: 020-7379 7767*
Dine amid a dazzling array of stage props, gilt furniture, and silk drapes to the sound of opera in this eccentric establishment in the heart of the West End (you can even book a box!) Mediterranean cuisine—strong on fish, vegetarian, and Turkish dishes.

**Spiga** ($)
*84-86 Wardour Street, W1*
*tel: 020-7734 3444*
Pizzas from a wood-fired oven form the core, but simple pasta and fish dishes are highly recommended. Great atmosphere.

**Stephen Bull Restaurant** ($$)
*5-7 Blandford Street, W1 tel: 020-7486 9696*
Intimate restaurant noted for smooth, professional service and innovative cooking. Short menus reveal a straightforward approach, and the lightest touch. Reservations essential.

**T.G.I. Friday's** ($$)
*6 Bedford Street, WC2 tel: 020-7379 0585*
Lively steak, burger and Tex-Mex restaurant, with special children's menu and entertainment on Sunday.

**Yming** ($$)
*35-36 Greek Street, W1 tel: 020-7734 2721*
Excellent Chinese with the cooking predominantly from the north, around Beijing, plus some regional Szechuan dishes.

### Cafés and bars

**MASH** ($$)
*19-21 Great Portland Street, W1*
*tel: 020-7637 5555*
Modernistic bar, light, expensive second-floor restaurant and state-of-the-art micro brewery rolled into one. Wide-ranging menu with imaginative pizzas and lots of global influences.

**Mezzo** ($$–$$$)
*100 Wardour Street, W1 tel: 020-7314 4000*
Gigantic Conran eatery—one of the largest in Europe. The lively Mezzonine specializes in Pacific-Rim food while the flagship basement restaurant, Mezzo, expands the theme, adding modern European twists.

**Monmouth Coffee Company** ($)
*27 Monmouth Street, WC2*
*tel: 020-7836 5272*
One of Soho's best kept secrets: from the front it is nothing more than a store selling bags of coffee. At the back are eight tables, newspapers to read, and a selection of pastries.

**Museum Street Café** ($)
*47 Museum Street, WC1 tel: 020-7405 3211*
A clean-cut, plain café with closely spaced tables, open from breakfast to tea and strong on good baking and wholesome dishes. The short lunch menu is vegetarian, except for occasional fish dishes.

**Patisserie Valerie** ($)
*44 Old Compton Street, W1*
*tel: 020-7437 3466*
Cramped, old-fashioned tea room; a Soho institution. Patisserie is superb, but there are also good salads, croque monsieur and savory quiches.

**Planet Hollywood** ($$)
*Trocadero, 13 Coventry Street, W1*
*tel: 020-7287 1000*
More a movie theme park (with souvenir store alongside) than a restaurant, but popular with the young.

**Union Café and Restaurant** ($$)
*96 Marylebone Lane, W1 tel: 020-7486 4860*
Stylish, casual and very popular. Here simple ideas are translated into great food.

## HOLBORN, THE STRAND, AND THE CITY



**Alba** ($-$$)
*107 Whitecross Street, EC1*
*tel: 020-7588 1798*
Smart, modern Italian restaurant a short walk from the Barbican, noted for excellent value at lunch and pre-theatre.

**Break for the Border** ($)
*5 Goslett Yard, WC2 tel: 020-7437 8595*
Tex-Mex and Cajun food, huge burgers plus vegetarian dishes and Mexican beer. The music and the partying crowds make for a noisy atmosphere.

**Le Café du Marché** ($$)
*22 Charterhouse Square, EC1*
*tel: 020-7608 1609*
Reservations are essential at this restaurant on the fringes of the City in a converted warehouse. Expect an adventurous range of dishes on the daily set menu.

**City Miyama Restaurant** ($$$)
*17 Godliman Street, EC4 tel: 020-7489 1937*
Just by St. Paul's churchyard, this Japanese is crowded at lunch and less frequented in the evening. It's typically minimalist in style, with a sushi bar and *teppan-yaki* counter and a main dining area downstairs.

**City Rhodes** ($$$)
*1 New Street Square, EC4*
*tel: 020-7583 1313*
T.V. celebrity chef Gary Rhodes brings stunning presentation to his imaginative reworking of classic English dishes. Save room for traditional desserts such as the signature bread-and-butter pudding.

**The Eagle** ($$)
*159 Farringdon Road, EC1*
*tel: 020-7837 1353*
Famous food-lovers' pub specializing in mainly Spanish and Portuguese-influenced dishes. Lively and often crowded, arrive early to secure a table (no reservations). Great value.

**Gaudi Restaurante** ($-$$)
*63 Clerkenwell Road EC1*
*tel: 020-7608 3220*
Brightly colored tiles, mirrors, stained glass and much wrought iron give the interior a Gaudi-esque feeling, and the staff, professional and friendly, are as Spanish as the menus. Lunch is great value.

**The Hothouse** ($$)
*78–80 Wapping Lane, E1 tel: 020-7488 4797*
The setting is unusual—a converted warehouse with exposed bricks, timbers, and a stripped floor softened by colorful wall hangings and ethnic cotton tablecloths. The cooking style is modern English, with both formal and less formal meals on offer.

**Imperial City** ($$)
*Royal Exchange, EC3 tel: 020-7626 3437*
Within the cavernous vaults of the Royal Exchange, off Cornhill, T.V. chef Ken Hom's menus include some less familiar dishes.

**Joe Allen** ($$)
*13 Exeter Street, WC2 tel: 020-7836 0651*
The Covent Garden haunt of journalists, publishers, and theatergoers, Joe Allen serves chic modern food among some American classics and is particularly renowned for its Bloody Marys.

**Moro** ($$)
*34–36 Exmouth Market, EC1*
*tel: 020-7833 8336*
An informal, lively setting for food that is largely Spanish and Arabic in origin – the bar serves great tapas. Good raw materials, chargrilled or roasted in a wood-burning oven, produce such great results that it is essential to reserve a table well in advance.

**Quality Chop House** ($$)
*94 Farringdon Road, EC1 tel: 020-7837 5093*
Much of the original character remains intact at this former Victorian chophouse. The menu offers a fashionable mix of updated traditional English dishes and French brasserie classics.

**Savoy Grill** ($$$)
*Strand, WC2 tel: 020-7836 4343*
Many regard the Savoy Grill as their private club, but it is equally accessible to all who wish to experience a real British institution. Regular daily items include the likes of roast rib of beef on Thursdays.

**St John** ($$)
*26 St John Street, EC1 tel: 020-7251 0848/7251 4998*
Clerkenwell hotspot close to Smithfield meat market where Fergus Henderson reworks traditional old English recipes as well as exploring modern Mediterranean dishes.

### Cafés and bars

**Cranks Express** ($)
*Adelaide Street, WC2 (no telephone bookings*
A pioneer of vegetarian cuisine in London, Cranks has rejuvenated its menu while sticking true to its principles of top quality, healthy food at affordable prices. Branches (take-out and eat-in) also at Marshall Street, Covent Garden Market, St. Christopher's Place, Great Newport Street, Tottenham Street.

## WESTMINSTER, BANKSIDE, AND DOCKLANDS

**Bengal Clipper** ($$)
*Butlers Wharf, SE1 tel: 020-7357 9001*
An old cardamom warehouse next to the Conran gastrodome at Butlers Wharf is a fitting setting for this respected Indian restaurant. The short menu specializes mainly in Bengal and Goan dishes.

**Blue Print Café** ($$$)
*The Design Museum, Shad Thames Street, SE1 tel: 020-7378 7031*
This riverside eatery on the mezzanine floor of the Design Museum is part of Sir Terence Conran's "Gastrodome." Eat in the minimalist dining room with its appropriately arty décor, or on the terraces overlooking Tower Bridge. The cooking is modern, the services professional, and the wine list lively.

**Butler's Wharf Chop House** ($$$)
*Butler's Wharf Building, 36e Shad Thames, SE1 tel: 020-7403 3403*
One of Terence Conran's growing chain of restaurants (see also pages 89 and 193), this one serves traditional English dishes (steak, kidney and oyster pudding), with a stunning view of the river.

**Cantina del Ponte** ($$)
*The Butler's Wharf Building, 36c Shad Thames, SE1 tel: 020-7403 5403*
The mainly Italian-inspired menu brings a simple choice of grilled or roasted meats and fish at this busy, informal Conran eaterie on the quayside by Tower Bridge.

**People's Palace** ($$)
*Level 3 Royal Festival Hall, SE1*
*tel: 020-7928 9999*
Best seats are those by the huge windows overlooking the Thames, so reserve a table early to enjoy the strong Mediterranean- and Asian-influenced dishes. Pre-theater dinners are excellent value.

**Le Pont de la Tour** ($$–$$$)
*The Butler's Wharf Building, 36d Shad Thames, SE1 tel: 020-7403 8403*
In the shadow of Tower Bridge, a large yet surprisingly intimate restaurant, part of Sir Terence Conran's restaurant empire. Expect excellent modern Mediterranean food and spectacular views from the riverside terrace.

**RSJ, The Restaurant on the South Bank** ($$)
*13a Coin Street, SE1 tel: 020-7633 0881*
An invaluable South Bank destination that is a good choice for after the theater—a comfortable, contemporary setting with modern Anglo-French cooking, that is strong on seasonal ingredients.

### Cafés and bars

**Konditor & Cook** ($)
*Young Vic, 66 The Cut, SE1*
*tel: 020-7620 2700*
Open for breakfast through till dinner, the menu is a mix of classics such as scrambled eggs and smoked salmon to Cal-Ital pasta dishes. Cakes are hard to resist, made by their own bakery. Coffee is excellent.

## CHELSEA AND KNIGHTSBRIDGE, KENSINGTON AND NOTTING HILL, HYDE PARK

**Adam's Café** ($)
*77 Askew Road, W12 tel: 020-8743 0572*
Award-winning restaurant in Shepherd's Bush, specializing in couscous served with tender grilled meats and chunky vegetable stew. Good value.
**Chinon** ($$$)
*23 Richmond Way, W14 tel: 020-7602 5968*
The atmosphere of this idiosyncratic bistro-style restaurant near Shepherds Bush Green is largely in the French provincial tradition, with a few fashionable, exotic influences and some brilliant vegetarian dishes.
**Chutney Mary** ($$)
*535 King's Road, SW10 tel: 020-7351 3113*
Imaginative cooking that draws on regional-Indian cuisine (salmon kedgeree, spicy crab cakes, and salads, for example) as well as more conventional Indian dishes.
**Clarke's** ($$)
*124 Kensington Church Street, W8*
*tel: 020-7221 9225*
Simple set menus (vegetarian dishes only by advance arrangement) usually based around charcoal-grilled meat or fish and served with delicious homemade breads (also sold in the store next door).
**Fifth Floor at Harvey Nichols** ($)
*Harvey Nichols, Knightsbridge, SW1*
*tel: 020-7235 5250*
The top floor of the designer-label department store—a cool, chic space that forms part of a food emporium and popular bar. Henry Harris's cooking reveals imaginative Italian, Middle Eastern, and Oriental influences. Way above the average department store restaurant.
**Kensington Place** ($$)
*201–205 Kensington Church Street, W8*
*tel: 020-7727 3184*
Lively, young, and fashionable restaurant serving adventurous combinations (fish dishes are usually excellent). The place to be seen (and overheard—the tables are placed awfully close together).
**Leith's** ($$$)
*92 Kensington Park Road, W11*
*tel: 020-7229 4481*
Haute cuisine in a discreet environment. Expect complicated and very rich concoctions, using imaginative ingredients, and a wealthy, middle-aged clientele.
**Vama** ($$)
*438 King's Road, SW10 tel: 020-7351 4118*
Explore the cuisine of India's North-West Frontier, including interesting vegetarian dishes, at this smart Chelsea haunt.
**Veronica's** ($$)
*3 Hereford Road, W2 tel: 020-7229 5079*
This Bayswater restaurant is worth seeking out for historically researched English food (the menu will explain what goes into delicious dishes such as salmagundy and watersouchy) plus a very good choice of British cheese and wines.
**Vong** ($$$)
*The Berkeley Hotel, Wilton Place, SW1*
*tel: 020-7235 1010*
Fashionable, modern Far Eastern cooking designed by New Yorker Jean-Georges Vongerichten.
**Wilson's** ($$)
*236 Blythe Road, W14 tel: 020-7603 7267*
Despite an out-of-the-way location (in Shepherd's Bush), food lovers flock here (reservations essential) for consistently high quality food with a Scottish bias.
**Zafferano** ($$)
*5 Lowndes Street, SW1 tel: 020-7235 5800*
An air of classy informality permeates Giorgio Locatelli's understated restaurant. He specializes in up-to-date interpretations of simple Italian country cooking.

### Cafés and bars

**The Orangery** ($)
*Kensington Palace, Kensington Gardens, W8*
*tel: 020-7376 0239*
Stunning setting for a classic English afternoon tea—the grandest includes champagne. There's a delicious selection of cakes and light lunches are available between 12 and 2:30.



## OUTSIDE THE CENTER

**Ayudhya Thai Restaurant** ($$)
*14 Kingston Hill, Kingston-upon-Thames, KT2*
*tel: 020-8549 5984*
You get reliably authentic Thai food at this workmanlike restaurant on London's southwestern fringe. The menu listing more than 90 dishes covers most aspects of Thai cuisine from satays and stir-fries to noodles, and the flavors usually come through well.
**Laicram Thai Restaurant** ($$$)
*1 Blackheath Grove, SE3 tel: 020-8852 4710*
There is a disarming hospitality and cheerfulness about this neighborhood Thai restaurant, where diners sit at tightly packed candlelit tables. Children are particularly welcome but reservations are essential.
**Kastoori** ($$)
*188 Upper Tooting Road, SW17*
*tel: 020-8767 7027*
Family-run vegetarian restaurant specializing in freshly prepared Gujarati, and Kathihwadi dishes. The varied menu also includes some African-inspired dishes.
**Osteria Antica Bologna** ($$)
*23 Northcote Road, SW11*
*tel: 020-7978 4771*
This Italian restaurant in Clapham proved amazingly successful when it opened because of the huge range of novel dishes served at honest prices. Lively atmosphere.
**Rani** ($$)
*7 Long Lane, N3 tel: 020-8349 4386*
This Finchley restaurant has won awards and high praise because everything is home-made (including the pickles and desserts), and because the vegetarian menu contains so many unusual dishes (all well explained). A connoisseurs' curry restaurant; good value.

# Index

## I



## J



## K



## L



## M

## N



## O



## P

## Q



## R



## S

## Acknowledgments

**ALLSPORT (UK) LTD** 206 London Marathon (S Bruty), 206–7 Lord's Cricket Ground ( A Murrell), 207 Ball girl Wimbledon (B Martin). **BANQUETING HOUSE** 46 Int Banqueting House. **BRITISH LIBRARY** 133 Int British Library. **BRITISH MUSEUM** 131 Gold Alloy Torc, 132 Exhibit. **COURTAULD INST. GALLERIES** 156 Manet's A Bar at the Folies-Bergère. **CROWN COPYRIGHT, HISTORIC ROYAL PALACES** 197 Beefeater, 222 Henry VIII's Armour, 223 Great Hall Hampton Court. **HARRODS LTD** 87 Harrod's Food Hall. **HULTON DEUTSCH COLLECTION LTD** 38 Wearing Smog Masks, 38–9, 39 Festival of Britain. **ILLUSTRATED LONDON NEWS** 34 Queen Victoria, 87 Harrods Advertisment. **IMPERIAL WAR MUSEUM** 36–7 Aerial view of London. **LINLEY SAMBOURNE HOUSE, LONDON:** The Drawing Room 114, Victorian Society, Linley Sambourne House, UK Bridgeman Art Library. **KENSINGTON PALACE** 112 Court Dress Collection. **LONDON DUNGEONS** 194 The London Dungeon. **MADAME TUSSAUD'S** 120 Chamber of Horrors. **MAGNUM PHOTOS LTD** 37 London at War (G Rodger). **MARY EVANS PICTURE LIBRARY** 69 Athenaeum Club. **MUSEUM OF LONDON** 24a Carving. **NATIONAL GALLERY** 51 Van Eyck's Giovanni Arnolfini and his Wife. **NATIONAL TRUST** 90 Carlyle's House. ORDE **ELIASON/LINK PHOTOGRAPHY** 108 Doll, Commonwealth Inst. **PERFORMING ARTS LIBRARY** 180–1 Ballet. **PLANETARIUM** 121 Planetarium. **RADIO TIMES** 1950's Radio Times. **REX REATURES LTD** 15 Queen Elizabeth II,16 Beatles, Punk,17 Mary Quant. **JOHN ROGERS (COURTESY OF THE ROYAL BOROUGH OF KENSINGTON & CHELSEA** 109 Leighton House. **ROYAL GEOGRAPHICAL SOCIETY** 22–3 Old Map, London. **SCIENCE MUSEUM** 100 Flight, 101 Exploring Space. **SHAKESPEARE'S GLOBE** 202 Globe Museum. **SPECTRUM COLOUR LIBRARY** 12–13 Traffic, 74 Tessiers, 91 Chelsea Physic Garden, 93 Chelsea Flower Show, 156–7 Somerset House. **TATE GALLERY** © Tate Gallery, London 1999 JWM Turner "Norham Castle, Sunrise" 57; © Tate Gallery, London, 204; © Tate Gallery, London 1999/David Hockney "Bigger Splash", 1967 acrylic on Canvas 96″ x 96″, © David Hockney 205. **THE MANSELL COLLECTION LTD** 25 Boudicca, 27 Chaucer, 28–9 16C Plan of London, 28 London Tower in Tudor times, 29 Henry VIII, 30 Plague, 32 Christopher Wren, 34–5 Great Exhibition. **THE THEATRE MUSEUM** 147 Wind in the Willows, "Props" department. **VICTORIA & ALBERT MUSEUM** 104 Italian Cast Court, 105 "Acanthus" Wallpaper, 178–9 Engine, Carriage & Tank in Bethnal Green Museum of Childhood. **WALLACE COLLECTION** 126 Sèvres Tea Service, 127 The Laughing Cavalier, 224–5 Kenwood House. **ZEFA PICTURE LIBRARY (UK) LTD** 3 Aerial view of London, 235 Rugby.
All remaining pictures are held in the AA's own photo library (**AA PHOTO LIBRARY**) with contributions from: **P BAKER** 6,168a, 196. **M BIRKITT** 209, 211. **P ENTICKNAP** 18–19, 19. **D FORSS** 223a. **R MORT** 9, 12, 26b, 35, 72, 97,116, 135, 136c, 137, 146, 162–3, 164, 165, 171, 175, 176, 183a, b, 213, 216a, b, 240a, b, 241a, b, 242a, b, 247, 249, 254, 265b, 268, 272a, b, 275, 276, 278, 279. **S & O MATHEWS** 21a, 210, 219. **B SMITH** 34a, 64, 66, 78, 84, 96b, 143a, 144b, 182–3, 200b, 201, 217, 226, 227, 229a, 245a, 255, 263, 267, 269b, 270, 277. **R STRANGE** 4a, b, 5a, b, 7b, 10–11, 10, 11, 13, 21b, 22, 30–1, 31, 40–1, 40, 48, 49, 52, 53, 55a, 59, 60, 70, 74–5, 76–7, 76a, b, 77, 78–9, 79, 80–1, 81a, b, 82, 83, 85, 86a, b, 88a, b, 89, 92, 93a, 95a, b, 98, 98–9, 102–3, 102, 104, 106, 107, 110–11, 111, 112–13, 113, 114, 115a, b, 117, 118a, b, 119b, 122a, b, 123, 124c, 125a, b, 126a, 128, 129, 130–1, 134a, b, 136a, b, 138, 139, 140, 148–9, 152–3, 155b, 158, 159a, 160, 162, 168b, 169, 172, 173b, 178a, 181, 184, 185, 186, 187, 191, 198, 224a, 225, 231a, b, 235b, 236, 236–7, 237, 238a, b, 239b, 244a, 245b, 246a, b, 250, 251, 252, 253, 256a, b, 259a, b, 261, 262, 265a, 266, 271, 274. **M TRELAWNY** 47, 63, 68–9, 155a, 159b, 170a, 190, 195a, 202, 212, 228a, b, 232, 233, 269b. **R VICTOR** 18, 170b, 174–5, 195b, 218b, 243b, 248, 280. **W VOYSEY** 20–1, 45, 54, 66–7, 67, 124b, 142–3, 142, 143b, 144–5, 145, 180b, 188, 192, 192–3, 193, 197a, 203c, 205a, b, 238b. **T WILES** 7a, 14–15, 14, 65, 273. **P WILSON** 50–1, 56, 96a, 150, 151, 174, 200a, 203a, b, 264. **T WOODCOCK** 20, 24b, 26a, 33, 55b, 56, 71, 124a, 166, 208, 214, 216a.

## Contributors

Copy editor: Nia Williams   Verifier: Louise Nicholson
Revisions editor: Grapevine Publishing Services